Gerry
Frank's
Oregon

Gerry Frank's Oregon

Printed in the United States of America

ISBN: 978-1-879333-27-7

First Edition, 2012

Second Edition, 2014

Third Edition, 2016

No fees were paid or services rendered in exchange for inclusion in this book.

Although every effort was made to ensure that all information was accurate and up-to-date at the time of publication, neither the publisher nor the author can be held responsible for any errors, omissions or adverse consequences resulting from the use of such information.

It is recommended that you call before your visit to verify the information for individual business listings.

Gerry Frank's
Oregon

Gerry's Frankly Speaking, Inc.
P.O. Box 2225
Salem, OR 97308
503/585-8411
800/692-2665
email: gerry@teleport.com
oregonguidebook.com

To the reader,

If the state ever bestows the title of "Mr. Oregon," Gerry Frank probably wins in a landslide.

For nearly 30 years, he's been filing a weekly column for *The Oregonian* and also now for our website OregonLive. He's never missed a deadline. Never filed late. Back in 1987, former *Oregonian* editor Bill Hilliard asked Gerry to begin writing his weekday column. It shifted to Sunday in 2003. "I don't think he's ever missed a Sunday," Hilliard told me recently. And he's right. The column has taken Gerry to every nook and cranny of our state. Week in and week out, readers have come to depend on him to unearth buried treasure or reconnect with iconic destinations from Astoria to Pendleton and from Ashland to Wallowa Lake. His guidebook to Oregon, now in its third edition, is an indispensable resource for visitors and residents alike.

Gerry's roots and institutional knowledge run deep. He served for 26 years under U.S. Sen. Mark Hatfield – 20 years as chief of staff. He's owned his own restaurant in Salem for 34 years. For more than a century, the family operated the Meier & Frank department store chain in Oregon. His great uncle Julius Meier was our 20th governor. "I've had eight generations of my family in this state. And I have a very deep love affair for it," he says, offering some of the motivation behind his weekly "Gerry Frank's picks" column. "And I've always felt that the people of western Oregon in particular don't realize that there is a big state out there." Gerry travels around the state relentlessly. But he's also counted upon his faithful readers to send tips and suggestions. "It's impossible for one guy to know about all these places so you have to rely on others and that has been a great joy," he relayed late last year.

His book includes roughly 1,000 mentions of diners, lodges, spas, bakeries, candy stores, delis, coffee shops and wineries. They range from his old favorites like the Tu Tu' Tun Lodge in Gold Beach to places he's discovered more recently like Majestic Mountain Retreat at the base of Mt. Hood. Along the way, he's introduced readers to the inn keepers, chefs and owners behind each of these Oregon landmarks and small businesses. "It's really about meeting the people whether they make doughnuts or run a lodge or have a wine store. That's the fun part of it for me," he says.

I think you'll enjoy meeting them too, courtesy of the ultimate Oregon tour guide, Gerry Frank.

Mark Katches
Editor and Vice President of Content
The Oregonian/OregonLive

Contents

About price categories

Restaurants mentioned in this book fall into four price ranges, based on the combined cost of an appetizer and entree (excluding drinks):

Inexpensive: $12 and under per person

Moderate: $13 to $20 per person

Moderately expensive: $21 to $34 per person

Expensive: $35 and up per person

Hotels are categorized by nightly room tariff (excluding taxes and surcharges) based upon double occupancy as follows:

Inexpensive: $125 and under

Moderate: $126 to $249

Expensive: $250 to $399

Very expensive: $400 and up

Activity fees are based on adult admission (optional features and activities are not included):

Nominal: $9 and under

Reasonable: $10 to $19

Expensive: $20 and over

From the Author

Dear Readers,

I have been overwhelmed by the positive response to the first two editions of *Gerry Frank's Oregon* (2012 and 2014). The title has been a huge success! Wherever I travel throughout the state, longtime friends, former colleagues, retail associates and readers share heartwarming anecdotes and fond memories and suggest their favorite places to visit. The experience continues to be an exciting journey around Oregon and a wonderful trip down memory lane!

My new discoveries and many of those newly shared places are included in this third volume, and all entries have been updated; more photos from my personal photo albums are shared. Again I am featuring my very comprehensive and exclusive list of restaurants and lodgings — Gerry's Exclusive List — with a nod to the best places in Oregon to eat, drink and stay. You will also learn interesting facts and read about some of Oregon's fascinating personalities who have helped shape our remarkable state.

It requires a hard-working team to accomplish a revision such as this. I want to recognize the following individuals whose skills and diligence helped me accomplish this edition: Jan Boutin, Nancy Burke, Nancy Chamberlain, Linda Chase, Cheryl Johnson and Olga Polyakova. Each of these ladies has my sincere gratitude for another job well-done!

I hope that you enjoy using this book as you explore Oregon's highways and byways, and if I am lucky, we'll meet along the way!

Gerry Frank, Author

Gerry's **exclusive list**

... the best places in Oregon to eat, drink and stay

Barbecue

Adam's Rib Smoke House (1210 State St, Salem; 503/362-2194)
Apple Valley BBQ Restaurant and Catering (4956 Baseline Dr, Parkdale; 541/352-3554)
Cowboy Dinner Tree (East Bay Road, Silver Lake; 541/576-2426)
Pig Feathers BBQ (300 S Main St, Toledo; 541/336-1833)
Reverend's BBQ (7712 SE 13th Ave, Portland; 503/327-8755)
Ribslayer BBQ To Go (575 NE 2nd St, McMinnville; 503/472-1309)
Slick's Que Co. (442 E Hood Ave, Sisters; 541/549-4227)
Storrs Smokehouse (310 E 1st St, Newberg; 503/538-8080)
Sundown Grill & Bar-B-Q (223 SE 4th St, Pendleton; 541/276-8500)
Uncle Jack's Bar-B-Que (416 S Trade St, Amity; 503/835-5225)

Bars and Pubs with Good Eats

23Hoyt (529 NW 23rd Ave, Portland; 503/445-7400)
Bar Mingo (811 NW 21st Ave, Portland; 503/445-4646)
Block 15 Restaurant and Brewery (300 SW Jefferson Ave, Corvallis; 541/758-2077)
Brewers Union Local 180 (48329 E 1st St, Oakridge; 541/782-2024)
Buffalo Gap Saloon & Eatery (6835 SW Macadam Ave, Portland; 503/244-7111)
Cannon Beach Hardware and Public House (1235 S Hemlock St, Cannon Beach; 503/436-4086)
Deschutes Brewery & Public House (1044 NW Bond St, Bend; 541/382-9242)
Elements Tapas Bar & Lounge (101 E Main St, Medford; 541/779-0135)
Fort George Brewing & Public House (1483 Duane St, Astoria; 503/325-7468)
Full Sail Brewing (506 Columbia St, Hood River; 541/386-2247)
Gilgamesh Brewing (2065 Madrona Ave SE, Salem; 503/584-1789)
The Haul (121 SW H St, Grants Pass; 541/474-4991)
Les Caves Bier & Kitchen (308 SW 3rd St, Corvallis; 541/286-4473)
Lostine Tavern (125 Hwy 82, Lostine; 541/569-2246)
Mutiny Brewing Company (600 N Main St, Joseph; 541/432-5274)
Oxenfre Public House (631 Chetco Ave, Brookings; 541/813-1985)
Pig & Pound Public House (427 SW 8th St, Redmond; 541/526-1697)
Seven Brides Brewery and Tap Room (990 N 1st St, Silverton; 503/874-4677)

Stammtisch (401 NE 28th Ave, Portland; 503/206-7983)
Standing Stone Brewing Co. (101 Oak St, Ashland; 541/482-2448)
Terminal Gravity Brewing and Public House (803 SE School St, Enterprise; 541/426-3000)
Thirsty Lion Pub and Grill (71 SW 2nd Ave, Portland; 503/222-2155; 10205 SW Washington Square Road, Tigard; 503/352-4030 and 2290 NW Allie Ave, Hillsboro; 503/336-0403)
Trader Vic's (1203 NW Glisan St, Portland; 503/467-2277)
The Verdict Bar & Grill (110 8th St, Oregon City; 503/305-8429)
Wild River Brewing & Pizza Company (595 NE E St, Grants Pass; 541/471-7487)

Best Sleeps
The Allison Inn & Spa (2525 Allison Lane, Newberg; 503/554-2525)
Awtrey House (38245 James Road, Manzanita; 503/368-5721)
The Benson Hotel (309 SW Broadway, Portland; 503/228-2000)
Cannery Pier Hotel & Spa (10 Basin St, Astoria; 503/325-4996)
Geiser Grand Hotel (1996 Main St, Baker City; 541/523-1889)
The Grand Hotel (201 Liberty St SE, Salem; 503/540-7800)
Jacksonville Inn (175 E California St, Jacksonville; 541/899-1900)
The Ocean Lodge (2864 S Pacific St, Cannon Beach; 503/436-2241)
Salishan Spa & Golf Resort (7760 Hwy 101 N, Gleneden Beach; 541/764-2371)
The Sentinel (614 SW 11th Ave, Portland; 503/224-3400)
Sheraton Portland Airport Hotel (8235 NE Airport Way, Portland; 503/281-2500)
Steamboat Inn (42705 N Umpqua Hwy, Idleyld Park; 541/498-2230)
Stephanie Inn (2740 S Pacific St, Cannon Beach; 503/436-2221)
Tu Tu' Tun Lodge (96550 North Bank Rogue, Gold Beach; 541/247-6664)
The Whaler (155 SW Elizabeth St, Newport; 541/265-9261)

Breads and Bakery Goods
Angeline's Bakery & Cafe (121 W Main St, Sisters; 541/549-9122)
Baker & Spice Bakery (6330 SW Capitol Hwy, Portland; 503/244-7573)
Bob's Red Mill Whole Grain Store (5000 SE International Way, Milwaukie; 503/607-6455)
The Bread Board (404 N Main St, Falls City; 503/787-5000)
Bread and Ocean (154 Laneda Ave, Manzanita; 503/368-5823)
Dave's Killer Bread (5209 SE International Way, Milwaukie; 503/335-8077)
Grand Central Bakery (numerous locations, Greater Portland; grandcentralbakery.com)
The Grateful Bread Bakery (34805 Brooten Road, Pacific City; 503/965-7337)
Heaven on Earth Restaurant & Bakery (703 Quines Creek Road, Azalea; 541/837-3700)
Home Baking Co. (2845 Marine Dr, Astoria; 503/325-4631): Finnish
Pacific Way Bakery & Cafe (601 Pacific Way, Gearhart; 503/738-0245)
Panini Bakery (232 NW Coast St, Newport; 541/265-5033)
Pearl Bakery (102 NW 9th Ave, Portland; 503/827-0910)
St. Honoré Boulangerie (numerous locations, Portland; sainthonorebakery.com)
Tomaselli's Pastry Mill & Cafe (14836 Umpqua Hwy, Elkton; 541/584-2855)

Breakfast

Annette's Westgate (1311 Edgewater St NW, Salem; 503/362-9588)
The Broken Yolk Cafe (119 SW 3rd St, Corvallis; 541/738-9655)
Buster's Main Street Cafe (811 Main St, Cottage Grove; 541/942-8363)
Cousins Restaurant & Saloon (2114 W 6th St, The Dalles; 541/298-2771)
Crescent Cafe (526 NE 3rd St, McMinnville; 503/435-2655)
Egg River Cafe (1313 Oak St, Hood River; 541/386-1127)
The Klamath Grill and Pancake House (715 Main St, Klamath Falls; 541/882-1427)
Maggie's Buns (20072 21st Ave, Forest Grove; 503/992-2231)
Momma Jane's Pancake House (900 W 6th St, The Dalles; 541/296-6611)
Morning Glory (1149 Siskiyou Blvd, Ashland; 541/488-8636)
Nelscott Cafe (3237 SW Highway 101, Lincoln City; 541/994-6100)
Off the Waffle (2540 Willamette St, Eugene; 541/515-6926 and 840 Willamette St, Eugene; 541/654-4318)
The Original Pancake House (8601 SW 24th Ave, Portland; 503/246-9007; 4685 Portland Road NE, Salem; 503/393-9124 and 4656 Commercial St SE, Salem; 503/378-0431)
Otis Cafe (1259 Salmon River Hwy, Otis; 541/994-2813)
The Palm Court Restaurant and Lobby Bar (The Benson Hotel, 309 SW Broadway, Portland; 503/228-2000)
The Pump Cafe (710 Main St, Springfield; 541/726-0622)
The Reedville Cafe (7575 SE Tualatin Valley Hwy, Hillsboro; 503/649-4643)
Roosters (1515 Southgate, Pendleton; 541/966-1100)
Slappy Cakes (4246 SE Belmont St, Portland; 503/477-4805)
The Victorian Cafe (1404 NW Galveston Ave, Bend; 541/382-6411)
Wanda's Cafe (12870 Hwy 101 N, Nehalem; 503/368-8100)
Word of Mouth Neighborhood Bistro (140 17th St NE, Salem; 503/930-4285)

Brunch

Bellino Trattoria Siciliana (1230 NW Hoyt St, #B, Portland; 503/208-2992)
Bridgewater Bistro (20 Basin St, Astoria; 503/325-6777)
Cedar Plank Buffet (Spirit Mountain Casino, 27100 SW Salmon River Hwy, Grande Ronde; 503/879-2350)
Delaney Madison Grill (5745 Inland Shores Way N, Keizer; 971/273-0495)
Irving St. Kitchen (701 NW 13th Ave, Portland; 503/343-9440)
Orchard Heights Winery (6057 Orchard Heights Road NW, Salem; 503/391-7308)
Portland City Grill (111 SW 5th Ave, 30th floor, Portland; 503/450-0030)
Redfish (517 Jefferson St, Port Orford; 541/366-2200)
Salty's on the Columbia (3839 NE Marine Dr, Portland; 503/288-4444)
Simon's Cliff House (Columbia Gorge Hotel, 4000 Westcliff Dr, Hood River; 541/386-5566)
Stockpot Broiler (8200 SW Scholls Ferry Road, Beaverton; 503/643-5451)
Tasty n Sons (3808 N Williams Ave, Suite C, Portland; 503/621-1400)
Verdigris (1315 NE Fremont St, Portland; 503/477-8106)

Burgers (see list on page 45 of chapter 1)

Candy

Bruce's Candy Kitchen (256 N Hemlock St, Cannon Beach; 503/436-2641)
Cary's of Oregon (413 Union Ave, Grants Pass; 888/822-9300)
The Chocolate Box (115 N Water St, Silverton; 503/873-3225)
Enchanté (10883 SE Main St, Milwaukie; 503/654-4846)
Honest Chocolates (575 NE 3rd St, McMinnville; 503/474-9042 and 312 E 1st St, Newberg; 503/537-0754)
Moonstruck (numerous locations, Greater Portland; moonstruckchocolate.com)
The Sycamore Tree (2108 Main St, Baker City; 541/523-4840)

Cheap Eats

Buster's Main Street Cafe (811 Main St, Cottage Grove; 541/942-8363)
Goose Hollow Inn (1927 SW Jefferson St, Portland; 503/228-7010)
The Horse Radish (211 W Main St, Carlton; 503/852-6656)
Indian Creek Cafe (94682 Jerry's Flat Road, Gold Beach; 541/247-0680)
Little Brown Hen Cafe (435 Hwy 101, Florence; 541/902-2449)
Maggie's Buns (2007 21st Ave, Forest Grove; 503/992-2231)
Mustard Seed Cafe (130 N 5th St, Jacksonville; 541/899-2977)
RJ's Restaurant (Hwy 20 East Hwy 395, Burns; 541/573-6346)
Sno Cap Drive In (380 W Cascade Ave, Sisters; 541/549-6151)
Stepping Stone Cafe (2390 NW Quimby St, Portland; 503/222-1132)
Turnaround Cafe (7760 3rd St, Turner; 503/743-1285)
Zigzag Mountain Cafe (70171 E Hwy 26, Rhodendron; 503/622-7684)

Cheese

Blue Heron French Cheese Company (2001 Blue Heron Dr, Tillamook; 503/842-8281)
Pholia Farm (9115 W Evans Creek Road, Rogue River; 541/582-8883)
Rogue Creamery (311 N Front St, Central Point; 541/665-1155)
Tillamook Cheese Factory (4175 Hwy 101 N, Tillamook; 503/815-1300)
Willamette Valley Cheese Co. (8105 Wallace Road NW, Salem; 503/399-9806)

Clam Chowder (see list on page 215 of chapter 3)

Coffee and Tea

Archive Coffee & Bar (120 Liberty St NE, Suite 120, Salem; 971/701-6266)
Boyd's Coffee (19730 NE Sandy Blvd, Portland; 503/666-4561; boyds.com)
Green Salmon Coffee and Tea House (220 Hwy 101 N, Yachats; 541/547-3077)
Lovejoy's Restaurant & Tea Room (195 Nopal St, Florence; 541/902-0502)
Mt. Hood Roasters (73451 E Hwy 26, Rhododendron; 503/622-6574)
The Pendleton Coffee Bean and Bistro (241 S Main St, Pendleton; 541/379-3663)
Sleepy Monk Coffee Roasters (1235 S Hemlock St, Cannon Beach; 503/436-2796)
Steven Smith Teamaker (1626 NW Thurman St, Portland; 503/719-8752)
Stumptown Coffee (numerous locations, Portland; stumptowncoffee.com)
World Cup Coffee & Tea (1740 NW Glisan St, Portland; 503/228-5503)

Comfort Food
Barley Brown's Brew Pub (2190 Main St, Baker City; 541/523-4266)
Barlow Trail Roadhouse (69580 E Hwy 26, Welches; 503/622-1662)
Buffalo Gap Saloon & Eatery (6835 SW Macadam Ave, Portland; 503/244-7111)
Café 22 West (5152 Salem-Dallas Hwy, Salem; 503/363-4643)
Community Plate (315 NE Third St, McMinnville; 503/687-1902)
Copper River Restaurant and Bar (7370 NE Cornell Rd, Hillsboro; 503/640-0917)
Depot Cafe (250 W Cascade Ave, Sisters; 541/549-2572)
Gerry Frank's Konditorei (310 Kearney St SE, Salem; 503/585-7070)
Inland Cafe (2715 10th St, Baker City; 541/523-9041)
Oswego Grill at Kruse Way (7 Centerpointe Dr, Lake Oswego; 503/352-4750)
Oswego Grill at Wilsonville (30080 SW Boones Ferry Road, Lake Oswego; 503/427-2152)
The Reedville Cafe (7575 SE Tualatin Valley Hwy, Hillsboro; 503/649-4643)
River Lodge and Grill (6 Marine Dr, Boardman; 541/481-6800)
Side Door Café and Eden Hall (6675 Gleneden Beach Loop Road, Gleneden; 541/764-3825)
Tad's Chicken 'n Dumplins (1325 E Historic Columbia River Hwy, Troutdale, 503/666-5337)

Deli
Bread and Ocean (154 Laneda Ave, Manzanita; 503/368-5823)
Josephson's Smokehouse & Specialty Seafood (106 Marine Dr, Astoria; 503/325-2190)
Kenny & Zuke's Delicatessen (1038 SW Stark St, Portland; 503/222-3354)
Little Lois Cafe (1211 Edgewater St NW, Salem; 503/362-8422)
Otto's Sausage Kitchen (4138 SE Woodstock Blvd, Portland; 503/771-6714)

Desserts
The Cakery (6306 SW Capitol Hwy, Portland; 503/546-3737)
Gerry Frank's Konditorei (310 Kearney St SE, Salem; 503/585-7070)
Ida's Cupcake Cafe (1314 NW Galveston Ave, Bend; 541/383-2345 and 1155 SW Division St, A-7, Bend; 541/678-5057)
Mehri's Bakery & Cafe (6923 SE 52nd Ave, Portland; 503/788-9600)
Sweet Life Patisserie (755 Monroe St, Eugene; 541/683-5676)
Tebo's Restaurant (19120 McLoughlin Blvd, Gladstone; 503/655-6333)

Doughnuts
Joe's Donut Shop (39230 Pioneer Blvd, Sandy; 503/668-7215)
Sisters Bakery (251 E Cascade Ave, Sisters; 541/549-0361)
Voodoo Doughnut (22 SW 3rd Ave, Portland; 503/241-4707; 1501 NE Davis St, Portland; 503/235-2666 and 20 E Broadway, Eugene; 541/868-8666)

Fireside

Beasy's on the Creek (51 Water St, Ashland; 541/488-5009)
Dundee Bistro (100-A SW 7th St, Dundee; 503/554-1650)
Hall Street Grill (3775 SW Hall Blvd, Beaverton; 503/641-6161)
McKay Cottage Restaurant (62910 O.B. Riley Road, #340, Bend; 541/383-2697)
RingSide Steakhouse Uptown (2165 W Burnside St, Portland; 503/223-1513)
Rudy's Restaurant (2025 Golf Course Road SE, Salem; 503/399-0449)
Stonehedge Gardens (3405 Wine Country Ave, Hood River; 541/386-3940)
Tollgate Inn Restaurant & Bakery (38100 Hwy 26, Sandy; 503/668-8456)

Fish and Seafood

Baked Alaska (1 12th St, Astoria; 503/325-7414)
Barnacle Bill's Seafood Market (2174 NE Hwy 101, Lincoln City; 541/994-3022)
Bay House (5911 SW Hwy 101, Lincoln City; 541/996-3222)
Bowpicker Fish & Chips (1634 Duane St, Astoria; 503/791-2942): tuna fish & chips
Bridgewater Ocean Fresh Fish House and Zebra Bar (1297 Bay St, Florence; 541/997-1133)
Dan & Louis Oyster Bar (208 SW Ankeny St, Portland; 503/227-5906)
Delaney Madison Grill (5745 Inland Shores Way N, Keizer; 971/273-0495)
Depot Restaurant (1208 38th Pl, Seaview, WA; 360/642-7880)
Fisherman's Market (830 W 7th St, Eugene; 541/484-2722)
Gracie's Sea Hag Restaurant and Lounge (58 N Hwy 101, Depoe Bay; 541/765-2734)
Jake's Famous Crawfish (401 SW 12th Ave, Portland; 503/226-1419)
Lord Bennett's (1695 Beach Loop Dr, Bandon; 541/347-3663)
Luna Sea Fish House and Village Fishmonger (153 NW Hwy 101, Yachats; 541/547-4794)
Newman's Fish Market (City Market, 735 NW 21st Ave, Portland; 503/227-2700)
Norma's Seafood & Steak (20 N Columbia St, Seaside; 503/738-4331)
Oregon Lox Company (4828 W 11th Ave, Eugene; 541/726-5699): smoked salmon, lox and trout
Portside Restaurant (63383 Kingfisher Dr, Charleston; 541/888-5544)
Redfish (517 Jefferson St, Port Orford; 541/366-2200)
RingSide Fishhouse (838 SW Park Ave, mezzanine level, Portland; 503/227-3900)
Saffron Salmon (859 SW Bay Blvd, Newport; 541/265-8921)
Silver Salmon Grille (1105 Commercial St, Astoria; 503/338-6640)
Spinners Seafood, Steak & Chophouse (29430 Ellensburg Ave, Gold Beach; 541/247-5160)
Tidal Raves (279 NW Hwy 101, Depoe Bay; 541/765-2995)
Tom's Fish & Chips (240 N Hemlock St, Cannon Beach; 503/436-4301)
Tony's Crab Shack & Seafood Grill (155 1st St, Bandon; 541/347-2875)
Umpqua Oysters (723 Ork Rock Road, Winchester Bay; 541/271-5684)

Foreign Flavors

- BOSNIAN: **Drina Daisy** (915 Commercial St, Astoria; 503/338-2912)
- BRAZILIAN: **Fogo de Chão** (930 SW 6th Ave, Portland; 503/241-0900)

- **BRITISH: Pig & Pound Public House** (427 SW 8th St, Redmond; 541/526-1697)
- **CHINESE: Kwan's Original Cuisine** (835 Commercial St SE, Salem; 503/362-7711); **Marco Polo Global Restaurant** (300 Liberty St SE, Salem; 503/364-4833) and **Seres Restaurant and Bar** (1105 NW Lovejoy St, Portland; 971/222-0100)
- **FRENCH: Bistro Maison** (729 NE 3rd St, McMinnville; 503/474-1888); **Cuvee** (214 W Main St, Carlton; 503/852-6555); **La Maison Bakery & Cafe** (315 SW 9th St, Newport; 541/265-8812), **Marché** (296 E 5th Ave, Eugene; 541/342-3612) and **Verdigris** (1315 NE Fremont St, Portland; 503/477-8106)
- **GERMAN: Frau Kemmling Schoolhaus Brewhaus** (525 Bigham Knoll Dr, Jacksonville; 541/899-1000); **Glockenspiel Restaurant & Pub** (190 E Charles St, Mt. Angel; 503/845-6222) and **Stammtisch** (401 NE 28th Ave, Portland; 503/206-7983)
- **HUNGARIAN: Novak's Hungarian Restaurant** (208 2nd Ave SW, Albany; 541/967-9488) and **Vali's Alpine Restaurant** (59811 Wallowa Lake Hwy, Joseph; 541/432-5691)
- **INTERNATIONAL: Castaways Restaurant & Tiki Bar** (316 N Fir St, Cannon Beach; 503/436-8777)
- **IRISH: 4 Daughters Irish Pub** (126 W Main St, Medford; 541/779-4455); **The Irish Table** (1235 S Hemlock St, Cannon Beach; 503/436-0708); **Mackey's Steakhouse & Pub** (111 SW 1st St, Ontario; 541/889-3678) and **Nana's Irish Pub** (613 NW 3rd St, Newport; 541/574-8787)
- **ITALIAN: a Cena** (7742 SE 13th Ave, Portland; 503/206-3291); **Bellino Trattoria Siciliana** (1230 NW Hoyt St, #B, Portland; 503/208-2992); **Benetti's Italian Restaurant** (260 S Broadway, Coos Bay; 541/267-6066); **Beppe & Gianni's Trattoria** (1646 E 19th Ave, Eugene; 541/683-6661); **Fiorano Ristorante** (18674 SW Boones Ferry Road, Tualatin; 503/783-0727); **Gamberetti's Italian Restaurant** (325 High St SE, Salem; 503/339-7446); **Gilda's Italian Restaurant** (1601 SW Morrison St, Portland; 503/688-5066); **La Pomodori Ristorante** (1415 7th St, Florence; 541/902-2525); **Macaroni's Ristorante** and **Martino's Restaurant and Lounge** (58 E Main St, Ashland; 541/488-3359); **Mama Mia Trattoria** (439 SW 2nd Ave, Portland; 503/295-6464); **Mangiare Italian Restaurant** (114 S Main St, Independence; 503/838-0566); **Mucca Osteria** (1022 SW Morrison St, Portland; 503/227-5521); **Nick's Italian Cafe** (521 NE 3rd St, McMinnville; 503/434-4471); **Nonni's Italian Bistro** (831 Broadway St, Seaside; 503/738-4264); **Nostrana** (1401 SE Morrison St, Portland; 503/234-2427); **Piazza Italia** (1129 NW Johnson St, Portland; 503/478-0619); **Ristorant di Pompello** (177 E Historic Columbia River Hwy, Troutdale; 503/667-2480); **Ristorante Roma** (622 SW 12th Ave, Portland; 503/241-2692); **Trattoria Sbandati** (1444 NW College Way, Bend; 541/306-6825) and **Tucci Ristorante** (220 A Ave, Lake Oswego; 503/697-3383)
- **JAPANESE: Kanpai Sushi & Saké Bar** (990 NW Newport Ave, Bend; 541/388-4636) and **Syun Izakaya** (209 NE Lincoln St, Hillsboro; 503/640-3131)
- **LATIN: Del Alma Restaurant** (136 SW Washington Ave, Corvallis; 541/753-2222) and **OBA Restaurant** (555 NW 12th Ave, Portland; 503/228-6161)
- **MEDITERRANEAN: April's at Nye Beach** (749 NW 3rd St, Newport; 541/265-6855); **Cafe Soriah** (384 W 13th Ave, Eugene; 541/342-4410) and **Romuls West** (315 Oak St, Hood River; 541/436-4444)
- **MEXICAN: Diego's Spirited Kitchen** (447 SW 6th St, Redmond; 541/316-2002);

Left Coast Siesta (288 Laneda Ave, Manzanita; 503/368-7997) and **Pancho's Restaurante Y Cantina** (1136 Chetco Ave, Brookings; 541/469-6531)
- **MOROCCAN: Dar Essalam** (29585 SW Park Pl, Suite A, Wilsonville; 503/682-3600)
- **PERUVIAN: Andina** (1314 NW Glisan St, Portland; 503/228-9535)
- **SICILIAN: Bellino Trattoria Siciliana** (1230 NW Hoyt St, #B, Portland; 503/208-2992)
- **SPANISH: La Rambla Restaurant & Bar** (238 NE 3rd St, McMinnville; 503/435-2126) and **Toro Bravo** (120 NE Russell St, Portland; 503/281-4464)
- **THAI: Pok Pok** (3226 SE Division St, Portland; 503/232-1387 and 1469 NE Prescott St, Portland; 503/287-4149); **Thai Bay** (250 SW Hwy 101, Depoe Bay; 541/765-2497) and **Thai Bloom** (3800 SW Cedar Hills Blvd, Beaverton; 503/644-8010)

Game
Alchemy Restaurant and Bar (35 S 2nd St, Ashland; 541/488-1115)
Beast (5425 NE 30th Ave, Portland; 503/841-6968)
Gary West Meats (690 N 5th St, Jacksonville; 800/833-1820)
Jaspers Café (2739 N Pacific Hwy, Medford; 541/776-5307)
Kokanee Cafe (25545 SW Forest Service Road, Camp Sherman; 541/595-6420)
Le Pigeon (738 E Burnside St, Portland; 503/546-8796)
Recipe – A Neighborhood Kitchen (115 N Washington St, Newberg; 503/487-6853)
Red Hills Provincial Dining (276 N Hwy 99W, Dundee; 503/538-8224)
Thistle Restaurant & Bar (228 NE Evans St, McMinnville; 503/472-9623)
Tim Garling's Jackalope Grill (750 NW Lava Road, Bend; 541/318-8435)

Hot Dogs and Sausage
Langlois Market (48444 Hwy 101, Langlois; 541/348-2476)
Mt. Angel Sausage Co. (105 S Garfield St, Mt. Angel; 503/845-2322)
Otto's Sausage (4138 SE Woodstock Blvd, Portland; 503/771-6714)

Ice Cream and Other Frozen Treats
BJ's Ice Cream Parlor (1441 Bay St, Florence; 541/902-7828 and 2930 Hwy 101, Florence; 541/997-7286)
Bontà (920 NW Bond St, Suite 108, Bend; 541/306-6606
Charley's Ice Cream Parlor (2101 Main St, Suite 101, Baker City; 541/524-9307)
East Wind Drive-In (395 Wa Na Pa St, Cascade Locks; 541/374-8380): insanely large ice cream cones
Prince Pückler's Gourmet Ice Cream (1605 E 19th Ave, Eugene; 541/344-4418)
Salt & Straw (2035 NE Alberta St, Portland; 503/208-3867; 3345 SE Division St, Portland; 503/208-2054 and 838 NW 23rd Ave, Portland; 971/271-8168)
Serendipity Ice Cream (502 NE 3rd St, McMinnville; 503/474-9189)

Lamb and Goat
The Blue Goat Restaurant (506 S Trade St, Amity; 503/835-5170)
Clarke's Restaurant (455 2nd St, Lake Oswego; 503/636-2667)

Gogi's Restaurant (235 W Main St, Jacksonville; 541/899-8699)
Porters – Dining at the Depot (147 N Front St, Medford; 541/857-1910)
Trader Vic's (1203 NW Glisan St, Portland; 503/467-2277)

Liquid Libations

Blue Mountain Cider Company (235 E Broadway Ave, Milton-Freewater; 541/938-5575)
Multnomah Whiskey Library (1124 SW Alder St, Portland; 503/954-1381)
Pearl Specialty Market & Spirits (900 NW Lovejoy St, Portland; 503/477-8604): spirits
Sakéone (820 Elm St, Forest Grove; 503/357-7056): saké

Meats

Gartner's Country Meat Market (7450 NE Killingsworth St, Portland; 503/252-7801)
Gary West Meats (690 N 5th St, Jacksonville; 800/833-1820)
Langlois Market (48444 Hwy 101, Langlois; 541/348-2476)
Laurelhurst Market (3155 E Burnside St, Portland; 503/206-3097)
Mt. Angel Sausage Co. (105 S Garfield St, Mt. Angel; 503/845-2322)
Otto's Sausage Kitchen (4138 SE Woodstock Blvd, Portland; 503/771-6714)
Tillamook Country Smoker (8250 Warren Ave, Tillamook; 503/377-2222)

Outdoor Dining

Beaches (1919 SE Columbia River Dr, Vancouver, WA; 360/699-1592)
Beasy's on the Creek (51 Water St, Ashland; 541/488-5009)
Castagna Restaurant (1752 SE Hawthorne Blvd, Portland; 503/231-7373)
Driftwood Restaurant & Lounge (179 N Hemlock St, Cannon Beach; 503/436-2439)
Helvetia Tavern (10275 NW Helvetia Road, Hillsboro; 503/647-5286)
Loft Brasserie & Bar (18 Calle Guanajuato, Ashland; 541/482-1116)
Stone Cliff Inn Restaurant & Bar (17900 S Clackamas River Dr, Oregon City; 503/631-7900)
Taprock Northwest Grill (971 SE 6th St, Grants Pass; 541/955-5998)

Personal Favorites

Copper River Restaurant and Bar (7370 NE Cornell Road; Hillsboro; 503/640-0917)
Hall Street Grill (3775 SW Hall Blvd, Beaverton; 503/641-6161)
The Irish Table (1235 S Hemlock St, Cannon Beach; 503/436-0708)
Jake's Famous Crawfish (401 SW 12th Ave, Portland; 503/226-1419)
Jory (The Allison Inn & Spa, 2525 Allison Lane, Newberg; 503/554-2525)
Newmans at 988 (988 S Hemlock St, Cannon Beach; 503/436-1151)
Oba Restaurant (555 NW 12th Ave, Portland; 503/228-6161)
The Painted Lady (201 S College St, Newberg; 503/538-3850)
Paley's Place (1204 NW 21st St, Portland; 503/243-2403)
Portland City Grill (111 SW 5th Ave, 30th floor, Portland; 503/450-0030)
Silver Grille (206 E Main St, Silverton; 503/873-8000)

Picnic Fixin's
Bread and Ocean (154 Laneda Ave, Manzanita; 503/368-5823)
Downtown Market Co. (231 E Main St, Medford; 541/973-2233)
Grand Central Bakery (numerous locations, Greater Portland; grandcentralbakery.com)
The Horse Radish (211 W Main St, Carlton; 503/852-6656)

Pie
Baker & Spice Bakery (6330 SW Capitol Hwy, Portland; 503/244-7573)
Blue Raeven Farmstand (20650 S Hwy 99W, Amity; 503/835-0740)
Mother's Bistro & Bar (212 SW Stark St, Portland; 503/464-1122)
Oxbow Restaurant & Saloon (128 W Front St, Prairie City; 541/820-4544)
Pacific Pie Co. (1520 SE 7th Ave, Portland; 503/381-6157 and 1668 NW 23rd Ave, Portland; 503/894-9482)
Tebo's Restaurant (19120 McLoughlin Blvd, Gladstone; 503/655-6333)
Willamette Valley Pie Company (2994 82nd Ave NE, Salem; 503/362-8678)

Pizza
3rd Street Pizza Co. (433 NE 3rd St, McMinnville; 503/434-5800)
The Cafe on Hawk Creek (4505 Salem Ave, Neskowin; 503/392-4400)
Giovanni's Mountain Pizza (146 NW Santiam Blvd, Mill City; 503/897-2614)
Kaleidoscope Pizzeria & Pub (3084 Crater Lake Hwy, Medford; 541/779-7787)
Ken's Artisan Pizza (304 SE 28th Ave, Portland; 503/517-9951)
Mia & Pia's Pizzeria & Brewhouse (3545 Summers Lane, Klamath Falls; 541/884-4880)
Nostrana (1401 SE Morrison St, Portland; 503/234-2427)
Pacific Way Bakery & Cafe (601 Pacific Way, Gearhart; 503/738-0245)
Padington's Pizza (5255 Commercial St SE, Salem; 503/370-7556 and 410 Pine St NE, Salem; 503/378-0345)
Pizza a' fetta (231 N Hemlock St, Cannon Beach; 503/436-0333)
Ratskeller Alpine Bar &Pizzeria (88335 E Government Camp Loop, Government Camp; 503/272-3635)
Solstice Wood Fire Café & Bar (501 Portway Ave, Hood River; 541/436-0800)
Via Chicago (2013 NE Alberta St, Portland; 503/719-6809)
Wild River Brewing & Pizza Company (numerous locations in Southern Oregon; wildriverbrewing.com)

Produce
Aspinwall's Nursery & Produce (5152 Salem-Dallas Hwy, Salem; 503/363-4643)
Bauman's Farm & Garden (12989 Howell Prairie Road NE, Gervais; 503/792-3524)
Bear Creek Artichokes (19659 Hwy 101, Hemlock; 503/398-5411)
E.Z. Orchards (5504 Hazel Green Road NE, Salem; 503/393-1506)
French Prairie Gardens & Family Farm (17673 French Prairie Road, St. Paul; 503/633-8445)
Minto Island Growers (3394 Brown Island Road S, Salem; 503/931-6840)

Mt. Hood Organic Farm (7130 Smullin Dr, Mt. Hood; 541/352-7492)
New Seasons Market (numerous locations in Greater Portland)

Romantic Settings
Amuse (15 N 1st St, Ashland; 541/488-9000)
Bistro Restaurant (263 N Hemlock St, Cannon Beach; 503/436-2661)
Bluehour (250 NW 13th Ave, Portland; 503/226-3394)
Georgie's Beachside Grill (744 SW Elizabeth St, Newport; 541/265-9800)
Newmans at 988 (988 S Hemlock St, Cannon Beach; 503/436-1151)
Riverview Restaurant (29311 SE Stark St, Troutdale; 503/661-3663)
Simon's Cliff House (Columbia Gorge Hotel, 4000 Westcliff Dr, Hood River; 541/386-5566)
Stephanie Inn (2740 S Pacific St, Cannon Beach; 503/436-2221)
Stonehedge Gardens (3405 Wine Country Ave, Hood River; 541/386-3940)

Sandwiches
Boda's Kitchen (404 Oak St, Hood River; 541/386-9876)
Buffalo Gap Saloon & Eatery (6835 SW Macadam Ave, Portland; 503/244-7111)
Court Street Dairy Lunch (347 Court St NE, Salem; 503/363-6433)
Macadangdangs Reefside Bar & Grill (3521 SW Hwy 101, Lincoln City; 541/614-0970)
Neskowin Trading Company (48880 Hwy 101 S, Neskowin; 503/392-3035)
Pine State Biscuits (2204 NE Alberta St, Portland; 503/477-6605)
The Pink House Cafe (242 D St, Independence; 503/837-0900)
Red Fox Bakery (328 NE Evans St, McMinnville; 503/434-5098)

Soups
Canyon Way Bookstore & Restaurant (1216 SW Canyon Way, Newport; 541/265-8319)
Fishtails Cafe (3101 Ferry Slip Road, Newport; 541/867-6002)
McKay Cottage Restaurant (62910 O.B. Riley Road, #340, Bend; 541/383-2697)

Southern
Pine State Biscuits (2204 NE Alberta St, Portland; 503/477-6605)
Zydeco Kitchen & Cocktails (919 NW Bond St, Bend; 541/312-2899)

Steaks
Bigfoot's Steakhouse (2427 S Roosevelt Dr, Seaside; 503/738-7009)
The Blacksmith Restaurant (211 NW Greenwood Ave, Bend; 541/318-0588)
Bob's Texas T-Bone (101 E 1st St, Rufus; 541/739-2559)
Brickhouse (412 SW 6th St, Redmond; 541/526-1782)
Cowboy Dinner Tree (50962 E Bay Road, Silver Lake; 541/576-2426): by reservation only
El Gaucho Portland (The Benson Hotel, 319 SW Broadway, Portland; 503/228-2000)
Fogo de Chão (930 SW 6th Ave, Portland; 503/241-0900)

Haines Steak House (910 Front St, Haines; 541/856-3639)
Hamley Steak House (8 SE Court Ave, Pendleton; 541/278-1100)
Mr. B's Steakhouse (3927 S 6th St, Klamath Falls; 541/883-8719)
Norma's Seafood & Steak (20 N Columbia St, Seaside; 503/738-4331)
Porters – Dining at the Depot (147 N Front St, Medford; 541/857-1910)
RingSide Steakhouse Eastside (14021 NE Glisan St, Portland; 503/255-0750)
RingSide Steakhouse Uptown (2165 W Burnside St, Portland; 503/223-1513)
Rodeo Steak House & Grill (2015 1st St, Tillamook; 503/842-8288)
Rudy's Restaurant (2025 Golf Course Road SE, Salem; 503/399-0449)
Ruth's Chris Steak House (850 SW Broadway, Portland; 503/221-4518)
Sayler's Old Country Kitchen (10519 SE Stark St, Portland; 503/252-4171)
Shirley's Tippy Canoe (28242 E Columbia River Hwy, Troutdale; 503/492-2220)
The Snaffle Bit Dinner House (830 S Canyon Blvd, John Day; 541/575-2426)
Virgil's at Cimmiyotti's (137 S Main St, Pendleton; 541/276-7711)

Sushi
Kanpai Sushi & Saké Bar (990 NW Newport Ave, Bend; 541/388-4636)
Sushi Mazi (2126 SE Division St, Portland; 503/432-8651)
Syun Izakaya (209 NE Lincoln St, Hillsboro; 503/640-3131)

Unique
Camp 18 (42362 Hwy 26, Elsie; 503/755-1818)
Cowboy Dinner Tree (East Bay Road, Silver Lake; 541/576-2426)
Fogo de Chão (930 SW 6th Ave, Portland; 503/241-0900)
Kokanee Cafe (25545 SW Forest Service Road, Camp Sherman; 541/595-6420)
McMenamins (70 unique properties in Oregon and Washington; mcmenamins.com)
Oregon Electric Station (27 E 5th Ave, Eugene; 541/485-4444)
Pine Tavern Restaurant (967 NW Brooks St, Bend; 541/382-5581)
Voodoo Doughnut (22 SW 3rd Ave, Portland; 503/241-4707; 1501 NE Davis, Portland; 503/235-2666 and 20 E Broadway, Eugene; 541/868-8666)

Vegan and Vegetarian Options
Clemente's Cafe & Public House (175 14th St, Astoria; 503/325-1067)
Natural Selection (3033 NE Alberta St, Portland; 503/288-5883)
Nearly Normal's (109 NW 15th St, Corvallis; 541/753-0791)
The Painted Lady (201 S College St, Newberg; 503/538-3850)
Ten Depot Street (10 Depot St, La Grande; 541/963-8766)
Tina's Restaurant (760 Hwy 99W, Dundee; 503/538-8880)
Vault 244 (244 1st Ave W, Albany; 541/791-9511)

View Restaurants
Baked Alaska (1 12th St, Astoria; 503/325-7414)
Bay House (5911 SW Highway 101, Lincoln City; 541/996-3222)
Cascade Dining Room (Timberline Lodge, 27500 E Timberline Road, Timberline; 503/272-3311)

Greg's Grill (395 SW Powerhouse Dr, Bend; 541/382-2200)
The Loft (315 1st St SE, Bandon; 541/329-0535)
Nor'wester Steak & Seafood (10 Harbor Way, Gold Beach; 541/247-2333)
Ona's Restaurant and Lounge (131 Hwy 101 N, Yachats; 541/547-6627)
Pelican Pub & Brewery (33105 Cape Kiwanda Dr, Pacific City; 503/965-7007)
Portland City Grill (111 SW 5th Ave, 30th floor, Portland; 503/450-0030)
Redfish (517 Jefferson St, Port Orford; 541/366-2200)
Restaurant Beck (Whale Cove Inn, 2345 S Hwy 101, Depoe Bay; 541/765-3220)
Riverside (1108 E Marina Dr, Hood River; 541/386-4410)
Roseanna's Cafe (1490 Pacific Ave, Oceanside; 503/842-7351)
Salty's on the Columbia (3839 NE Marine Dr, Portland; 503/288-4444)
Stone Cliff Inn Restaurant & Bar (17900 S Clackamas River Dr, Oregon City; 503/631-7900)
Tidal Raves (279 NW Hwy 101, Depoe Bay; 541/765-2995)
The Waterfront Depot Restaurant (1252 Bay St, Florence; 541/902-9100)
Wayfarer Restaurant & Lounge (1190 Pacific Dr, Cannon Beach; 503/436-1108)

Wine

Abacela Vineyard and Winery (12500 Lookingglass Road, Roseburg; 541/679-6642)
Carlton Winemakers Studio (801 N Scott St, Carlton; 503/852-6100)
Dusky Goose (8355 NE Warren Road, Dundee; 503/857-5776): tasting room set to open early in 2016
Equestrian Wine Tours (6325 NE Abbey Road, Carlton; 541/864-2336)
Helvetia Winery (23269 NW Yungen Road, Hillsboro; 503/647-7596)
Hood River Vineyards and Winery (4693 Westwood Dr, Hood River; 541/386-3772)
King Estate Winery (80854 Territorial Road, Eugene; 541/942-9874)
Orchard Heights Winery (6057 Orchard Heights Road NW, Salem; 503/391-7308)
The Pines Tasting Room (202 Cascade Ave, Suite B, Hood River; 541/993-8301)
Stoller Family Estate (16161 NE McDougall Road, Dayton; 503/864-3404)
Sunshine Mill Artisan Plaza and Winery (901 E Second St, The Dalles; 541/298-8900)
Weisinger Family Winery (3150 Siskiyou Blvd, Ashland; 541/488-5989)
Willamette Valley Vineyards (8800 Enchanted Way SE, Turner; 503/588-9463)
Youngberg Hill Vineyards & Inn (10660 SW Youngberg Hill Road, McMinnville; 503/472-2727)

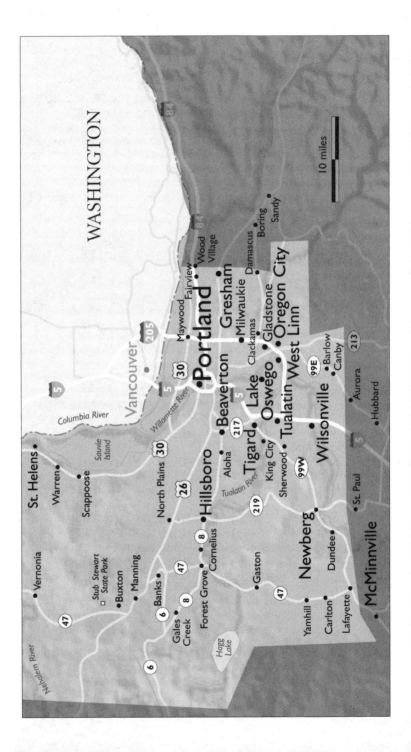

BEAVERTON

decarli

4545 SW Watson Ave
Dinner: Tues-Sun
Moderate

503/641-3223
decarlirestaurant.com

Jana and Paul Decarli are talented and attentive hosts at their Italian ristorante. With a wealth of cooking experience, Chef Paul creates sophisticated and rustic dishes influenced by his Swiss-Italian-American background amalgamated with Northwest fresh bounty. The daily-changing menu includes wonderful salads and pasta, meat, fish and seafood entrees. Fascinating and delicious ingredients and accompaniments turn ordinary offerings into gourmet fare; happy hour selections and desserts receive similar treatment. The warm dining room is lighted by a large brass chandelier which, in another life, illuminated the historic Benson Hotel; private dining room available. Around the corner, the Decarlis have another business: **Watson Hall** (12655 SW 1st St, 503/616-2416) is open for lunch, dinner and Sunday brunch (closed Monday).

Hall Street Grill

3775 SW Hall Blvd
Lunch: Mon-Fri; Dinner: Daily
Moderate to expensive

503/641-6161
hallstreetgrill.com

Hall Street Grill is not only the pinnacle of fine dining in Beaverton, but they also have the best happy hour menu in the neighborhood. Patio seating is great for nice days. Menu options are ever-evolving and feature a Northwest-inspired cuisine; in order to prepare quality dishes, focus remains on local, in-season produce and products. Possible menu items include their signature crispy coconut prawns, salmon, prime rib and a variety of soups, salads, starters and more entrees. The cocktail list is innovative and crafted using only the freshest local juices, herbs and specialty ingredients for unique quality drinks; bartender classic cocktails are just $5.

BED & BREAKFASTS

If you are looking for a cozy lodging option when visiting Portland, here are some great bed and breakfasts:

Evermore Guesthouse (3860 SE Clinton St; 503/206-6509; evermoreguesthouse.com): 1909 Arts and Crafts house in Division/Clinton neighborhood

Friendly Bike Guest House (4039 N Williams Ave; 503/799-2615; friendlybikeguesthouse.com): cyclist-oriented accommodations less than two miles from downtown; inside bike lockup

Heron Haus Bed & Breakfast (2545 NW Westover Road; 503/274-1846; heronhaus.com): beautifully restored 1904 English Tudor in Nob Hill

Lion & the Rose (1810 NE 15th Ave; 503/287-9245; lionrose.com): 1906 Queen Anne mansion in historic Irvington District; on National Register of Historic Places

Mayor's Mansion (3360 SE Ankeny St; 503/232-3588; pdxmayorsmansion.com): four-room 1912 Albee House at Laurelhurst Park; on the National Register of Historic Places

The White House (1914 NE 22nd Ave; 503/287-7131; portlandwhitehouse.com): 1911 Greek Revival mansion in historic Irvington District

La Provence Bakery and Bistro

15151 SW Barrows Road   971/246-8627
(See detailed listing with Petite Provence, Portland)

Stockpot Broiler

8200 SW Scholls Ferry Road   503/643-5451
Lunch, Dinner: Daily; Brunch: Sat, Sun   stockpotbroiler.com
Moderate

When you want a delicious meal, don't forget the always-busy Stockpot Broiler for an elegant lunch or dinner. Chef **Joshua Murphy** features a consistently good menu using Northwest ingredients. You won't be disappointed with dinner from the grill, especially the tender, flavorful steaks. Entree salads are filling, soups are fresh and meals are made to order. In addition to sandwiches and burgers, you can also enjoy Korean bento or seasonal seafood. On weekends, a trip to a buffet of fresh fruit, rich pastries and other treats accompanies brunch favorites like eggs and crab Benedict, German pancakes, classic shrimp and grits and other creative vittles.

FOREST GROVE

Maggie's Buns

2007 21st Ave   503/992-2231
Mon-Fri: 6-5:30; Sat: 7-1:30   maggiesbuns.com
Inexpensive

The slogan at Maggie's Buns is "too hot to handle." The restaurant offers exciting full breakfast and lunch menus; breakfast to 11 midweek and until 1 p.m. on Saturday. Sandwiches are made on Maggie's freshly-baked breads and salads are healthy and tasty; homemade soups change daily and lunch entrees run the gamut from pasta dishes to pork loin and salmon. Giant cinnamon buns are always served piping hot, straight from the oven — as advertised. Maggie's also offers catering and specializes in corporate and wedding events. Come as you are; this is a favorite "gal pal" coffee-and-more spot.

Montinore Estate

3663 SW Dilley Road
Daily: 11-5
Inexpensive

503/359-5012
montinore.com

Father and daughter team, **Rudy and Kristin Marchesi**, run this 210-acre certified biodynamic and organic estate. For those who are not familiar with biodynamic farming, it is said to be one of the most sustainable forms of agriculture resulting in healthier food. Their values lie in that of a well-lived life, which includes good food and wine with friends and family, as well as creating quality wine. Seven grape varieties are grown including Pinot Noir, Pinot Gris, Gewürztraminer, Riesling, Müller-Thurgau, Teroldego and Lagrein. For tastings, the current $10 flight features six wines that change with the seasons. The vineyard is located near the foothills of the Coast Range with views of the mountains; the beautifully appointed tasting room is perched overlooking a stretch of the lush grape vines. Grounds are spacious and picnics are encouraged if visiting on a nice day.

RIVER GUIDES

Our state offers amazing opportunities for guided river adventures — whether it's via canoe, raft, drift boat, jet boat, ocean charter or hiking and fishing. **Oregon Outfitters & Guides** (541/617-9090, ogpa.org) is a non-profit organization that provides a comprehensive list of over 50 guide services on their website; choose your outdoor activity and the region you want to explore. A less extensive list of outfitters and guides is available at **Travel Oregon** (traveloregon.com). Click on "recreation" and your preferred activity. Whether you're planning a day or overnight trip, let your selected guide take care of the details for a safe river outing.

SakèOne

820 Elm St
Daily: 11-5

503/357-7056
sakeone.com

This is a different kind of craft brewery. SakéOne brews saké for America, based on more than 500 years of Japanese history and traditions. Production includes six traditional Junmai Ginjo sakés (premium grade, including two organic), a super-premium saké brand called g Saké and a fruit-infused saké under their Moonstone brand. All are available nationally and, increasingly, internationally. In the tasting room, choose from three saké tasting flights; you will also find imported Japanese saké, saké glassware and logo apparel. Enlightening guided afternoon tours are conducted daily at 1, 2 and 3. Kanpai!

Stecchino Bistro

2014 Main St   503/352-9921
Lunch, Dinner: Wed-Sat   stecchinobistro.com
Moderately expensive

Nestled in a historic Main Street storefront, Stecchino Bistro is as good as its metropolitan counterparts and serves well-prepared French and Italian fare. Wherever possible ats and produce are locally-sourced and soups, pastas a s are always made in-house. The day's specials are a large chalkboard until they run out. You'll find ppings for each of the three crusty bruschetta sli catches-of-the-day, fresh sausages and the night's pre on of duck or chicken breast. Don't miss out on the scrumptious desserts by pastry chef and owner **Randy Reeder**. Executive Chef **Jeremy McMurtry**'s interpretations of such treats as the butternut squash tart and chicken saltimbocca receive

MAGNIFICENT MANSION

Beautiful **Pittock Mansion** (3229 NW Pittock Dr, Portland; 503/823-3624; pittockmansion.org) was completed in 1914 for **Henry Pittock**, Portland businessman and founder of *The Daily Oregonian*. Pittock built an empire in real estate, banking, railroads, steamboats, sheep ranching, silver mining and the pulp and paper industry; talk about diversification! The French Renaissance house is furnished with 18th- and 19th-century European and American antiques. Sitting atop 46 acres, it offers panoramic views of the city. Christmas is a particularly fun time to visit as rooms are filled with holiday decorations, lights and Christmas trees.

high marks and elicit repeat requests. Reservations are strongly recommended on Friday and Saturday evenings.

GALES CREEK

OutAZAblue Market & Cafe

57625 NW Wilson River Hwy   503/357-2900
Breakfast, Lunch, Dinner: Wed-Sun   outazablue.com
Moderate

Chef **Gabriel Barber** chose this small Washington County spot to perform his European-honed culinary talents. The ambitious menu offers everything from attractively presented sandwiches and wraps to pizzas, pastas, burgers, steaks, fish and poultry dishes; pizzas and calzones are fashioned on fresh pizza skins with unique ingredients. AZA breakfasts are advertised as extraordinary and sweets and healthy breads are homemade. Youngsters feel grown up when they are offered a choice of kid-favorite ingredients and sauces for their special pasta dishes. Chef Gabriel says that the meaning behind OutAZABlue is "to create anything from A to Z." Catering is available off-site and for intimate on-site events. This countryside market also sources take-home organic produce, breads, meats and dairy products.

GLADSTONE

Tebo's Restaurant

19120 McLoughlin Blvd   503/655-6333
Lunch, Dinner: Daily   tebos.net
Moderate

What started out as Gene & Joe's years ago has only improved with Tebo's new owners, **Craig Klein** and **John Karlik**, bringing you better food and desserts. Menu offerings are hot-off-the-grill hamburgers, fresh-cut fries, healthy salads, delicious homemade desserts such as pies and their famous strawberry shortcake (in season from spring until early fall); *Willamette Week* awarded a "best bite" to Tebo's shortcake and stated that it is "the best and only reason to go to

WHO'S BREWING

As of 2015, Oregon has some 194 brewing companies (and more than 16 cideries) in 72 towns. In Portland alone there are 61 breweries; more than any other city in the world. Our state's fast-growing craft beer industry has gained much respect, not only for its quality, but also for its variety. For tasting opportunities be sure to check out annual events like the **Oregon Brewers Festival**. A list of breweries, festivals and events is available (by area) at oregoncraftbeer.org.

Gladstone." Craig and John have worked at the restaurant for 25 years and hold on strong to traditions of serving the highest quality food using fresh ingredients and knowing thousands of their customers by name; a place where you can truly feel at home. Freshly-baked pies are available by special order on their website.

HILLSBORO

Copper River Restaurant and Bar

7370 NE Cornell Road
Lunch, Dinner: Daily
Moderate

503/640-0917
copperriverrestaurant.com

I am a big fan of the two Oswego Grills and it's no wonder I am now a devotee of Copper River, too. After all, they are locally-owned and -operated by the same Burnett tribe that so successfully runs the Oswego Grills. With the help of other members of the family and expert advice from David's mentor, the late Bob Farrell (of Farrell's Ice Cream Parlours), **Christie and David Burnett** have now opened a huge sparkling room in the shadows of Hillsboro's Intel and Nike. Copper River is a sure crowd pleaser with an attractive atmosphere, a huge and inviting menu and superbly-trained help, managed by very able family member **Kristen Burnett**. The 300-seat facility includes a private dining area for any occasion, offers ample parking and two happy hour menus and delicious food using the finest and freshest ingredients. Included on the menu are 21 appetizers, varying from traditional fried chicken tenderloins to corn fritters, more than 52 featured craft beers, a variety of canned and bottled beers, local wines that are sure to satisfy any taste, hearty salads, sandwiches and just about everything else a hungry family might want without spending a fortune. When customers are treated like family, as is the case with the Burnett tribe, success is assured.

Helvetia Tavern
10275 NW Helvetia Road   503/647-5286
Lunch, Dinner: Daily   Facebook
Inexpensive to moderate

It's interesting to note that Helvetia Tavern opened the day that the Prohibition Era came to a close. Decades later, beer continues to flow with domestic, imported, draft and micros by the pint or pitcher. While the rustic, rural locale is part of the draw, foremost are burgers, all made with freshly-ground beef, cooked to perfection and finished with the usual fixings and special sauce (bacon, jalapenos and ham are extra). Don't pass on an order of hand-cut fries and onion rings (or both). If you visit on a warm day you'll want to sit outside on the patio. Note that this is a "cash only" business, but there is an ATM conveniently on-site.

The Reedville Cafe
7575 SE Tualatin Valley Hwy   503/649-4643
Breakfast, Lunch, Dinner: Daily   reedvillecafe.com
Moderate

The Reedville Cafe is a local institution that started as the Shack Tavern in 1934; it has been owned and operated by the Van Beveren family since 1950. With a name change in 1990, the building has seen several remodels in order to serve ever-growing numbers of loyal customers. Breakfast, lunch, dinner and happy hour menus are served daily and there is outdoor seating in season. For breakfast there's hearty, slow-roasted corned beef hash and eggs with horseradish sauce along with plenty of other good options such as omelets, pancakes, French toast combos and biscuits with country gravy. The lunch and dinner menus feature backyard burgers and

CHALLENGING EAT FEATS

Adam's Rib Smoke House (1210 State St, Salem; 503/362-2194): Eat the two-pound burger (with trimmings and one pound of fries) within 60 minutes and get it free along with an "I conquered Goliath" T-shirt and bragging rights!

Paizano's Pizza (2940 10th St, Baker City; 541/524-1000): Eat a 24-inch giant pizza within 30 minutes and get the pizza free plus $100.

Roxy Dawgs (1425 NW Monroe Ave, Corvallis; 541/207-3351): Take the Dawg Pack Challenge and eat 9 specialty dogs in 30 minutes; dogs are free if you succeed!

Sayler's Old Country Kitchen (10519 SE Stark, Portland; 503/252-4171): This challenge is to eat a 72-ounce steak with all the trimmings within 60 minutes and it is free-of-charge.

Stepping Stone Cafe (2390 NW Quimby St, Portland; 503/222-1132): Indulge in the Great Pancake Challenge, eat three giant pancakes and earn your pic on the "wall of shame."

Voodoo Doughnut (22 SW 3rd Ave, Portland; 503/241-4704): Eat the Tex-Ass Challenge doughnut (equal to six regular-sized ones) in 80 seconds or less and you get your money back.

For seasonal offerings, check out pie-eating contests during harvest festival at **E.Z. Orchards** (5504 Hazel Green Road NE, Salem; 503/393-1506) and at other farm festivals.

tasty seafood baskets. Monthly specials include Crabfest in January, Steakfest in April, Sizzlin' Summer BBQ in July and Oktoberfest in the fall. A full bar offers craft beers, wine and cocktails. It's no wonder this cafe continues to be a busy place.

Rice Northwest Museum of Rocks and Minerals
26385 NW Groveland Dr   503/647-2418
Wed-Fri: 1-5; Sat, Sun: 10-5   ricenorthwestmuseum.org
Nominal

This educational attraction is home to one of the world's best collections of crystals and petrified wood, plus a fascinating showing of fluorescent minerals. The working collection of over 20,000 specimens includes the "Alma Rose" Rhodochrosite, dinosaur eggs, meteorites and an impressive chunk of gold and exotics. Don't miss what is perhaps Oregon's largest state rock, a one-ton thunder egg. The gift shop is like no other museum outpost with high-end faceted gemstone jewelry as well as rare books and polished stones. Saturdays offer regularly scheduled guided tours (private group tours available by request).

A PARTY FOR THE ELEVATOR GIRLS

A friend asked me the other day if I knew where he could get a Santa suit to surprise his grandchildren at Christmas. I have one that has been put away for many years. I had to smile at the thought of the last time I wore the Santa suit; it was a disaster!

I was a rather young fellow working in the downtown Portland Meier & Frank store. We had a bank of twenty elevators which were manned by Portland's most attractive and personable young ladies. Being a co-worker, I was excited to be invited to their Christmas breakfast. Just one catch in the invitation; I was to be the entertainment!

What better, I thought, than to appear as the spirit of Christmas himself, Santa Claus. But what would I do once I was in the proper outfit? I spent days coming up with feeble rhymes that included colorful stories in the lives of these elevator operators.

All was going well, when in the middle of my presentation, my audience erupted into sustained laughter. The stories were not really that funny, it seemed to me. My Santa Claus outfit included a pillow stuffed in my pants, held together with a safety pin attached to the top portion of my trousers. All of a sudden in the midst of the uproar, I felt a distinct draft in my lower extremities. You guessed it. The safety pin had broken, and my Santa pants were sitting on the floor. There I was, in my underwear, the boss' son, half naked in front of all those thoroughly amused co-workers. It took several weeks before I was once again able to ride the store's elevators!

*(From **Gerry Frank's Friday Surprise**)*

Syun Izakaya

209 NE Lincoln St   503/640-3131
Lunch: Mon-Sat; Dinner: Daily   syun-izakaya.com
Moderate

The feature at this quaint Japanese pub-style restaurant in Hillsboro's former Carnegie Library is stupendous sushi. Lovers of this delicacy will find a large selection of dishes: raw fish, sashimi, sushi rolls and delicious daily specials that include hot dishes and noodles. Patrons unfamiliar with the cuisine on this expansive menu are well-served by the knowledgeable and attentive staff; recommendations for food are on the mark. They'll also steer you toward fine sakés from their impressive inventory or you may opt for your familiar favorite from the full bar. Enter the brownstone under the green awning; seasonal outdoor seating.

Thirsty Lion Pub and Grill

2290 NW Allie Ave   503/336-0403
(See detailed listing with Thirsty Lion Pub and Grill, Tigard)

LAKE OSWEGO

Baird's on B

485 2nd St   503/303-4771
Lunch: Mon-Fri; Dinner: Daily   bairdsonb.com
Moderate

Baird's on B is an attractive space in downtown Lake Oswego that includes a patio for outdoor dining in nice weather. **Baird Bulmore** has put together an interesting well-priced menu that includes smaller plates and snacks for those not wanting a full meal; some offerings are seasonal. Items include crab cakes, fish and chips, mac and cheese, housemade potato chips and more. For heartier appetites, fresh salads, grilled salmon, seared scallops, steak and burgers are offered. Roasted chicken is a delicious choice; filling and tasty desserts include lemon and chocolate mousse. One word of information: access is up a flight of rather steep steps.

KIDS' ACTIVITIES: IN AND AROUND TOWN

GASTON
Tree to Tree Adventure Park (503/357-0109, tree2treeadventurepark. com): seasonal; reservations required
HILLSBORO
Hillsboro Ballpark (503/640-0887, hillsborohops.com): seasonal
Rice Northwest Museum of Rocks & Minerals (503/647-2418, ricenorthwestmuseum.org)
MILWAUKIE
North Clackamas Aquatic Park (503/557-7873, ncprd.com/aquatic-park)
Portland Aquarium (503/303-4721, portlandaquarium.net)
PORTLAND
Lloyd Center Ice Rink (503/288-6073, lloydcenterice.com)
Oaks Amusement Park (503/233-5777, oakspark.com): seasonal
OMSI (503/797-4000; omsi.edu)
Oregon History Museum (503/222-1741, ohs.org)
Oregon Rail Heritage Center (503/233-1156, orhf.org)
Oregon Zoo (503/226-1561, oregonzoo.org)
Portland Aerial Tram (503/494-8283, gobytram.com)

Clarke's Restaurant

455 2nd St   503/636-2667
Dinner: Mon-Sat   clarkesrestaurant.net
Expensive

With sophisticated surroundings and delicious dinners, **Laurie and Jonathan Clarke**'s upscale restaurant is a go-to spot in Lake Oswego. Rack of lamb is a reliable favorite and is as good as I've tasted anywhere; lobster and shrimp risotto is also popular. Beef, fish and pork entrees are seasonally prepared to benefit from the freshest fruits, vegetables and herbs befitting this gourmet fare. Among several appetizer choices, you won't go wrong with the artisan cheese platter. The bar area is a cheerful stop for late afternoon happy hour with moderately-priced casual bar grub. Banquets and private dining occasions are easily accommodated. Busy Laurie pulls double duty with her artistic celebration cake business (503/662-2533, laurieclarkecakes.com).

KIDS' ACTIVITIES, CONTINUED

Portland Art Museum (503/226-2811, portlandartmuseum.org)
Portland Children's Museum (503/223-6500, portlandcm.org)
Portland Police Museum (503/823-0019, portlandpolicemuseum.com)
Portland Public Parks (503/823-7529, portlandparks.org): Jamison Square (810 NW 11th Ave) and Keller Fountain (SW 3rd Ave and Clay St) are summertime favorites.
Portland Saturday Market (503/241-4188, portlandsaturdaymarket.com)
Portland Spirit River Cruise (503/224-3900, portlandspirit.com)
Powell's City of Books (503/228-4651, powells.com)
World Forestry Center's Discovery Museum (503/228-1367, worldforestry.org)

SAUVIE ISLAND

Sauvie Island (sauvieisland.org)

TIGARD

The House of Reptiles & Venomous Reptile Museum (503/722-1992, house-of-reptiles.com)

WILSONVILLE

Family Fun Center and Bullwinkle's Restaurant (503/685-5000, fun-center.com/wilsonville)

La Provence Bakery and Bistro

16350 SW Boones Ferry Road   503/635-4533
(See detailed listing with Petite Provence, Portland)

Oswego Grill at Kruse Way

7 Centerpointe Dr   503/352-4750
Lunch, Dinner: Daily   oswegogrill.com
Moderate

Experienced local ownership is evident here with the winning ingredients of well-trained and friendly wait staff. The varied menu includes twice daily happy hour specials, fresh salads, burgers, first-rate prime rib sandwiches, pot pies, hand-selected steaks and more American classics. The hardwood grill's distinctive smoky mesquite and apple wood flavor is found on the romaine lettuce salad, meats, chicken and fish with Cajun, Southwest and Thai influences spicing up the menu. Desserts like warm, rich scratch-made doughnuts and hot-from-the-oven cookies and ice cream top off an amazing meal. A sister location, **Oswego Grill at Wilsonville** (30800 SW Boones Ferry Road) and newly-opened **Copper River Restaurant and Bar** (7370 NE Cornell Road, Hillsboro), are equally attractive and as charming as hardworking owners **Christie and David Burnett** and **Kathy and Bud Gabriel.**

St. Honoré Boulangerie

315 1st St   503/496-5596
(See detailed listing with St. Honoré Boulangerie, Portland)

Tucci Ristorante

220 A Ave   503/697-3383
Lunch: Mon-Fri; Dinner: Daily   tucci.biz
Moderate

Tucci Ristorante is a delightful casually elegant dining spot featuring authentic Italian fare prepared in an open kitchen. The evolving menu changes seasonally and features homemade artisanal pastas, quality meats, fresh and sustainable Northwest foods and local Italian-inspired foods. Changing dessert selections might include plates of assorted sweet bites or salted caramel chocolate cake. Alfresco dining is offered in summer. The recently-expanded Lido Bar features "Hollywood-style" booth seating.

MILWAUKIE

Bob's Red Mill Whole Grain Store

5000 SE International Way   503/607-6455, 800/349-2173
Mon-Sat: 6-6 (restaurant till 3)   bobsredmill.com

Since 1978 **Charlee and Bob Moore** have been grinding out flours, mixes, cereals, vegetarian-friendly products and other good-for-you eats (including gluten-free goods). The 15,000 square-foot red barn is a popular retail store that features all of Bob's Red Mill foods (packaged and bulk) and culinary-related items, a casual restaurant

PORTLAND MUSICAL TALENT

Pink Martini (pinkmartini.com) is the musical vision of very talented Portlander **Thomas Lauderdale**. While working in politics and attending lots of fundraisers, Thomas became acutely aware of the disappointing music at such events. He was inspired to form Pink Martini, his "little orchestra," with the goal of providing beautiful music for political events supporting important causes such as the environment, civil rights, education, affordable housing and others. The talented group currently features a dozen musicians performing a multilingual repertoire on concert stages and with symphony orchestras in Europe, Asia, the Middle East and North and South America. The music crosses genres such as classical, jazz and old-fashioned pop. Lead vocalists include **China Forbes**, a fellow Harvard classmate of Lauderdale, and **Storm Large**, who joined the band in 2011. The group has released ten albums to date, the most recent, *Dream a Little Dream*; some recordings include guest artists. If you have yet to experience Pink Martini, check online for their next local performance as this is an Oregon must. Thomas is a gem!

serving breakfast and lunch and in-house bakery. Nutritious recipes and essential techniques are taught in cooking classes also emphasizing whole grains. It's mighty difficult to resist the bakery which turns out dozens of healthy breads, muffins, cookies and vegan goodies; you'll spot them on the breakfast and lunch menus as well as other choices made with Bob's products. Beautifully landscaped grounds, super products, helpful suggestions and knowledgeable employees make this a true Oregon winner. The state-of-the-art milling, packaging and distribution operations are one mile down the road (15321 SE Pheasant Ct). Guests learn the ins-and-outs of the business with a smattering of the industry's history on a free tour of the facility conducted Monday through Friday mornings at 10.

Dave's Killer Bread

5209 SE International Way
Mon-Sat: 7:30-6

503/335-8077
daveskillerbread.com

Dave's Killer Bread is currently the best-selling organic, sliced bread in the U.S., with 17 varieties of whole grain. DKB revolutionized the healthy bread industry in 2005 when it first pioneered the organic seeded bread category. That year the resulting product was first introduced at Portland Farmers Market. Delicious slices are packed with nutritious grains, nuts and seeds, but no artificial preservatives. Not only are the breads nutritious, but they make fabulous toast and sandwiches. The company continues its commitment to the power of second chances; one in three employee-partners have a criminal background and are being helped to transform their lives.

Enchanté
10883 SE Main St   503/654-4846
Tues-Fri: 11-5:30; Sat: 11-4   enchantechocolatier.com

Enchanté is a Parisian-style chocolatier, located in the heart of historic downtown Milwaukie. Husband-and-wife duo **Kim and Bill Cairo** proudly handcraft their own chocolates in a tradition that has lasted 85 years. Additionally, several varieties of caramel corn are still made in a traditional copper candy kettle. When you visit this enchanting store you will be drawn in by exquisite displays that include confections from around the globe. There is a beautiful selection of gift items including treasures from Paris flea markets. *USA Today* named Enchanté one of the top ten candy stores in the country.

OREGON CITY

Stone Cliff Inn Restaurant & Bar
17900 S Clackamas River Dr   503/631-7900
Lunch, Dinner: Daily   stonecliffinn.com
Moderately expensive to expensive

Built from Douglas fir logs on the remains of a basalt quarry, Stone Cliff Inn Restaurant & Bar is a nod to Carver and the rock quarry and logging industries. The menu options at Stone Cliff Inn are abundant and prepared from scratch. Smoked salmon chowder is always available as well as a soup of the moment followed by side and entree salads (Caesar, spinach, warm beet with goat cheese and more). Interesting and appetizing rubs, spices and glazes are used in steak and seafood preparations; favorites of the house include cioppino, baby back ribs, bacon-wrapped meatloaf and hazelnut chicken. Pasta dishes are laden with goodies from the land and sea with the option to add chicken, salmon, prawns or steak to an already hearty dish. Try the lamb shank or duck ravioli if you are lucky enough to visit when these savory dishes are available. Lunch choices include many of the same items and a nice selection of sandwiches and entrees. If you have room, marionberries are in two desserts: crème brûlée and apple berry strudel. *Twilight* movie fans may recognize the property as a backdrop for several scenes.

The Verdict Bar & Grill

110 8th St · 503/305-8429
Lunch, Dinner: Daily · Facebook
Moderate to moderately expensive

Owner **Ryan Smith** remodeled Oregon's oldest commercial building and created his friendly Verdict restaurant across from the

OREGON WONDERS

Though they may be missing from the "Seven Wonders of the World" list, Oregon has its own amazing noteworthy attractions.

Columbia River Gorge: National Scenic Area; 80 mile stretch of Columbia River canyon (4,000 feet deep)
Crater Lake: deepest lake in the United States at 1,943 feet
Mt. Hood: the 11,245-foot peak offers hiking and snow sports; panoramic views from historic Timberline Lodge
Oregon Coast: 363 breathtaking miles of public coast; thus called the "people's coast"
Painted Hills: colorful geological layers; part of John Day Fossil Beds National Monument
Smith Rock State Park: 3,000-foot tower of compressed volcanic ash in high desert; hiking and climbing
Wallowa Mountains: 10,000-foot peaks also known as "Little Switzerland"

Clackamas County Courthouse. The reasonably-priced lunch and dinner menus are broken down as "Opening Statements" (delicious bacon-wrapped shrimp and hot artichoke dip), "Lighter Sentence" (soups and salads), "In the Jury Box" (classic sandwiches and burgers) and "Order in the Court" (fish and chips, fish tacos, pasta). "Night Court" options include braised pork osso bucco and black truffle scallops; "Guilty as Charged" refers to the fresh dessert options. Flat screen TVs, free Wi-Fi, hand-crafted cocktails and Oregon brews and spirits round out the docket. Smith's next door casual coffee shop, the **Caufield House** is convenient to downtown workers for breakfast, lunch and a quick cuppa joe. Banquet and private party space are available at **The Verdict** and **The Holding Cell**, appropriately named for its location between the two entities.

PORTLAND

3 Doors Down Café & Lounge
1429 SE 37th Ave   503/236-6886
Dinner: Tues-Sun   3doorsdowncafe.com
Moderate to moderately expensive

    This Italian sanctuary is serious about two things: wine and food. The list of imported and Northwest wines, sparkling wines and champagnes is impressive; specialty cocktails are artfully composed. Some wines by the glass are straight from the barrel and there are cocktails and cider on tap. You can cut to the chase and order full-bodied pasta dishes and flavorful roast chicken or linger over reasonably-priced antipasto, appetizers and happy hour small plates while you navigate the bar offerings. Bring this bite of Italy to your next party with group-size appetizers, entrees and desserts (arrange in advance).

23Hoyt
529 NW 23rd Ave   503/445-7400
Dinner: Daily; Brunch: Sat, Sun   23hoyt.com
Moderate to moderately expensive

    Sophisticated New American tavern, 23Hoyt (so named for its location at 23rd and Hoyt), has a birdseye view of this hip neighborhood. The two-story front windows bathe the first floor bar and upstairs dining room in natural light. It's no secret that this is a hot spot for daily happy hour snacks (priced between $2 and $9). Segue to dinner and choose from the chef's farm-to-table menu of interesting soups and salads, charcuterie made in-house and entrees accompanied by seasonal sides given an updated twist; the listing changes daily. Brunch kicks off with eye-opening mimosas and delivers punched-up doughnuts, burgers, omelets, salads and sandwiches.

a Cena

7742 SE 13th Ave   503/206-3291
Lunch: Tues-Sat; Dinner: Daily   acenapdx.com
Moderately expensive to expensive

Enjoy lunch or dinner at a Cena (Italian meaning "come to supper"), reminiscent of an Italian country kitchen. On a changing menu, freshly-baked focaccia bread, pizzas and cured meats are favorites. Fabulous pasta dishes are made in-house; lasagna varieties change daily and tender ravioli are stuffed with housemade ricotta cheese. Second courses of duck, braised short ribs, lamb, trout and seafood are equally enticing with exquisite fresh ingredients. For the finale, enjoy espresso or after-dinner coffee drinks and savor affogato, cannoli or tiramisu; all desserts are made daily from scratch.

Alpenrose Dairy

6149 SW Shattuck Road   503/244-1133
Events are seasonal   alpenrose.com

One of the great family names in Oregon is Cadonau, who own and operate Alpenrose Dairy in southwest Portland. Since its beginning in 1891 when Florian Cadonau began delivering milk in a horse-drawn wagon, this family has provided top-quality dairy products. In 1916 during the next-generation operation that included Florian's son, Henry, the business was officially named "Alpenrose" after the national Swiss flower. Family entertainment became an integral part of the business, including the annual Easter Egg Hunt that generations of children fondly remember; Dairyville

BEST FOR CRAB AND OTHER SEAFOOD

Fresh Dungeness crab and crab feeds are synonymous with winter in Oregon. I make the rounds of roll-up-your-sleeves-and-crack-your-own crab feasts at local establishments. While crab is almost always on seafood menus, the top season runs from December to mid-August, peaking in February. Check out the tasty offerings at these favorite places:

Baked Alaska (1 12th St, Astoria; 503/325-7414; bakedak.com): outstanding crab cakes for lunch or dinner; great Columbia River view

Barnacle Bill's Seafood Market (2174 NE Hwy 101, Lincoln City; 541/994-3022 and 41600 Oretown Road, Cloverdale; 541/994-3022; barnaclebillsseafoodmarket.com): very friendly service and good prices; fresh from the ocean; superb smoked salmon

Bell Buoy of Seaside (1800 S Roosevelt Dr, Seaside; 800/529-2722; bellbuoyofseaside.com): specialty seafood store; online and phone orders

Ecola Seafoods Restaurant & Market (208 N Spruce, Cannon Beach; 503/431-9130; ecolaseafoods.com): quality, fresh Pacific wild seafood, plus smoked salmon jerky and homemade clam chowder

Fitt's Seafood (1555 12th St, Salem; 503/364-6724; fitts.net): reliable source for all types of fresh seafood

Jake's Famous Crawfish (401 SW 12th Ave, Portland; 503/226-1419; jakesfamouscrawfish.com): the long-running, top seafood restaurant in Portland (reservations suggested)

Local Ocean Seafoods (213 SE Bay Blvd, Newport; 541/574-7959; localocean.net): full-service restaurant; fresh seafood

Newman's Fish Market at City Market (735 NW 21st St, Portland; 503/227-2700 and **Newman's Fish Company** (1545 Willamette St, Eugene; 541/344-2371; newmansfish.com): outstanding selection; special orders; seafood salads, accompaniments and more

Oregon Lox Company (4828 W 11th Ave, Eugene; 541/726-5699; oregonlox.com): assorted smoked salmon, lox and trout

Sportsmen's Cannery & Smokehouse (182 Bayfront Loop, Winchester Bay; 541/271-3293; sportsmenscannery.com): full array of fresh fish and seafood; overnight shipping; delicious meals

Tony's Crab Shack & Seafood Grill (155 1st St, Bandon; 541/347-2875; tonyscrabshack.com): whole crabs served with drawn butter; crab ring rentals

is a replica frontier town; the Alpenrose Stadium provides baseball facilities for Little League and the girls' Little League Softball World Series; the Alpenrose Velodrome (bicycle race track) is Olympic-class and one of only 20 in the United States and a Quarter Midget Racing arena attracts speedster enthusiasts. All recreational facilities offer free admission (check with Alpenrose for a detailed calendar). 2016 marks the 100th anniversary as Alpenrose Dairy. What an amazing accomplishment!

Andina

1314 NW Glisan St
Lunch, Dinner: Daily
Moderate to expensive

503/228-9535
andinarestaurant.com

Andina is a standout Peruvian restaurant in the Pearl. Celebrating the country's culture and cuisine, the space is bold, warm and beautiful and masterfully appointed to showcase the atrium. A large menu lists various Andean tapas — meats, fish, vegetables and cheeses. Plates are offered in two sizes to savor or share. You won't be disappointed with the extensive wine list (Northwest, Spanish, South American) and imaginative cocktails served in the lounge or dining room. Dressed-up family recipes and traditional entrees are served for both lunch and dinner; each presentation is a visual masterpiece. Meat and fish headliners are deliciously married with herbs, spices, quinoa and sundry elements creating unforgettable flavors as in the double rack of lamb served with a Peruvian potato side and roasted pepper demi-glace. The wait staff is knowledgeable and gracious; their Spanish pronunciation of menu items is music to my ears.

Baker & Spice Bakery

6330 SW Capitol Hwy
Tues-Fri: 6-6; Sat, Sun: 7-6

503/244-7573
bakerandspicepdx.com

Sugar and spice and all things nice describe Baker & Spice's retail bakery operation and cafe in the Hillsdale Shopping Center. Breads, pastries and lunch items are made in small batches from scratch with European-style butter, Belgian chocolate and the best local, organic and imported ingredients. The displays are overflowing with hearty scones, buttery croissants, housemade granola, fruit-laden hand pies, cookies, tarts and daily variations of bread pudding. Pies are available Friday and Saturday or any day by pre-order. Baguettes, buns, rolls, loaves and rounds are baked daily and Andina loaves (potato quinoa loaf) are available periodically. For lunch, enjoy savory meat or vegetarian sandwiches made with the fresh breads or homemade soups and salads. Grab-n-go sandwiches are available to pick up at 8:30 for later lunch. Visit their cake annex and retail bakeware store, **The Cakery** (6306 SW Capitol Hwy, 503/546-3737), just eight storefronts up.

Bar Mingo
811 NW 21st Ave   503/445-4646
Dinner: Daily   barmingonw.com
Moderate

If you are looking for a bar that specializes in casual Italian fare, then look no further than Bar Mingo. There are plenty of easy-priced hot and cold sharable plates and daily happy hour specials between 4 and 6. Substantial dinner choices are listed on the giant chalkboard featuring several fresh pasta dishes. This attractive watering hole offers sidewalk seating, perfect on warm evenings. Come early, it is always crowded! Next door, **Caffe Mingo** (503/226-4646) is open daily for dinner with comforting zuppa (soup), pasta of the day and other tempting Italian plates.

Beaches Restaurant and Bar
Portland International Airport
7000 NE Airport Way   503/335-8385
Breakfast, Lunch, Dinner: Daily   beachesrestaurandandbar.com
Moderate

For innovative and satisfying meals at the Portland Airport, step into Beaches. Owner/operator **Mark Matthias** has a superbly-trained wait staff that operates efficiently and makes customers feel welcome. The tempting menu has something for everyone's taste: Asian, American and Italian choices including an inexpensive kids' menu. The long hours accommodate travelers' breakfast, lunch and dinner appetites; breakfast is offered all day, ideal for surviving jet lag. If you're in a hurry, stop by their quick-service **Beach Shack** (5 a.m. to 9 p.m.) on the airport's main concourse for to-go food to take aboard your flight. Both outlets have delicious options and marvelous caramel corn that is made fresh daily. The main Beaches location is on the Columbia River in Vancouver (1919 SE Columbia River Dr, 360/699-1592). Beaches is a topnotch operation!

Beast

5425 NE 30th Ave
Dinner: Wed-Sun; Brunch: Sun
Expensive

503/841-6968
beastpdx.com

Best to plan ahead for this one! Diners are offered a choice of two seatings Wednesday through Saturday, one seating on Sunday night and a six-course *prix-fixe* menu (one menu for the week; substitutions politely declined) four nights a week. Scrumptious meals are inspired by fresh and intriguing ingredients from local sources; the charcuterie plate (braised duck, beef cheeks, terrines) is generous and immensely flavorful. Main courses are at the chef's whim according to the season and varying cuts from whole lambs, pigs and other beasts. Vegetable garnishes and accompaniments are oh-so-good. Special dinners are offered twice a month including vegetarian meals and meals with special cocktail pairings. Cheese and dessert courses warrant saving room and wine pairings are carefully chosen to best complement each course. Four-course Sunday brunches (10 or noon) are similarly composed.

Bellino Trattoria Siciliana

1230 NW Hoyt St, #B
Lunch, Brunch: Fri-Sun; Dinner: Daily
Inexpensive to moderately expensive

503/208-2992
bellinoportland.com

The space once known as the Fratelli restaurant, located in the Pearl District, has been transformed into Portland's only Sicilian restaurant. Native Sicilian executive chef and owner, **Francesco Inguaggiato**, brings authentic Sicilian culture to the table serving traditional street food such as *Assaggini*, also known as Sicilian tapas, *Arancini* (fried rice balls with various fillings), Crochette and *Panelle* (garbanzo bean fritters). Other menu options include meat, fish and vegetarian dishes as well as freshly-prepared pasta dishes; local and sustainable ingredients are always used. Classic Sicilian dishes are served for weekend brunch and lunch. On Mondays, Festa Italiana, a weekly supper club, features cuisine from different Italian regions. An extensive beverage menu, including a variety of imported Italian wines, is served daily.

The Benson Hotel

309 SW Broadway   503/228-2000, 800/663-1144
Moderate and up   bensonhotel.com

The Benson is one of Portland's most elegant landmarks where guests are greeted by debonair doormen. For over 100 years it has been the "residence of the presidents," graciously accommodating each U.S. president from William Howard Taft to Barack Obama (and many celebrities, too). This elegant property features original Austrian crystal chandeliers, Italian marble floors and historical Circassian walnut imported from the forests of Imperial Russia. Guests unwind in 287 sophisticated guest rooms and suites; most are outfitted with a comfortable Tempur-Pedic mattress. There are also specially designed eight-foot pillow-top mattresses in select rooms and suites and luxurious amenities by Gilchrist & Soames along with organic bamboo bathrobes and slippers, umbrellas, in-room safes and modern technology. Lavish ballrooms have been the scene of memorable soirees for Portland's elite and the setting for impressive business meetings. **El Gaucho Portland** steakhouse offers old-school tableside service perfect for special occasions while **The Palm Court**

> ### DID YOU KNOW...?
>
> ...the famous White Stag sign in downtown Portland now reads Portland Oregon. At one time, it used to say Made in Oregon — a bone of contention among many Portlanders. The day after Thanksgiving a red bulb is lit on the stag's nose to welcome the holiday season.
>
> ... Portland has been home to many famous bands/musicians such as The Kingsmen, The Dandy Warhols, Everclear, Pink Martini, The Shins, Blitzen Trapper, The Decemberists and the late Elliott Smith.

Restaurant and Bar offers relaxing lobby dining featuring sumptuous menu options for breakfast, lunch and dinner along with twice-nightly happy hours and live entertainment. Exemplary accommodations and service are first-class.

Bistro by Truss
1401 SW Naito Pkwy   503/226-7600
(See detailed listing with Portland Marriott Downtown Waterfront)

Bluehour
250 NW 13th Ave   503/226-3394
Lunch: Mon-Fri; Dinner: Daily   bluehouronline.com
Expensive

Under the direction of restaurateur **Bruce Carey**, Bluehour continues to wow patrons in a modern yet intimate setting. The Pacific Northwest seasonal menu with Mediterranean influences features the area's rich bounty. Expect terrines, salads, pastas, fish and seafood, duck confit and more; opt for a tasting menu for optimal flavor exposure. "Happy Bluehour" eats are casual and range from fried green tomatoes to gnocchi with arugula and scallions and the signature burger. Satisfying desserts include plum and sour cream cake, citrus coconut macaroons and nectarine and berry sorbet.

Buffalo Gap Saloon & Eatery
6835 SW Macadam Ave   503/244-7111
Breakfast, Lunch, Dinner: Daily   thebuffalogap.com
Moderate

Every neighborhood deserves a place like the Buffalo Gap: fun, laid-back, extended hours, consistently good food and a jam-packed menu. Breakfast choices are hearty (housemade biscuits and gravy) or sensible (Paleo breakfast tacos) and gigantic cinnamon rolls are baked each morning. Soups are made from scratch; specialty salads are indeed special and laden with lots of tasty ingredients and intriguingly-named sandwiches and burgers are served with a choice of sides. Not to be overlooked are pizzas, pastas and full-meal-deal dinner platters. There's plenty of seating inside and out, upstairs and down with live music Friday and Saturday nights, billiards and other games plus every saloon beverage you can think of. The Attic area is available for private parties and banquets.

The Cakery

6306 SW Capitol Hwy   503/546-3737
Tues-Sat: 9-6; Sun: 9-3   bakerandspicepdx.com

Baker & Spice's cake annex and retail bakeware store, The Cakery, might be considered the proverbial icing, or sprinkles, on the cake. This shop, eight doors down from the bakery, creates and sells lots and lots of cake – whole or by the slice. During the holidays they make an amazing Yule log as well as peppermint patties, marshmallows, caramels and killer ginger snaps. The shelves are brimming with quality baking supplies (including sprinkles and edible decorations), aprons, tea towels, handmade candles, vintage kitchenwares and hand-selected baking books. In the afternoons there are sometimes book signings with cooking demonstrations by the author.

Castagna Restaurant

1752 SE Hawthorne Blvd   503/231-7373
Dinner: Wed-Sat   castagnarestaurant.com
Expensive

Monique Siu has created one of my favorite fine dining houses in Portland. Elegantly-presented courses take center stage in this sleek, modern establishment where service reigns supreme. Choose from the seasonal tasting menu or the chef's tasting menu with optional wine pairings. The chef defines the cuisine as "seasonal and progressive" with unexpected twists created by incorporating uncommon ingredients. Next door, **Café Castagna** (503/231-9959) is the happening spot for dinners Tuesday through Sunday and happy hours (5 to 6 and 9 to close Tuesday through Friday) with a moderately-priced menu of casual renditions of sandwiches, pastas, pizzas and steaks. Seasonal outdoor dining is delightful; restaurant and cafe reservations are recommended for groups of any size.

PENDLETON BRAND

The **Pendleton** brand (pendleton-usa.com) is certainly one of the best known names in Oregon manufacturing. Originally the maker of high-quality Native American themed woolen blankets and tough men's shirts, the company branched out to include the same quality in additional men's and women's apparel, accessories, home decor and gifts. The company was founded in 1909 by brothers Clarence, Roy and Chauncey Bishop. The Bishop family has been a leader in the commercial and social life of both Portland and Pendleton. In early days they were associated with the Thomas Kay Woolen Mills, now the site of Salem's Willamette Heritage Center. Presently, fourth-generation **Mort Bishop III** is President of the close-knit family management team. Long admired for its corporate citizenship, participating in countless civic activities, the Pendleton brand and the Bishop family are true Oregon treasures. Besides the Pendleton Mill store located in Pendleton, the Portland metro area offers four retail stores, including apparel at the Downtown and Portland Airport Pendleton stores; blankets and home products at Pendleton Home store and The Woolen Mill store. Lincoln City, Bend, Pendleton, Seaside and Troutdale have outlet stores. Pendleton products are available through select retailers worldwide; also through direct-to-consumer channels, including the Pendleton website.

Dan & Louis Oyster Bar

208 SW Ankeny St
Lunch, Dinner: Daily
Moderate to expensive

503/227-5906
danandlouis.com

Five generations of the Wachsmuth family have been shucking oysters at this landmark since 1907. A prominent green and red striped awning over the gleaming brass and glass front doors and large windows frame the interior. What to eat? Oysters, of course; on the half-shell, Rockefeller, in stew, as a sandwich, broiled, fried or combined with other fresh seafood like prawns, scallops, clams and calamari. A specialty of the house is cioppino which blends the best fresh fish of the ocean in a delicious broth. Delicious preparations of salmon, steak and halibut are not to be ignored. For decades, this has been a go-to restaurant for client dinners, company parties and celebrations.

Departure Restaurant + Lounge

525 SW Morrison St   503/802-5370
(See detailed listing with The Nines)

El Gaucho Portland

The Benson Hotel
319 SW Broadway   503/227-8794
Dinner: Daily   elgaucho.com
Very expensive

An extraordinary evening at El Gaucho, where no detail is overlooked, will impress your clients or significant other. The well-orchestrated exhibition kitchen is in full swing turning out melt-in-your-mouth dry-aged prime steaks, meats, seafood and poultry expertly prepared on a charcoal grill or rotisserie. Elaborate tableside preparations include Caesar salad and carved chateaubriand. The showmanship continues with a flaming sword of brochettes of tenderloin. Flambéed desserts of Bananas Foster and cherries jubilee turn any occasion into a special occasion. A nice touch: a fruit and cheese dish served "on the house" after your table finishes their entrees. Enjoy nightly live music in the bar or retire to the clubby Cigar Lounge for single malt scotches, after-dinner drinks and imported cigars from the humidor. The tab will be pricey, but visit this old-school destination when only the best will do.

Filson

526 NW 13th Ave   503/246-0900
Mon-Sat: 10-6; Sun: noon-6   filson.com

Since 1897, the creed and motto that this company has lived up to is "might as well have the best." The recreational outdoorsman and -woman, or those whose profession puts them in the elements, will find high-quality clothing and accessories at Filson's flagship store. Boots can be re-soled and garments repaired (contact customer service; 800/624-0201). Filson luggage is proudly handed down to next generations. Only the finest from Filson for canines, too: coats, beds, dog mats, leashes and even dog dishes are made from Filson's proprietary Tin Cloth.

ONE OF AMERICA'S GREAT STORIES ... IN OREGON!

Aaron Meier was born in Bavaria, Germany, in 1831. At age 24, drawn by the California gold rush, he immigrated to California in 1855. There he worked long hours in his brother's store. Two years later, the gold rush boom times had diminished, and Aaron headed north to Oregon Territory where he sold dry goods from a pushcart on Portland's waterfront. Remember, Oregon was not yet a state until 1859.

Aaron's dad died in 1864 in Bavaria. Aaron traveled to Germany to collect his inheritance of $14,000, which was a fortune at the time. While in Bavaria, Aaron married a lovely local woman, 22-year-old Jeannette Hirsch. There was no Transcontinental Railroad or completed Panama Canal at the time so chances are Aaron traveled by steamship around South America to New York and from New York to Germany. It was expensive and slow! After two years of being away, Aaron and Jeannette arrived in Portland only to find that his partner, Mr. Meriholtz, had bankrupted the business and left town. Did he give up? No, he started over!

Aaron formed a partnership with Emil and Sigmund Frank under the name **Meier & Frank**. They began selling merchandise that arrived by steamer from San Francisco and from covered wagons that rolled in along the Oregon Trail. In the early days, the store was often paid in eggs, potatoes, pickles, salmon and furs.

Tragedy struck in 1878 when a large fire burned 20 blocks of downtown Portland including the Meier & Frank store. In 1894 the Willamette River flooded leaving three feet of water in the store. Always resilient, Jeannette Meier organized rowboats and customers continued to shop on raised walkways. In spite of major setbacks, Meier & Frank continued to thrive and eventually located at 5th and Morrison streets.

Aaron Meier died in 1889 at age 58. From a pushcart he had successfully built M&F, a successful Portland department store, in just 34 years. It was a real Horatio Alger "Rags to Riches" story.

Jeannette Meier continued to run the store with the help of her children Fannie, Abe and Julius. Jeannette was brilliant and an iron fist in the velvet glove who worked behind the counter and behind the scene. In her later years, she loudly banged her cane on the floor to emphasize her demands. From the beginning, she was the boss and everyone knew it! Jeannette's influences were significant. At the turn of the century she guided the store into its lovely 5th Street building. In 40 years the store went from 1,750 square feet to 120,000 square feet and offered an unheard of "money-back guarantee!"

Meier & Frank celebrated their 50th anniversary in 1907. Now the largest retail department store in the West, the eight-story building of steel and concrete cost about $350,000. M&F had gone from a one-room store to the largest retail merchandise firm of its kind, west of Chicago.

Store buyers now took the four-day train ride to New York on buying trips. They left in the evening and rode the Portland Rose train two nights to Chicago. After an overnight in Chicago they changed trains and stations to take the New York Central one more night to New York. Remember, it was also a long four-day return. M&F was one of only a few stores to have their own buying offices in New York. Sales representatives joked that there were four major cities on the West Coast: Los Angeles, San Francisco, Seattle and Meier & Frank!

Gerry Frank's dad, Aaron Frank, was the son of Fannie Meier and Sigmund Frank. He was described as smart, dedicated, brilliant and tough. A few years after Aaron took over as president of Meier & Frank, World War II began. For 1,207 days on the back page of the first section of *The Oregonian*, M&F ran full-page ads, not to sell merchandise, but to urge citizens to buy war bonds and support the war effort. Patriotic M&F conducted the largest single sale of war bonds in the nation. It was a $32 million sale that lasted two weeks in the store auditorium. Federal officials acknowledged Meier & Frank's support of the war effort as the most outstanding of any department store in the entire United States.

During his years as store president, one of Aaron Frank's landmark achievements was initiating branch expansion with the opening of a store in Salem in 1955, and then a store at the Lloyd Center in 1960. Aaron Frank led M&F to great success and was the most important businessman in Oregon for 40 years!

By 1957, Meier & Frank celebrated its 100th anniversary. Two years later, 102-year-old M&F and their 4,000 associates joined in celebrating Oregon's 100th year of statehood. Descendants of Aaron Meier and Sigmund Frank were still actively involved in the management of Meier & Frank; it all happened between 1857 and 1959. It was quite a celebration for the Meier and Frank families. They had worked hard for four generations through early incompetent partners, floods, enormous competition, the Great Depression (which left customers without jobs or money), world wars and bank closures. Yet with perseverance, they had survived to celebrate over 100 years.

Aaron Frank wasted no time getting his talented son, Gerry, into the family business. The first day home from Cambridge University, Gerry's dad put him to work in the Portland store. He started in the receiving room opening boxes, then got promoted to opening larger boxes! He also sold men's furnishings, was in charge of the bargain counters on the street floor and moved up to manage the mail order department.

In the 1950s, the M&F family decided to expand. On Sundays, Gerry and his Dad drove around Salem and Eugene; Aaron Frank would put his coat collar up so no one would recognize him. They wanted to ascertain which community would be best. The old Salem High School property was available, and it offered one entire block. M&F also had 10,000 charge accounts in Salem, therefore, Salem would be the best choice for the first branch store.

Gerry was selected manager, and his dad sent him on a year-long trip around the world to look at major department stores across the United States, Europe and Asia. He traveled to England, Sweden, France, Tokyo and Hong Kong. The store was meticulously planned from information Gerry gathered, down to every fixture specially designed for the merchandise it would hold. Opening on October 27, 1955, the Salem store was the largest per capita business of any store of its size in America.

The May Company bought the store in 1965; the decision to sell the store involved a very contentious Meier and Frank family battle. The sale was very hard on Gerry's dad who went to the store every day. M&F was his life; he never really recovered from the family split and store sale. It killed him; Aaron Frank died two years later of a broken heart.

Gerry has often said that the sale of M&F was the saddest day of his life, "I thought I would be in the family business all my life." It was tragic to think of the four generations of family that struggled, sacrificed and worked tirelessly to build a successful store for generations to come. In the end, the May Company destroyed Meier & Frank. In 2006 the stores became a part of **Macy's**, America's greatest department store chain. With superb management, Macy's is now working very hard to bring back the great traditions of the original Meier & Frank store. The Macy's executive team, led by CEO **Terry Lundgren**, is the best in the business.

(This article was compiled from **Oregon's Own Gerry Frank**, *with permission from author Jan Boutin.)*

Fink's Luggage & Repair Co.
517 SW 12th Ave   503/222-6086
Mon-Fri: 8:30-6; Sat: 9-5   finksluggage.com

For over 40 years, travelers have been outfitted with Fink's savvy packing products. Luggage brands in every price range, wallets, briefcases, handbags and other travel necessities are offered, plus outstanding repair service, knowledgeable staff and personal attention. **Alex Fink** and crew repair all makes of luggage and leather jackets, replace linings, recondition leather items and work magic on handbags and briefcases. For excellent service, Fink's is the best!

Fogo de Chão
930 SW 6th Ave   503/241-0900
Lunch: Mon-Fri, Sun; Dinner: Daily   fogodechao.com
Expensive

One of the very successful restaurant trends is the Brazilian steakhouse, based on the original tastes of Southern Brazil. This is not just an Americanized take on that nation's food, the founders of Fogo de Chão bring you authentic cuisine straight from Southern Brazil. The food is plentiful and unusual, the service friendly and efficient and the whole experience very pleasant, even if the tab is on the high side. Lunch is easier on the pocketbook, the salad bar is plentiful and fresh with special pricing available for youngsters. Brazilian-trained gaucho chefs bring delicious skewers, warm and tender, of prime sirloin cuts, house-specialty picanha sirloin, filet mignon wrapped in bacon, leg of lamb, pork loin filets, pork sausages, beef or pork ribs and bacon-wrapped chicken breasts and chicken legs. You can ask for more as long as your appetite holds up. These folks have finely crafted an authentic and very delicious meal; truly a feast for the eyes and the stomach.

Forktown Food Tours

Office: Tues-Sat: 9-5
Expensive

503/234-3663
forktownfoodtoursportland.com

Rain or shine, Forktown Food Tours explore Portland's impressive food culture. The three-hour walking tours feature good eats with a side dish of commentary by restaurant owners, chefs and food crafters. Samples vary and may include microbrews or other libations, dishes made with locally-sourced ingredients, unusual desserts and only-in-Portland food cart cuisine. Current tours are The Alphabet District, North Mississippi Avenue and The Pearl District, Division Street and Downtown and the Farmer's Market (available seasonally); reservations necessary.

Gartner's Country Meat Market

7450 NE Killingsworth St
Tues-Sat: 9-6; Sun: 10-4

503/252-7801
gartnersmeats.com

More than 51 years ago, the late Jack Gartner opened his butcher shop with the mission statement of "People come for what's inside the case; they come back for the service behind the counter." From Jack's parents to his children, they all pitched in over the years; Jerry Minor came on as a business partner in 1965. The company has passed along generationally and today **Sheri Gartner Puppo** and **Rick Minor** (the "kids") continue this Portland institution with the same commitment. It's a busy and popular spot for always-fresh beef, pork, poultry, lunch meats and cheeses along with Traeger grills and pellets for just-right barbecuing; custom cutting and game processing are also offered. Three full smokehouses turn out the best handcrafted sausages (many also fresh or unsmoked), hams, bacon and specialties.

SCENIC BIKEWAYS

With Oregon passing its first Bicycle Bill in 1971, it led the state in designating the first official Scenic Bikeway. Now there are fourteen "official" bikeways consisting of tested, signed and mapped highways and back roads running through the countryside. Go to rideoregonride.com/bikeways for maps of these designated bikeways as well as recommended biker-friendly lodging and dining.

Blue Mountain Century Scenic Bikeway: 109-mile loop (advanced) starting/ending at Heppner

Cascade Siskiyou Scenic Bikeway: 55 miles of steep, winding terrain

Cascading Rivers Scenic Bikeway: 70 miles of dramatic water and rock views

Covered Bridges Scenic Bikeway: 38 miles in Lane County

Grande Tour Scenic Bikeway: 135-mile, figure-eight ride in northeastern Oregon; mountain views and wildlife

Madras Mountain Views Scenic Bikeway: 130-mile loop; peaceful Central Oregon views

McKenzie Pass Scenic Bikeway: 36 miles of strenuous biking over McKenzie Pass

Metolius Loops Scenic Bikeway: four loops of varying length centering around the Metolius River

Old West Scenic Bikeway: 175 miles for serious touring cyclists; multi-day trip

Sisters to Smith Rock Scenic Bikeway: 37 miles (intermediate) with beautiful views of the Cascades

Tualatin Valley Scenic Bikeway: 50 miles through fertile farmland

Twin Bridges Scenic Bikeway: 36-mile ride (intermediate) in Central Oregon

Wild Rivers Coast Scenic Bikeway: 61 miles of scenic coastal views

Willamette Valley Scenic Bikeway: 132 miles through agricultural valleys

Or opt to see Oregon via guided bike tours and excursions with outfits like **Cog Wild** (255 SW Century Dr, Bend; 866/610-4822; cogwild.com) and **Pedal Bike Tours** (133 SW 2nd Ave, Portland; 503/243-2453, pedalbiketours.com).

Gilda's Italian Restaurant

1601 SW Morrison St   503/688-5066
Lunch: Mon-Fri; Dinner: Daily   gildasitalianrestaurant.com
Moderate

Grandma Gilda's home cooking influenced chef-owner **Marco Roberti** to pursue his passion for Italian food and entertaining. That enthusiasm led him to Italy where he immersed himself in cuisine, culture and cooking family dishes with his aunts and cousins, ultimately earning his master's degree in Italian Culinary Arts. With those experiences under his belt, he returned to Portland to open his own restaurant featuring his beloved grandmother's signature family dishes. Lunch features a number of smaller dishes, along with grilled paninis, pastas and risottos, plus a delicious lemon chicken breast with a dash of sherry. I like the *Sformatino* at dinnertime, a fabulous artichoke flan in a parmesan cheese sauce. The beloved Italian dish of prosciutto and melon is excellent; several veal dishes are house favorites and Italian black cherries served over housemade ice cream make a nice ending to a good meal. Gilda's Old World specialties will leave you satisfied and enamored with this family business which includes next-door Gilda's Lounge, a cozy spot for pizza, handcrafted cocktails and local beers and wines.

Goose Hollow Inn

1927 SW Jefferson St   503/228-7010
Lunch, Dinner: Daily   goosehollowinn.com
Inexpensive

The history of the Goose Hollow Inn is as interesting as its proprietor, **Bud Clark**, Portland's colorful mayor from 1985 to 1992. Bud's first tavern venture was the Spatenhaus (which was replaced by the Ira Keller Fountain). Spatenhaus' menu, using a pizza oven to toast sandwiches, was developed with imagination by Bud and customers. The soul and simplicity of those days has been retained as Goose Hollow has evolved to match today's modern palates and interests. The Reuben sandwich is still referred to as "the best on the planet," vegetables, meats and other menu items are freshly-prepared on premise and there are no fried foods or hamburgers. Soups are homemade and fresh as are the salads (quinoa-beet, crab and shrimp Louis, spinach) with homemade dressings. Locally-produced hard liquor and wine join the lineup of 14 on-tap beers and ciders. Outside, the Portland Timbers Army has found a welcome watering hole on the deck; inside, framed historical photos and posters add to the cabin atmosphere. Bud's other notorieties are his enthusiastic "Whoop! Whoop!!" greeting and as the trench coat-clad model for the famous poster entitled *Expose Yourself to Art.*

Grand Central Bakery

2230 SE Hawthorne Blvd	503/445-1600
3425 SW Multnomah Blvd	503/977-2024
7987 SE 13th Ave	503/546-3036
714 N Fremont St	503/546-5311
4440 NE Fremont St	503/808-9877
4412 SE Woodstock Blvd	503/953-1250
12595 NW Cornell Road	503/808-9878
Daily: Hours vary	grandcentralbakery.com

These artisan bakeries are conveniently situated around town and at local farmers markets. They craft breads to perfection: crusty on the outside, chewy on the inside and at their prime when eaten warm and generously buttered. Muffins, croissants, fruit tarts, cookies, pies and cakes are sweet choices; purchase one or be a hero and bring treats for the office. Ingredients for all breads and pastries are natural and top-quality. All locations serve sandwiches for breakfast and lunch, from-scratch soups, salads and seasonal specials; sack lunches are a specialty. Busy home cooks get a helping hand with balls of U-Bake pizza dough, rolls of puff pastry, pre-formed cookie dough and disks of pie dough ready to be transformed into "homemade" meals and desserts.

The Heathman Hotel

1001 SW Broadway	503/241-4100, 800/551-0011
Expensive and up	heathmanhotel.com

Service is still an art at this luxurious downtown property. Built in 1927, for the past 25-plus years it has earned four diamonds from

AAA. This independently-owned 150-room luxury boutique hotel is a proud member of Historic Hotels of America (it was recognized by that group as the #1 historic hotel in the country). The classically-elegant guest rooms are tastefully furnished with modern accents, technology and amenities; a full array of upscale services is offered including a floor dedicated to guests with four-legged companions. Exquisite artwork is exhibited throughout the building; works from the Vanderbilt Estate grace the charming Tea Court. Unbeknownst to many Portlanders, overnight guests of the property have access to a cataloged lending library of over 2,500 books signed by author-guests. **Heathman Restaurant & Bar** executive chef **Michael Stanton** blends fresh-daily Northwest cuisine into dishes that capture the taste of this abundant region. The breakfast, lunch, dinner and brunch menus change to accommodate seasonal choices and may offer bouillabaisse, local beef, pork, poultry, fish and seafood – all prepared with panache; the wine selection features over 6,000 bottles from 20 of the world's wine regions. Casual fare is served in the Marble Bar, Tea Court (live jazz Wednesday through Saturday evenings) and seasonal sidewalk cafe. Culture and beauty permeate the ten-story brick landmark under the leadership of talented GM **Steve Hurst**.

PORTLAND'S SOUTH WATERFRONT

Portland's South Waterfront is Portland's newest neighborhood. While the Great Recession of 2009 severely slowed down its development, the neighborhood has seen tremendous growth since 2012. There has been the addition of numerous residential and medical office buildings, including the new building for the relocation of the Oregon School of Dentistry. Oregon Health & Science University is an important part of the identity of South Waterfront and OHSU will continue to shape the future of the neighborhood in the coming years. From the iconic aerial tram, to Caruthers Park, to retail and restaurants, to the newly-completed Greenway and MAX train access, South Waterfront is a vibrant part of Portland.

Hilton Portland & Executive Tower

921 SW 6th Ave   503/226-1611
Moderate and up   hilton.com

Your author has spent many a night away from home as a guest in this downtown hotel. The management and staff are wonderful ambassadors — cheerful, helpful and provide quick service. That is no small feat considering this is Oregon's largest hotel; 782 rooms in two separate buildings. The main building was constructed in 1963 and was remodeled in 2006. The on-site restaurant, **HopCity Tavern**, offers savory, hearty comfort foods, local handcrafted beers on tap and wine by the glass sourced from 12 local Northwest wineries; the lounge is open until 11:30 p.m. daily and offers a lavish happy hour. Across the street is the Executive Tower; the rooms are more contemporary and spacious with business king suites on the top floor. **Porto Terra Tuscan Grill & Bar** offers a sumptuous daily breakfast buffet and creative Northern Italian cuisine for lunch and dinner that features housemade pastas and gelatos. The popular lounge is open until 11:30 p.m. daily. Both entities offer valet parking, complimentary fitness center with pool and free Wi-Fi in the lobbies. All guest rooms and suites are equipped with work desks, luxurious bath amenities and coffeemakers. Elegant ballrooms and more intimate conference rooms accommodate important meetings and informal occasions; the incredible staff will work magic to make your event memorable.

Hotel Eastlund

1021 NE Grand Ave   503/235-2100
Moderate to moderately expensive   hoteleastlund.com

Downtown Portland's eastside neighborhood welcomes you to stay at their new hotel located across from the Convention Center. This luxury boutique hotel is modern chic with many well-thought-out touches such as the beautiful art and faux fur throws in each room. Amenities and services are topnotch and include all that any full-service luxury hotel would have; high speed internet, Keurig coffee makers, smart refrigerators, HD TVs, soaking tubs in select rooms, concierge service, a fitness center and plenty of meeting/event space. Within the hotel, restaurateur **David Machado** runs **Altabira City Tavern** (503/963-3600, altabira.com) and **Citizen Baker**

(503/963-3610, citizenbaker.com). Altabira is a rooftop restaurant and bar perched above Portland's Lloyd district, a perfect match for the hotel's atmosphere. The beautiful panoramic views surround you as you lounge on outdoor sofas by the fire pits or take a seat in one of five private dining rooms with the same stunning views through floor-to-ceiling windows. The restaurant serves fresh, seasonal American cuisine with a creative twist and smart pairings of food and drink. Extensive drink options consist of European and Northwest wines, locally-distilled spirits and 16 tap handles of local craft beers. Don't leave without stopping by the bakery for a fresh breakfast pastry!

Hotel Monaco Portland
506 SW Washington St   503/222-0001, 888/207-2201
Expensive   monaco-portland.com

For a luxurious night in downtown amid museums, boutiques and large shops, amazing restaurants, nightclubs and entertainment, stay at Hotel Monaco Portland. A vibrant, ornate lobby, the site of morning coffee and tea service, greets guests at this Kimpton Hotel property. Each of the 221 rooms and suites are awash with a tasteful assortment of colorful furnishings and Italian Frette linens atop deep pillow top beds. Classy French doors separate sleeping and living areas in the roomy suites, a nice touch when enjoying in-room spa services. Standard conveniences include flat-panel TVs, private mini-bars, personal coffeemakers, laptop-compatible safes and fun animal print bathrobes. A hosted evening wine reception, 24/7 fitness center, newspapers, morning coffee in the lobby and use of bicycles (seasonal) are complimentary to guests. Four-legged companions are welcome on the pet-friendly floor with special services. Guests with allergies can enjoy one of three hypo-allergenic floors that have never seen a pet. These floors feature synthetic comforters and foam pillows (no down), special HEPA filter vacuums and room air filters and allergen- and scent-free cleaning products; hypo-allergenic toiletries are available on request. Adjacent to the Monaco, **Red Star Tavern** (503/222-0005, redstartavern.com) provides round-the-clock room service; but to experience the Portland vibe, head on over for phenomenal American cuisine with a twist; creative cocktails and an impressive bourbon selection.

BEST FOR GIFTS IN PORTLAND

Looking for a unique gift for someone special? A plethora of specialty gift shops exist in the Portland area.

Alder & Co. (616 SW 12th Ave, 503/224-1647, alderandcoshop.com): one-stop shop for items from handmade soaps and ceramics to cashmere scarves and carpet boots

Betsy & Iya (2403 NW Thurman St, 503/227-5482, betsyandiya.com): stunning hand-crafted jewelry, bags and cards

Finnegan's Toys & Gifts (820 SW Washington St, 503/221-0306, finneganstoys.com): toys, games and books

Land (3925 N Mississippi Ave, 503/451-0689, landpdx.com): art gallery plus a collection of funky, hand-crafted gifts and books from over 100 artists

Memento (3707 SE Hawthorne Blvd, 503/235-1257, mementopdx.com): eclectic gifts, jewelry, candles, cards and local art

Noun (3300 SE Belmont St, 503/235-0078, shopnoun.com): exquisite jewelry gifts, upscale vintage furniture and glassware

Paxton Gate (4204 N Mississippi Ave, 503/719-4508, paxtongate.com): like a natural history museum, but with jewelry and art featuring taxidermy, fossils and insects

Presents of Mind (3633 SE Hawthorne Ave, 503/230-7740, presentsofmind.tv): jewelry, accessories, baby items and greeting cards; featuring local and independent designers

Redux (811 E Burnside St, #110, 503/231-7336, redux.pdx.com): handmade, local and indie jewelry, accessories and art from re-purposed and recycled objects

Tender Loving Empire (412 SW 10th Ave, 503/243-5859; 3541 SE Hawthorne Blvd, 503/548-2927 and 525 NW 23rd Ave, 503/964-6592, tenderlovingempire.com): prints, posters, mugs, magnets, flasks and more by local artists; shop online and "pay what you want" with 5% towards a chosen charity

Huber's Cafe

411 SW 3rd Ave   503/228-5686
Lunch: Mon-Sat; Dinner: Daily   hubers.com
Moderate

Huber's was established in 1879 and is Portland's oldest-operating restaurant. The original location was at the corner of First and Alder and named The Bureau Saloon; this domain with a magnificent arched leaded-glass ceiling is on the ground floor of the Historic Oregon Pioneer Building. The history is an interesting read and stars Frank Huber, Jim Louie, turkey sandwiches, Prohibition and Spanish Coffee. The latest chapter of Huber's continues the Louie family's involvement, a tradition of turkey (sandwiches and turkey cuisine are prominent on the menu) and Spanish Coffee (the signature drink) is still prepared tableside. Each week about 1,000 pounds of roasted turkey is served as entrees (picatta, marsala, enchiladas, wings, drumsticks) along with salads made with organic field greens, Certified Angus Beef steaks, seafood and pasta. Interesting fact: Huber's is said to use more Kahlua than any other independent restaurant in the United States.

Irving St. Kitchen

701 NW 13th Ave   503/343-9440
Dinner: Daily; Brunch: Sat, Sun   irvingstreetkitchen.com
Moderate

Irving St. Kitchen is one of the Pearl District's growing list of eateries. The space is large and airy and nice weather brings outdoor dining. Interesting snacks along with a reasonably-priced mix of charcuterie are good meal-starters. The New American menu includes about a dozen delicious first courses like meatballs with Yukon Gold mashed potatoes and sauce au poivre, barbecued shrimp or a tasty Bibb lettuce salad with Rogue blue cheese dressing. The menu changes regularly, but delicious fried chicken is always available. Desserts are inspired, including the ever-present butterscotch pudding with caramel sauce.

Jake's Famous Crawfish

401 SW 12th Ave   503/226-1419
Lunch, Dinner: Daily   jakesfamouscrawfish.com
Moderate to expensive

I love Jake's crawfish; just the thought makes my mouth water! If I've set my heart on a big 1½-pound bowl of the freshwater crustaceans boiled in a spicy broth, I call ahead to make sure

FAVORITE FULL-SERVICE PIT STOP

Since 1952, a favorite stop of truck drivers for fuel, truck services and much more is **Jubitz Travel Center** (10210 N Vancouver Way, Portland; 503/283-1111; jubitztravelcenter.com). Within the 26-acre property are the **Portlander Inn & Marketplace** (503/345-0300, portlanderinn.com). The Marketplace offers a variety of traveler amenities: an 80-seat digital cinema and handy services for travelers including laundry, hair salon, medical clinic, chiropractor, mailing services, shoe repair, arcade and convenience store. Fresh breads are baked daily at **Moe's Deli** for sub sandwiches, hot and cold. **Cascade Grill** is a 24/7 full-service restaurant with homestyle food and daily specials cooked-to-order, or stop in for a drink and entertainment at country honky-tonk bar **Ponderosa Lounge. Fred Jubitz** heads up this family endeavor which was founded by his father, **Moe Jubitz**. You don't have to be a truck driver to stop in; everyone is welcome.

they are fresh and on the menu (the season is roughly Easter to Halloween). Other delicious preparations are in pasta, cooked and chilled, Cajun-style or "popcorn" fried tails. The best, however, is the famous live crawfish boil. Lunch and dinner menus are printed daily to reflect the freshest bivalves, seafood and steaks; fresh catch is listed with the source of origin. Check out the daily Blue Plate lunch special and catch of the day priced at $8.95. Jake's clam chowder is legendary and you can't go wrong with a fabulous crab or shrimp cocktail or salad for lunch or dinner; sandwiches (turkey, crab, shrimp, chicken) are served for lunch. Dinner steaks are superb with the option of adding a lobster tail or jumbo scampi prawns to create a surf and turf combo to your liking. Chocolate truffle cake and bread pudding with bourbon anglaise have become famous in the dessert department. If you want just a bite, consider Jake's dessert trio with mini-portions of berry cobbler, truffle cake and a cream puff. The bar is a popular downtown after-work watering hole; a great venue for groups and banquets. Jake's has rightfully earned a spot in the top ten seafood restaurants in America and has been a Portland fixture since 1892.

Joy's Uptown Style
1627 NW Glisan St   503/223-3400
Mon-Fri: 10-6; Sat: 10-5   joysuptown.com

Joy Walker has an eye for fashion, especially mother-of-the-bride (or groom) dresses and formal attire. Most ensembles may be ordered in a full spectrum of bright or subdued colors. An expert seamstress can take a tuck here or there, reposition buttons, raise hemlines or modify sleeves and collars to customize the piece for the desired look. Just as attractive are the unique and classy daytime, casual fashions and accessories that fill the lovely boutique. At Joy's the seemingly lost art of personalized customer service is superb!

Kenny & Zuke's Delicatessen
1038 SW Stark St   503/222-3354
Breakfast, Lunch, Dinner: Daily
2376 NW Thurman St   503/954-1737
Breakfast, Lunch: Daily   kennyandzukes.com
Moderate

There are delis, then there is Kenny & Zuke's! And now there are two locations! They arguably have the best pastrami sandwich in town, made with brisket that is cured for a week, smoked for ten hours and steamed for three hours. It is served between slices of housemade rye bread or toast, or with chopped liver and cole slaw. The most popular version is a glorious Reuben with sauerkraut, Swiss cheese and Russian dressing, then grilled and served with K&Z's pickles and potato salad. Other hearty hot and cold sandwiches (such as meatloaf and create-your-own double deckers) round out the lunch and dinner menu. There's much more: smoked and pickled fish, noodle kugel, rugelach, hot dogs, burgers and fries, salads and homemade desserts. Breakfasts feature deli case meats with eggs, bagels or in omelets as well as latkes, blintzes and weekend Benedicts and biscuits. Eat in, take out, rent the deli for your private event or arrange for the crew to cater your party; any way you slice it, these places are winners.

Ken's Artisan Bakery

338 NW 21st Ave   503/248-2202
Mon-Sat: 7-6 (Mon till 9:30); Sun: 8-5   kensartisan.com

Boulangerie and patisserie proprietor, **Ken Forkish**, has honed his craft as an artisan baker exceptionally well and has justifiably been recognized in the local and national media for his rustic breads and luscious pastries. The latter are jaw-dropping creative works of art, handmade with real butter, fresh fruits, rich chocolate and other fine ingredients. Lunch fare (sandwiches, soups, salads) is served in the cafe in addition to the anytime bakery items and coffee drinks. Ken thoroughly researched flours and settled upon a local, sustainable product for his breads, croissants and pizzas. Pizzas are so popular that they have made Monday "Pizza Night" with extended hours to 9:30. You'll find Ken's breads on the tables of some of Portland's best restaurants and at select retailers; or the best selection, visit the bakery. **Ken's Artisan Pizza** (304 SE 28th Ave, 503/517-9951) was opened to accommodate the demand for the Italian pies — thin, crisp and baked in a wood-fired oven; open daily for dinner.

Kidd's Toy Museum

1301 SE Grand Ave   503/233-7807
Mon-Thurs: noon-6; Fri: 1-6   kiddstoymuseum.com
Free

As a youngster I spent many hours in the toy department of my family's Meier & Frank store. I had my eyes on the latest shiny cars, games and other playthings, and wrongly assumed that I had my pick of anything my heart desired at any time. My father vowed not to spoil me, and I only received toys as gifts on special occasions. Portlander **Frank Kidd** has amassed an enviable collection of vintage toys, mostly from the years 1869 to 1939. Mechanical and other banks, die-cast vehicles as well as toys from later years; Disney figurines, dolls, trains and much more are displayed in glass-front cases. Kidd has traveled near and far and has acquired assortments from friends to add to his impressive accumulation of toys and related items. There's much to see and memories to recall. Groups and additional times by appointment.

VERY BEST BURGERS IN OREGON

Helvetia Tavern (10275 NW Helvetia Road, Hillsboro; 503/647-5286) is consistently voted the best burger in the Portland area because of its jumbo cheeseburger served with fries and onion rings; this according to Travel Oregon. Located west of Hillsboro on Helvetia Road, customers rave. Cash only.

Following is my list of additional top picks for burgers:

The Canyon Grill (8825 SW Canyon Road, Beaverton; 503/292-5131): canyon burger

Cheesy Stuffed Burgers (1545 NW Monroe Ave, Corvallis; 541/286-5335): three-cheese burger; food truck near OSU campus

Cornerstone Pub & Grill (2307 Pacific Ave, Forest Grove; 503/357-4742): lumberjack burger

Jasper's Café (2739 N Pacific Hwy, Medford; 541/776-5307): Popper burger

Jimmy's Classic Drive-In (515 NE E St, Grants Pass; 541/479-3850): Cryin' Shame burger

The Local Cow (336 N Main St, Gresham; 503/489-5116): Pendleton burger

pFriem Family Brewers (707 Portway Ave, Suite 101, Hood River; 541/321-0490): Mt. Shadow cheeseburger

Pilot Butte Drive-In (917 NE Greenwood Ave and 320 SW Century Dr, Suite 410, Bend; 541/382-2972 both locations): bacon cheeseburger

Plateau Restaurant (Wildhorse Resort & Casino, 46510 Wildhorse Blvd, Pendleton; 541/966-1610): Plateau burger with smoked fries

Laurelhurst Market

3155 E Burnside St	503/206-3097
Restaurant: Dinner: Daily	laurelhurstmarket.com
Moderate	
Butcher shop: Daily: 10-10	503/206-3099

The name is a bit deceiving; it is not where you shop for eggs, butter or bread. Most of the day it is a first-rate butcher shop featuring all-natural, and hormone- and antibiotic-free meats plus sausages (12 flavors), cured meats, duck confit, housemade lard and other uncommon items. Special requests are not a problem. Tuesday is fried chicken day in the butcher shop (starting at 11 until it's gone) and deli-style and daily special sandwiches are prepared each day between 11 and 5. The steakhouse-inspired brasserie serves an intriguing selection of hors d'oeuvres, including a charcuterie plate, marrow bones and beef tartare. Steaks and chops, though, are the signature dishes with varied a la carte side dishes.

Le Pigeon
738 E Burnside St   503/546-8796
Dinner: Daily   lepigeon.com
Expensive

True to Portland's persona, Le Pigeon is fine dining in a hole-in-the-wall establishment. Cuisine is French-inspired and features inventive game dishes such as rabbit, duck, pigeon and quail as well as beef and fish. Chef **Gabriel Rucker** offers five- and seven-course tasting menus. Every nook and cranny of the small restaurant is used with pigeonholed wine bottles becoming part of the decor. The open kitchen is in full view and best observed from the Chef's Counter; reservations are accepted for two or more people at three communal tables. Sister restaurant, **Little Bird** (219 SW 6th Ave, 503/688-5952; littlebirdbistro.com) is open weekdays for lunch and daily for dinner — fine dining in more refined surroundings.

Made in Oregon
Pioneer Place, 340 SW Morrison St, Suite 1300   503/241-3630
Lloyd Center, 1017 Lloyd Center   503/282-7636
Washington Square, 9571 SW Washington Square Road   503/620-4670
Clackamas Town Center, 12000 SE 82nd Ave   503/659-3155
Portland International Airport, Oregon Market   503/282-7827
Portland International Airport, Concourse C   503/335-6563
Portland International Airport, Concourse D   503/493-5970
Hours vary   madeinoregon.com

These stores are about Oregon! Since 1975, Made in Oregon has been the source for the best Oregon products under one roof. The product mix is fabulous; Pendleton blankets and clothing, gourmet foods (cheese, candies, nuts, salmon, cookies, jams and jellies), wines, jewelry, home accessories, books, T-shirts, Oregon State University and University of Oregon paraphernalia, souvenirs and gifts. Many of these items are assembled into attractive boxes and baskets which are ideal for gift giving; customize your choices for specific occasions or buy a single item (order online or from eye-catching mail order catalogs). At the helm of Made in Oregon is legendary **Sam Naito**. The Naito family has a long history of community service, philanthropy and commerce in Oregon (previously Norcrest China Company). Share the love and bounty of Oregon with gifts from this notable Oregon company. Note that outside of the Portland area there are three additional locations; one in Salem (Salem Center, 480 Center St, #242; 503/362-4106), one in Eugene (296 E Fifth Ave, #119; 541/393-6891) and another one in Newport (342 SW Bay Blvd; 541/574-9020).

Mama Mia Trattoria
439 SW 2nd Ave   503/295-6464
Lunch, Dinner: Daily; Brunch: Sat, Sun   mamamiatrattoria.com
Moderate

This busy downtown trattoria is located just off the Morrison Bridge. Crystal chandeliers, marble-top tables and gilded mirrors create a warm and inviting destination for the whole family. Food is traditional Italian — slow-cooked, made from scratch and plentiful. Housemade mozzarella and desserts are some of the many items that are prepared daily. Lunch choices include salads, paninis, Italian gourmet burgers, sandwiches, pizzas and homemade pastas. As the sun sets, offerings include cioppino, chicken marsala, chicken and veal parmesan, jumbo prawns scampi and traditional pastas with marinara sauce simmered to perfection and married with cheeses, sumptuous meatballs and other fine additions. The extensive bar menu includes Chianti, Prosecco, Northwest wines, beers and specialty cocktails; happy hour eats are value priced. Try sinful amaretto cheesecake, rich cannolis or delicate sorbets for dessert.

The Meadow

3731 N Mississippi Ave	503/288-4633, 888/388-4633
Daily: 10-8	
805 NW 23rd Ave	503/305-3388
Sun-Thurs: 10-8; Fri, Sat: 10-9	themeadow.com

Question: If you mix craft cooking and finishing salts, some of the world's great chocolates, throw in an interesting selection of Oregon and European wines, handcrafted bitters and fresh-cut flowers, what do you get? Answer: A very beautiful business called The Meadow. **Mark Bitterman** turned his love of food and travel into this unique shop. Exploring over 120 of the world's salt varieties, an array of more than 500 chocolate bars, 200 bitters for cocktails and delicious Oregon pinot noirs (so good with chocolate) makes for quite a mix-and-match experience. Tastings and classes are held at the shop from time to time. If you're in New York City, another Meadow location is in Manhattan's West Village (523 Hudson St, 212/645-4633); sans wine.

Mehri's Bakery & Cafe

6923 SE 52nd Ave	503/788-9600
Mon, Tues: 7-3; Wed-Fri: 7-7; Sat: 8-5; Sun: 8-2	mehris.com

Check out Mehri's for specialty cakes and desserts just like mom used to make: apple, berry and pumpkin chiffon pies; fruit cobblers and company's coming chocolate fudge cake. Not only does Mehri produce spectacular sweets (and custom wedding cakes), but she also offers the unusual twist of Persian delights (pomegranate chicken stew, shish kabobs and crusty bottom rice to name a few), along with more traditional fare for breakfast and lunch. At this time a large focus of the business is on wedding cakes and catering needs.

Mother's Bistro & Bar

212 SW Stark St	503/464-1122
Breakfast, Lunch, Dinner: Tues-Sun	mothersbistro.com
Moderate	

Mother always said to clean your dinner plate before dessert. Fortunately, this mother does not make that admonishment! The oh-so-good pies vary according to the season and are baked fresh.

In fact, all desserts are made with rich butter, cream, local fruits and quality ingredients. The devil's food cake with chocolate ganache is good and gooey! Mom would approve of the comfort food meals, often updated to appease more sophisticated tastes. For example; wild salmon hash, chicken salad, macaroni and cheese, meatloaf, beef pot roast and greens (salads and side dishes). Successful chef-owner **Lisa Schroeder** brings a wealth of experience from her training and experience on the East Coast, the Mediterranean and Europe. Specials change monthly to reflect the background cuisine of assorted mothers. This is a comfortable and dependable breakfast, lunch or dinner spot to take business associates, family and mom for people-pleasing meals "made with love."

Mucca Osteria

1022 SW Morrison St	503/227-5521
Dinner: Mon-Sat	muccaosteria.com
Moderately expensive	

This is a success story about a Rome native who relocated in Portland to open an Italian osteria featuring indigenous wines and authentic fare. The beautiful restaurant is welcoming and permeated with the enticing aroma of bread fresh from the oven. An interesting side note is that they make their own natural yeast derived from the fermentation of raisins. Homemade pasta and rich seasonal dishes include winners such as slow-braised wild boar ragu, stewed rabbit and fish, seafood and poultry preparations. Multi-course tasting menus are served at lunch and dinner and are best enjoyed with outstanding wines or signature cocktails.

Multnomah Whiskey Library

1124 SW Alder St	503/954-1381
Mon-Thurs: 4 p.m. to midnight;	multnomahwhiskeylibrary.com
Fri, Sat: 4 p.m. to 1 a.m.	

Portland has a very innovative whiskey bar, the inspiration of Portland real estate owner and civic promoter **Greg Goodman** and his nephew, **Alan Davis**. In a smallish upstairs space they have created one of the most appealing rooms in the city. With painted glass skylights, period pieces from abroad, historic pictures and leather banquets, the place is a real charmer. Along the walls are 1,600 whiskey bottles (including after-dinner drink selections) and wines and beers to choose from. Extremely polite mixologists will prepare your drink at the table. The menu includes plates to be shared like oysters, a *salumi* (pork cold cuts) board, fried cauliflower, pork and octopus along with razor clam linguini, oysters, a cheeseburger and steaks; all meant to be paired with fine libations and conversation. Memberships (at $600 per) sell out in a hurry; they allow the bearer to make reservations and access other perks. Otherwise, best you arrive before 4 p.m. Monday through Saturday, as the line is long. Educational seminars and special events (some for members only) are offered periodically.

CULINARY OPTIONS

Besides providing professional training in restaurant management, the culinary arts, baking and pastry, the **Oregon Culinary Institute** (1701 SW Jefferson St, Portland; 503/961-6200; oregonculinaryinstitute.com) has a fine-dining restaurant open to the public five days a week (when school is in session). Students participate in all aspects of the meal planning, preparation and presentation. Offerings include watermelon gazpacho, pickled shrimp salad and Cajun trout grenobloise; finish with chocolate dream torte or cheesecake. The three-course, $9 lunch or four-course, $18 dinner is a fun opportunity to interact with enthusiastic young chefs while enjoying a tasty, reasonably-priced meal. Reservations required.

Natural Selection
3033 NE Alberta St 503/288-5883
Dinner: Wed-Sat
naturalselectionpdx.com
Moderately expensive

At this dinner house Chef **Aaron Woo**, a graduate of the California Culinary Academy and the proud owner of Natural Selection, presents the best in vegetables, fruits and grains. Served in a warm European-style setting with an open kitchen, the flavors of France, Italy and Spain inspire the cuisine. The changing menu items are available a la carte or choose a four-course dinner for $45; wine pairings, add $29. Tasty vegan/vegetarian choices might include cream of fennel and tomato soup, butternut squash risotto or spaghetti with heirloom peppers, turnips and crispy eggplant; desserts might be fall fruit crumble with coconut ice cream or lemon and hazelnut cake with banana pudding and chocolate sauce. The food is delicious as well as healthful and beautifully presented. Even if you are not a practicing vegetarian or vegan, Chef Woo is sure to please your palate.

New Seasons Market

7300 SW Beaverton-Hillsdale Hwy	503/292-6838
3495 SW Cedar Hills Blvd	503/641-4181
15861 SE Happy Valley Town Ctr Dr	503/558-9214
1214 SE Tacoma St	503/230-4949
14805 SW Barrows Road, Suite 103, Beaverton	503/597-6777
1453 NE 61st Ave, Hillsboro	503/648-6968
3 Monroe Pkwy, Lake Oswego	503/496-1155
7703 SW Nyberg St, Tualatin	503/692-3535
2100-B SE 164th Ave, Vancouver	360/760-5005
6400 N Interstate Ave	503/467-4777
3210 NE Broadway St	503/282-2080
5320 NE 33rd Ave	503/288-3838
2170 NW Raleigh St	503/224-7522
4034 SE Hawthorne Blvd	503/236-4800
1954 SE Division St	503/445-2888
4500 SE Woodstock Blvd	503/771-9663
3445 N Williams Ave	503/528-2888
Daily	newseasonsmarket.com

On Leap Day 2000, Raleigh Hills welcomed an upstart grocer to their community. Now 18 New Seasons Markets in the Pacific Northwest are committed to providing an easy, fun and friendly neighborhood shopping experience — one that meets customers' needs for both national brand staples and local sustainable products. You'll find quality merchandise in all departments: bakery, beer and wine, bulk, cheese, deli, floral, grocery, meat, pastry, produce, seafood and wellness. But the neighborhood stores are about more than just groceries — they are about people. By supporting New Seasons and the local economy, they in turn, give grants and donations back to the area while their employees volunteer. In 2014 New Seasons partnered with more than 900 local nonprofits dedicated to addressing hunger, public education and conservation.

FESTIVAL OF ROSES

Portland's annual **Rose Festival** (rosefestival.org) is a source of pride and community spirit that brings millions of dollars to Portland and surrounding communities. For over a century the event has kicked off each year in March with court selections from city high schools with one of the princesses named Queen of Rosaria at the highly-anticipated coronation event. Fun runs and walks, the Starlight Parade, dragon boat and milk carton boat races, fireworks, Naval fleet participation, the Junior Parade and many more activities make up the four-month celebration, culminated with the Grand Floral Parade. **Jeff Curtis** is the able chief executive officer — and it's a big job!

The Nines

525 SW Morrison St   877/229-9995, 503/222-9996

Moderate and up   thenines.com

Of course I maintain a keen interest in the goings on at Meier & Frank Square; afterall, I spent a good part of my life here. The Nines opened as a modern luxury hotel in 2008, filling the floors above **Macy's** retail space with 331 guest rooms and 13 suites, meeting facilities, an atrium, fitness center, library and rooftop dining. It is spectacular and a great addition to Portland's downtown. Oregon artists are featured in the eighth-floor lobby, also the location of a charming library. Guest rooms and suites are tastefully appointed, sleek and tranquil. Guests on the 12th-floor club level receive light breakfasts, snacks and evening libations. The one bedroom Meier & Frank Suite affords spectacular city views from the comfortable living room; the dining room accommodates up to eight. During the summer, it's hard to beat the two view patios that add to the spectacular ambience at **Departure Restaurant + Lounge**. Here you can enjoy dinner or a late night visit in the rooftop setting; more private, classy seating is available inside. Small plates of sushi and dim sum, with specialties like Kobe meatballs and barbecue short rib buns are available. Chef **Gregory Gourdet**'s kushiyaki grill and wok dishes feature a variety of chicken and meats; a favorite is Ishiyaki steak, a stone-grilled Wagyu strip steak served on a sizzling hot stone. The **Urban Farmer** is a first-rate steakhouse with inviting country-chic decorative touches. A huge table in the middle seats up to 16 diners; make a friend at breakfast, lunch, dinner or weekend brunch. Yes, my friends, the top floors of my family's department store have been spiffed up "to the nines."

Northwest Film Center
1219 SW Park Ave   503/221-1156
(See detailed listing with Portland Art Museum)

Nostrana
1401 SE Morrison St   503/234-2427
Lunch: Mon-Fri; Dinner: Daily   nostrana.com
Moderate

Nostrana is large and extremely busy, with an energy level as high as any dining spot in Portland. This rustic Italian eatery, meaning "ours" in Italian, features a daily changing menu of simple homemade food from locally-grown produce. For starters try roasted shitake mushroom soup, house charcuterie, fried oyster salad and interesting pastas made in-house. Fish, seafood, chicken, pork and beef plates are delicious and accompanied with fingerling potatoes, lentils or other Italian preparations. In traditional style, uncut pizzas are delivered to your table along with a pair of scissors for cutting (fun for kids). Fine wines and baked-to-order seasonal fruit crisps complete the meal.

Oba Restaurant
555 NW 12th Ave   503/228-6161
Dinner: Daily   obarestaurant.com
Moderate

Chef **Luis Contreras** excels in authentic Nuevo Latino cuisine and he knows the best way to serve it is in a full-on festive environment. OBA is renowned for tableside-prepared guacamole, grilled fresh fish, wood-fired grilled prime rib, scallop ceviche and an abundance of jalapenos, tomatoes, chilies, spices, fresh fruits and vegetables; all are natural, organic and regional, as available. Special dietary requests are accommodated and nutritious, low-fat options are suggested on the menu. Latin street food is served in the lounge where spirited conversations are fueled by potent potables and wines from around the world — Spain, Argentina, Chile and a large selection of Oregon pinot noir. Several rooms accommodate private dining groups.

Oregon History Museum

1200 SW Park Ave   503/306-5198
Mon-Sat: 10-5; Sun: noon-5   ohs.org
Reasonable

For anyone wanting to understand the Oregon story, the Oregon History Museum is a required stop. Operated since 1898 by the Oregon Historical Society, the museum includes the award-winning "Oregon My Oregon" permanent exhibit that traces Oregon's history from the first Native Americans to the Lewis and Clark expedition to the iconic Conestoga wagons of the Oregon Trail. The interactive "Oregon Voices" exhibit highlights 20th century history. Recent exhibits have highlighted the priceless American historical treasures and Presidential documents and artifacts that are part of the **Melvin "Pete" Mark** collection, a Portland business leader and philanthropist. The museum also houses the Oregon Historical Society Research Library, which contains one of the country's most extensive collections of state history materials, including approximately 25,000 maps, 30,000 books, over 8 million feet of film and videotape and more than 2 million photographic images. OHS also sponsors an extensive series of educational programs and lectures. Executive Director **Kerry Tymchuk** is like Oregon, one-of-a-kind.

Oregon Zoo

4001 SW Canyon Road   503/226-1561
Daily   oregonzoo.org
Reasonable

Lions and tigers and bears — oh, yes! And an elephant named Packy! You, your family and friends will want to visit all of the animal friends at the Oregon Zoo. The zoo's origins date back to 1888 with a few animals collected from a Portland pharmacist's seafaring friends. Today, the menagerie has grown from one "she grizzly" to over 2,200

FAVORITE PORTLAND ATTRACTIONS

Among Portland's myriad attractions, here are a few of my favorites:

International Rose Test Garden (850 SW Rose Garden Way, 503/227-7033, rosegardenstore.org/thegardens): beautiful in bloom; fragrant

Lan Su Chinese Garden (239 NW Everett St, 503/228-8131, lansugarden.org): traditional garden and koi pond; tea house

Oregon History Museum (1200 SW Park Ave, 503/2221741, ohs.org): a great taste of past Oregon

Pittock Mansion (3229 NW Pittock Dr, 503/823-3623, pittockmansion. org): 1914 home of Henry and Georgiana Pittock; tours

Portland Art Museum (1219 SW Park Ave, 503/226-2811, portlandartmuseum.org): founded 1892, visual and media arts

Portland Japanese Garden (611 SW Kingston Ave, 503/223-1321, japanesegarden.com): authentic

Portland Saturday Market (North Waterfront Park and Ankeny Plaza, 503/222-6072, portlandsaturdaymarket.com): outdoor arts and crafts market, March to December 24

animals. The zoo encompasses 64 acres of exhibits (Great Northwest, Fragile Forests, Asia, Pacific Shores, Africa), exotic plants, a one-mile loop railway, eateries, gift shops and a petting zoo for the pint-size set. The zoo's focus centers on animal enrichment, zoological knowledge, education, sustainable operations and conservation. Over 1.6 million folks visit this animal kingdom each year; other popular events include summertime concerts on the lawn and the annual holiday ZooLights extravaganza. Back to Packy; in 1962 he was the first Asian elephant to be born in this country in over four decades and overnight became the zoo's star attraction. His 50th birthday party (in 2012) was fit for a king!

Otto's Sausage Kitchen

4138 SE Woodstock Blvd   503/771-6714
Mon-Sat: 9:30-6; Sun: 11-5   ottossausage.com

Since 1929 the Eichentopf family has produced smoked and fresh sausages; one of Portland's best sausage purveyors. Over 40 different kinds of sausage (including wieners and bockwurst) are made on-site including Otto's own recipes brought over from Germany. The neighborhood deli is a reliable source for imported cheeses, craft beers and wines, condiments, homemade salads, candies, sandwiches and catering. Both sausages and merchandise can also be purchased online.

Pacific Fish & Oyster
3380 SE Powell Blvd   503/233-4891
Mon-Fri: 9-6   pacseafood.com

You know the fish is fresh if you shop here. Begun by the Dulcich family more than 70 years ago, these folks showcase fresh shrimp, salmon, oysters and crab. The business has expanded to nearly 40 fish and seafood processing and distribution facilities from Alaska to Texas. From those plants and worldwide imports, customers enjoy one of the largest selections in this area. In addition they supply Dungeness crabs for fundraising crab feeds and ship Northwest fish and seafood across the country.

Pacific Pie Co.
1520 SE 7th Ave   503/381-6157
1668 NW 23rd Ave   503/894-9482
Lunch, Dinner: Daily   pacificpieco.com
Moderate

If you have a craving for pie, sweet or savory, head to one of the Pacific Pie Co. locations. **Sarah Curtis-Fawley** and **Chris Powell** first introduced their baked goods at seasonal farmers markets in 2009. They soon found that the demand for their mouthwatering pastries necessitated a storefront, then another. The assortment of handmade savories includes classic beef (and mushroom variations), steak and cheese, creamy chicken and shepherds pies as well as a roast lamb version and spinach and cheese pasties. Order an outstanding pie floater which features your favorite meat pie or pastie floated in a bowl of homemade pea soup (this dish is a nod to Chris' Aussie roots). Salads, potatoes and other sides complete the hearty meal. Oh, those dessert pies! Fresh, local fruits are turned into delectable creations and sold whole or by the slice. A sample of the weekly selections includes apple sour cream streusel and key lime pies, chocolate salted caramel tarts, lamingtons (sponge cake covered in chocolate icing and coconut) and ANZAC biscuits (both are Australian favorites). Desserts are an integral part of many dinner parties; please give the busy bakers 48-hour notice ahead of time so you and your guests won't be disappointed.

Paley's Place

1204 NW 21st Ave	503/243-2403
Dinner: Daily	paleysplace.net
Expensive	

Though culinary duo **Kimberly and Vitaly Paley** perfected their roles as general manager and executive chef at fine establishments in New York and France, the lure of this area's sustainable and seasonal products brought them to Portland. In a beautiful house with two dining rooms and a wide front porch they showcase their talents at Paley's Place. Picture perfect charcuterie (order a single serving or tastes of three, five or one of each) and desserts are delicious. Superb entrees are planned factoring in seasonal availability of main and complementing ingredients. To bring out the best flavors and qualities, preparations are braised, roasted or grilled. Relax and unwind at the cozy full-service bar with Oregon and French wines, handcrafted cocktails or an always-popular Paley's Burger.

The Palm Court Restaurant and Bar

309 SW Broadway	503/228-2000
(See detailed listing with The Benson Hotel)	

Park Kitchen

422 NW 8th Ave	503/223-7275
Dinner: Daily	parkkitchen.com
Moderate	

Located on the North Park Blocks in Portland's Pearl District, Park Kitchen provides inspired American fare utilizing Oregon's own farmers and producers to craft seasonal food and wine menus.

DIVISION STREET DINING

One of the city's exciting dining areas is southeast Division Street (and nearby Clinton Street) where you can find a variety of food options any time of day. Check out the area's tasty offerings at these restaurants:

Ava Gene's (3377 SE Division St; 971/229-0571; avagenes.com): A Northwest-inspired menu features great local produce and meats grown by local ranchers and farmers. Guests are welcomed with a wood-burning fire and rustic charm.

Block & Tackle (3113 SE Division St; 503/236-0205; blockand tacklepdx.com): This casual seafood restaurant (also called B&T by regulars) presents classic shrimp Louie and clam chowder alongside creative seafood items. Look for **Roe**, a small intimate restaurant located at the back of Block & Tackle.

Broder (2508 SE Clinton St; 503/736-3333; broderpdx.com): A small Swedish restaurant with a scrumptious Scandinavian brunch.

Little T. American Baker (2600 SE Division St; 503/238-3458; littletbaker.com): Breadmaker **Tim Healea** creates delicious baked inspirations from around the world.

Nuestra Cocina (3715 SE Division St; 503/232-2135; nuestracocina. com): Translated, Nuestra Cocina means "our kitchen." This classic restaurant serves authentic Mexican recipes passed down through many generations.

Off the Waffle (2601 SE Clinton St; 503/946-1608; offthewaffle. com): This spot features a variety of amazing Belgian waffle creations. Eugene-based, the restaurant also has two locations there.

Pok Pok (3226 SE Division St; 503/232-1387; pokpokpdx.com): Award-winning chef **Andy Ricker** began this Northern Thai pub as a food cart. His superb menu includes grilled offerings, curries, noodle soups and more.

Roman Candle Baking (3377 SE Division St; 971/302-6605; roman candlebaking.com): This great cafe stop serves pizzas, sandwiches and pastries; owned by **Duane Sorenson**, also Stumptown Coffee's owner.

Sen Yai (3384 SE Division St; 503/236-3573; pokpoksenyai.com): Offerings at this partner to Pok Pok include authentic Asian street noodles and spicy Thai cuisine.

Tidbit Food Farm and Garden (2880 SE Division St; Facebook): A family-friendly food cart pod offers 20 exceptional food carts, a

DIVISION STREET DINING, CONT.

beer garden, firepit, picnic tables and a vintage dress shop in a double-decker bus.

Whiskey Soda Lounge (3131 SE Division St; 503/232-0102; whiskeysodalounge.com): Across the street find sister eatery to Pok Pok; many of the same menu items and shorter lines!

Xico (3715 SE Division St; 503/548-6343; xicopdx.com): Xico is a Mexican restaurant serving a fresh, seasonal menu including small plates, vegetarian and a walk-up window serving rotisserie food. Chicken dinner pick-up is available 5 to 9 daily.

Chef/owner **Scott Dolich** is a true genius in the kitchen with original compositions as well as updated favorites. Small hot plates (chickpea fries with pumpkin ketchup, asparagus soup with marinated mushrooms), small cold plates (duck ham, halibut carpaccio, lamb tartare), large plates (seared salmon, sorrel, potatoes, leeks) and desserts (apple butter crepes or a selection of cheeses) are uniformly delicious. Visit on a warm evening when you can sit outside and enjoy a view of the park and busy bocce ball court.

Pearl Bakery

102 NW 9th Ave   503/827-0910
Mon-Fri: 6:30-5:30; Sat: 7-5; Sun: 8-3   pearlbakery.com

Fragrant fresh loaves of bread fill the space at family-owned Pearl Bakery. Unique flavors and textures are achieved using different leavening methods to extend fermentation, and as a result, each variety of bread has its own unique flavor. Pugliese is the signature variety, characterized by its chewy crust and dense holes and a hint of extra-virgin olive oil. Loaves vary in size and shape from petite French rolls up to the four-pound Pugliese and are sold as baguettes, rounds and in decorative shapes. Other breads include dried fruit, nuts, olives, spices and/or herbs. In addition to the daily breads, bakers turn out diet-breaking breakfast pastries, cookies and shortbreads, cupcakes, tarts, layer cakes and bundt cakes. At the top of my list are the oh-so-elegant Parisian macarons; cookie and filling flavors are ever-changing. For lunchers on the run, the retail case is filled each morning with sandwiches made with Pearl's breads and natural meats, imported cheeses and organic greens; stop in anytime for coffee and sweet treats. Small batches of handcrafted bonbons and chocolate bars are a more recent addition to the enterprise (pearlbakerychocolate.com)

Pearl Specialty Market & Spirits
900 NW Lovejoy St   503/477-8604
Mon-Sat: 9 a.m.-10 p.m.; Sun: noon-8   pearlspecialty.com

Talk about a liquor store on steroids! By the numbers it has over 1,000 spirits, 500 wines, 500 beers and 300 cigars. Those are labels, not actual pieces! They carry an impressive array of top-shelf bottles and imported and locally-produced wines, spirits and beers; champagnes; sakés; bitters; syrups and barware. The more exclusive (read very expensive) products, including a bottle of Remy Martin Louis XIII cognac, are in a specialty case behind lock and key; special orders are welcome. Unlike run-of-the-mill Oregon Liquor Control Commission outlets, Pearl Specialty stocks all these items including an extensive selection of craft beers, world wines, hard-to-find vermouths, mixers and bitters under one roof. They also have a glass-walled, temperature- and humidity-controlled walk-in humidor that pairs well with the extensive bourbon and scotch selection.

Petite Provence
1824 NE Alberta St   503/284-6564
4834 SE Division St   503/233-1121
7000 NE Airport Way   503/493-4460
Daily: Hours vary   provencepdx.com

Originally from France, the owners of these bistros strive to create a nostalgic French atmosphere in their establishments and become an integral part of neighborhoods. Menus are similar at each location, but chefs operate in their own creative styles. Omelets, French toast, Benedicts, hash and more for breakfast; lunch can spill over into the dinner hour with salad, sandwich and soup choices. Throughout the day enjoy wonderful fresh bakery goods from cases filled with yummy croissants, chocolate treats galore and fruit tarts. Additionally, check out sister locations **La Provence Bakery and Bistro** (16350 SW Boones Ferry Road, Lake Oswego; 503/635-4533; 15151 SW Barrows Road, #153, Beaverton; 971/246-8627) and **Petite Provence of the Gorge** (408 E 2nd St, The Dalles; 541/506-0037).

Piazza Italia

1129 NW Johnson St   503/478-0619
Lunch, Dinner: Daily   piazzaportland.com
Moderate

For an authentic Italian meal, visit this fun Pearl District eatery. In 2000, the late Gino Schettini and Kevin Gorretta, a fellow Italian descendant, realized their dream for their own restaurant. Now members of Gino's family (Amy and Brian) carry on his vision of providing fantastic food from a large menu. Start with bruschetta with sautéed mushrooms, pancetta, fresh garlic, parsley and white wine. Order flavorful sauces like garlic marinara and wild boar meat sauce to accompany your chosen pasta. Linguine *squarciarella* is highly recommended. Adding to the appeal is good friendly service, lively Italian conversations and an obvious bent for celebrating soccer. You can easily stock your fridge with the large selection of Italian wines and meats and cheeses from the deli counter. Ciao!

The Picnic House

723 SW Salmon St   503/227-0705
Lunch, Dinner: Mon-Sat   picnichousepdx.com
Moderate

Picnic House, in the nearly century-old lobby of the original Heathman Hotel, is the project of **Aaron and Jessica Grimmer**. The classical two-story interior boasts the original hand-tiled floors and rich wood. Colorful mosaics of old printing plates embellish the walls and stair risers and retain the historical local flavor. Choose a seat at a table or the bar where locally-influenced and -named cocktails are crafted with regional spirits. The lunch menu lists interesting homemade soups, salads (green, vegan and pasta) and sandwiches (kimchi chicken or charred tomato and goat cheese). Small plates and appetizers center around seasonal roasted vegetables, charcuterie and artisanal cheeses. Seasonal entrees may include black truffle mushroom lasagna with sage cream sauce or ponzu-braised lamb ribs with roasted garlic potatoes.

Pine State Biscuits

2204 NE Alberta St	503/477-6605
1100 SE Division St, Suite 100	503/236-3356

Mon-Wed: 7-3; Thurs-Sun: 7a.m.-11 p.m.

125 NE Schuyler St	503/719-9357
Daily: 7-3	pinestatebiscuits.com

Inexpensive to moderate

Don't miss the sumptuous buttermilk biscuits at Pine State Biscuits! Order just one (I dare you) or a dozen, then slather on butter, honey or jam. The sausage gravy is out of this world, and so are the biscuit sandwiches made with bacon, housemade sausage, ham, fried chicken, flank steak, eggs and assorted greens, cheeses and sauces. You'll probably tackle your towering concoction (multi-layers dripping with melted cheese atop creamy gravy) with a knife and fork. Southern food extras like fried green tomatoes and hush puppies or desserts baked on-site like pecan pie and bourbon cinnamon rolls are hard to resist.

Pok Pok

3226 SE Division St	503/232-1387

Lunch, Dinner: Daily

Pok Pok Noi

1469 NE Prescott St	503/287-4149
Lunch: Sat, Sun; Dinner: Daily	pokpokpdx.com

Moderate

Accolades to Chef **Andy Ricker** who mastered the art of Thai cooking during a lengthy sojourn in Southeast Asia. His hard work has not gone unrecognized; he earned the James Beard Award for Best Chef Northwest and continues to add to his realm. Specialties of the house at his two Portland locations include flavorful rotisserie-roasted game hen, papaya Pok Pok salad and deep-fried Vietnamese fish sauce wings; all are best enjoyed with sticky rice. Other

ACHIEVEMENTS IN ATHLETICS

For more than two decades, **Oregon Sports Authority** has tirelessly served the state in the field of sports economic development. The goal of this non-profit organization is to enhance Oregon's economy and quality of life by securing amateur and professional sports events and franchises. CEO **Drew Mahalic**, former football linebacker for the San Diego Chargers and the Philadelphia Eagles, has had an important hand in successfully landing the NCAA Men's Basketball Tournament, Davis Cup World Final, U.S. Figure Skating Championships and Women's World Cup Soccer. Kudos to the more than 150 members for their ongoing efforts!

Additionally, since its inception in 1978, the **Oregon Sports Hall of Fame** (503/227-7466, oregonsportshall.org) has recognized and honored Oregon's rich athletic history. From auto racing to wrestling with 30 other sports and related athletic contributions in between, the organization is currently looking for a new bricks-and-mortar home in the Portland metro area where the achievements of Harrington, Simonton, Buckwalter, Brooks, Schollander, Baker, Prefontaine, Fosbury, Salazar, Drexler, Sitton, Walton, Schonely, Jacobsen and other greats will again be publicly showcased in the halls of a museum. An annual induction ceremony welcomes new honorees to Oregon's Sports Hall of Fame. The organization is dedicated to education and continues to award a number of collegiate scholarships annually with the underlying message that hard work and dedication reap benefits for any life path.

authentic dishes utilize pork belly and ribs, sausage, boar collar and fish; preparations may be grilled or incorporated into noodle dishes. Out-of-state diners can choose from several Pok Pok locations in Manhattan and Los Angeles.

Portland Art Museum

1219 SW Park Ave   503/226-2811
Tues, Wed, Sat, Sun: 10-5; Thurs, Fri: 10-8   portlandartmuseum.org
Reasonable

Oregon's premier art museum just happens to be the Pacific Northwest's oldest art museum and is an anchor in Portland's Cultural

District in the South Park Blocks. Founded in 1892, there are over 42,000 items. The majority of the gallery spaces contain pieces from the impressive permanent collections of modern and contemporary art, English silver, graphic arts and art of the native peoples of North America. Check the schedule for interesting and stunning exhibitions and public tours; free to members or with paid admission. The **Northwest Film Center** (503/221-1156, nwfilm.org) is also a part of the Portland Art Museum and is home to a variety of festivals, exhibitions and a film school. Museum Director **Brian Ferriso** is a treasure!

Portland City Grill

111 SW 5th Ave, 30th floor   503/450-0030
Lunch: Mon-Fri; Dinner: Daily; Brunch: Sun   portlandcitygrill.com
Moderate and up

The Portland City Grill is one of Portland's most popular award-winning restaurants, and if you've seen the breathtaking views then you know why. Atop the 30th floor of what is one of downtown's tallest towers are panoramic views of the city and the Cascade Mountains; there are not many places you can access these great views. This grill is famous for much more. It has one of the busiest happy hours in the city with cheap eats and delicious cocktails, just in time for the sunset. Their menu primarily consists of fresh seafood prepared with Northwest, Island and Asian influences and steak as well as soups, salads and appetizers. The signature dish is a chili-rubbed Kobe flat iron steak with poblano romesco, mustard marble potatoes (caviar-studded) and creamy charred corn with citrus. Their extensive drink menu features wines, cocktails and an assortment of beers; *Wine Enthusiast* magazine crowned them as one of the best 100 wine restaurants in the country.

Portland Marriott Downtown Waterfront

1401 SW Naito Pkwy   503/226-7600
Moderate to expensive   portlandmarriott.com

For those visiting downtown Portland for business or pleasure, this luxury hotel is an excellent choice. The hotel is ideally located in the heart of the city at the waterfront with easy to-and-from freeway access. Rooms are recently renovated with modern amenities including movable desktops, walk-in showers, ambient lighting, flat-screen TVs and Thaan natural bath products. Large windows afford picture postcard views of the Willamette River, Mt. Hood and the City of Bridges. A selection of rooms with bike storage is also available. The property also offers a completely new, modern fitness center and **M Club Lounge**, Marriott's new 24/7 concierge lounge. **Truss** restaurant is open for breakfast, serving a "Purely Portland" inspired buffet including a fresh selection of fruits, made-to-order omelets, waffles and local jams and butters. **Bistro by Truss**, the property's prime dining outlet, embraces the Portland tradition of sourcing the best local and seasonal products to create familiar American favorites. The menu is moderately priced and designed to offer shareable choices for a perfect meal. A unique feature transforms the coffee bar into a contemporary bar where bartenders create exciting cocktails using freshly-squeezed juices and local liquors and their newest specialty bourbon flights. The hotel offers over 45,000 square feet of meeting space, of which over 2,000 square feet on the second floor is complemented with outstanding views; very nice, indeed.

Porto Terra Tuscan Grill & Bar

830 SW 6th Ave   503/944-1090
(See detailed listing with Hilton Portland & Executive Tower)

Powell's Books

City of Books, 1005 W Burnside   503/228-4651 (all stores)
Books on Hawthorne, 3723 SE Hawthorne Blvd
Books for Home and Garden, 3747 SE Hawthorne Blvd
Books at PDX, 7000 NE Airport Way
Cedar Hills Crossing, 3415 SW Cedar Hills Blvd, Beaverton   powells.com
Hours vary by location

One could say if it is printed on paper, it may just be at Powell's. Founded in 1971, Powell's Books remains a family-owned and -operated business, with **Emily Powell** serving as the company's third-generation leader. This Northwest Portland fixture has expanded numerous times to make room for more shelves of every ilk of book — new and used, fiction, non-fiction, hard back, soft cover, rare, reference, collectible, signed and audio, plus toys and gifts. Over 1 million tomes are housed in the Burnside flagship location; each genre is shelved in the labyrinth of rooms. Over the years the popularity of Powell's and the burgeoning supply necessitated growth to other Portland buildings; additionally, the Beaverton store has over a half million selections. Travelers appreciate the three shops at PDX for last minute reading material before boarding flights or to grab a quick gift on the way in or out of town. Two neighboring businesses are on Hawthorne Boulevard, one dedicated to home and garden material as well as cooking utensils, accessories and related merchandise; the other store carries a full spectrum of reads. Powell's is a leader in book-buying and selling, in stores or online. This is another quintessential Portland institution!

Ringside Fish House

838 SW Park Ave, mezzanine level   503/227-3900
Lunch: Mon-Fri; Dinner: Daily   ringsidefishhouse.com
Moderate and up

This business branched out from its historic Portland custom of providing the "best steaks in town" to celebrate Oregon's proximity to fresh fish and seafood with the creation of RingSide Fish House in the Fox Tower downtown overlooking Director Park. You'll find a raw bar, seafood platters, sandwiches (including non-seafood) and changing entrees of halibut, cioppino, lobster, trout and many other fish choices with a sprinkling of beef, pasta and poultry. This space is warm, classy and inviting and offers early and late happy hours in the busy bars; private dining.

Ringside Steakhouse Uptown

2165 W Burnside St   503/223-1513
Dinner: Daily

Ringside Steakhouse Eastside at the Glendoveer Golf Course

14021 NE Glisan St   503/255-0750
Lunch: Mon-Fri; Dinner: Daily   ringsidesteakhouse.com

The RingSide Steakhouse Uptown has been a Portland tradition for more than 70 years. For decades they have been providing great steaks, fabulous onion rings and other delectables. The evolving menu features select steaks that are dry-aged and carved on-premises. The space is airy and cozy with a welcoming fireplace. Service, as always, is highly professional. The 10,000-bottle wine cellar is fabulous. Across town, expect the same fine dining and impeccable service in a relaxed, clubby atmosphere at the Glendoveer Golf Course. In an era of chain restaurants, it is refreshing to boast about a homegrown winner; great credit goes to the members of the Peterson family who keep watchful eyes on every phase of the business.

Ristorante Roma
622 SW 12th Ave   503/241-2692
Lunch: Mon-Fri; Dinner: Mon-Sat   ristoranteromaportland.com
Moderate

A dozen or so tables enhance the intimate and friendly atmosphere at Ristorante Roma. Conversation is easy in this casual trattoria where platters are quite tasty and where prices are also easy on the wallet. The antipasti choices range from salads and minestrone soup to seafood plates. The authentic Italian dishes combine shrimp, clams and mussels in a variety of impressive dishes. Pastas are wide-ranging: rigatoni, fettuccine, ravioli, gnocchi, spaghetti and more — all made fresh. A filet steak is available, as well as beef tenderloin and chicken; from-scratch sauces are made daily. Reservations are recommended for busy Thursday through Saturday nights.

RiverPlace Hotel
1510 SW Harbor Way   503/228-3233, 800/227-1333
Moderate to very expensive   riverplacehotel.com

This is one of Portland's finest settings — downtown Portland along the Willamette River. The city and river vistas are stunning, but never more so than on a sunny day when watercraft navigate the sparkling waterway. Miles of walking paths front the RiverPlace connecting pedestrians with bustling or tranquil neighborhood eateries and shops (complimentary guest use of hotel bicycles). Consider staying here when you attend events at adjacent Tom McCall

Waterfront Park or book a riverview room for the annual parade of Christmas ships alternating between the Willamette and Columbia rivers. Luxury abounds in the 84 spacious rooms and suites at this Kimpton Craftsman-style boutique hotel; upscale in-room features are the norm as well as refrigerators stocked with local and organic snacks, yoga mats, umbrellas and electronic conveniences. Seasonal cooking has diners looking forward to breakfast, lunch, dinner and weekend brunch at **Three Degrees Waterfront Bar & Grill** (503/295-6166; threedegreesportland.com).

Ruth's Chris Steak House

850 SW Broadway   503/221-4518
Dinner: Daily   ruthschris.com
Expensive

This prestigious steakhouse chain does things in a big way; Portland's warm yet spectacular location is no exception. Classic seafood appetizers are the perfect way to start dinner. The beefsteak tomato salad is superb, baked potatoes are gigantic and other potato dishes are more than generous. Beef lovers have their choice of USDA Prime cuts; tender, juicy and delicious every time. My preference, though, are the grilled lamb chops; cut extra thick and very flavorful. Fresh lobster is always on the menu as are other seafood and fish selections. Desserts include homemade cheesecake, crème brûlée, chocolate cake, bread pudding and seasonal berries with cream. Weekday happy hours are between 4 and 7, a very pleasant way to ease into the evening.

Salt & Straw

2035 NE Alberta St   503/208-3867
3345 SE Division St   503/208-2054
Daily: 11-11
838 NW 23rd Ave   971/271-8168
Daily: 10 a.m.-11 p.m.   saltandstraw.com

Salt & Straw is a farm-to-cone ice cream shop which makes small batches of seasonal and classic flavors. Each scoop is chock-full of real ingredients; no artificial flavorings or manufactured particles are to be found. Savor the goodness in winning combinations of pear with blue cheese, strawberry with cracked pepper, chocolate with brownies, almond brittle with salted ganache or single-origin Woodblock chocolate ice cream. For a distinctive touch to any party, Salt & Straw's website offers catering options or order a five-pint gift pack delivered to your door.

Salty's on the Columbia

3839 NE Marine Dr

503/288-4444

Lunch: Mon-Sat; Dinner: Daily; Brunch: Sat, Sun

saltys.com/portland

Moderate

The mighty Columbia flows past this local landmark restaurant. Alfresco dining on the wraparound deck is spectacular in summer and window seats are coveted when the Christmas ships sail past in December. Salty's arguably presents the busiest and best weekend champagne brunch buffet in the state. Prawns, Dungeness crab, salmon, clams, mussels, omelets, crepes, waffles, fruits, cheeses, baked ham (excellent), prime rib and much more make choosing a real dilemma; a four-foot tall fountain of gurgling chocolate sauce is irresistible for dipping fruits and cookies (kids love to swirl marshmallows). The impressive sea and land lunch and dinner menus feature entries such as sustainable seafood, live Maine lobster, cioppino and Certified Angus beef. Lighten up during the bar's weekday happy hours with great bar eats and drinks or join in the fun at Salty's entertaining cooking classes and special events.

HARDWARE PLUS

These businesses offer something beyond the typical trappings of your ordinary hardware store:

Ace Hardware (706 Madrona Ave SE, Salem; 503/763-6323): extraordinary gifts, too!

Cannon Beach Hardware & Public House (1235 S Hemlock St, Cannon Beach; 503/436-4086): affordable hardware plus brews

Wichita Feed & Hardware (6089 SE Johnson Creek Blvd, Portland; 503/775-6767): huge inventory of gadgets for electrical, plumbing and repairs, with superior service

Sayler's Old Country Kitchen
10519 SE Stark St   503/252-4171
Dinner: Daily   saylers.com
Moderate and up

For years, wise steak lovers have made one-of-a-kind Sayler's Old Country Kitchen crowded every day of the week. Reasonable prices for top-quality meals bring customers back again and again. Although steaks are in the main here, those who prefer seafood or chicken can find a number of entrees. The crab Louis salad is especially appealing and delicious. Don't miss the fabulous onion rings — right at the top of any offered in the Portland area. Steak offerings include filet mignon, top sirloin, T-bone, porterhouse, ribeye (bone-in or not), New York and ground sirloin. Since 1948, the 72-ounce top sirloin dinner ($65.00) has been served free to anyone who can eat the steak and trimmings within one hour (weekdays only). Why (or how) anyone could do this is beyond me. Value-priced senior dinners are offered as well as prime rib plates and sandwiches. Sayler's is a true quality Portland tradition; look for the revolving steak sign.

Seres Restaurant and Bar
1105 NW Lovejoy St   971/222-0100
Lunch: Mon-Sat; Dinner: Daily; Brunch: Sat   seresrestaurant.com
Moderate

This Pearl District restaurant serves tasty Szechuan and multi-regional Chinese cuisines. The surrounds are modern, neat and clean and the staff is informed. Start your meal with the chicken and lotus lettuce wraps or scallion pancakes — delicious. Classic dishes, like sesame chicken or peppered lamb, are made with fresh, locally-sourced ingredients (free of hormones, antibiotics and MSG) and prepared on flaming woks. Order the flavorful curry lamb claypot for something a bit more interesting. Eat in, take out or have your order delivered. While you're in the area, enhance your cultural experience with a visit to the remarkable **Lan Su Chinese Garden** in Old Town Chinatown before or after your meal.

Serratto

2112 NW Kearney St   503/221-1195
Lunch, Dinner: Daily   serratto.com
Moderately expensive

Serratto is a busy Alphabet District favorite recognized for Mediterranean and Northwest fare. The extensive, eclectic menu features homemade pastas, family-pleasing delicious pizzas, risotto and locally-sourced meats, seafood and produce. Portland's best artisan bakeries provide the breads. A bittersweet chocolate cobbler served warm with vanilla bean gelato is on the dessert menu; other seasonal sweets and housemade gelato and sorbetto are also satisfying. You'll feel like part of the neighborhood at this cozy corner spot; the outside tables are charming.

Sheraton Portland Airport Hotel

8235 NE Airport Way   503/281-2500, 800/325-3535
Moderate   sheratonpdx.com

The guest rooms, meeting facilities and the restaurant at this convenient hotel are most inviting. **Columbia Grill and Bar** offers appealing meals from 6 a.m. to midnight; room service is available until 10 p.m. Complimentary Wi-Fi is available for all guests throughout the 212-room hotel. The Sheraton also features great Starwood amenities such as the Sweet Sleeper Bed, Sheraton Fitness by Core Performance and the Sheraton Club which offers continental breakfast and evening reception for a nominal fee. Hardworking, civic-minded hotelier **Harold Pollin**'s portfolio includes two other airport properties. Next door to the Sheraton is **Hampton Inn Portland Airport** (8633 NE Airport Way, 503/288-2423, hamptoninn.com) and **Aloft Portland Airport at Cascade Station** (9920 NE Cascades Pkwy, 503/200-5678, alofthotels.com). Complimentary shuttle service to the airport runs 24/7 making these convenient stays for travelers in and out of PDX; also great as jumping-off-points for exploring southwest Washington or the Gorge.

LUXURY DOWNTOWN LODGING

Portland offers many choices in luxury lodging, all with tastefully and magnificently appointed guest rooms and impeccable service. Some of the best include:

The Benson Hotel (309 SW Broadway; 503/228-2000, 800/663-1144; bensonhotel.com): elegant landmark; El Gaucho steakhouse and The Palm Court Restaurant & Lounge

The Heathman (1001 SW Broadway; 503/241-4100, 800/551-0011; heathmanhotel.com): charming; historic Heathman Restaurant offers Pacific Northwest fare and elegant Tea Court Lounge, one of the hotel's original features

Hotel deLuxe (729 SW 15th Ave; 503/219-2094, 866/895-2094; hoteldeluxe.com): retro-chic; classic fare at Gracie's restaurant; Manhattans in the iconic Driftwood Room

Hotel Eastlund (1021 NE Grand Ave; 503/235-2100; hoteleastlund.com): modern- chic eastside boutique; rooftop Altabira City Tavern and bakery/cafe Citizen Baker

Hotel Lucia (400 SW Broadway; 503/225-1717, 877/225-1717; hotelucia.com): warm and contemporary; chef Vitaly Paley's Imperial restaurant and the Portland Penny Diner

Hotel Monaco Portland (506 SW Washington St; 503/222-0001, 888/207-2201; monaco-portland.com): classic tasteful Kimpton property

Hotel Vintage Portland (422 SW Broadway; 503/228-1212; hotelvintage-portland.com): boutique flavor Kimpton property; Italian-inspired Pazzo Ristorante and Baccus Bar, featuring Oregon wines

Sentinel (614 SW 11th Ave; 503/224-3400; sentinelhotel.com): formerly the Governor Hotel; home to Jake's Grill and Jackknife, a hip, classic lobby lounge

The Westin Portland (750 SW Alder St; 503/294-9000, 888/627-8401; westinportland.com): top-of-the-line beds and baths; seasonal American fare at next-door Daily Grill or refreshing drinks at The Lobby Bar

Slappy Cakes

4246 SE Belmont St   503/477-4805
Breakfast, Lunch: Daily   slappycakes.com
Inexpensive

Scratch pancakes and other breakfast items are the order of the day here. Guests have the option of making their pancakes on tabletop griddles or leaving the cooking to the kitchen. Emphasis is on organic and their own garden supplies many ultra-fresh ingredients. Pick a batter (buttermilk, chocolate, peanut butter, gluten-free and seasonal); then the fixins (chocolate or butterscotch chips, fruits, nuts, mushrooms, bacon); add a lavender honey, peanut butter, lemon curd or maple syrup topping — and you'll have a memorable pancake breakfast made at your table. A host of additional creative breakfast choices, including eye-opening cocktails, chicken-fried steak, seasonal vegetable scrambles and a classic egg breakfast are available every day.

St. Honoré Boulangerie

2335 NW Thurman St   503/445-4342
Daily: 6:30 a.m.-8 p.m.
3333 SE Division St   971/279-4433
Daily: 7 a.m.-9 p.m.
315 1st St, Lake Oswego   503/496-5596
Mon-Fri: 7-7 (till 8 in summer);
Sat, Sun: 7 a.m.-8 p.m.   sainthonorebakery.com

Cruising down northwest Thurman Street be on the lookout for flags which identify this traditional French bakery evocative of the French countryside. The wonderfully rustic establishment sets the stage for specialty items (raisin and fennel benoitons, rolls, the signature Miche Banal loaves and cranberry hazelnut bread and rolls), baguettes and other breads. Not to be overlooked are the pain au chocolat (chocolate-filled croissant) and other decadent pastries. Croissant and other sandwiches, quiches, soups, salads and oh-so-good desserts are served in these neighborhood cafes at communal harvest or Parisian-style tables; the atmosphere is truly delightful. **Dominique Geulin**'s Lake Oswego cafe is elegant and the Division Street locale features a nice selection of craft beers and cider.

Stammtisch

401 NE 28th Ave   503/206-7983

Mon-Fri: 3 p.m.–2:30 a.m.; Sat, Sun: 11 a.m.–2:30 a.m.   stammtischpdx.com

Moderate

There seems to be an uprising in beer connoisseurs and who could blame them; what is better than a refreshing cold beer at the end of the day? Germany is widely recognized as one of the greatest beer centers in the world and Stammtisch is a perfect example of what Germany has to offer. This new brew pub carries a large collection of German brandies and liquors, traditional German biers and truly authentic German food such as Bretzels (a Bavarian pretzel) and Hausgemachte Wurst (bratwurst, weisswurst or knackwurst with sauerkraut and house mustard). Now that's a mouthful. Some of the more popular bier selection includes Andechs Hell and Ayinger Bräu Weisse with tastes of light and floral to citrus and vanilla. No matter the craving, Stammtisch is the place to experience a part of Germany's culture. The open yet cozy atmosphere is welcoming, staff is friendly and attentive and the restaurant is very upbeat as if it's Oktoberfest every day. You can also fill your stein at sister location, **Prost** (4237 N Mississippi Ave, 503/954-2674).

LOCAL BUSINESS NEWS

The *Portland Business Journal* has been the primary source of critical local business news, data and strategies to help Portland area businesses grow for some 31 years. This entity engages with its regional executive audience through three platforms: the weekly print newspaper, read by more than 55,000 executives weekly; digitally through websites trafficking more than 1.5 million page views per month; and through 40 local events and programs giving more than 13,000 regional executives the chance to connect and engage throughout the year. The publisher, **Craig Wessel**, began his publishing career at the launch of the *Portland Business Journal* in 1984. He has worked across the country in a variety of publishing roles before returning to Portland to resume his position in 2001. Bravo!

Stepping Stone Cafe

2390 NW Quimby St   503/222-1132
Breakfast, Lunch, Dinner: Daily   steppingstonecafe.com
Inexpensive

Breakfast at all hours, every day! Enter hungry and leave stuffed! Here's another Portland eatery that has earned a national reputation. Casual Stepping Stone is famous for its dinner-plate-size mancakes (aka pancakes); one will probably do, but order a stack if you dare. There are plenty of other choices, some with interesting names like the Grazing Goat (spinach, portabella, artichoke, feta) and Neo Bobcat (tomato, avocado, choice of cheese) omelets and One-Eyed Jack (fried egg) burgers. Lunch sandwiches, soups and salads are served starting at 10:30 and comfort food dinners begin at 5; meatloaf and chicken-fried steak are full-meal-deals. You'll probably need a shoe horn to get into this small quirky cafe on weekends!

Sushi Mazi

2126 SE Division St   503/432-8651
Lunch: Tues-Fri; Dinner: Tues-Sun   sushimazipdx.com
Moderate

Chef Marc takes great pride in preparing and presenting sushi using fresh fish and vegetables to create culinary works of art. The coconut shrimp roll, real grasshopper sushi and Buddha crunchy roll with mango, asparagus and avocado are appealing and interesting. Platters of sushi and sashimi are served with miso soup; beer, wine and saké are available. Expect friendly service at this casual and quiet restaurant.

Thirsty Lion Pub and Grill

71 SW 2nd Ave   503/222-2155
(See detailed listing with Thirsty Lion Pub and Grill, Tigard)

Toro Bravo

120 NE Russell St   503/281-4464
Dinner: Daily   torobravopdx.com
Moderately expensive

This vibrant Spanish-inspired tapas restaurant offers plenty of choices. For tiny bites, order toasted almonds, cheese and salads from the Pinchos section. Tapas selections change daily and might include griddled shrimp, sauteed spinach, grilled flat bread and other small plates great for sharing or a light meal. Several whole meals are offered; paella, meatballs, fish and seafood and vegetable options. For a special evening, order the chef's choice for your party, complemented with Spanish wine and desserts such as olive oil cake or churros and chocolate.

Trader Vic's

1203 NW Glisan St   503/467-2277
Dinner: Daily; Brunch: Sat, Sun   tradervicspdx.com
Expensive

Longtime Portlanders fondly recall the original Trader Vic's, tucked away in The Benson Hotel from 1959 until 1996. Oh, the stories that went away with it! In 2011, local booster Clayton Hering wooed this Polynesian escape back to Portland. The splendid bar is open every day between 4 and 10 (till midnight on Friday and Saturday). Order a famous Mai Tai or other exotic cocktail that is sure to bring visions of a Tahitian vacation. Traditional pupus like beef cho cho, crab rangoons and the cosmo tidbit platter are tasty hors d'oeuvres that are meant to be shared. A custom-built Chinese wood-fired oven turns out delicious seafood, beef, pork and chicken permeated with the light sweet, smoky flavor. Sweet cravings are satisfied with the chef's inspirations, housemade of course. Service is exceptional in this tiki-adorned, Polynesian-style hot spot with plenty of seating inside and out.

Truss

1401 SW Naito Pkwy   503/226-7600
(See detailed listing with Portland Marriott Downtown Waterfront)

Urban Farmer

525 SW Morrison St   503/222-4900
(See detailed listing with The Nines)

AIRPORT HOTELS

These are a sampling of the hotels conveniently located near the Portland Airport that offer frequent airport shuttle service:

Aloft Portland Airport at Cascade Station (503/200-5678, aloft portlandairport.com): on-site restaurant, pet-friendly

Clarion Hotel Portland Airport (503/252-2222, stayclarion.com): free breakfast

Courtyard Portland Airport (503/252-3200, marriott.com): on-site restaurant

Embassy Suites by Hilton Portland Airport (503/460-3000, portlandairport.embassysuites.com): free breakfast, pet-friendly

Fairfield Inn & Suites Portland Airport (503/253-1400, marriott. com): free breakfast

Hampton Inn Portland Airport (503/288-2423, hamptoninn.com): free breakfast

Hilton Garden Inn Portland Airport (503/255-8600, portlandairport. hgi.com): on-site restaurant, free *USA Today*

Hyatt Place Portland Airport/Cascade Station (503/288-2808, hyattplaceportlandairport.com): on-site restaurant, free breakfast

LaQuinta Inn & Suites Portland Airport (503/382-3820, lq.com): free breakfast, pet-friendly

Radisson Hotel Portland Airport (503/251-2000, radisson.com): on-site restaurant

Red Lion Hotel Portland Airport (503/255-6722, redlionpdx.com): on-site restaurant, pet-friendly

Residence Inn Portland Airport at Cascade Station (503/284-1800, marriott.com): newly renovated, free breakfast, pet-friendly

Sheraton Portland Airport Hotel (503/281-2500, sheraton.com/ Portland): on-site restaurant, pet-friendly, outstanding

SpringHill Suites Portland Airport (503/253-4095, marriott.com/ springhill): breakfast buffet, mini kitchen

Verdigris

1315 NE Fremont St   503/477-8106
Dinner: Tues-Sun; Brunch: Sat, Sun   verdigrisrestaurant.com
Moderate

Whether you are looking for a warm and cozy restaurant or somewhere more intimate, the candlelit dining room, casual elegance and minimalist decor of this funky French-inspired restaurant is sure to please. The menu and the wine list are ever-changing, making for a new, refreshing experience each time. The rotating selection of appetizers and entrees includes items such as housemade pork terrine, Idaho trout, grilled top sirloin steak and crispy pork confit. A recent vegetarian option was a delicious potato gnocchi. The cuisine doesn't skip steps either; every dish is cooked to order and breads made in-house and local produce help ensure freshness. Verdigris is ideal for a brunch with friends or a classic dinner.

DID YOU KNOW...?

... that Portland's **Multnomah Athletic Club** (themac.com) is the largest (in terms of membership) private athletic club in the world? With over 22,000 members and a staff of 500, eight levels encompass 610,000 square feet over a two-block area. The facility offers three pools; multiple tennis, handball and racquet-ball courts; three gyms (one for rock climbing); an indoor track; batting cage; exercise rooms; three restaurants, private dining, a grand ballroom and more. The MAC has been a focal point of the city since 1891; by invitation, non-members are always welcome for dining and at the many social and political events held at the club. The location overlooking **Providence Park** (providenceparkp-dx.com) — home of the **Portland Timbers** (portlandtimbers.com) — offers special stadium views. Although membership is at capacity, periodic admission lotteries are held. Prima Chef **Philippe Boulot** oversees the exceptional club food operations. Get an invitation from a member!

Veritable Quandary

1220 SW 1st Ave   503/227-7342
Lunch: Mon-Fri; Dinner: Daily; Brunch: Sat, Sun   veritablequandary.com
Moderately expensive

Legions of loyal patrons affectionately refer to this delightful restaurant as the "VQ." The fare is fresh from Northwest farms and prepared with a nod to Chef **Annie Cuggino**'s New Orleans and New York culinary experiences. What to order? Bacon-wrapped dates, housemade pierogi, seafood stew, osso bucco and other dishes from around the world; try the shrimp and grits for weekend brunch. You'll find a large selection of superb desserts such as a peanut butter banana split, tarts, soufflés and housemade ice creams and sorbets. Enjoy the patio's sensational spring and summer blooms; a table in the glass-walled dining room is the next best seating. Classy private dining for up to eight friends is available in the wine cellar.

Voodoo Doughnut

22 SW 3rd Ave   503/241-4707
1501 NE Davis St   503/235-2666
24/7   voodoodoughnut.com

It seems the whole world knows about Voodoo Doughnut thanks to the magic of the media and faithful foodies. These are no ordinary doughnuts, probably the best known variety is the signature Voodoo doughnut; a raspberry jelly-filled raised yeast doughnut in the shape of a Voodoo Doll, frosted with chocolate icing, embellished with details and presented with a pretzel stake to the heart! It has a cult following of its own! There over 50 more varieties, from plain to over-the-top creations, some with names and descriptions inappropriate for this book. When you visit one of their almost-anything-goes shops, keep in mind that they accept cash only (ATM inside). Look for the Voodoo Doughnut pink cart in Cartlandia (8145 SE 82nd Ave); open daily, but with limited hours. Eugene also has an outpost (20 E Broadway, 541/868-8666). One more thing: they also perform legal and non-legal wedding ceremonies at all locations!

West Cafe

1201 SW Jefferson St   503/227-8189
Lunch: Mon-Fri; Dinner: Mon-Sat; Brunch: Sun   westcafepdx.com
Moderate

Chef **Sean Concannon** and partner **Doug Smith** offer brunch, lunch and dinner at their contemporary New American restaurant. Great selections of scrumptious small-plate appetizers (or make a meal of them) are reasonably priced, ditto the soups and salads. Dinner choices such as chicken pot pie, North African spiced leg of lamb, laurel and chili herb-rubbed hangar steak and various locally-sourced preparations are joined by daily fish and vegetarian specials; all are served with interesting fresh and seasonal accompaniments. A little of this and that is on the sweets menu — assorted mini-cupcakes, housemade chocolate truffles and cookies, bread pudding, crème brûlée, key lime pie and other desserts. Stop in on the second and fourth Saturdays for live jazz or anytime for handcrafted cocktails featuring local distillers.

The Westin Portland

750 SW Alder St   503/294-9000, 888/627-8401
Moderate to expensive   westinportland.com

The Westin's convenient downtown location is most appealing. Original art works from a private collection embellish the lobby and common areas. Westin's famous Heavenly beds and baths are standard in all 205 tranquil guest rooms and are stocked with spa-like bath products. A full range of features and amenities are offered including concierge service, multilingual staff, valet parking, free Wi-Fi in the lobby, 24-hour room service from the next-door **Daily Grill** and other courtesies. You may want to take a seat at **The Lobby Bar** for a refreshing drink and use one of the built-in iPads or step outside into the center of Portland. The MAX light rail, museums, concert halls and shopping at Nordstrom, Macy's, outdoor markets and fashionable boutiques are just a short walk away.

CRAFT SPIRITS

Oregon's craft spirits industry is alive and growing. **Oregon Distillers Guild** was formed in 2007 to promote the quality of liquers and liquors produced by our state's craft artisans. There are now well over 30 distilleries around the state; many creations reflect the spirit and landscape of Oregon with such names as Trails End Bourbon, Snake River Stampede Whiskey, Crater Lake Vodka and Hazelnut Spice Rum. The guild's website (oregondistillerytrail. com) lists the distillery locations and offerings as well as recipes, festivals and other special events. Of special mention is **TOAST** (The Original Artisan Spirits Tasting), a spring spirits festival offering an opportunity to taste whiskey, rum, gin, vodka, tequila and brandy; you name it, they got it, from some 40 distillers (held at the Left Bank Annex in 2015).

Willamette Jetboat Excursions

1945 SE Water Ave	503/231-1532, 888/538-2628
May-Sept: Daily: 9:30-4:30	willamettejet.com
Expensive	

Take a thrilling trip up to Oregon City Falls or a shorter tour of the downtown area and harbor. Portland's version of jet boating gives guests a different perspective of the city's bridges by passing under a dozen bridges. Tour prices range between $20 and $51 (lower prices for kids), varying between scenic and downtown/harbor tours. Special packages include an all-inclusive lunch on the Columbia River.

Zupan's Markets

2340 W Burnside St	503/497-1088
3301 SE Belmont St	503/239-3720
7221 SW Macadam Ave	503/244-5666
16380 Boones Ferry Road, Lake Oswego	503/210-4190
Daily	zupans.com

Founded by the late John Zupan in 1975, Zupan's is a locally- and family-owned market that serves Portland's food-loving community.

Likened to farmers markets, Zupan's focuses on quality, selling everything from the best meats and wines to the freshest produce, baked goods, gourmet deli products, specialty foods, flowers and more. Touting a unique grocery shopping experience, Zupan's stores are meant to indulge the senses, inviting customers to see, smell, taste and learn. Regularly scheduled beer, wine and cheese tastings are among customer favorites. Full-service floral departments have beautiful fresh-cut flowers year-round and provide custom design, wedding and event services. The deli features handmade, home-style items with grab-n-go meals, gourmet sandwiches and catering. Bakery items are delivered from 35 of the best bakeries around the Portland area.

SAUVIE ISLAND

Blue Heron Herbary

27731 NW Reeder Road 503/621-1457
March-Oct: Fri-Sun: 10-5 blueheronherbary.com
Dec holiday hours: check web

Take a trip to Sauvie Island and explore the meandering roads passing by farms and wildlife refuges. Blue Heron Herbary is worth a stop to learn about the magic of herbs. Nearly 300 unusual and household herbs are planted in specialty beds: Mediterranean, salad, tea, bee and butterfly. You'll find great-smelling lavenders of varying sizes, colors and shapes, medicinal herbs, culinary additives and ornamentals grown under the loving care of the Hanselman family. In the gift shop you'll find herbal plants for growing at home (over 350 varieties of herbs and more than 100 lavender variations), plus pottery, wind chimes, birdhouses, honey, spices and seasonings. Herbal and/or lavender wreaths, bath and beauty products, herbal cookies for dogs, catnip for felines and home decor and accessories (many items also available online) are crafted at the farm. Plan a visit to the beautiful grounds that are abuzz with bees, butterflies and songbirds.

SHERWOOD

Sleighbells Gift Shop
23855 SW 195th Pl   503/625-6052
July-Dec: Daily: 10-6   Facebook

Although the name implies Christmas, this shop is packed with attractive displays of decorative (traditional, whimsical, stylish) merchandise for other occasions as well; patriotic, St. Patrick's, Hanukkah, Halloween, but especially Christmas. Lines represented: Christopher Radko, Bethany Lowe, Department 56 Villages, Jim Shore, Byers Carolers, Old World Christmas and more. A tradition for many families is searching the 75-acre tree farm for the perfect Frasier fir tree. Starting in September, customers may preselect trees and have them ready on the predetermined day; of course, tromping through the farm with kids and dog in tow and saw in hand is also an option. Sleighbells is a delightful stop; note their seasonal hours.

ST. HELENS

Nob Hill Riverview Bed and Breakfast
285 S 2nd St   503/396-5555
Moderate and up   nobhillbb.com

Three luxurious guest rooms at this bed and breakfast are descriptively named the Paris Apartment, French Suite and Casablanca Retreat. Accommodations in the turn-of-the-century Craftsman-style home vary and may include a private entrance, fireplace, jetted tub, kitchenette or separate living or dining area. Standard features include robes, lavish linens, down comforters and refrigerators. Relax on the front porch with views of the mighty Columbia River, passing ships and romantic sunsets or enjoy complimentary afternoon tea or beverages in the parlor. Each morning, the organic gourmet breakfast is served in the formal dining room or, upon prior request, in your suite. To augment your stay, choose from additional specials and packages.

STATE OF OREGON FUN FACTS

Capital. . . . . Salem

Motto . . . . "She flies with her own wings."

Animal. . . . . Beaver

Beverage. . . . . Milk

Bird . . . . Western meadowlark

Colors . . . . Navy blue and gold

Dance . . . . Square dance

Fish . . . . Chinook salmon

Flower. . . . . Oregon grape

Fruit. . . . . Pear

Gem . . . . Oregon sunstone

Insect. . . . . Swallowtail butterfly

Mushroom . . . . Golden chanterelle

Nut. . . . . Hazelnut

Rock. . . . . Thunder egg

Song . . . . *Oregon My Oregon* by J.A. Buchanan
and Henry B. Murtagh

Tree . . . . Douglas fir

Flag . . . . The only state flag with different
pictures
on each side; on the back is a beaver

Largest city. . . . . Portland

Deepest gorge. . . . . . . Hells Canyon; deepest gorge in the U.S.

Deepest lake . . . . Crater Lake; deepest lake in the U.S.
at 1,943 feet

Highest mountain. . . . Mt. Hood; 11,239 feet

Lowest elevation. . . . . Sea level

Number of lakes 6,000

Shortest river. . . . . D River in Lincoln City; 121 feet long

Seawright House Luxury Retreat

134 N 2nd St   503/366-3035
Moderate   seawrighthouse.com

You or your group will be the only (very spoiled) guests during your stay. This restored home, built in 1910, offers a 1,700 square-foot private suite with three bedrooms, two baths, a complete kitchen, living room with fireplace and formal dining room. But there's more: jacuzzi tub, full laundry room, mini-office area, sunroom and inviting sundeck with private hot tub, water garden and views of Mt. St. Helens, the Columbia River and marina. Gracious hostess **Melinda Beville** offers exceptional hosted, extended-stay or vacation rental accommodations; rented by the week, month or longer and will help you begin a relaxing vacation with a "she-thought-of-everything" feeling upon your arrival at this well-appointed home.

TIGARD

Bridgeport Village

7455 SW Bridgeport Road   503/968-1704
Daily   bridgeport-village.com

Bridgeport Village is one of the Northwest's premier shopping and dining destinations. Located just 15 minutes south of downtown Portland, this outdoor location offers mega retail therapy with over 75 stores and restaurants to explore. It is home to Oregon's only Crate & Barrel, Tommy Bahama, Eileen Fisher, Z Gallerie, Container Store and Saks Fifth Avenue OFF 5th. Hungry visitors have a dozen sit-down eateries from which to choose including PF Chang's China Bistro, McCormick & Schmick's Grill, California Pizza Kitchen and Twigs Bistro & Martini Bar. First-class amenities include valet parking, free Wi-Fi, strollers, wheelchairs and an outdoor playground for kids. Catch a first-run flick at Regal Cinema; 18 screens and a 3-D IMAX. Additional big-name shopping venues are in the immediate area.

ICE RINKS AROUND OREGON

ASHLAND

Rotary Centennial Ice Rink (95 Winburn Way, 541/488-9189, centennialicerink.com): across from Lithia Park; admission specials midweek; open through February

BEND

Seventh Mountain Skating Rink (18575 SW Century Dr, 541/225-5123, rinkatseventhmtresort.com): an outdoor rink at Seventh Mountain Resort; lessons for all ages and skating levels; $7 admission, $5 skate rental

EUGENE

The Rink Exchange (Lane Events Center, 796 W 13th Ave, 541/225-5123, therinkexchange.com): birthday party packages and lessons for all ages; $7 admission, $5 for seniors, students, military

KLAMATH FALLS

Ice Sports (Running Y Ranch, 5075 Fox Sparrow Dr, 541/850-5758): classes in curling, broomball, hockey; $4 all ages after school, $7.50 for 18+, $6.50 for six to 17, $3.50 skate rental

MEDFORD

The RRRink (1349 Center Dr, 541/770-1177, therrrink.com) learn to skate program for ages three to adult; hockey and figure skating, too

PORTLAND

Lloyd Center Ice Rink (Lloyd Center Mall, 503/288-6073, lloydcenterice.com): remodeled rink with skating program for every level and age; $11.50-$14.50 admission, $3.50 skate rental

Winterhawks Skating Center (9250 Beaverton Hillsdale Hwy, 503/297-2521, winterhawksskatingcenter.com): a skating school for adults and youth; $8 admission, $3 skate rental

ICE RINKS AROUND OREGON, CONT.

REDMOND

Redmond Ice Rink (downtown Redmond Plaza at SW 7 St, 541/977-7841): ice skating across from Centennial Park; $4 admission with skate rental, $12 admission family rate; open daily in winter; 10–1 free skate (with your own skates)

SHERWOOD

Sherwood Ice Arena (20407 SW Borchers Dr, 503/625-5757, sherwoodicearena.com): skate time for pros and families; lessons for all ages and abilities, plus hockey lessons; $7 adult admission, $3 skate rental

SILVERTON

Oregon Garden Skating Rink (879 W Main St, 503/874 -8100, oregongarden.org): outdoor ice rink under the tent through January 3; the little German village will charm you; $5 parking, $5 admission, $12 skating, $45 unlimited skating

SUNRIVER

The Village at Sunriver Ice Arena (57100 Beaver Dr, 541/593-5948, sunrivervillagefun.com): a covered rink open to the public during the winter months; $9 admission, $3.50 skate rental

VANCOUVER

Mountain View Ice Arena (14313 SE Mill Plain Blvd, 360/896-8700, mtviewice.com): arena in Washington offering lessons for every age; $13 admission and skates for two

The Grand Hotel at Bridgeport

7265 SW Hazel Fern Road   503/968-5757, 866/968-5757
Moderate to very expensive   grandhotelbridgeport.com

Travelers and shoppers call The Grand Hotel their home away from home in this Portland suburb; the location is ideal for business or pleasure. Package deals combine superb lodging with golf, hot air balloon adventures, shopping and romantic stays. The 124 luxurious rooms and suites offer first-class service and amenities and complimentary covered parking, Internet service, shuttle service and a delicious breakfast buffet. Nearby Bridgeport Village and adjacent complexes offer splendid local, regional and national retailers and irresistible boutiques. Unwind after a flurry of activities in comfortable rooms, conveniently furnished with leather couches and coffee tables, microwaves, refrigerators, coffee stations, work desks with ergonomic chairs and the outstanding hospitality of The Grand Hotel. **Steve Johnson**, president of parent company VIP's Industries, is an expert in the hospitality arena.

Thirsty Lion Pub and Grill

10205 SW Washington Square Road   503/352-4030
Lunch, Dinner: Daily   thirstylionpub.com
Moderate

Head here if you are hungry as a lion. Burgers start with a half-pound of ground beef, then grilled and dressed with different cheeses, sauces, onions, bacon, guacamole, peppers or mushrooms. Slaw, salad or hand-cut fries accompany burgers and other great sandwiches (chicken, turkey club, pulled pork, French dip, Reuben) with delicious components. The grilled pear and gorgonzola starter salad is superb and fresh entree salads (ahi, chicken Caesar, Cobb) are a full meal. Eclectic sharable appetizers include Scotch eggs, garlic sesame edamame and favorites like pretzels and artichoke spinach dip. Entrees are also varied: mac and cheese, artisan pizzas, pastas, chicken and fish dishes, ribs, steaks and more. Fare is seasonal and made from scratch; daily specials emphasize local ingredients. They pride themselves on a large offering of craft beers; signature cocktails are pretty tasty, too. There are three locations in the metro area; check listings for Hillsboro and Portland.

TUALATIN

Cabela's
7555 SW Nyberg St   503/822-2000
Mon-Sat: 8 a.m.-9 p.m.; Sun: 9-6   cabelas.com

Cabela's is the mega-sporting goods emporium along Interstate 5 just south of Portland. You'll find everything related to the good ol' outdoors, plus a wide assortment of museum-quality wildlife displays, an indoor archery test area, a gun library and an aquarium stocked with local fish. Even if you're not an outdoorsman, you may be tempted to take up an activity just so you can amass the latest and greatest equipment, clothing and accessories for yourself, home, cabin, tent or pet. Cabela's has over 60 stores throughout the country; each one a bit unique to fit the location.

Fiorano Ristorante
18674 SW Boones Ferry Road   503/783-0727
Lunch: Mon-Fri; Dinner: Mon-Sat   fioranos.com
Moderate

Inviting Tualatin Commons Lake is the setting for this traditional and infused Italian ristorante. For starters, order one of Chef Shan's daily appetizer specials. Robust pasta dishes are enhanced with traditional red or cream sauces, chili flakes or optional chicken, shrimp, Italian sausage or meatballs. Entrees are priced easy on the wallet and are accompanied by pasta or polenta. Try the lamb ragu or medallions of filet mignon with creamy madeira sauce. A sunny midday or a balmy evening is the perfect time to enjoy Fiorano's lakeside dining; catering at your site or theirs.

Hayden's Lakefront Grill
8187 Tualatin-Sherwood Road   503/885-9292
Breakfast, Lunch, Dinner: Daily   haydensgrill.com
Moderate

Hungry? Step into Hayden's for quality meals in a relaxed atmosphere (inside or outside seating along the man-made lake).

Breakfast choices appeal to light or hearty eaters; lunches include meal-sized salads and generously-portioned sandwiches with fries. Classic comfort food dinners of meatloaf, pork tenderloin, pastas and stews are made with fresh local ingredients and updated for today's palates; specialty burgers include Oregon elk and Kobe beef. Most of the delicious desserts are offered full-size or mini!

VERNONIA

Coastal Mountain Sport Haus
66845 Nehalem Hwy N   503/429-6940
Moderate   coastalmountainsporthaus.com

Load up your friends and bikes for a great escape to this European-style inn offering four spacious guest rooms, a bunk room, custom outdoor soaking spa and a yoga session. Great biking trails abound or simply enjoy the peaceful surroundings; laid-back or active — you choose. Built in 1999, this locale easily accommodates retreats, girls' getaways, man-cations and family groups. The tariff includes well-prepared breakfasts and dinners using fresh and local ingredients. (Two-night minimum May 15 to September 15; children 14 and older; no pets.) Recognized by Travel Oregon as "Bike Friendly" and "Oregon Forever" sustainability practices.

WEST LINN

(five-O-three)
21900 Willamette Dr, Suite 201   503/607-0960
Lunch: Tues-Fri; Dinner: Daily   restaurant503.com
Moderately expensive

A lunch or dinner at (five-O-three) is a pleasant experience. Note that the restaurant's name is its area code and represents their commitment to source local ingredients. Not only is the food very good, but the service is personal, the atmosphere cordial and the prices are reasonable. The menu changes seasonally and many favorites come and go. At lunch try the grilled Asian salad or buttermilk fried chicken with spoonbread and house slaw. Recommended dinner entrees include the chicken and shrimp gumbo, breaded pork schnitzel or the signature burger (house-ground chuck, white cheddar, housemade bacon and caramelized onions on an artisan bun). For dessert, try a deep dish chocolate chip cookie with salted caramel ice cream made in-house.

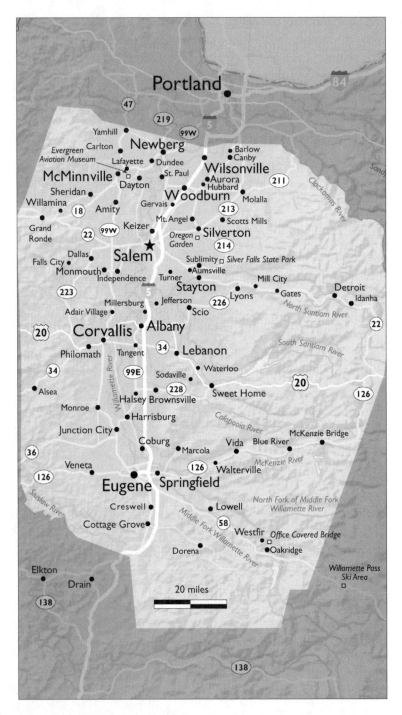

Willamette Valley

ALBANY

First Burger

210 1st Ave W
Lunch: Mon-Sat; Dinner: Tues-Sat
Inexpensive

541/704-1128
thefirstburger.com

Janel and Matt Bennett, owners of Sybaris, have the bases covered on First Avenue with both an upscale restaurant and a casual one, because there is a time and a place for both! First Burger is more of a casual outpost for hand-formed, made-to-order hamburgers. There are a dozen choices with names like The Smokestack, The Uncle Sam, The Iron Woman and The Whole Farm. If those don't strike your fancy, build your own from a list of patties made with house-ground beef, chicken, buffalo or half bacon and half beef; fresh, grilled or pickled vegetables; cheeses and such. The more you add, the more you pay. All sandwiches are served with hand-cut French fries. In addition, there are shakes, malts, soups, salads, onion rings and deep-fried pickles. Don't miss this burger joint as it has been voted the best in the Valley four years running.

The Depot Cafe

822 SE Lyon St   541/926-7326
Lunch, Dinner: Daily   depotrestaurantinc.com
Inexpensive to moderate

Since 1976, The Depot has been a landmark in town and known to have the best fish and chips around! The atmosphere is casual with a quirky interior; it resembles a cafe you might find at the coast. Menu options range from fish and fresh-cut fries to shrimp salads, award-winning housemade chowder and a variety of delicious appetizers. Aside from the best fish and chips and chowder, Bonnie's shrimp crunch salad is a crowd pleaser; a mix of shredded carrots, celery and green onions blended with tender shrimp, mayo, crunchy noodles and sunflower seeds. Beer and wine options are available including an array of bottled beers, rotating taps of domestic and craft beers and varietal wines of Riesling, chardonnay, merlot and pinot gris.

Nichols Garden Nursery

1190 Old Salem Road NE   541/928-9280, 800/422-3985
Mon-Sat: 9-5   nicholsgardennursery.com

Two generations of this family business continue to take pride that they never buy or sell genetically-engineered seeds or plants. All garden varieties are home tested so vegetables grown from Nichols seed or stock are delicious and healthy. Their picture-perfect herb garden is a mid-summer delight; visitors are welcome and photographers are encouraged to snap away. In addition to new and unusual seeds (vegetable, herb and flower), plants, bulbs and roots, Nichols maintains many discontinued varieties of seeds, lawn mixes, books and other garden essentials. Non-garden products include supplies for making beer, wine and cheese, herbs, spices, oils, soaps and lotions.

Novak's Hungarian Restaurant

208 2nd Ave SW   541/967-9488
Lunch, Dinner: Daily; Breakfast: Wed-Sun   novakshungarian.com
Moderate

Guests are treated like family at Novak's Hungarian Restaurant where traditional European fare is featured for breakfast, lunch and dinner. Ukrainian pancakes, späetzle and gravy, homemade sausages and egg and griddle dishes make up the breakfast menu. Lunch specialties include savory cabbage rolls, chicken paprika, pork schnitzel sandwiches and vegetarian specials; combination plates, specials and an expanded list of entrees are served for dinner. If you'd like to sample a bit of everything, opt for the buffets: dinner Monday through Thursday and brunch on Sunday. Irresistible Dobosh torte, crème horns and other rich pastries and eye-popping desserts are made on-site.

Sybaris Bistro

442 1st Ave W   541/928-8157
Dinner: Tues-Sat; Brunch: Sat   sybarisbistro.com
Moderate to moderately expensive

Sybaris Bistro is a spacious, upscale dining establishment in what was once a historic downtown industrial building. Chef **Matt Bennett** creates a new menu each month using the freshest goods from growers and farmers in the heart of the Willamette Valley. The Northwest cuisine is an innovative and eclectic interpretation of classic meat, seafood and poultry dishes. Seasonally-adapted choices may include green bean almondine, duck breast stroganoff with wild mushrooms or slow-cooked smoked pork osso buco and burnt apples. Housemade is the rule, not the exception, right down to catsup and daily bread. The restaurant's decor is always fresh, too; partner and wife **Janel Bennett** arranges displays of local artists' works.

Vault 244

244 1st Ave SW   541/791-9511
Dinner: Mon-Sat   vault244.com
Moderately expensive

With his parents **Kathy and Mike Brown**, **Lane Brown** renovated the historic Cusik Bank building and opened Vault 244. This downtown place has settled into a popular cocktail and dining gathering spot that feels much more metro than one would expect in Albany. You can readily make a meal from a dozen tapas choices or go for full entrees of salads, pastas, land and sea menu items; vegetarian, too.

The wine and cocktail menu is extensive and the chocolate flourless torte is indeed as decadent as advertised. Plan to visit on a warm summer evening; outdoor seating is delightful.

ALSEA

Leaping Lamb Farm Stay
20368 Honey Grove Road   541/487-4966
Moderate   leapinglambfarm.com

Scottie and Greg Jones continue the original 19th-century Honey Grove Farm homestead tradition as a working farm and grow hay, raspberries, blueberries, grapes, plums, pears, apples, lettuce and onions, all while raising chickens, turkeys and sheep. A unique aspect to this farm is the two-bedroom rental cottage for bed and breakfast guests. The space sleeps up to six people; a flat rate is the same for parties of two or six. The kitchen comes fully stocked with breakfast items (seasonally fresh) for guests to prepare as they wish. Guests have the option to help feed the farm animals, harvest fruits and vegetables, collect fresh eggs or wander the trails throughout 64 acres. Of course, lazing by the creek or curling up with a good book is always an option. Urban kids dig the opportunity to be on the farm for a taste of rural life.

AMITY

The Blue Goat Restaurant
506 S Trade St   503/835-5170
Lunch, Dinner: Wed-Sun (seasonally adjusted);
Brunch: Sun   amitybluegoat.com
Inexpensive to moderate

This wee restaurant offers affordable upscale simple dining with Old World eclectic charm. Owners **Cassie and Dave VanDomelen** source local products for the daily-changing menu. At lunch, you'll find soups, salads and other starters, plus sandwiches, burgers and pizza. Dinner brings some of the same with added entrees (maybe braised beef gnocchi and housemade pasta), many are prepared in a special wood-fired earthen oven; several gluten-free dishes are also available. Diet-splurge desserts range from chocolate caramel tart to fresh baked pastries. Fresh daily rustic bread, a diverse selection of local wines and eight taps pouring Northwest microbrews complete your meal. Reservations are suggested for Sunday brunch.

Blue Raeven Farmstand
20650 S Hwy 99W   503/835-0740
Daily: Hours vary   blueraevenfarmstand.com

Step inside this farmstand and you'll be greeted by tantalizing aromas emanating from freshly-baked bread and pies. Owners **Jamie and Ron Lewis** bring fresh berries from their 140-acre berry farm three miles down the road. For pie-lovers, dozens of varieties of five- and nine-inch pies will fulfill the hankering; many are seasonal to capture the essence of the freshest fruits. Berries and fruits are enveloped in golden crust, sometimes solo or in interesting and delicious combinations. There is also a generous list of cream pies; on request, most pies can be prepared sugar-free. (It's best to call ahead if you're craving a certain flavor.) Fresh produce, jams, jellies, syrups, gifts and other local products round out the merchandise selection.

Uncle Jack's Bar-B-Que
416 S Trade St   503/835-5225
Lunch, Dinner: Mon-Sat   Facebook
Inexpensive to moderate

Janell Temple-Rolston shares her dad's barbecue magic in this 20-seat restaurant which is filled with "Uncle Jack's" history and family photos. The atmosphere is casual and relaxed, a place for great food and beer as you throw peanuts on the floor! Turkey, chicken, pork, brisket, sausage and baby back ribs are prepared out back on three smokers. Meats are dry-rubbed with a mixture of spices and slowly cooked at low temperatures; regular and spicy sauces are offered on the side. Choose one or two side dishes with dinner portions; combination dinners of two meats and a side feed one to two people; and family-style combos include two to five meats and two large sides—enough for three to four people.

Smoked meats are also made into hot or cold sandwiches and can be added to green salads to create a lighter meal. Catering and takeout orders are also offered.

BLUE RIVER

Pacific Tree Climbing Institute

Office: 605 Howard Ave, Eugene   541/461-9410
Prices vary   pacifictreeclimbing.com

With Oregon's abundance of trees, and with the coaching of these well-trained professionals, you can learn the art of tree climbing. Go on an old-growth expedition using state-of-the-art equipment specifically designed for this activity; the low guest-to-guide ratio provides plenty of individual attention. Overnighters are rewarded with dinner; bed down high among the branches in a comfortable canvas hammock fitted with a two-inch thick air mattress. Morning begins with a hot beverage and refreshing peppermint-aroma hot towel followed by an organic breakfast back on terra firma. Day climbers relish the organic lunch. No particular age or experience is required.

McMENAMIN HOLDINGS

McMenamins (mcmenamins.com) has become a household word in Oregon and Washington. Brothers **Mike McMenamin** and **Brian Mc-Menamin** are pioneers in both the Northwest microbrew and historic hotel industries. They currently hold more than 50 properties that house brew pubs, full-blown restaurants, breweries, wineries, distilleries, coffee-roasting houses, spas, hotels, movie theaters and music venues. Part of their vision has been to reincarnate and literally save some buildings in order to "keep the past in the present." The first pub, Barley Mill, opened in Portland in 1983, with interests now strewn across the Willamette Valley, the Oregon Coast, Central Oregon and many Washington state holdings. Check their website for good grub and pub stops and overnight options for your next trip.

BROWNSVILLE

The Living Rock Studios
911 W Bishop Way   541/466-5814
Tues-Sat: 10-5 (or by reservation)   livingrockstudios.org
Free (donations accepted)

The Living Rock Studios offers a look back into history with a fabulous showing of rocks, historic artifacts, carvings of Oregon native woods, life-size bird paintings, hundreds of mineral specimens and other fascinating objects. Visionary artist and naturalist Howard B. Taylor spent over 30 years creating this unique attraction, made with more than 800 tons of stone and concrete. Visitors marvel at seven biblical scenes made of translucent rocks, perhaps more beautiful than stained glass windows. A tree of petrified wood pieces, lined with sparkling crystals, reaches two stories high, crowned by a fiber-art canopy. Look high and low as many items are built into walls, ramps and the stairway; flashlights are provided to highlight special details and to make agates glow.

CARLTON

Abbey Road Farm
10501 NE Abbey Road   503/852-6278
Moderate to very expensive   abbeyroadfarm.com

Owners **Judi and John Stuart** preside over an 82-acre farm, offering guests a choice of five tastefully appointed "silo suites" or a renovated three-bedroom farmhouse which works well for families or couples traveling together. The suites are unique in that they are built into grain silos with windows on the curved walls that open to stunning views of the cherry orchard, vast grass seed fields, a neighboring vineyard and an English garden. Breakfast in the old farmhouse is served at 8:30, just a short stroll away. Animal lovers will be entertained with the collection of llamas, sheep, goats and chickens. The inviting parlor and outdoor observation deck are conducive to fun times with family and friends.

Carlton Winemakers Studio

801 N Scott St   503/852-6100
Daily: 11-5 (till 4 Dec-Feb)   winemakersstudio.com

Visit this cooperative winemaking facility where 14 small, independent vintners produce and sell bottles of some of the best that Oregon's wine country has to offer. Wineries represented may be as small as operations producing only 200 cases a year with treasures exclusive to this innovative location; the large selection of red and white wines range between $19 and $72 a bottle. Creative uses of repurposed, recycled and green materials in the building's design and construction led to its impressive status as the first winery to be registered with the U.S. Green Building Council. You'll see many of these features in the state-of-the-art tasting room and in the production areas.

Cuvee

214 W Main St   503/852-6555
Dinner: Days and hours vary   cuveedining.com
Moderately expensive

Chef-owner **Gilbert Henry** wanted to find a place reminiscent of his home region in Alsace, France where he could set up a fine country French restaurant. He decided that Carlton was just that locale. So he set to work to create a dinner house with a distinct French accent, a large wine list (French imports and Oregon favorites), classic cocktails and a restaurant drawing diners to his tables because of its sophisticated ambience. Lovers of true French cuisine will appreciate many traditional favorites such as bouillabaisse, escargots, coquille St. Jacques, steamed mussels and boeuf bourguignon with ingredients sourced from local farms and vendors. Two signatures of a real French dinner house are crisp pomme frites and warm, crunchy French bread with that just-out-of-the-oven aroma. In both cases, Cuvee excels. Informed diners visit Cuvee on Wednesday, Thursday and Sunday evenings for Chef Henry's scrumptious three-course prix-fixe dinner; it's a real bargain at $30 per person.

Equestrian Wine Tours

6325 NE Abbey Road
Year round, by reservation
Prices vary

503/864-2336
equestrianwinetours.com

Head to the Dundee Hills for a super family or romantic outing exploring the wine country via horseback or carriage. If you'd just like to sit back and enjoy yourself, opt for a carriage ride; choose from an antique surrey, a white "Central Park" carriage, a circa 1890 black carriage or a 12-passenger carriage (ideal for small groups). If you are more ambitious, ride one of their Tennessee Walkers and wind your way between vineyards for a two-hour guided tour and wine tasting. To complete your memorable outing, arrange with the Prices for a gourmet picnic served in high style.

The Horse Radish

211 W Main St
Lunch: Daily; Dinner: Fri, Sat
Inexpensive to moderate

503/852-6656
thehorseradish.com

Superb artisan cheeses from around the Northwest reign at this restaurant and wine and cheese bar. I love great cheese and there is no shortage of sweet and savory choices made with milk from cows, goats or sheep. The knowledgeable staff assists in creating custom meat and cheese platters from any of the offerings to take along on a wine tasting sojourn or enjoy in-house with wine or a meal. Standard soup, salad and sandwich fare prevails on the brief lunch menu, and dinner specials are offered Friday and Saturday nights in conjunction with weekly live music performances. Yes, horseradish is on the menu in a blue cheese dip and the horseradish mayo accompanying several entrees.

R.R. Thompson House Bed & Breakfast

517 N Kutch St
Moderate

503/852-6236
rrthompsonhouse.com

This stately 1930s Colonial Revival estate is within walking distance of over two dozen Carlton wineries and tasting rooms plus Carlton restaurants and shops. The historic home features five floral-themed guest rooms and suites with private marble and granite bathrooms, whirlpool tubs and luxurious mattresses for restful slumber. Breakfast in the dining room is a feast for the senses and morning appetites; the signature brie cheese omelet or French toast with homemade fruit compote may be the choice du jour. A thoughtful selection of light beverages from the well-stocked dining room refrigerator is handy for guests to raid day or night.

FIELDS IN BLOOM

The beautiful colors of Oregon's flower industry are manifested in these Willamette Valley fields; some farms celebrate the peak of the season with special events (family activities, festivals, barbecues). Cut flowers are for sale during bloom season and varieties are shown in catalogs for convenient ordering throughout the year. Bring your camera (and perhaps boots).

BROOKS
Adelman Peony Gardens (503/393-6185, peonyparadise.com): May to mid-June

INDEPENDENCE
Lavender Lake Farms (503/804-3574, lavenderlakefarms.com): mid-June to mid-July; gift shop open all year

SALEM
Schreiner's Iris Gardens (503/393-3232, schreinersgardens.com): May to early June

ST. PAUL
Heirloom Roses (503/538-1576, heirloomroses.com): March to August

WOODBURN
Wooden Shoe Tulip Farm (503/634-2243, woodenshoe.com): Tulip Fest in April; Pumpkin Fest in October; gift shop open all year

Republic of Jam

211 W Main St   503/395-5261
Daily: noon-5   republicofjam.com

The artisan spreads at Republic of Jam are not your mother's preserves. Jam master **Lynnette Shaw** has paired local fruits, herbs and spices to create gourmet combinations such as blackberry lime, chocolate cherry, cranberry ginger, plum cinnamon walnut and raspberry anise. On an inspired whim, she'll toss in bacon, tomatoes, figs, mint and whatever else is in the kitchen to make outstanding jams and syrups. Lemons preserved in salt, spices and lemon juice are a staple in Middle Eastern dishes; delicious with salmon and vegetables, too. Shaw freely dispenses samples, recipes and serving suggestions. The tasting room serves swanky tastes on weekends (sweet and savory tidbits, drinks and flights of jam) using her products; check the schedule for occasional cocktail parties in the compact Main Street store.

CORVALLIS

Big River Restaurant

101 NW Jackson Ave   541/757-0694
Lunch: Mon-Fri; Dinner: Daily   bigriverrest.com
Moderate

A big hit since it first opened, Big River features eclectic, fresh Northwest cuisine using local organic produce, natural meats, sustainable seafood and Big River artisan breads from the on-site bakery. Award-winning pastry chef **Loretta Verdugo** also creates hard-to-resist desserts. Sandwiches made on these breads and stuffed with pulled pork, turkey or house-cured beef brisket layered with sauerkraut are extra delicious. Specialty martinis, single malt scotch and local and regional wines are featured at the bar; weekends are punctuated with live jazz. The crew strives to bring good, honest food directly from the Valley with the menu supporting many of the area's hard-working farmers, ranchers and foragers.

Block 15 Restaurant and Brewery
300 SW Jefferson Ave   541/758-2077
Lunch, Dinner: Daily   block15.com
Inexpensive

Located on a busy corner in downtown Corvallis with well over a dozen specialty and seasonal lagers, IPAs, stouts and barrel-matured ales always on tap, it's no wonder this is a well-known and popular hangout. The menu features casual pub food with a few twists to the usual offerings. Instead of a BLT sandwich, try the BMT—bacon, mozzarella cheese, tomato and hazelnut pesto on grilled sourdough; all sandwiches and burgers are accompanied by beer-battered fries, salad or soup. Great tasting salads can also be found on the menu; dress them up with housemade dressings and the addition of chicken, salmon, pulled pork or smoked tempeh which can also be added to pasta dishes. Monthly and weekend specials feature the best local bounty. Here at Block 15, they are always evolving and constantly searching for new and effective ways to bring you the highest quality beer and food in a more sustainable manner.

The Broken Yolk Cafe
119 SW 3rd St   541/738-9655
Breakfast: Daily   broken-yolk.com
Inexpensive

Many Corvallis residents and Oregon State University alumni fondly remember Burton's Sunny Brook Restaurant, a popular eatery spanning five decades. With a nod to the nostalgic past, owners **Brooke and Brandon Dale** retained Burton's familiar booths and tables during their acquisition upgrade. The building is a home-style breakfast spot until 3 every afternoon. Eggs, of course, take top billing in skillet and scramble dishes or alongside or atop crispy chicken-fried steak or corned beef hash. Creamy sausage gravy and other sauces complement just about any entree, and Grandma Dale's strawberry jam is the perfect topper for toast or fluffy hotcakes. Homemade "cinn-ful" cinnamon rolls are always an option. Gramps built a fun play area for young kids in this family-friendly and collegiate favorite.

Del Alma Restaurant

136 SW Washington Ave 541/753-2222
Dinner: Daily delalmarestaurant.com
Moderate

At this Latin fusion dinner house and waterfront bar, the tapas menu is anything but boring. Guacamole is made with house-cured bacon, apples, hazelnuts and avocados and served with homemade chips; Mexican meatballs are delicious with spices, pine nuts, cheese, raisins, ground beef and pork. You could have a very satisfying and tasty meal from the tapas menu or select entrees such as roasted duck breast, lamb molé, Yucatan-style barbecue pork, grilled fish or beef. Three-course dinner specials are the order of the day on Wednesdays; choose from three first and second courses and dessert, specially priced at $25 per person. Owners **Kinn Edwards** and **Carolyn Krueger** have assembled a notable wine selection representing Spain, Portugal, France, Germany, Chile and Oregon; most are sold by the bottle and a limited number are poured by the glass. Frequent dinners with wine or cocktail pairings are delightful additions to this intimate, fine dining venue. An expansion into the adjoining **Dulce del Alma** wine bar offers a casual venue for desserts, sweets and espresso (dinner from the restaurant upon request).

Hanson Country Inn

795 SW Hanson St 541/752-2919
Moderate hcinn.com

One of the Valley's oldest country inns enjoys a charming knoll-top setting. The five-acre estate was built in 1928 by J.A. Hanson and also functioned as a poultry breeding ranch. The home has been brought back to its original style and class by the Covey family and adorned with attractive antiques, art and a well-stocked library. Four spacious guest rooms feature original built-ins, sitting rooms and private baths; a cozy two-bedroom cottage is equipped with a private kitchen and modern electronic conveniences. Each morning, the aroma of homemade muffins entices guests into the sunny dining room for a full gourmet breakfast. The facilities are ideal for garden receptions, parties and meetings.

Les Caves Bier & Kitchen

308 SW 3rd St
Dinner: Tues-Sun; Brunch: Sat, Sun
Inexpensive to moderate

541/286-4473
biercaves.com

The owners of Block 15, **Kristen and Nick Arzner**, also operate this European bier tavern, located next door above Block 15's barrel cellar. Belgian beers are on tap as well as Block 15 brews, rotating local and imported craft beer and an impressive selection of bottled beer and bourbons. Regional farms are tapped to provide food offerings for the European/American menu, because nearly everything is prepared fresh daily the menu varies with the season. A sampling includes house-pickled vegetables served with bread and cheese, smoked German sausage, beef filet wrapped in bacon and mussels with pommes frites. Brussels-style waffles, pulled pork pancakes, fried chicken Benedict and other hearty breakfasts and morning drinks are weekend brunch favorites (until 2 p.m.) at this sister location.

Luc

134 SW 4th St
Dinner: Wed-Sun
Moderate

541/753-4171
i-love-luc.com

It's all about food and wine at this casually elegant eatery. Chef **Aaron Evans** often changes the menu, featuring inventive yet down-to-earth savory gourmet delights; owner **Ian Johnson** oversees the vino. Their teamwork turns out great tasting meals such as pork shoulder au poivre with creamy polenta, Dungeness crab fritters and goat cheese tiramisu. Come for a special wine-paired dinner, or just because, and enjoy the culinary efforts of these serious foodies.

Nearly Normal's

109 NW 15th St
Breakfast, Lunch, Dinner: Mon-Sat
Inexpensive and up

541/753-0791
nearlynormals.com

This handcrafted vegetarian restaurant has been evolving to "nearly normal" since 1979, producing "gonzo cuisine" — the outcome of using the freshest, often organic, ingredients; many original recipes "born from chaos;" and careful preparation and presentation of dishes. The large menu offers eggs, potatoes, pancakes, soups, salads, veggie burgers (try the famous Sunburger), falafel and a "nearly nasty" burrito; kids' menu, too. Enjoy your meal in either the upstairs or downstairs dining rooms or outside in good weather.

New Morning Bakery

219 SW 2nd St   541/754-0181
Breakfast, Lunch, Dinner: Daily   newmorningbakery.com
Inexpensive to moderate

Purchasing the business in 2012, **Tristan and Keara James** have tried to enhance New Morning Bakery as the "go to" downtown bakery spot. The oversized iced cinnamon rolls are irresistible along with tantalizing pecan sticky buns, scones, bear claws, coffee cakes and several varieties of quiche. The lunch and dinner menus include homemade soups, stews, chowders, sandwiches (made on freshly-baked bread), salads and plentiful entrees. Since a common dilemma is what to order; try a salad sampler plate for lunch—two or three salad choices plus delicious bread. There is a long list of entrees such as lasagna, roasted vegetable polenta casserole, wraps and daily specials with local beers and wines also available. Complete your meal with a decadent piece of cake, seasonal tarts and pies, cream puffs, bread pudding, cookies and cheesecake. Thursdays offer a $9.95 three-course dinner option. When holidays roll around, the bakers pull out all stops to turn out magnificent Irish soda bread and Christmas creations like rich fruitcakes, German stollen, candy cane-shaped coffeecakes, sweet breads and gingerbread houses and kits.

COTTAGE GROVE

Buster's Main Street Cafe

811 Main St   541/942-8363
Breakfast, Lunch: Daily   bustersmainstreetcafe.com
Inexpensive to moderate

Cottage Grove and vicinity have been on the silver screen as early as 1927 when Buster Keaton starred in *The General* and the town is infamous for its Main Street parade scene in *National Lampoon's Animal House*. So, accordingly comes the name Buster's Main Street Cafe, paying homage to this great comedian. Breakfast offerings include traditional, griddle and plenty of egg dishes plus blood orange mimosas and white peach bellinis. Sandwiches, burgers, homemade soups and salads are on the small lunch menu. Of particular interest is the selection of craft sodas (Mt. Angel's hazelnut cream soda, North Carolina's cheerwine and Illinois' Green River soda and more) served by the bottle or glass or made into a float.

Stacy's Covered Bridge Restaurant & Lounge

401 E Main St   541/767-0320
Lunch: Tues-Fri; Dinner: Mon-Sat (Sun: March-Sept)   Facebook
Moderate

For 17 years Stacy's has operated downtown next to the Centennial Covered Bridge in a building that originally housed the Bank of Cottage Grove. With just 14 tables, the dining area fills up quickly. Owner **Stacy Solomon** prides himself on good service, comfortable prices and a menu of fresh seafood, prime rib, pastas and fresh salads. A good selection of appealing lunch sandwiches, reasonably-priced early-bird dinner specials and warm-weather outdoor seating add to the appeal.

Victoriana Antiques & Costumes

501 E Main St   541/767-0973
Tues-Sat: 10-5; Sun: 11-4   Facebook

When you're poking around Cottage Grove, browse through **Lesley Neufeld**'s unusual shop. Talented Lesley traded her busy life in Hollywood as a costume designer, for a quiet spot in small-town America (she worked on movies such as Pirates of the Caribbean). Customers rave at her helpfulness in selecting just the right trappings for parties, theater productions and more; for rent or purchase. The shop also sells interesting antique jewelry and furniture items.

DALLAS

Latitude One

904 Main St

Dinner: Thurs-Sat

Moderate to moderately expensive

503/831-1588

latitudeonedallas.com

This delightful dinner spot is housed in a historic 1892 downtown Dallas building. A somewhat limited menu lists half a dozen small plates like crab-filled mushrooms caps, tomato tart and fish tacos. Fresh Northwest entrees include several pasta dishes in addition to chef's choice of beef, pork loin chops and steamer clams, all accompanied by salad or homemade soup; seasonal specials are offered each week. The house lasagna is five layers of rich marinara and meat sauce balanced with pasta and cheese; all portions are generous. Arrive early enough to assure a seat on Friday evenings for live music entertainment beginning at 6:30.

SUSTAINABLE AT STAHLBUSH

Stahlbush Island Farms (Corvallis, stahlbush.com) is an environmentally-friendly farm and food processor, passionately committed to sustainable agriculture, and as such it is worthy of a mention! Since 1985, **Karla and Bill Chambers** have operated their family enterprise with the philosophy that their farming practices leave the soil, air, water, plant life, animals and people healthier. With 100% biodegradable packaging (featuring Karla's own artwork) and a biogas plant for energy, they continue as a leader in earth-friendly agriculture. Amazingly, the biogas plant consumes 77 tons of agricultural by-product per day creating electricity (twice the amount needed) to power the food processing plant, steam for the boilers, hot air to dry pumpkin seeds, hot water for sanitation and a rich fertilizer for the crops. Their premium frozen vegetables, fruit, legumes and grains are sold at Roth's Fresh Markets, Whole Foods Market, New Seasons Market, LifeSource Natural Foods and others; check the website's store locator.

DAYTON

Red Ridge Farms

5510 NE Breyman Orchards Road   503/864-2200
Store: Daily: 10-5   redridgefarms.com
Lodging: Expensive to very expensive

Red Ridge Farms is a 2001 creation of **Penny, Ken and Paul Durant**. The family began growing wine grapes in the early 1970s; today they farm over 60 acres of prime wine grapes and tend to approximately 13,000 olive trees. In 2005, they began growing cold-hardy olive trees. The **Oregon Olive Mill** building houses a state-of-the-art Italian Alfa Laval press and bottling facilities where olives are pressed mid- to late-November. The weekend before Thanksgiving, the Durants host a public Olio Nuovo party with tastings of fresh olive oil, bruschetta and samples of their wines. Visit the **Red Ridge Shop** and nursery for specialty vinegars, gourmet salts, teas, wines, local products, houseplants, lavender and rosemary plants, perennials, annuals, herbs, shrubs and trees. Lodging accommodations include a charming Garden Suite above the store and beautiful **Stoneycrest Cottage** situated in the vineyard.

Stoller Family Estate

16161 NE McDougall Road   503/864-3404
Expensive to very expensive   stollerfamilyestate.com

Stoller Family Estate is one of Oregon's most highly regarded vineyards and wineries. Pioneering Oregonian and founder, **Bill Stoller**, purchased his family's second-generation farm in 1993 with the vision of cultivating an enduring legacy for the land and Oregon's wine industry. Over the last 20 years, he has patiently transformed the 373-acre property into the largest contiguous vineyard in the Dundee Hills. Longtime winemaker, **Melissa Burr**, works in concert with vineyard manager, **Robert Schultz**, to oversee the site's continued refinement and steward Stoller's legacy of growing exceptional pinot noir and chardonnay grapes. Stoller Family Estate features the world's first LEED Gold certified winery, three guest homes and a new state of the art tasting room with panoramic vineyard views.

Wine Country Farm Bed & Breakfast and Armonéa Winery

6855 NE Breyman Orchards Road   503/864-3446, 800/261-3446
Moderate to expensive   winecountryfarm.com

Although this is a working farm where delicious grapes are grown and beautiful Arabian horses are raised, guests come for the peace, quiet and relaxation. Nine rooms and suites are outfitted with private baths, down comforters and Wi-Fi. Guests are welcomed at check-in with wine tasting as they familiarize themselves with their room and discover the beautiful views and grounds from the decks. At their adjacent boutique winery and cellars, guests receive a complimentary tasting of the estate wines. Spend an hour or all day on the property wine tasting, wandering the lovely grounds or exploring the trails on foot. Breakfast is a superlative start to the day at this beautiful estate.

DUNDEE

Black Walnut Inn & Vineyard

9600 NE Worden Hill Road   503/538-8663, 866/429-4114
Expensive to very expensive   blackwalnut-inn.com

It seems that Italy's Tuscan region meets Oregon's wine country at this jewel set in Dundee's Red Hills. The inn is a labor of love for the **Karen and Neal Utz** family where special care and attention to detail is evident throughout the nine suites with upscale Italian linens, quality bath amenities, spa soaking tubs and meticulously decorated suites. Rooms are both spacious and restful. Organic vegetable gardening has been Karen's passion since she was a child. Now her impressive gardens yield fresh herbs and fruits that are part of the full gourmet breakfast; she considerately provides several selections. A brood of hens is the source of fresh eggs used in the delicious egg dishes. Don't end your memorable stay without purchasing a bottle or so of their estate-grown Black Walnut Inn pinot noir and Utz Wines chardonnay. Consult the innkeepers for superb concierge services and intimate weddings at the inn. Hint: the secret season is December through April when rates are moderately priced.

Dundee Bistro

100-A SW 7th St   503/554-1650
Lunch, Dinner: Daily   dundeebistro.com
Moderately expensive

Mention the name Ponzi in Oregon and it will probably receive instant recognition as one of the leaders in the Oregon wine industry. It is no surprise that Ponzi's Dundee restaurant and wine bar are winners as well. With more than a decade's success hosting locals and the ever-increasing number of wine country visitors, the Bistro's kitchen continues to present fresh ideas and casual dishes inspired and executed by Executive Chef **Christopher Flanagan**. The Bistro consistently sources ingredients from neighboring farms, ranches, orchards, fishermen and wild mushroom foragers; the result is a constantly-changing menu. Designed and built by the Ponzi clan, the Italianate complex features murals and artwork by Oregon artists. Guests enjoy cozy fireside seating and summer courtyard dining; a private dining room accommodates up to 50 people. At the adjacent **Wine & Bubble Bar**, a rotating selection of sparkling wines and grower champagnes, wines from local producers, cider and beer as well as cocktails are showcased. To complement your tasting, choose from an array of small bites like cheeses, fresh raw oysters and pizzas.

Dundee Manor

8380 NE Worden Hill Road   503/554-1945, 888/262-1133
Expensive   dundeemanor.com

Well-traveled hosts **Brad Cunningham** and **David Godfrey** put fond memories and experiences from around the globe to good use in their 1908 Edwardian estate. Accommodations consist of four rooms with Asian, European, African and North American motifs and accessories acquired on their journeys. Upon arrival, guests are welcomed with a glass of local wine. In-room snacks and refreshing beverages are offered nightly with turndown service. Carve out some time to take in views of Mt. Hood, Mt. Jefferson and Mt. Bachelor and enjoy the wooded and landscaped areas with gazebos, pergolas and private sitting areas, complete with attractive lighting and soothing music. En suite amenities are sure to please even finicky guests:

LEAP YEAR'S MOST ELIGIBLE BACHELOR

It was leap year 1952 when Gerry Frank and Mark Hatfield (soon to be Oregon's governor and senator), were both named on the "Most Eligible Bachelor" list in Oregon. The event was held at the weekly Lipman Wolfe fashion luncheon at the Multnomah Hotel.

When asked for comments, the one that brought down the house was Gerry Frank's, "What are all these lovely ladies doing here? Don't they know it's Friday Surprise day at Meier & Frank?"

The Oregon Journal newspaper was quoted as saying, "Gerry Frank was one of the most attractive and eligible bachelors to pose for the society page layout. The photos picture young men of distinction and charm, who have not yet taken marriage vows."

Blushing, Gerry did confess that he had been the recipient of many proposals since the photos appeared. "The power of the press," sighed Gerry.

The fact is, Gerry received many "mash notes" during the "Most Eligible Bachelor" days, and though he never called any of his admirers, he enjoyed all the letters! The following letter is just one example ...

Feb. 29, 1952

Dear Mr. Frank,

I have seen you so many times at Meier and Frank and wondered who you were. After seeing your picture in the bachelor column, I surely agree that you are a dreamboat. I would consider myself indeed fortunate if you would allow me to become better acquainted with you. I am not matrimonially inclined at present, but of course, better girls than me have been swept off their feet by the right kind of salesmanship.

I would feel honored to have lunch with you, or even to have you speak to me. I am on the smallish side, and my friends say I am loaded with personality though not beautiful.

I am loathe to sign my name, but if you are interested call EV. 1-2443 and ask for Tootsie. I shall listen with accelerated heartbeat.

Fond Admirer

*(Excerpted from **Oregon's Own Gerry Frank**, with permission from author Jan Boutin.)*

down comforters, extra comfy queen beds, luxury linens, fleece spa robes and daily fresh flowers. The seemingly unending pampering continues at candlelit breakfasts — wonderful gourmet courses, beautiful presentation and special attention by your hosts.

Red Hills Provincial Dining

276 N Hwy 99W   503/538-8224
Dinner: Tues-Sun   redhills-dining.com
Moderately expensive to expensive

A changing seasonal menu in a charming restored Craftsman-style house is the forte of **Nancy and Richard Gehrts**. The attractive setting becomes more resplendent in the spring when massive rhododendrons are in bloom; the classy dining room is pleasingly done in black and taupe, setting off crisp white tablecloths. Nancy warmly welcomes diners at the front of the house while Richard prepares soups, sauces, stocks, desserts, breads, charcuterie and ice creams from scratch, relying upon family recipes for inspiration. Richard pulls double duty tending organic gardens at the restaurant locale and at Gehrts Vineyard in the hills of Dundee. The fruits, herbs and vegetables of his labor often find their way onto the menu. For example, you may find smoked duck breast with marionberry catsup, tenderloin of pork with riesling sauce and späetzle, pastas and game dishes. Definitely delightful!

Tina's Restaurant

760 Hwy 99W   503/538-8880
Lunch: Tues-Fri; Dinner: Daily   tinasdundee.com
Expensive

Capable **Dwight McFaddin** and **Michael Stiller** combine their passion for food and its preparation in this small 50-seat restaurant, whose customers often return to the two intimate dining rooms and familiar bar. Weekday lunches include salads, sandwiches and soups; dinner entrees list duck, salmon, lamb, beef, vegetarian, vegan or gluten-free offerings like soufflé and risotto. Most dishes are prepared using European techniques. Menus are developed around organic, healthy, high-quality, fresh and regional foods from nearby farmers and neighbors. A substantial wine list is offered from vintners just a stone's throw away; spirits and beer, too.

EUGENE

Caddis Fly Angling Shop
168 W 6th Ave   541/505-8061
Mon-Fri: 9-6; Sat: 9-5; Sun: 10-3   caddisflyshop.com

Since 1975, novice or professional fishermen (and fisherwomen) have been visiting this amazing 4,000-square foot emporium for fishing gear. This Eugene institution not only offers the best brands of equipment (Echo, Orvis, Winston, Bauer, Rio, Sage and more), but also provides advice on just about anything you'd want to know about one of Oregon's great recreational activities. As a fly-fishing shop, they specialize in flies for all types of fish and stock all necessary supplies and materials if you choose to tie your own. Don't go near the water without the appropriate waders, inflatable watercraft, clothing, books and accessories that you may not have known even existed (convenient online shopping, too). Lastly, book a trip with one of their licensed and experienced guides for an unforgettable experience — rain or shine.

Café 440
440 Coburg Road   541/505-8493
Breakfast: Sun; Lunch, Dinner: Mon-Sat   cafe440eugene.com
Moderate

When you're in the mood for a relaxed lunch or dinner at a friendly place, head to this stop on busy Coburg Road. You'll find topnotch comfort food like burgers, meatloaf and other sandwiches, delicious salads with housemade dressings, soups and "gourmet" mac and cheese. The dinner menu expands to include steaks, Northwest salmon, pastas and more. There is plenty of action on Sundays for breakfast consisting of omelets, Benedicts, homemade biscuits and gravy (topped with Tillamook cheese) and shrimp and grits. The sizable menu is bursting with old-standbys, many given updated treatment with unexpected and tasty ingredients. Owner **Todd Schuetz** adheres to his philosophy "keep it simple and make it better than everyone else." Sounds like the right idea.

Café Soriah

384 W 13th Ave   541/342-4410
Dinner: Daily   cafesoriah.com
Moderately expensive

This longtime dinner house continues to please patrons with Mediterranean dishes. Old World spice blended with Northwest-fresh is Soriah's trademark on its varying menu. You might find Greek and Middle Eastern favorites like souvlaki (marinated beef skewers) or fattoush (romaine lettuce mix) that pair nicely with chicken, steak, fish and seafood, lamb entrees or vegetarian plates of spanakopita (spinach pastry) and aubergine (eggplant). Chef **Ib Hamide** enjoys mingling with his diners; order a flambé entree or dessert and he will dazzle you tableside (any day except Sunday and Tuesday). The cafe's backyard garden provides a great seating venue (heated to ward off a bit of chill if necessary).

Cascades Raptor Center

32275 Fox Hollow Road   541/485-1320
Tues-Sun: Hours vary   eraptors.org
Nominal

Take your children to this nature center and wildlife hospital for educational fun. Some 50 resident birds of nearly 30 species are viewable in roomy outdoor aviaries as part of the permanent exhibition. Other injured, ailing or orphaned birds of prey are elsewhere on the property and away from public view. These birds are rescued, rehabilitated and released back into the wild. A combination of special permits, exemplary medical care and adherence to stringent standards, has allowed the dedicated staff and volunteers to return over half of their patients to their rightful environments.

Creative Clock

730 Conger St   541/344-6359
Mon-Sat: 10-5:30   creativeclock.com

My fascination with watches and clocks of all kinds makes me a booster of this timepiece emporium featuring one of Oregon's biggest and best selections of new, rare and traditional clocks. The shapes and sizes are seemingly endless: cuckoo, grandfather, mantle, wall, gallery, anniversary, nautical and animated clocks. Handsome Black Forest cuckoo clocks can cost up to a staggering $10,000. The adjoining **Conger Street Clock Museum** (open Tuesday through Saturday) is a popular destination for all ages with its fascinating window exhibits: clocks (of course), cameras, pigeon timers, telephones, toys and many other intriguing treasures from the past.

Fiddler's Green

91292 Hwy 99N   541/689-8464, 800/548-5500
Daily: Hours vary   fiddlersgreen.com

If it is golf-related, it can be found at this family-owned and -operated business. Since 1976, Fiddler's has been a golfer's "candy store" with 250 models of demo clubs; 20 fitting specialists assure the best fit. Everything you might possibly need for this sport is here: carts, balls, bags, books; well-priced lines for novices and pros. A full array of men's and women's apparel, shoes, rainwear and accessories help you dress the part. To play the game, sign up for individual or group lessons, participate in popular clinics or initiate customized instructions. The on-property 18-hole executive course and driving range are open year round; ideal for testing the latest equipment. Fiddler's also provides service, repair and an online store.

Fisherman's Market

830 W 7th St   541/484-2722
Daily: 10-8   eugenefishmarket.com
Restaurant: Moderate

Ask about the catch of the day and you're sure to hear where it was caught, by whom and perhaps a fish tale or two. The owners,

Debbie and Ryan Rogers, have long been part of the Alaskan fishing scene and are proud to have supported local fishing families for over 30 years. They know fresh fish and the best ways to prepare cod, halibut, salmon, clams, oysters, scallops and other ocean denizens. The market serves tasty appetizers, fried or grilled combos with criss-cut fries, tacos and chowders. Crab salads are loaded with succulent Dungeness morsels and fresh veggies accompanied by housemade

RODEOS AND POWWOWS

Across the entire state there are opportunities to enjoy traditional rodeo events and tribal celebrations. Oregon has a long tradition of displaying its Western heritage through these long-enduring rodeos and powwows.

Chief Joseph Days (Joseph, chiefjosephdays.com): last full weekend in July

Fort Dalles Days Pro Rodeo (The Dalles, fortdallesdays.com): July

Mill Luck Salmon Celebration (Coos Bay, themillcasino.com/entertainment/salmon): September

Molalla Buckeroo PRCA Rodeo (Molalla, molallabuckeroo.com): five days surrounding July 4

Pendleton Round-Up and Happy Canyon Indian Pageant and Wild West Show (Pendleton, pendletonroundup.com): second full week of September; "The king of them all!"

Philomath Frolic & Rodeo (Philomath, philomathrodeo.org): July

Pi-ume-sha Treaty Days Powwow (Warm Springs, calendar. powwows.com/events/pi-ume-sha-treaty-days): the weekend nearest June 25

Sisters Rodeo (Sisters, sistersrodeo.com): June

St. Paul Rodeo (St. Paul, stpaulrodeo.com): July 1-4

Veterans Powwow (Grand Ronde, grandronde.org): July

Wild Rogue Pro Rodeo (Central Point, attheexpo.com): late May

Louis dressing. Several types of fish and chips and Cajun crawfish pie are customer favorites. If you'd rather prepare fish your way, shop at the well-stocked fish counter; there are plenty of options for seafood gift baskets and samplers.

Inn at the 5th

205 E 6th Ave   541/743-4099
Moderate to expensive   innat5th.com

The Inn at the 5th is ideally positioned across a courtyard from the 5th Street Public Market, a crafters' destination since 1976 and home to unique shops and eateries. The sophisticated and sumptuous decor in this 70-room boutique hotel features Oregon artworks melded with interesting glass fixtures and artfully rustic furniture. Window seats and balconies afford striking views of the Emerald City and grounds; gas fireplaces are thoughtfully placed in most guest quarters. Room service is proficiently handled by the neighboring **Marché** (541/342-3612) restaurant through an unobtrusive butler door. If that isn't enough pampering, rejuvenate down a block at **Gervais Salon and Day Spa** (248 E 5th Ave, 541/334-6533) for professional body, hair, nail, waxing and makeup treatments; in-room services also offered. The staff is extra friendly!

King Estate Winery

80854 Territorial Road
Tasting Room: Daily: 11-8   541/942-9874
Restaurant: Lunch: Mon-Fri; Dinner: Daily; Brunch: Sat, Sun   541/685-5189
Moderately expensive to expensive   kingestate.com

For a special occasion in a very impressive Oregon setting, make plans to enjoy this family-owned, 1,000-plus-acre certified organic wine operation. The main facility of the stunning European-style winery sits on the rolling south Willamette Valley hills offering breathtaking vistas. Sustainable and organic farming practices are used in the vineyards and also in fruit, vegetable and flower gardens to protect and nourish this prime agricultural land. Daily informative tours of the production facilities depart on the hour from the visitors center or you may choose to settle into the expansive tasting room to sample flights of award-winning wines. Connoisseurs will surely want to stop in the wine library to appreciate King Estate standouts from past vintages (difficult to find at retailers). The culinary end of the business turns out superlative gourmet fare incorporating estate and local ingredients. What a winning combination: excellent food, a phenomenal setting and world-class wines!

Koho Bistro

2101 Bailey Hill Road   541/684-8888
Dinner: Tues-Sun   kohobistro.net
Moderately expensive

The sleek, contemporary interior showcases executive chef **Jeff Strom**'s love of fine food. Begin your evening with bistro small bites of pan-seared scallops in carmelized onion hash and apple grastrique, charcuterie and house-cut thin fries or imaginative salads incorporating fresh greens, fruits, grains and nuts dressed with harmonizing vinaigrettes. As much as possible, every part of the animal and seasonal produce is used in palate-pleasing dinners resulting in layers of flavors. Entrees on a changing menu might feature slow-braised beef and pork tomato bolognese tossed with linguini, basil and walnut-encrusted Oregon coho salmon or a seasonal special of the day. For a final sweet bite, try smokey chocolate ganache if available. A hand-selected wine list and specialty house cocktails pair well with the menus. Kudos to chef Strom for garnering Oregon Iron Chef titles in 2012 and 2013.

Made in Oregon

5th Street Pubic Market
296 E Fifth Ave, #119   541/393-6891
(See detailed listing with Made in Oregon, Portland)

Marché

5th Street Public Market
296 E 5th Ave   541/342-3612
Breakfast, Lunch, Dinner: Daily   marcherestaurant.com
Moderate (breakfast, lunch), Expensive (dinner)

Marché is the place to go for French market fare that is well-prepared, beautifully presented, fresh, healthful, seasonal and regional. Start with a signature artisan cocktail or glass of European or American wine and perhaps share a Provisions charcuterie plate while choosing from the mouthwatering fish, seafood, duck, beef and pork entrees flavorfully seasoned and accompanied by special vegetables, roots, grains, pastas and cheeses. The house steak dish is superb and the likes of mussels, steelhead and pizzetta are even better prepared in the wood-fired oven. The expanded bar serves a casual bar menu all day – a smashing success. Next to the fountain in the market, Marché has expanded **Provisions Market Hall** (541/743-0660, provisionsmarkethall.com) encompassing an artisan bakery and emporium for wines, gifts, cookware, fresh produce, meat and fish, specialty foods, pantry goods, a casual eatery (morning pastries, pizzas and more) and a fun spot for popular cooking classes. At the **Jordan Schnitzer Museum of Art** (541/346-3027, jsma.uoregon.edu) on the UO campus, **Marché Museum Cafe** (541/346-6440) is the scene of a small plate, quiche and sandwich casual eatery and a convenient meeting place for espresso and dessert. Bon appétit!

Off the Waffle

2540 Willamette St	541/515-6926
840 Willamette St	541/632-4225
Breakfast: Daily	offthewaffle.com
Inexpensive	

Waffle lovers take notice! Two brothers were introduced to Liège waffles while living in Belgium, and their desire to recreate this flavorful experience resulted in Off the Waffle. Richer and sweeter than your normal Belgian waffle, variations of Liège treats can make a complete and satisfying meal. Beyond the expected accompaniments of bacon and maple syrup, request toppings of avocado, fresh basil, mozzarella, tomato and more. The "bully waffle" includes Belgian chocolate chips, fresh strawberries and a swirl of housemade dark chocolate sauce. Or try the healthier "fruit party" waffle with a selection of fresh fruits topped with whipped cream. Leave all of your troubles behind and come to a place where waffles roam free and taste buds are a-frolicking. The menu also lists omelets, organic salads, tea infusions, wood-roasted coffee and freshly squeezed orange juice. There is a satellite location in Southeast Portland (2601 Clinton St, 503/946-1608). These are one-of-a-kind restaurants!

Oregon Electric Station

27 E 5th Ave   541/485-4444
Lunch: Mon-Fri; Dinner: Daily   oesrestaurant.com
Moderately expensive to expensive

When you have a yen for juicy prime rib or fresh seafood, the Oregon Electric Station will fill the bill. The large menu offers much more, from starters such as halibut ceviche or prawn cocktails to soups, salads, poultry and pasta. Generously portioned desserts are homemade; warm apple tart and decadent cheesecake are worth the extra calories. Warm brick and paneled walls, gleaming brass and replica light fixtures evoke memories of the station's heyday; dine next to and inside of an antique railcar. Located in Eugene's historic depot area, the Oregon Electric Station served the Great Northern and Northern Pacific Willamette Valley electric train system, circa 1912.

The Oval Door Bed and Breakfast Inn

988 Lawrence St   541/683-3160
Moderate   ovaldoor.com

Gracious and accommodating innkeepers **Nicole Craig** and **Melissa McGuire** oversee The Oval Door, which is within easy walking distance of downtown restaurants and shops. The six spacious guest rooms with private bathrooms are well appointed. A warm welcome begins with tea and homemade cookies by the fireplace or on the front porch with a cool drink, depending on the weather. Soda, beer and wine are complimentary and a hospitality refrigerator holds other goodies for guests to enjoy. Mornings start out right with locally-roasted coffee delivered to the guestrooms. Follow the aroma of just-out-of-the-oven baked goods to the dining room for a full gourmet breakfast. Main dishes feature a choice of two entrees made with seasonal ingredients (including a healthier option) such as eggs Benedict and eggnog French toast. Fruit and breakfast meats complement the superb main dishes.

Owen Memorial Rose Garden

300 N Jefferson St
541/682-4800
Daily: 6 a.m.-1 a.m.
skinnersbutte.com/rose-garden

Flower lovers can enjoy over 4,500 flowers and roses at one of Eugene's major flower parks. The collection includes around 400 varieties (modern, hybrid, heritage). About 8.5 acres have been dedicated to the roses, flowers, the state heritage Owen cherry tree, walking paths, an arbor picnic area, a gazebo and a beautiful pergola-lined walkway. Find this oasis nestled next to the Willamette River to give your senses a relaxing treat!

WORLD-CLASS WINES

As the third-largest wine producing state in the U.S., Oregonians should be proud to know that Oregon is considered a world-class wine region. Over 900 vineyards produce 72 varieties of grapes in the 18 approved winegrowing regions. Top-notch pinot noir, pinot gris, pinot blanc, chardonnay, riesling, syrah, merlot, cabernet and dulcet dessert wines are some of the wines produced at some 600 wineries. Several websites offer wine reviews and details on tours, tastings and events at specific wineries:
- oregonwine.org
- oregonwineryadvisor.com
- oregonwines.com
- traveloregon.com

Pewter Rabbit Antiques

136 E Broadway   541/344-1710
Mon-Sat: 10-5:30   pewterrabbit.com

Shelley Maynard developed her fondness for antiques when she lived in Pennsylvania. Her shop specializes in quality vintage goods, collectibles, antique jewelry and antique toys; she also buys individual items or entire estates. Regulars agree she has earned a 30-year reputation for top customer service and high integrity.

Prince Pückler's Gourmet Ice Cream

1605 E 19th Ave   541/344-4418
Daily: noon-11   princepucklers.com
Inexpensive

Sprint, don't walk, to this longtime really cool ice creamery that has been satisfying locals since 1975. Top quality ingredients are blended into just over 40 best-selling and unusual gourmet ice cream flavors such as Galaxy and Muddy River (both chocolate malt ice creams), fresh banana brownie, raspberry truffle, espresso and Chai tea ice creams. Euphoria Chocolate Company's ultra-chocolate sauce is the crowning touch to just about any ice cream dish or sundae that you concoct.

Science Factory Children's Museum & Exploration Dome

2300 Leo Harris Pkwy   541/682-7888
Wed-Sun: 10-4   sciencefactory.org
Nominal

Kids will want plenty of time to navigate and discover the fascinating Exploration Dome (seasonal star gazing shows and full dome movies), educational exhibits and informative hands-on entertainment at Lane County's only general science center. Located in Alton Baker Park, activities are continuously rotating to encourage youngsters' formative minds as they explore science, technology and humanity. The museum offers science camps, classes and special events delving into a wide variety of scientific disciplines specifically for children and their families; a fun birthday party locale.

Secret Garden Inn

1910 University St   541/484-6755
Moderate and up   secretgardenbbinn.com

This spacious mansion, one block south of the University of Oregon campus, has been transformed into a ten-room boutique hotel with several sitting areas, a large sunroom and gardens befitting special celebrations. Each of the elegant en suites is individually appointed and has a TV, other modern electronics and a refrigerator. Morning coffee and tea are conveniently located in the common areas followed by a full breakfast in the dining room. Good restaurants and Hayward Field are within easy walking distance. The Inn offers catering to groups gathering for weddings, meetings and other events. This attractive property was once home to Eugene's distinguished Baker family; it also housed a sorority and fraternity. And, yes, there really is a secret garden!

Sweet Life Patisserie
755 Monroe St　　　　　　　　　　　541/683-5676
Mon-Fri: 7 a.m.-11 p.m.; Sat, Sun: 8 a.m.-11 p.m.　　sweetlifedesserts.com

As the sole judge of the annual chocolate cake contest at the Oregon State Fair, I feel somewhat qualified to pass opinion on sweets throughout the state. This bakery passes muster, in spades! There are magnificent handmade cakes, tortes, scones, sticky buns, muffins, croissants and other delectables (gluten-free, too) that help make life a bit sweeter. A few savory choices complete the menu. Favored cake flavors include chocolate fudge, champagne chiffon, orange sour cream, pistachio nut and caramel. Each month features a quartet of specials: cakes, cheesecakes, petit sweets and pies or tarts that are often made with exotic or only-in-season ingredients. The bakery also accommodates the wedding cake part of the business providing topnotch service to couples planning one of the most important occasions of their lives.

Voodoo Doughnut
20 E Broadway　　　　　　　　　　　541/868-8666
(See detailed listing with Voodoo Doughnut, Portland)

FALLS CITY

The Bread Board
404 N Main St　　　　　　　　　　　503/787-5000
Fri, Sat: 10-4　　　　　　　　　　　thebreadboard.net

Falls City may be a trek for a loaf of bread, but this artisan bakery is worth the detour if you're in the vicinity. The ever-changing varieties are made with the owners' special wild yeast sourdough starters. Country sourdough, roasted garlic and sundried tomato, olive and rosemary, walnut sourdough and fennel with raisins are frequently in the rotation of loaves. Sweet sticky buns, pastries and scones delight early-morning customers. For those hiking, biking or wine tasting at the area's many wineries, there is a tempting lunch menu of fresh, homemade soups and salads, oven-toasted sandwiches and more in a warm, cozy atmosphere. The owners claim to bake the goods in Oregon's largest wood-fired bread oven. You may also find The Bread Board's hearth-baked products at select farmers markets throughout the Valley.

GERVAIS

Bauman's Farm & Garden

12989 Howell Prairie Road NE   503/792-3524
Spring, Summer: Mon-Fri: 9-6, Sat: 9-5;   baumanfarms.com
Fall: Mon-Fri: 9-6, Sat, Sun: 9-5;
Winter: Mon-Sat: 9-5

This is a year-round operation, with each season showcasing the best there is to offer. The original buildings contain mouthwatering displays of fresh fruits and vegetables; shelves of fresh baked pies, breads, muffins and cookies; flavorful fudge and tempting doughnuts (apple cider, strawberry, pumpkin or other seasonal flavors). Tastes of the bakery's freshest goods are strategically placed for sampling and bites of fudge are cheerfully offered at the coffee counter. Packaged gourmet products and a vast array of gifts and housewares are integrated throughout. Step into the greenhouse for an overwhelming profusion of colorful seasonal plants, already planted in attractive containers and ready to dress up patios and porches or buy individual plants for do-it-yourself gardening. Exciting and fun family events are scheduled throughout the year with something for everyone: classes, Easter egg hunt,

> **DID YOU KNOW...**
>
> ... just north of Salem is the 45th parallel, marking the point equidistant from the North Pole and the equator?
>
> ... the Willamette River was named for a native American village? It flows northward from the mountains southeast of Eugene and then joins the Columbia River at Portland.

pancake breakfast, fall harvest events, holiday activities and so much more.

INDEPENDENCE

Mangiare Italian Restaurant

114 S Main St   503/838-0566
Lunch: Mon-Sat; Dinner: Daily   mangiarerestaurant.com
Moderate

Independence's historic Sperling Building has housed many businesses since it was built as a hotel in 1913. Now, over a century later, Mangiare Italian Restaurant occupies a spot in the prominent corner location across from Riverview Park. Whether you opt for traditional spaghetti and meatballs or special pasta preparations, you'll find something to satisfy on the sizable menu listings. Lasagna and baked sausage with penne pasta are hearty with robust flavors. Mangiare alla Casa (shrimp in a lemon and white wine sauce with capers and artichokes over linguine) and chicken picatta liberally seasoned with garlic are delicious; vegetarian choices are equally appetizing. Nearly a dozen fresh salads contain greens, pancetta, cheeses, vegetables and other fresh ingredients in interesting combinations. Portions are more than adequate, prices are good and service is professional and friendly. A short list of beers, wines and desserts complement the menu. Outside seating is available in warmer months.

The Pink House Cafe

242 D St   503/837-0900
Breakfast, Lunch, Dinner: Wed-Sun   Facebook
Inexpensive to moderate

Just across from the Independence Cinema is a charming pink and white Victorian house adorned with gingerbread trim. Inside several rooms create an intimate, relaxing ambience. The appealing, consistently good menu is filled with hearty breakfasts (a generous side of pan-fried spuds is included), lunches, dinners and desserts.

Exceptional soups, salads, sandwiches and burgers are offered for both lunch and dinner; a serving of a green or homemade potato salad accompanies sandwiches. Movie patrons will find other tasty comfort food choices for date night such as fish, Mt. Angel Sausage Co. bratwurst, ravioli or short rib entrees; save room for berry cobbler, bread pudding or other desserts.

KEIZER

Delaney Madison Grill

5745 Inland Shores Way N   971/273-0495
Lunch, Dinner: Daily; Brunch: Sun   delaneymadisongrill.com
Moderate to moderately expensive

Enjoy the best waterfront dining venue in Salem-Keizer, overlooking Staats Lake! You may recognize the setting as it is the previous home to Caruso's Italian Cafe. Lunch offerings consist of favorites such as hearty salads, street tacos made with beef tenderloin, soup of the day and sandwiches (meatloaf, chicken avocado club) and the "killer" burger. The menu changes over to dinner at 4; start with pan-seared scallops, crab and shrimp croquettes, chicken lollipops or fresh salad before venturing onto the primarily meat and seafood menu. The filet mignon and lamb chop entrees are very good as are the braised boneless short ribs and halibut au gratin. Pasta dishes and entree salads are also very satisfying; vegetarians are fond of their gluten-free, vegetarian lasagna. Desserts are made in-house with old-fashioned apple pie and ice cream a top choice.

LYONS

Opal Creek Ancient Forest Center

33435 N Fork Road SE   503/897-2921
Seasonal   opalcreek.org

Take a one-hour, scenic drive east of Salem for an old-growth experience at Jawbone Flats, an historic 1920s mining town owned and operated by this local nonprofit group. In the heart of the Opal

Creek Wilderness and Scenic Recreation Area, hiking, swimming, backpacking and kayaking opportunities beckon in the largest remaining low-elevation old-growth forest left in Oregon. Rusty remnants of the mining era are still visible along the 3.1-mile hike to Jawbone Flats, nestled at the confluence of Battle Axe Creek and Opal Creek. The 15 acres are host to science-based outdoor school programs, a slate of overnight workshops for a range of ages, weeklong summer youth backpacking camps, wilderness medicine trainings and private cabin rentals. Call ahead to register for programs or to book seasonal lodging in the rustic cabins (sleeping from two to 16 and equipped with kitchens and bathrooms; not accessible by vehicle); or visit year-round for day hiking and backpacking.

McMINNVILLE

3rd Street Pizza Co.

433 NE 3rd St   503/434-5800
Lunch, Dinner: Daily   3rdstreetpizza.com
Inexpensive

These New York-style pizzas are cooked on a hearth stone in a traditional oven. House specialty toppings are added to create Thai, Mexican, Greek and barbecue flavor blends, but pizza aficionados can also choose from more traditional alternatives. The expanded menu includes salads, sandwiches on homemade bread, calzones and chicken wings. You might choose to enjoy your pie while watching a movie in the on-site Moonlight Theatre. There are three showings daily and Tuesday is bargain night with $5 tickets.

Bistro Maison

729 NE 3rd St   503/474-1888
Brunch, Lunch: Wed-Fri, Sun; Dinner: Wed-Sun   bistromaison.com
Expensive

A visit to this tiny bistro in the heart of Oregon wine country is reminiscent of a quaint countryside lunch in France of classic French onion soup gratinée, a Croque Monsieur sandwich and a glass of wine.

European-influenced entrees are enhanced with seasonal elements and Northwest flavors such as Emmentaler and Tillamook cheddar cheeses in white truffle fondue, classic Coq au Vin and cassoulet. Profiteroles au chocolat and tarte tartin are standout desserts. An unlikely but yummy treat is the build-your-own s'mores (customer participation required). The charmingly updated home-turned-bistro is furnished with comfortable banquettes and chairs (crisp white linens set an elegant tone); the front porch and garden patio are equally appealing.

Community Plate

315 NE 3rd St   503/687-1902
Breakfast, Lunch: Daily   communityplate.com
Inexpensive to moderate

This is the type of place to settle into whether you're a solo diner or are accompanied by your cadre of best friends. The restored space includes a long wooden communal table and classic counter seating— step up to take a seat on swivel stools or secure a spot at the front window counter and enjoy the street scene. A rotating seasonal menu includes breakfasts of buttermilk pancakes with local fruit compote, pork hash with caramelized onions and braised greens, a daily scramble creation, housemade granola, quiche and more. For a special treat, order a latte prepared by an experienced barista to go with a pastry from the tempting bakery case or a breakfast cocktail! At lunch, choose from updated sandwich favorites: chicken salad with pickled green beans, chickpea or grass-fed beef burger or a twist on the BLT ala bacon, greens and squash. And there are always hand-cut fries, homemade soups and fresh baked breads. A monthly supper club features seasonally-inspired three- or four-course dinners with beer and wine pairings; by reservation.

Crescent Cafe

526 NE 3rd St   503/435-2655
Breakfast, Lunch: Mon-Fri; Brunch: Sat, Sun   crescentcafeonthird.com
Inexpensive to moderate

Wheel in to this wonderful breakfast, brunch and lunch spot for fine daytime cuisine. Crescent Cafe is family-owned in a refined setting

SHOPPING WAREHOUSE-STYLE

Costco Wholesale (costco.com) has certainly changed the way the world shops! For many families, weekends begin with a trip to a Costco warehouse to stock up for the week and to nibble their way through the store grazing on ample samples. Headquartered in Issaquah, Washington and with its first warehouse in Seattle, Washington, Costco has grown to 690 locations worldwide; 484 in the U.S. alone. Now the second largest retailer in the country, there are currently 13 Oregon stores as listed below. These members-only warehouses stock brand name and reliable private label appliances, sporting goods, automotive needs, office needs, family clothing, books and movies, home goods and furniture, electronics and computers, health and beauty products, beer, wine and groceries. Top-quality meats are cut and packaged in stores, produce is always fresh and who can resist fresh-from-the-oven pies, cakes, cookies and pastries? Additional store services may include pharmacies, optical and hearing aid departments, photo services, tire centers, fueling stations and food courts (love the Costco-baked whole chicken!). Travel services, garage doors, flooring and much more, including cars, are added values to membership. Check the website periodically for a schedule of author signings that could include this author!

Albany (3130 Kildeer Ave, 541/918-7040)
Aloha (15901 SW Jenkins Rd, 503/644-7615)
Bend (2500 NE Highway 20, 541/385-9640)
Clackamas (13130 SE 84th Ave, 503/794-5500)
Eugene (2828 Chad Dr, 541/683-8126)
Hillsboro (1255 NE 48th Ave, 503/681-2800)
Medford (3639 Crater Lake Hwy, 541/734-4227)
Portland (4849 NE 138th Ave, 503/258-3700)
Roseburg (4141 NE Stephens St, 541/378-0020)
Salem (1010 Hawthorne Ave SE, 503/371-0483)
Tigard (7850 SW Dartmouth St, 503/639-0811)
Warrenton (1804 SE Ensign Lane, 503/338-4103)
Wilsonville (25900 SW Heather Pl, 503/825-4003)

with fresh flowers, classical music and attention to detail. To get the day properly started, try an amazing mimosa, chicken hash (a plate of crispy potatoes and large, tender pieces of chicken), an omelet or Benedict, fresh coffeecakes, buttermilk pancakes, pastries, breads and incredibly flaky and flavorful biscuits. The same attention is given to homemade soups and unusual sandwiches like grilled ham and chutney or lamb burgers for lunch. Be patient, there are only about a dozen tables which fill quickly (alas, they don't accept reservations), but you will be treated well in this ultra-friendly and popular downtown neighborhood destination.

Evergreen Aviation & Space Museum

500 NE Captain Michael King Smith Way   503/434-4185
Daily: 9-5   evergreenmuseum.org
Expensive

The home of Howard Hughes' Spruce Goose is one of Oregon's premier family attractions which inspires, educates, promotes and preserves aviation and space history. Besides this mammoth plane, there are other historic collections of general aviation, military aircraft (SR-71 Blackbird), space flight (replicas of the Lunar module and Rover), helicopters, firearms and more. Tours are self-guided or docent-led; knowledgeable docents are also stationed throughout the museum to enlighten visitors about these prized beauties. Continuing in a big way, the six-story tall digital 3D theater engrosses viewers with daily aviation-themed showings (one movie included with admission). Next door, **Evergreen Wings & Waves Waterpark** (503/434-4180) has ten water slides (appropriately named Tail Spin, Sonic Boom, etc.) departing from the rooftop Boeing 747, pools, a play structure and the educational H2O Hands-on Science Center. The waterpark is open daily between Memorial Day and Labor Day; other days and hours vary.

Golden Valley Brewery & Restaurant

980 NE 4th St   503/472-2739
Lunch, Dinner: Daily   goldenvalleybrewery.com
Moderate

This brewery-eatery sits in a historic setting with a gorgeous bar purported to be from Portland's famous Hoyt Hotel. Ten house beers on tap are named with seasonally descriptive and local connections. Choose from a large selection of appetizers, soups and salads, sandwiches, seafood, pork schnitzel, pastas and hand-cut steaks; the cuisine is fresh, local and made in-house. Owners **Celia and Peter Kircher**'s 76-acre Angus Springs Ranch provides much of the restaurant's meat and produce. A second location with similar offerings is in Beaverton (1520 NW Bethany Blvd, 503/972-1599).

Honest Chocolates

575 NE 3rd St   503/474-9042
Tues-Sat: 11-6   honestchocolates.com

At Honest Chocolates candies are crafted using high-quality, taste-tested chocolate, cooked in small batches and hand-dipped. What's not to love about (dark or milk) chocolate honey caramels with French sea salt or rocky road with handmade marshmallow? A niche they have deliciously filled is crafting chocolates to pair with Oregon's special wines. Dark chocolate ganache with berries and pinot noir is the candy to accompany a glass of pinot noir or your favorite wine. There are no fancy packaging or expensive marketing campaigns here which means prices are kept very reasonable. There are also locations in Carlton (217 E Main St, 503/852-0097) and Newberg (312 E 1st St, 503/537-0754).

La Rambla Restaurant & Bar

238 NE 3rd St   503/435-2126
Lunch, Dinner: Daily (Jan-March, closed Tues, Wed)   laramblaonthird.com
Moderate to expensive

This restaurant specializes in the cuisine of Spain's Iberian Peninsula and is named after a famous Barcelona boulevard. The historic Schilling Building (McMinnville's oldest brick building, circa 1884) was completely renovated to house this chic lunch and dinner house. Hot and cold tapas are a mainstay, affording opportunity for several taste treats; if you order traditional paella, allow 45 minutes. The wine list is extensive with both Oregon and Spanish wines. Retire upstairs in the luxurious two-bedroom **La Rambla Loft** (503/435-7189; expensive) with many amenities, including a gourmet kitchen, two fireplaces and laundry facilities. This is an ideal stay for four to six people touring the wine country. Owner **Kathy Stoler** provides more fun times next door at the **Gem Creole Saloon** (503/883-9194) where the cuisine is creole and the good times roll.

Nick's Italian Cafe

521 NE 3rd St   503/434-4471
Lunch, Dinner: Daily   Facebook
Moderately expensive and up

At this renowned pasta house you will not go away hungry! Local, sustainable produce and hormone- and antibiotic-free eggs and meats dominate the menu at Nick's. For lunch, who can turn down authentic thin-crust pizzas, oyster po' boys, classic minestrone soup or interesting paninis with housemade potato chips? You'll likely rub elbows with local vintners; they know that dinner choices from the a la carte fare or special five-course chef's tasting menu will be excellent and satisfying. Select from ragùs, pastas, seafood and vegetarian dishes or ask about the daily wood-fired oven lamb or pork preparations. An amazing wine list features Northwest and Italian tastings. Enter through the back door for the ambience of the comfy bar to enjoy wine, antipasti and perhaps a game of pool. It's no wonder that Nick's has been an integral part of McMinnville's dining scene since 1977.

Red Fox Bakery

328 NE Evans St   503/434-5098
Mon-Sat: 7-4   redfoxbakery.com

This artisan bakery uses local fresh ingredients as much as possible (even growing many of their own herbs), offering housemade jams and handcrafting breads and pastries. Flour is milled, produce grown and butter churned within miles of the bakery. Lunchtime (11-3) brings filling sandwiches, soups and salads. The bakery turns out coconut macaroons, with daily fresh batches sold on-site or shipped; brownies, too. Cinnamon rolls, coffee cakes and more make up the daily-changing pastry menu and "everything" scones are baked only on Thursday.

Ribslayer BBQ to Go

575 NE 2nd St   503/472-1309
Lunch, Dinner: Tues-Sat   ribslayer.com
Inexpensive to moderate

You'll know that you're near Ribslayer by the mouthwatering aroma emanating from the 9,000-pound custom-built behemoth smoker. This is one of the largest smokers in the area and can cook over 1,000 pounds of chicken, beef or pork at one time; all carefully seasoned and roasted long and slow. Homemade slaw, chips and pickles accompany orders of a half or whole bird, Carlton Farms pulled pork and award-winning beef brisket tri tip and beef ribs. If you're really famished, sink your teeth into the "XXX" sandwich: a juicy combination of thinly sliced beef brisket, pulled pork and corned beef. Housemade sides and salads round out the menu. Owners **Theresa and Craig Haagenson** also operate **Haagenson's Catering** (503/550-7388, haagensonscatering. com), a full-service (and barbecue) catering business.

Serendipity Ice Cream

502 NE 3rd St   503/474-9189
Lunch, Dinner: Daily   serendipityicecream.com
Inexpensive

Serendipity is much more than an ice cream shop! They have homemade waffle cones, baked-from-scratch cookies, sundaes and shakes made from hand-dipped Oregon ice cream. The diet-busting sundae surprise is made with a warm chocolate brownie, two scoops of ice cream, two toppings and mounds of whipped cream. The daily menu includes white bean chicken chili along with another homemade soup; the meal combination includes a steaming bowl of soup, warm cornbread and the choice of a scoop of ice cream or a cookie. An interesting sidebar: this business is owned and operated by MV Advancements which provides training and jobs for persons with developmental disabilities. Their hard work pays big dividends!

Thistle Restaurant & Bar

228 NE Evans St   503/472-9623
Dinner: Tues-Sat   thistlerestaurant.com
Moderately expensive

The ambience is warm and cozy in this smallish downtown storefront location, which is both eclectic and classically appointed. The compact kitchen is visible from the front window where nose-to-tail meat preparations are underway; a seat at the chef's bar offers a similar view accompanied by tantalizing aromas. A chalkboard lists Chef **Eric Bechard** and **Emily Howard**'s daily menu as well as the source from local farmers. The bar features classic cocktails and a smattering of Oregon's finest beers, wines and ciders. Seasonal entrees may include elk with winter squash and kale, pork with mushrooms and onions or seafood choices; surprisingly, bread is served with lard rather than butter. Thistle also offers a multi-course option, appropriately named the Chef's Whim, and requires participation of the entire party. Reservations are recommended.

Youngberg Hill

10660 SW Youngberg Hill Road   503/472-2727
Tasting Room: Daily: 10-4   youngberghill.com
Moderate to very expensive

Youngberg Hill creates authentic wines and experiences in their tasting room and inn. One of Oregon's premier wine country estates is set on a 50-acre hilltop surrounded by a 26-year old organic vineyard which produces award-winning pinot noir, pinot gris and chardonnay wines. The eight-room inn provides the perfect retreat including a two-course breakfast with salmon hash and poached pears as possible features. Centrally located in the Willamette Valley, there are over 100 wineries and tasting rooms within a 20-minute drive. In addition, Youngberg Hill specializes in exclusive, romantic and personalized wedding and elopement packages, everything you need in one fabulous location. They care for their wine and guests with the same respect and philosophy!

MILL CITY

Giovanni's Mountain Pizza

146 NW Santiam Blvd
Lunch, Dinner: Daily
Inexpensive

503/897-2614
Facebook

For over 20 years **Kathy and Jim Flack** have been feeding hungry travelers in the picturesque Santiam Canyon. Travelers return regularly for the New York-style pizzas made from fresh hand-rolled dough and plenty of tasty meat, vegetable and cheese toppings. The house specialty pizza, Fat Roman Delight, includes almost everything except the kitchen sink. Lasagna, spaghetti, calzones, homemade minestrone soup, salads, sub sandwiches and breadsticks round out the menu. This is a popular stop for recreationists heading back to the Valley after a day in the snow or on the lakes, rivers and trails.

MONMOUTH

MaMere's Bed & Breakfast

212 Knox St
Inexpensive to moderate

503/838-1514
mameresbandb.com

Book a stay at MaMere's if you're visiting a Western Oregon University student, touring wineries or taking a B&B break in the mid-Willamette Valley. The historic Howell House serves as the framework for this New Orleans-style accommodation, which is full of R&R and attentive service by owner **Terri Gregory**. You'll enjoy one of the best breakfasts this side of the Mississippi. Only two of the five vibrantly decorated rooms have private bathrooms. Borrow a bicycle and cruise through the quiet streets or plan a route to a winery or lavender field.

KIDS' ACTIVITIES: IN AND AROUND TOWN

BROOKS

Antique Powerland Museum (503/393-2424, antiquepowerland. com): March through October

EUGENE

Science Factory Children's Museum & Exploration Dome (541/682-7888, sciencefactory.org)

McMINNVILLE

Evergreen Aviation & Space Museum (503/434-4185, evergreen-museum.org)

Evergreen Wings & Waves Waterpark (503/434-4185, evergreen-museum.org/waterpark)

MOLALLA

Molalla Buckeroo PRCA Rodeo (503/829-8388, molallabuckeroo. com): five days surrounding July 4

Molalla Train Park (503/829-6866, pnls.org): May through October

Rosse Posse Acres (503/829-7107, rosseposseacres.com): ranch tours by appointment

SALEM

Gilbert House Children's Museum (503/371-3631, acgilbert.org)

Salem's Riverfront Carousel (503/540-0374, salemcarousel.org)

Willamette Heritage Center (503/585-7012, willametteheritage. org)

Willamette Queen (503/371-1103, willamettequeen.com)

SILVERTON

Oregon Garden (503/874-8100, oregongarden.org)

Silver Falls State Park (503/873-8681, oregonstateparks.org)

ST. PAUL

St. Paul Rodeo (503/633-2011, stpaulrodeo.com): July 1-4

TURNER

Enchanted Forest (503/371-4242, enchantedforest.com): spring to fall; check web calendar for schedule

WILSONVILLE

Family Fun Center & Bullwinkle's Restaurant (503/685-5000, fun-center.com)

MONROE

The Inn at Diamond Woods

96096 Territorial Road   541/510-2467
Moderate   theinnatdiamondwoods.com

This large facility features four en suite bedrooms and meeting rooms. Views of the Willamette Valley and Diamond Woods Golf Course are captured through soaring windows and from the expansive patio and sprawling lawn (ideal for large weddings or corporate events). Individual, group and whole-house reservations are accepted with special rates for several couples who would like to have the entire place to themselves for a football weekend, wine excursion or special occasion. Catering is available for guests, weddings and special events. Guests receive a 50% discount on golf at the 18-hole golf course.

MT. ANGEL

Glockenspiel Restaurant & Pub

190 E Charles St   503/845-6222
Lunch, Dinner: Daily   glockenspielrestaurant.net
Moderate

Hopefully you have experienced Mt. Angel coming alive for its annual Oktoberfest and German cultural activities every September; however, traditional cuisine is not just autumnal fare in this Bavarian-themed village. Start your meal by sharing a pot of fondue, twirling apple slices and baguette chunks in the melted Swiss national dish. Sweet and savory braised red cabbage accompanies platters of schnitzels, späetzle, wursts, potato pancakes, steaks, seafood and other specialties. While German lunch selections are hard to beat, salads, hearty homemade soups and sandwiches (Reuben, sausage and schnitzel) are equally as tempting, especially when washed down with German and Northwest brews and wines. Fish lovers show up on Friday evenings for Glockenspiel's popular weekly Fish Fry featuring beer-battered fish, German slaw and potato pancakes. It goes without saying that any time is the right time for delicious apple strudel. Before leaving, be sure to notice the unique clocktower; bells periodically chime as figures dance above the entrance. It's quite a place!

Mt. Angel Sausage Co.

105 S Garfield St   503/845-2322
Lunch, Dinner: Daily; Breakfast: Sat, Sun   ropesausage.com
Inexpensive to moderate

Robust Old World-style artisan sausages are expertly handmade by the Hoke family and served on-site at their restaurant. Chicken, beef, pork and assorted spices, cheese and loads of garlic are added to create distinctly flavored sausages before the curing process. Only high-quality natural products are used; no chemicals, fillers or by-products. This casual eatery offers over a dozen varieties of wursts in sandwiches or on a stick, schnitzel entrees, fondue and hearty dinners. Good food, German and domestic brews, wines, cocktails and refreshing Mt. Angel Brewing Company's root beer attract patrons to the comfortable outdoor deck on warm summer afternoons and evenings. Weekend breakfasters come for the German pancakes, omelets and heaping platters of schnitzel and fried potatoes. Their products are a staple at many nearby fairs and events. If you're not in the area, but need a bratwurst fix, they gladly fill and ship orders each week. Prost!

NEWBERG

The Allison Inn & Spa

2525 Allison Lane   503/554-2525, 877/294-2525
Expensive to very expensive   theallison.com

Words cannot adequately describe this magnificent haven built by Oregon entrepreneurs the late **Joan and Ken Austin**. The genius of this world-class retreat is in the attention to details. For instance, comfy throws on "living room" couches and fireplaces on automatic timers. There is a fabulous spa with every amenity, including a treatment room with an overhead "rain" feature. Every guest room in this 85-room wine country boutique resort has an outside view terrace; gorgeous landscaping blends with the setting. The casually elegant in-house Jory restaurant (503/554-2526) is of the same high caliber and honors Oregon's wine, microbrew, hand-crafted distilled spirit and agricultural industries with outstanding Oregon garden-to-table cuisine. For special occasions there are private dining rooms to accommodate small gatherings; the chef's table for ten boasts a customized menu; counter seating offers a view into the open kitchen. Any meal of the day is a guaranteed palate pleaser, especially the brioche French toast with berry compote at breakfast or midday interesting salads and charcuterie; the dinner menu's wood-grilled Wagyu striploin with cream-braised lobster mushrooms is as good as you will find anywhere. Superlative, indeed!

Chehalem Ridge Bed and Breakfast

28700 NE Mountain Top Road   503/538-3474
Moderate   chehalemridge.com

Perched high above the Willamette Valley floor is this appropriately named bed and breakfast with inspiring vistas. The five bedrooms offer private baths (some with jetted tubs and fireplaces) and private decks. If you oversleep or depart early you'll miss the three-course breakfast extravaganza. Experienced as a professional chef and baker, **Kristin Fintel** is busy each morning baking pastries, preparing fresh fruits and impressing guests with hazelnut waffles, crepes, salmon quiche or amazing Benedicts. No worries if you have special dietary needs; food allergies are pleasantly accommodated. The library offers reading material and HDTV (if you must); but first make a slight detour to the cookie jar full of home-baked goodies.

Critter Cabana

516 E 1st St   503/537-2570
Mon-Sat: 10-7; Sun: noon-5   crittercabana.com

You'll be absolutely amazed when you walk into this pet-and-more store. It is a charming place full of interesting products and lovable pets. You'll find dogs, cats, birds, fish, snakes, frogs, tortoises, lizards, teddy bear hamsters, rabbits and exotics such as hedgehogs, plus other curious creatures including birds. There is no shortage of high-quality pet supplies for your critters including food, toys, treats and everyday necessities. You have to see this menagerie to believe it; and keep your eyes open for the giant strolling tortoises! Here's a great idea for birthday parties: they will open at special hours or take their pets on the road. In Wilsonville, visit their second location (8406 SW Main St, #200, 503/682-9812).

Le Puy A Wine Valley Inn

20300 NE Hwy 240   503/554-9528
Expensive   lepuy-inn.com

A transitional contemporary bed and breakfast is the brainchild of owners, **Lea Duffy** and **Andy Kosusko**, who used their architectural backgrounds to build a holistic, sustainable inn incorporating the principles of feng shui. Le Puy has eight en suite guest rooms with magnificent views of Chehalem Ridge and picturesque vineyards, with peeks at the Coast and Cascade Range mountains. A restful night is nearly assured on king- or queen-size beds with luxurious Tempur-Pedic mattresses; your room choice may include a balcony or patio, spa tub or gas fireplace. An über private outdoor hot tub is featured with the Mountain suite, the Thunder suite is fully accessible and the Lake suite is spa-inspired and contains both a jetted tub and separate double-headed shower. Breakfast is served between 9 and 10:30 a.m.; guests may filter in at their convenience during that time and enjoy local and organic specialties, homemade scones and other treats. A two-night minimum stay is required and seasonal discounts are available December through April; electric car charging station.

The Painted Lady

201 S College St   503/538-3850
Dinner: Wed-Sun   thepaintedladyrestaurant.com
Expensive

Great things often come in small packages and this Willamette Valley dinner house is arguably one of the best in all of Oregon (awarded four stars from Forbes in 2013). Classy consistency with innovative cuisine and topnotch service continue to make this tiny Victorian home a huge winner. Owners **Jessica Bagley** and her husband **Allen Routt** are a model team: Jessica mainly takes care of the front of the house and Allen does magical things in the kitchen creating classic dishes updated for a modern, refined palate. Everything in the intimate 35-seat home-cum-gourmet-restaurant, from the initial greeting to the superb service, makes for a special experience. Your party can choose from five-, seven- and nine-course menus; the five- and seven-course menus can be vegetarian. Chef Allen offers a nine-course special chef's menu for the day with no printed menus and no substitutions. Optional local wine pairings are available with all menus. Signature dishes include potato gnocchi and miso custard; grounded on seasonal, local, quality ingredients, you won't be disappointed. Reservations are nearly a must unless you are very lucky...and tell Jessica and Allen that Gerry sent you!

The Painted Lady Guest Cottage

205 S College St   503/516-4382

Expensive   thepaintedladycottage.com

Following an excellent meal at The Painted Lady, opt to spend the night in a charming two-bedroom home next door, ample for four guests. You will find a comfortable living area, modern technology and many other amenities including proximity to the downtown area and Dundee Hills' wine country. The gourmet kitchen is fully stocked; help yourself to the restaurant's garden for herbs, berries and vegetable bounty. Additional culinary packages are available.

Rain Dance Marketplace

26355 NE Bell Road   503/538-0197

Tues-Sun: 11-5   raindancemarketplace.com

Owners **Celia and Ken Austin, Jr.** raise top-quality llamas, diversified in their utility as packers, pets and show animals and highly valued for their fine wool. Visit the acreage to see the Austin's outstanding stock. While there, enjoy the artsy and sophisticated farm store, filled with a range of changing merchandise including works by local artists, llama fiber products, home items, local foods and gifts; Ken is also a fine wood craftsman. There is now a tasting area within the Marketplace featuring its estate pinot noir.

Recipe — A Neighborhood Kitchen

115 N Washington St   503/487-6853
Lunch, Dinner: Tues-Sat   recipenewbergor.com
Moderately expensive

Paul Bachand and **Dustin Wyant** personally remodeled a home into an artisan restaurant and then morphed back into their other roles — Bachand as chef and Wyant in charge of operations. In the shade of a gigantic tree lies their Victorian that radiates charm and offers a fresh, seasonal and local menu. Riddlers Room is a fun gathering place; dine at a no-reservation communal table between the bar and the main dining area, or be seated in the main dining room. Menu choices range from homemade pastas, soups, sandwiches and salads for lunch to dinnertime fine dining. The changing dinner menu includes entrees such as leg of lamb with pesto-basted fingerling potatoes and nettle pesto, duck breast with red wine lentils and peppered rhubarb coulis, wild-caught steelhead, Wagyu beef steak with king trumpet mushrooms and golden potato puree and red wine-thyme sauce or perhaps a game or seafood offerings. You're sure to feel as comfortable as supping in a good friend's kitchen.

Storrs Smokehouse

310 E 1st St   503/538-8080
Breakfast, Lunch, Dinner: Wed-Sun   storrssmokehouse.com
Inexpensive to moderate

This Newberg barbecue joint opens bright and early just to serve homemade biscuits with creamy gravy that's loaded with chunks of sausage and brisket. The remainder of the day, Storrs, a "child" of the city's famous **The Painted Lady** restaurant, is the place for Texas-style beef brisket, southern-style pulled pork, ribs with a Midwest spice rub and saucy chicken wings. Meats are slow-cooked until they are fall-apart-tender and are accompanied by a choice of sauces: sweet pinot noir-laced Texas-style, soy-based Asian and vinegary Carolina-style. Meals are served with coleslaw, bread and pickle; optional side dishes include favorites such as mac and cheese, mashed potatoes and soup. Everything is homemade from family recipes including salted caramel and whiskey brownie ice cream and an excellent ice cream sandwich (peanut butter ice cream with chopped peanut butter cups sandwiched between slices of chocolate chiffon cake). Takeout orders and catering are also available; prepared meats are sold by the pound.

OAKRIDGE

Brewers Union Local 180

48329 E 1st St
Lunch, Dinner: Daily (hours vary)
Inexpensive to moderate

541/782-2024
brewersunion.com

This Anglo-American public house and brewery is lauded as Oregon's only real ale pub and brewery. When you ask for a pint you will receive the proper measure; it is served in a 10- or 20-ounce oversized, lined glass (certified with the Honest Pint Project) in the bar. Ales are conditioned in firkins (casks) and pumped from six beer engines; other beers, wine, ciders and brewed soft drinks are tapped from a keg or sold in bottles. For nourishment, try fish and chips, assorted sandwiches, soups and salads, vegetarian options or satisfying daily specials like grilled pork chop with corn pudding and collards. Families and kids are welcome at all times in the pub or on the outdoor patio. Come on in, lift a full pint, tell a tall tale and enjoy free pool, books and games.

RAINBOW

Holiday Farm Resort

54791 McKenzie Hwy
Moderate to expensive

541/822-3725
holidayfarmresort.com

Ideally situated on the scenic McKenzie River, the secluded resort is a mecca for fly-fishing, drift boating, bird watching, hiking and nearly unlimited outdoor recreation. Most are riverfront cabins and homes less than four miles from Rainbow; many are pet-friendly. Each accommodation is a bit different and individually named to reflect its character: log house, historical, Mediterranean-style, rustic, cozy or spacious; capacity ranges from two to ten occupants. Wood-burning fireplaces, kitchenettes, Wi-Fi and decks are standard in most units. Golfers may want to book a tee time at the 18-hole **Tokatee Golf Club** (tokatee.com), a Giustina family enterprise; views are incredible when not eyeballing your shot. Just a mile from the McKenzie Bridge, this stretch of the river is dotted with little burgs, parks and trails; a splendid region to explore for a day or longer.

TRY YOUR LUCK

With a statewide lottery and nine tribal casinos (most incorporate hotels, restaurants and resorts), there's plenty of gaming for Oregonians and visitors who want a chance at Lady Luck. The casinos are operated by individual Native American tribal councils and have been successful in bringing additional revenues and jobs to the state.

CANYONVILLE
Seven Feathers Casino Resort (541/839-1111, sevenfeathers.com)

CHILOQUIN
Kla-Mo-Ya Casino (541/783-7529, klamoyacasino.com)

COOS BAY
The Mill Casino (541/756-8800, themillcasino.com)

FLORENCE
Three Rivers Casino Resort (541/997-7529, threeriverscasino. com)

GRAND RONDE
Spirit Mountain Casino (800/760-7977, spiritmountain.com)

LINCOLN CITY
Chinook Winds Casino Resort (541/996-5825, chinookwindscasino. com)

PENDLETON
Wildhorse Resort & Casino (541/278-2274, wildhorseresort.com)

WARM SPRINGS
Indian Head Casino (541/460-7777, indianheadgaming.com)

SALEM

Annette's Westgate

1311 Edgewater St NW   503/362-9588
Breakfast, Lunch, Daily; Dinner: Mon-Sat   annetteswestgate.com
Inexpensive to moderate

Housed in the historic Kingwood Building, Annette's still holds the same old-fashioned charm that the building has held since 1928, but with many renovations. Tasty American cuisine is served up for breakfast, lunch and dinner in a casual, family-friendly environment. The breakfast menu will especially delight foodies with an impressive selection of sweet and savory items, not to mention their generous portions! Lunch and dinner offerings are equally impressive. Breakfast entrees include a large selection of egg omelets, traditional breakfast items such as eggs Benedict, waffles, French toast, pancakes and more; lunch items include massive burgers made with $1/3$ pound char-broiled beef patties, sandwiches, a salad bar and housemade soups. For dinner they serve it all; chicken, beef, pork or seafood, and the chicken-fried steak is a must-try. You can also find desserts, local wine, beer, cocktails and brews on their menu.

Archive Coffee & Bar

120 Liberty St NE, Suite 120
Daily: 7 a.m.-midnight   archivecoffeeandbar.com
Inexpensive to moderate

There are many good coffeehouses and bars in Salem but none quite like this one, bringing a fresh approach to downtown Salem. In fact, this is more of a coffee bar that you would expect to see in Portland. The atmosphere is youthful and laid back while remaining sophisticated. Creativity and passion are evident in all corners of the space from the decor and menu design to food and drink presentation. Archive prides itself on making high-end espresso as a form of art; no sugar-coating here. So, if you pride yourself on being a coffee connoisseur, your senses and taste buds will be highly satisfied. What sets them apart? From 7 a.m. to 6 p.m., Archive roasts and serves specialty coffee and a selection of fine teas; by night, they shift gears and feature quality spirits and innovative cocktails, food, wine and beer pairings—all of which have been carefully thought-out and concocted. Menu options are seasonal and ever-changing and feature a Northwest-style cuisine.

Assistance League Gift Shop at the Daue House

1095 Saginaw St S   503/364-8318
Mon-Sat: 10-4   assistanceleaguesalem.org

Savvy shoppers who frequent the Assistance League's two retail stores have a variety of merchandise from which to choose. The **Daue House,** on the National Register of Historic Places, has well-priced antiques, collectibles, gifts and quality women's used clothing and accessories. Merchandise includes china, wall decor and pictures, glassware, tchotchkes, fine and costume jewelry and small furniture pieces. A block away, **Encore Furniture** (1198 Commercial St SE, 503/581-3300) is in a large building with an eclectic selection of consigned furniture, decorating accessories and bargain-priced books. At both stores, unique pricing shows automatic price reductions of up to 75%. Most goods are consigned, some are donated; new gift shop merchandise is purchased to augment the product mix. These shops are the main fundraising activity of the Assistance League of Salem-Keizer whose endeavors support philanthropic programs benefitting children, most notably Operation School Bell which provides impoverished school age children with clothing. Other programs aiding children and adults are capably operated by the League members; this is an all-volunteer, nonprofit organization that has contributed to the community for over 50 years. The Salem-Keizer chapter is part of a national organization of 120 chapters.

Café 22 West

5152 Salem-Dallas Hwy   503/363-4643
Breakfast, Lunch: Daily; Dinner: Thurs-Sun   cafe22west.com
Inexpensive to moderate

For over 100 years the Aspinwall clan has tended the soil on this 40-acre property. Hard-working **Clyde Aspinwall** combines fresh produce from his next-door market with great comfort food.

For hearty breakfasts, try fruit-topped pancakes and waffles with a mound of whipped cream, a heaping platter of chicken-fried steak with taters or the Big Rig (biscuit, creamy sausage gravy, eggs, breakfast meat and taters). Platters, sandwiches and burgers with fries or beer-battered onion rings get afternoons off to a satisfying start and are tasty dinner choices, too. On weekends, the star attraction is the slow-roasted baby back ribs dinner special; sides of mac and cheese and baked beans can't be beat. If you're still hungry, there is always dessert, or saunter across the parking lot to **Aspinwall's Nursery & Produce** for summertime-favorite strawberry shortcake and ice cream. The restaurant is open year round and the market and greenhouse are seasonal. Aspinwall peaches are topnotch!

Court Street Dairy Lunch

347 Court St NE   503/363-6433
Breakfast, Lunch: Mon-Fri   Facebook
Inexpensive

Pop in any weekday for breakfast or lunch and you'll see folks from every walk of life ordering their "regular." Breakfast, served until 11, consists of sweets, omelets, fresh cottage-fried potatoes and egg dishes. Soups are homemade; one for each day. Great juicy burgers and special sandwiches are served with a choice of sides. There are also daily lunch specials and satisfying fried ham and egg, meatloaf (warm or cold) and PB&J sandwiches. Sweet daily goodies include ice cream, sundaes, milkshakes, malts, ice cream sodas and floats; dairy products were the mainstay of this business when it was founded in 1929. Every Tuesday at noon community members gather to "hold court" and share stories of what's happening in the area.

E.Z. Orchards

5504 Hazel Green Road NE   503/393-1506
Mon-Fri: 9-6; Sat: 9-5; Sun: 11-5 (Oct only)   ezorchards.com

On the eastern outskirts of Salem, friendly farmer **John Zielinski** leads his capable team and family business at E.Z. Orchards farm store. Much of the fresh produce comes from the family's orchards and other farms from around the Valley. Smart retailer that he is, upon entering the store customers are assailed with the aroma and samples of just-out-of-the-fryer seasonal doughnuts (apple cider, strawberry, raspberry, blueberry, pumpkin and gingerbread). The merchandise displays are full of mixes, sauces, preserves, seasonings, ingredients, condiments and gourmet staples to stock your pantry, plus housewares and gifts to outfit any kitchen. Cidre, a tasty Normandy French-style hard cider, is made by **Kevin Zielinski**. Outside, the Shortcake Stand (open May to October) is a beehive of activity selling strawberry, raspberry, blueberry, marionberry and peach desserts with hand-scooped ice cream and/or whipped cream. Events are held throughout the year; the harvest festival with a corn maze, pumpkin patch and lots of wholesome fun is many a family's tradition. Try to score a ticket to one of their five-course, farm-to-table alfresco meals in the orchards; space limited to 80 people. You can count on John for great customer service and a willingness to accommodate special orders.

Et Cetera Antiques and Art Gallery

3295 Triangle Dr SE, #140   503/581-9850
Tues-Sat: 11-5   etceteraantiques.com

Cindy Day is the dynamic owner at a shop bursting with antique furniture, glassware, china, silver and collectibles. A licensed appraiser, she grew up in Portland, took art courses at the Portland Art Museum and had early experiences with Oriental art and various furniture styles. All of this background has served her well. With ongoing buying and newly added treasures from estate sales, the inventory is kept fresh and interesting. The gallery features artwork of American and European artists from the 18th, 19th and 20th centuries and Oregon art from 1850 to 1970. You'll also find wood carvings by Oregon's renowned late Leroy Setzoil. As an impressive aside, Cindy is the widow of the legendary L.B. Day, a state legislator, labor chief and civic powerhouse. A loyal following of regular customers find the real joy of visiting Et Cetera Antiques is the chance to converse and learn from Cindy's wealth of knowledge; she offers antique classes in fall and spring.

STATE CAPITOL

It took some doing to make Salem the capital city of Oregon. In 1844, provisional government legislation chose Oregon City. When Salem was proclaimed the governmental seat in 1850, it created quite a ruckus; the matter was settled by an act of Congress in 1852. However, in 1855, the Oregon Territorial Legislature made a move to designate Corvallis as the capital city, though blocked by noting that it would take another congressional act to do so. When the statehouse burned down, also in 1855, the question was reopened and it was decided to put it to the people, giving the two cities receiving the most votes a runoff. Eugene and Corvallis won, but many ballots were invalidated putting Salem back in the running.

Even though Eugene won the runoff election, the turnout was so low that the election was ignored. After 1859 statehood, the legislature put the question to popular vote, and Salem was officially declared Oregon's capital city. Another fire disrupted state business in 1935 when only the outer walls remained of the building that had stood since 1876. Citizens and multiple community firefighters rushed to help (including then 12-year-old Mark Hatfield, who went on to become a two-term governor, five-term U.S. senator and one of our state's most beloved politicians).

Oregon's current structure is the fourth newest in the U.S., dedicated on October 1, 1938, with President Franklin D. Roosevelt attending. Much of the interior and exterior is made of marble. The rotunda features four large Depression Era murals depicting significant events in the state's history; the bronze state seal anchors the floor of the rotunda. The 1993 "Spring Break Quake" damaged the Capitol, which was repaired at a cost of several million dollars. In 2008, another fire did heavy damage to the governor's offices. Little known and keeping with Oregon's "green" culture, the Capitol is the first in the nation to produce solar power through the use of photovoltaic panels. The art, architecture and history of Oregon's state Capitol is worthy of many visits; it was placed on the National Register of Historic Places in 1988.

Guided tours are available or just stop in and wander the magnificent House and Senate chambers, ceremonial Governor's Office and grand Rotunda. A 23-foot statue symbolizing the Oregon pioneers tops the building. Weather permitting, hike the 121 steps to the observation deck to visit the Golden Pioneer and enjoy the view!

Gamberetti's Italian Restaurant

325 High St SE   503/339-7446
Lunch: Mon-Fri; Dinner: Daily   gamberettis.com
Moderate

Warm and affordable, robust Italian flavors emanate from the kitchen of this downtown restaurant. Big winners include molte carne tortellini (Bolognese sauce, marinara, Italian sausage and meatball on cheese tortellini), fra diavolo ravioli (shrimp, lobster and marinara over shrimp and leek ravioli) and grilled pizzas. Macaroni and cheese is featured on Monday evenings; not just any mac and cheese, but gourmet concoctions with steak, lobster, chicken or sausage. Tuesday night specials include soup or salad, a choice of entree and tiramisu for $12.95. Beer, wine, a full bar and outside seating attract diners to this popular location.

Gerry Frank's Konditorei

310 Kearney St SE   503/585-7070
Breakfast, Lunch, Dinner: Daily   gerryfrankskonditorei.com
Moderate

My good friend **Barney Rogers** (now retired) and I opened this sweet venture in 1982. Now a full-service restaurant, cake lovers have descended upon the 44-seat cake shop for over 30 years. Many customers linger at the display cases to make the biggest decision of their day: choosing from the 50 available layer cakes and cheesecakes. Choices include Gerry's chocolate, Barney's blackout, carrot, champagne, Mounds, poppy seed and seasonal preferences such as pumpkin, strawberry and others. Additional temptations made with the finest ingredients include cookies, bars, tortes and other delicious baked goods; all made with the finest ingredients. Each recipe has been personally tasted by a panel of discerning experts before it is sold to customers. In addition to sweet goodies, cakes by-the-slice and whole cakes, there are light breakfasts, lunches, dinners, beer and wine. Favorites like the famous **Meier & Frank** Cobb salad and old-fashioned Konditorei ribbon loaf (ham, turkey and egg salads layered on white and wheat bread and wrapped with cream cheese!) are Konditorei exclusives. The menu always includes daily quiche and soup specials, sandwiches, lasagna and more. Call ahead for special requests, orders to go, dessert catering or box lunches. With great service, the restaurant has earned a top recommendation from AAA and has consistently been named a Best of the Mid-Valley multi-category winner.

Gilbert House Children's Museum

116 Marion St NE   503/371-3631
Daily: 10-5; see website for seasonal hours   acgilbert.org
Nominal

The nonprofit, hands-on Gilbert House Children's Museum is named for Salem-born A.C. Gilbert, an Olympic athlete, creator of the erector set and a prolific inventor. The museum is comprised of three historic Victorian-style houses filled with over a dozen interactive exhibits, as well as a 20,000-square-foot outdoor discovery center.

Gilgamesh Brewing

2065 Madrona Ave SE   503/584-1789
Lunch, Dinner: Daily   gilgameshbrewing.com
Moderate

What was once a home-based business, Gilgamesh Brewing has morphed into a thriving operation. Dad, **Lee Radtke**, led the charge with sons **Mike, Nick and Matt** to build the brewery in a former warehouse. The campus includes the brewery and a craftsman-style restaurant pub and plays host to a variety of fun activities throughout the year. Outdoor patio seating is a summertime draw, too. The food choices are quite tasty: ahi salad, a Cuban sandwich with braised pork and housemade bacon, lamb flat bread sandwich, fish tacos, mussels and fries, seasonal pot pies and much more. You won't go away thirsty either as Gilgamesh claims to have a refreshing beer for everyone!

The Grand Hotel

201 Liberty St SE   503/540-7800, 877/540-7800
Moderate to expensive   grandhotelsalem.com

Grand it is, and provides Salem's most elegant lodging and flawless customer service under the direction of **Steve Johnson**. The prime downtown location is contiguous to the Salem Convention

Center; this combination is a major draw for visitors, meetings and conferences throughout the year. The nearly 200 rooms and suites are spacious, classically appointed and very comfortable. Suites are thoughtfully planned with separate bedrooms, microwave ovens and refrigerators; some suites have gas fireplaces, Jacuzzi tubs and wet bars. A complimentary full breakfast buffet is included with an

HISTORIC COVERED BRIDGES

With only hand tools, Oregon's pioneers began building covered bridges in the mid-1850s. Our state is blessed with 52 covered bridges; most are located in Lane and Linn counties. Since 1900, 398 of Oregon's original 450 covered bridges have simply worn out. The bridges were first covered to keep their huge truss timbers dry. The wet climate could take out a wooden bridge in just a few years, while a covered bridge could last for 80 or more years. Early covered bridge owners could recover construction costs by charging tolls; three cents for a sheep and five cents for a horse and rider. These grand covered structures were once called "Kissing Bridges." Courting couples could take a walk and privately steal a kiss under the cover of a wooden bridge.

There is a scenic loop to follow to see many of these covered bridges. It begins near the town of Scio; just follow the "Covered Bridge Tour Route." Exit off I-5 to Albany and follow Highway 226 east of town. Many of the bridges date as early as 1930.

Look for the **Shimanek Bridge** in Linn County. This bridge is a beauty; rebuilt in 1966, its predecessor dates back to 1891. Larwood Bridge was built in 1939 with a great picnic place near the creek bank.

Moving into Lane County, exit off I-5 to Cottage Grove to see two more covered bridges. Head east on Mosby Creek Road to see others. The **Mosby Creek Bridge**, circa 1920, is the only one open to traffic.

Visit **Drift Creek Bridge** off Highway 22 near Otis, on the way to Lincoln City; follow the Drift Creek Bridge sign near Rose Lodge. This bridge may have been destroyed by flood and rebuilt in 1933; the bridge was moved to this private property location in 1997.

Today Oregon's covered bridges (covered-bridges.org; travel oregon.com) are a treasure and a wonderful connection to our heritage.

overnight stay. Sharing the complex, **Bentley's Grill** (503/779-1660, bentleysgrill.com) offers Northwest ingredients on its regional fine dining and bar menu. Light appetizers, salads, pizzas and sandwiches are served beginning at lunch, with fresh seafood a prominent element; steaks, chops, chicken, pasta and ocean fare are on the dinner menu. This highly visible corner has served as a hospitality center since the Marion Hotel was completed in 1870.

Greenbaum's Quilted Forest
240 Commercial St NE   503/363-7973
Mon, Fri, Sat: 9:30-5:30; Tues-Thurs: 9:30-7; Sun: noon-5   quiltedforest.com

Greenbaum's is among the top 20 best quilt shops in the country. Third generation owner, **Sylvia Dorney**, continues her family's penchant for customer service and provides creative classes and quality merchandise. All things quilting-related are on hand in the welcoming historic 1889 building in downtown Salem. Beautiful examples are displayed in the ever-changing front windows and throughout the store and a talented staff are on hand to offer quilting and fabric expertise.

Hallie Ford Museum of Art
Willamette University
700 State St   503/370-6855
Tues-Sat: 10-5; Sun: 1-5   willamette.edu/arts/hfma
Nominal (free on Tues)

This museum supports the liberal arts curriculum of Willamette University with primarily regional historical and contemporary art, collections and objects. Works by Carl Hall, Ruth Dennis, C.S. Price and other well-known mid-century Oregon modernists are permanently on display in the gallery named for Willamette University art professor Carl Hall (consult the website for other collections and rotating exhibitions). Willamette University has a long presence in Salem, founded in 1842 by Methodist missionaries as the first university in the West. The inviting campus is between the Willamette Heritage Center and the State Capitol with the Mark O. Hatfield Library in the middle of the campus overlooking the millrace.

Kwan's Original Cuisine

835 Commercial St SE   503/362-7711
Lunch, Dinner: Daily   kwanscuisine.com
Moderate

My long association with **Bo and Kam Sang Kwan** goes back to the 1960s. Kwan's roots and work ethic started in Asia well before he ran the household of yours truly. In 1976 Kwan's Kitchen debuted in Salem's City Hall; six years later his restaurant moved down the street to a new 300-seat restaurant with a landmark pagoda, new name and banquet facilities. The extensive menu is excellent and full of curry, Szechuan and garlic options in vegetable, rice and noodle dishes combined with meats (chicken, beef, seafood, emu, lamb and pork) and prepared with mild, medium, hot or super-hot spice levels. The results are interesting, flavorful (without chemicals like MSG) and attractively presented. Special dietary requests such as gluten-free are honored to nourish the soul and body. Hard-working Kwan is always on the job taking only four days off each year: Memorial Day, Independence Day, Thanksgiving and Christmas! One of Kwan's many talents is deboning a chicken with a meat cleaver while blindfolded!

Made in Oregon

Salem Center Mall
480 Center St NE, #242   503/362-4106
(See detailed listing with Made in Oregon, Portland)

Marco Polo Global Restaurant

300 Liberty St SE   503/364-4833
Lunch, Dinner: Daily   marcopolosalem.com
Moderate

Aptly named, this restaurant enjoys spacious downtown quarters. Proprietors **Jackey and Cathay Cheung** serve a full slate of Chinese-Asian fare, European specialties such as pastas and raviolis, vegetarian and vegan offerings, tofu entrees and American favorites such as burgers; gluten-free selections are also available. Garlic green beans with choice of chicken, prawns or beef and the Marco Polo special crispy pan-fried egg noodles loaded with chicken, barbecue pork and shrimp with a substantial portion of good-for-you vegetables are especially satisfying.

Orchard Heights Winery

6057 Orchard Heights Road NW   503/391-7308
Lunch: Mon-Sat; Brunch: Sun   orchardheightswinery.com
Tasting Room and Wine Bar: Mon-Sat: 11-4; Sun: 9-4
Moderate

This relaxing place is a wonderful spot to bring your family and friends for Sunday brunch. The winery, tasting room and cafe sits amidst a five-acre Gewürztraminer vineyard. An ideal afternoon combines a bucolic drive through West Salem's orchards, vineyards and farmland with a break here for lunch of homemade soup, bread and caramelized pear salad, hot quiche or a panini sandwich. You may want to repeat the drive on a Sunday for their tasty brunch.; outstanding omelet and pasta bars, build-your-own waffles, breads and pastries, breakfast burritos, fresh seasonal fruits, cheeses and Orchard Heights' wines await. An assortment of Island Princess tropical wines start with a dry white wine mixed with juices (pineapple, passion fruit, mango). Owners **Gwen and Michael Purdy** also own a Hawaiian macadamia nut orchard and chocolate factory specializing in Island Princess gourmet chocolates and confections using macadamia nuts and Kona coffee beans. Needless to say, they carry an impressive line of the sister company's Hawaiian delights in the well-stocked gift shop.

The Original Pancake House

4685 Portland Road NE   503/393-9124
4656 Commercial St SE   503/378-0431
Breakfast: Daily: 6-2   originalpancakehouse.com
Moderate

The Original Pancake House now boasts 130 franchised locations including Seoul and Tokyo. Founded in Portland in 1953 by **Erma Heuneke** and **Les Highet**, these breakfast houses have long been a Frank family favorite. Whether you call them pancakes, griddlecakes, flapjacks or hotcakes, the menu offers almost every concoction of pancake imaginable: buttermilk, potato, buckwheat, sourdough, Swedish or wheat germ finished with fruits, nuts, bacon or other goodies. Add crepes, waffles, egg dishes, omelets, cereal and specialties such as the Dutch Baby (an oven-baked soufflé, served with lemon, whipped butter and powdered sugar) and, man oh man, you have breakfast for everyone. Other Oregon locations are in Portland, Bend, Redmond and Eugene; menu items may vary by location.

Riverfront Park
200 Water St NE   503/588-6336
                                                                cityofsalem.net

Now a beautiful downtown greenspace along the Willamette River, Riverfront Park was formerly industrial ground for a flour mill and more recently Boise Cascade's paper and cardboard-manufacturing plant. In the mid-1980s the City of Salem purchased the property and cleared the way for a carousel, heritage village, an amphitheater, covered pavilion, picnic tables, boat dock and miles of walking and biking paths. The park is host to numerous annual events like The Bite & Brew and World Beat Festival. One lasting vestige of the industrial past is a large pressurized acid ball which held acids for processing wood chips. A five-year endeavor transformed it into an artistic world globe depicted through 86,000 hand-crafted tiles. On the north end of the park a defunct railroad bridge is a popular pedestrian walkway across the river to West Salem and through Wallace Marine Park. Work is currently underway to connect the southern terminus of the park with Minto-Brown Island Park. Completion of the Peter Courtney Minto-Brown Bridge will open a continuous network of paths and trails, bypassing busy downtown traffic; completion is expected fall 2016.

Roth's Fresh Markets
Vista, 3045 Commercial St SE   503/364-8449
Sunnyslope, 4555 Liberty Road S   503/370-7833
Lancaster, 702 Lancaster Dr NE   503/585-5770
Hayesville, 4746 Portland Road NE   503/393-2345
West Salem, 1130 Wallace Road NW   503/370-3790
Daily: 6 a.m.-10 p.m.   roths.com

Known simply as Roth's by everyone in the mid-Willamette Valley,

Roth's Fresh Markets has been striving for and providing excellence since it was founded in 1962 by the late Orville Roth, a visionary leader, philanthropist and community supporter. Son **Michael Roth** continues the traditions of personal cheerful service and a high-quality product mix in well-maintained, modern stores. The company provides valued jobs to the area and has been a huge supporter to a myriad of good causes—all part of Roth's original mission. Currently there are five Salem stores and additional locations in the towns of Independence, McMinnville, Silverton and Stayton. The Roth family is outstanding!

Rudy's Restaurant

2025 Golf Course Road SE
503/399-0449
Breakfast, Lunch, Dinner: Daily
rudyssteakhouse.com
Moderately expensive

FARM-FRESH ORGANIC

Inspired and influenced by the Miller family multi-generational Mt. Jefferson Farms, **Elizabeth Miller** and **Chris Jenkins** jointly own **Minto Island Growers** (mintogrowers. com). Their organic fruits and vegetables along with native nursery stock are grown under strict organic guidelines. The fresh provisions and plants are available at farmers markets in Salem and Portland from May to late fall as well as at the on-site farm stand; U-pick is available, too. The separate food cart (open June through September) offers simple, seasonal fresh salads, soups and daily specials including locally-produced meats, cheeses and breads. Wood-fired pizzas with fresh toppings and fresh fruit milkshakes are favorites, all inspired and sourced from the bounty of the farm.

Rudy's is perhaps the premier steakhouse in Salem. Set on the first and tenth tee boxes at Salem Golf Club, it is hard to find a better landscape to gaze upon while dining. Rudy's takes pride in serving premium corn-fed, aged beef, hand cut in the restaurant daily. Soups, gourmet sauces and salad dressings are made from scratch from the finest ingredients. Be sure to try their famous marionberry cobbler or blueberry bread pudding! Service is always efficient and friendly at this reliable house.

PRIVATE COLLEGES

Besides seven public universities in the Oregon University System (ous.edu), Oregon has numerous well-honored private degree-granting institutions. Some of the more notable choices include:

Concordia University (Portland, cu-portland.edu): masters university
Corban University (Salem, corban.edu): baccalaureate college
George Fox University (Newberg, georgefox.edu): research university
Lewis & Clark College (Portland, lclark.edu): liberal arts college
Linfield College (McMinnville, linfield.edu): liberal arts college
Marylhurst University (Marylhurst, marylhurst.edu): masters university
Pacific University (Forest Grove, pacific.edu): research university
Reed College (Portland, reed.edu): liberal arts college
University of Portland (Portland, up.edu): masters university
Willamette University (Salem, Willamette.edu): liberal arts college

Seventeen community colleges are operated by locally-elected boards, including:

Blue Mountain Community College (Pendleton, bluecc.edu)
Central Oregon Community College (Bend, cocc.edu)
Chemeketa Community College (McMinnville and Salem, chemeketa.edu)
Clackamas Community College (Oregon City, clackamas.edu)
Clatsop Community College (Astoria, clatsopcc.edu)
Columbia Gorge Community College (The Dalles, cgcc.edu)
Klamath Community College (Klamath Falls, klamathcc.edu)
Lane Community College (Eugene, lanecc.edu)
Linn-Benton Community College (Albany, linnbenton.edu)
Mt. Hood Community College (Gresham, mncc.edu)
Oregon Coast Community College (Lincoln City, Newport and Waldport, oregoncoastcc.org)
Portland Community College (Portland, pcc.edu)
Rogue Community College (Grants Pass, roguecc.edu)
Southwestern Oregon Community College (Coos Bay, socc.edu)
Tillamook Bay Community College (Tillamook, tillamookbaycc.edu)
Treasure Valley Community College (Ontario, tvcc.cc.or.us)
Umpqua Community College (Roseburg, Umpqua.edu)

Salem's Riverfront Carousel

101 Front St NE   503/540-0374
Daily (seasonal hours)   salemcarousel.org
Nominal

A trip to the Riverfront Park is not complete without a ride on the locally hand-carved indoor carousel where 46 horses and friends prance to calliope music. The piece has become a Salem landmark and source of community pride. The adjacent gift shop is filled with unique and magical items.

Wild Pear

372 State St   503/378-7515
Lunch, Dinner: Mon-Sat   wildpearcatering.com
Inexpensive to moderate

Sisters and owners, **Jessica Ritter** and **Cecilia Ritter**, are known by their family as the "wild pair," hence the name of their restaurant. Walking in, you are welcomed by colorful and bold oil paintings of pears on the walls of this restaurant/catering establishment. The sisters take pride in bringing you flavorful American dishes made with the Pacific Northwest's bounty with a Vietnamese twist. Their selection of lunch items span appetizers, soups, salads, sandwiches, wraps, pizza and the traditional Vietnamese Pho dish (a family recipe). Popular dishes include an open-face lobster and seafood melt and the Wild Pear chicken pizza topped with pears, candied pecans, blue cheese crumbles, mozzarella and pesto. For more of a sampling across their menu, try one of their combinations varying from quiche with a soup or salad, a salad and soup or even two soups with a salad. Decadent desserts, specialty cocktails, wine and beer are also highlighted on the menu. A seasonal supper club allows diners to partake in a family-style dinner with other guests.

Willamette Heritage Center

1313 Mill St SE   503/585-7012
Mon-Sat: 10-5   willametteheritage.org
Tours: nominal

This history complex that began in 1896 as the Thomas Kay Woolen Mill, is a forerunner of the famous Pendleton Woolen Mills label. Restored, refurnished and moved to the manicured grounds are the oldest remaining wooden frame houses in the Northwest (the Jason Lee House and Methodist Parsonage), Salem's oldest single family dwelling (the John D. Boon house) and Pleasant Grove Church (the oldest remaining Presbyterian Church in Oregon). The mill, which closed in 1962, is the only woolen mill museum west of Missouri and was the last direct water-powered factory in the U.S. when it closed. In 2010, Mission Mill Museum Association merged with the Marion County Historical Society and established library, archives and collections divisions to oversee the combined collections and provide a vision for the future. The center has created interesting interpretive displays illuminating the area's history, from the days of interaction between Euro-American missionaries and Native Americans, to the time when blankets and textiles were made at the mill. A rushing millrace and the thump-thump sound of looms is part of the re-created working ambience. Self-guided tours for individuals and small groups and guided tours for larger groups are available. The warehouse building is home to several businesses including a gift shop, yarn and knitting supply store, a cafe and orientation center.

Willamette Valley Cheese Co.

8105 Wallace Road NW   503/399-9806
Tues-Sat: 10-5   wvcheeseco.com

Always on the lookout for good cheese, I discovered some tasty offerings at this delightful cheesery with sustainability-focused pastures and production facilities. This operation makes all-natural, handcrafted cheeses from a decades-old recipe. They produce cheddar, fontina, Gouda, creamy Havarti, Asiago, Eola Jack and brie-style French prairie; all can be sampled in the tasting room. Most of the cheeses are made with vat-pasteurized milk, but they do offer a small selection of raw milk cheese. Many cheeses are enhanced with herbs, spices, cranberries or blueberries, smoked or aged. You will also find their products at upper-end markets and seasonal farmers markets throughout Portland and the Valley.

Willamette Valley Pie Company

2994 82nd Ave NE   503/362-8678
Mon-Fri: -8-6; Sat: 9-5   wvpie.com
Check website for extended seasonal hours

This farm store offers an up-close glimpse into an incredible pie-making operation. Twenty or so folks produce thousands of pies that are sold locally and shipped throughout the western states (and beyond via their online store). Up to 30 local growers funnel fruits through this family-owned business to be used in not only pies, but cobblers, jams and jellies, freezer jams, syrups and fruit snack bars. The store offers other gourmet products, seasonal fresh produce, gift and garden items, frozen packaged fruit, freshly baked goods, milkshakes, lunch fare and more. Call by 8:30 a.m. to pick up a pie baked fresh for you that afternoon. A much-anticipated Harvest Festival and Christmas events are held at this rural locale between Salem and Silverton.

DESTINATIONS OF DISTINCTION

Loni Austin Parrish is a successful part of Newberg's hospitality scene with three luxury vacation rentals operated by **Distinctive Destinations** (503/476-2211, distinctivedestinations.net). Each home is tastefully and beautifully appointed with quality furnishings. There is a two-night minimum on weekends and a three-night minimum during the week; a discount is offered for weeklong stays. Exact locations will be provided at time of reservation.

The Lions Gate Inn is in Newberg's downtown Cultural District; four suites accommodate eight guests.

The Lake House is in the Yamhill/Carlton area and is sited on 3½ acres overlooking a private pond; three bedrooms; sleeps up to six guests.

Vineyard Ridge is on top of the Dundee Red Hills with breathtaking views of the vineyards, Cascades and Willamette Valley; two master suites; sleeps up to four guests.

Word of Mouth Neighborhood Bistro

140 17th St NE   503/930-4285
Breakfast, Lunch: Wed-Sun   wordofsalem.com
Moderate

There is almost always a waiting line for a table on the enclosed front porch, at the bar or in the main floor dining areas at this small house. Until mid-afternoon, owners/chefs **Becky and Steve Mucha** turn out seductive breakfast winners such as prime rib Benedict, the incredible flying biscuit (buttermilk biscuit, fried chicken, fried egg, melted cheese, bacon and sausage gravy with breakfast potatoes), omelets, hash (veggie, corned beef or prime rib), housemade sausage and crème brûlée French toast (thick slices of challah bread with a caramelized crunchy topping, ordered a la carte or with eggs and bacon). Complement your order with a Bloody Mary or mimosa for a special treat. Lunch service begins at 11 with soups, chowders, fresh salads (spinach, chicken bistro or chopped chicken), burgers and hearty specialty sandwiches with a nice assortment of sides. Don't tell your cardiologist about your cholesterol overload!

SILVERTON

The Chocolate Box

115 N Water St   503/873-3225
Tues-Sat: 11:30-5   silvertonchocolateboxshop.com

This boutique is all about my favorite food: chocolate. You'll find artisan handmade chocolates by award-winning Oregon chocolatiers including Moonstruck, Goody's, Extreme Chocolates, LillieBelle Farms, Ladybug Chocolates and The Brigittine Monks all under one roof. Buy these luscious chocolates by the piece or as many as you wish; custom gift baskets and boxes are no problem. The folks here will skillfully design a chocolate buffet or favors for weddings, showers, anniversaries and other celebrations. Dairy-free and vegan chocolates, chocolate sauces and gourmet hot cocoa, as well as Northwest produced wines, dessert wines and imported ports are also featured.

Creekside Grill

242 S Water St   503/873-9700
Lunch, Dinner: Daily   creeksidesilverton.com
Inexpensive to moderate

Silverton has an allure and charm all its own; small businesses are the fabric of downtown, colorful wall murals depict the town's history, and there is a sense of pride throughout the community. Creekside Grill is one such business that fits right in. Located beneath street level in the Hartman Building, the restaurant is situated along Silver Creek. On nice days, enjoy the delightful outdoor balcony. There are over a half-dozen sandwiches and sides to choose from for lunch, such as a thyme and house-roasted turkey salad sandwich, BLT with avocado as well as a classic cheeseburger and popular fish tacos. Flavorful dinners include several fish and seafood entrees, pork chop with seasonal tapenade, hickory-smoked pork ribs, grilled chicken breast with artichoke hearts and mushrooms as well as steak and pasta inventions; soups are made fresh daily. The unique zombie fries are made with tempura-fried Portobello mushrooms dusted with parmesan, chili flakes and truffle oil, accompanied by chipotle aioli dipping sauce. Meal-portioned salads include delectable tidbits, such as smoky steak with grilled onions or the fiesta chicken with avocado and black beans. The quinoa and warm autumn salad are a real hit.

Edward Adams House Bed & Breakfast

729 S Water St   503/873-8868
Moderate   edwardadamshousebandb.com

In one of Oregon's most picturesque towns, this cozy inn welcomes you to one of three lovingly restored bedrooms. Built by Swedish master craftsman Magnus Ek, the 1890 home is listed on the National Registry of Historic Places and is a Silverton Heritage Landmark. The home features antiques, a 1920 Steinway grand piano and vintage furnishings. Updated private baths are individualized with a whirlpool tub in the octagonal turret, vintage tub or a walk-in shower; all are stocked with sumptuous bathrobes and towels. Mornings start with a silver tray of coffee and tea set outside your bedroom door, followed by a delightful breakfast of homemade goodies, fruits and varying entrees (special dietary needs can be accommodated) in the dining room.

FESTIVALS AND FAIRS IN THE VALLEY

MARCH
McMinnville Wine and Food Classic (McMinnville, sipclassic.org)
APRIL
McKenzie River Wooden Boat Festival (Vida, woodenboatpeople. com)
Oregon Garden Brewfest (Silverton, oregongarden.org/events)
Wooden Shoe Tulip Fest (Woodburn, woodenshoe.com)
JULY
Lavender Festival (Vida, oregonlavenderdestinations.com)
Salem Art Fair & Festival (Salem, salemart.org)
AUGUST
McKenzie Art Festival (Leaburg, mckenziechamber.com/events)
Northwest Art & Air Festival (Albany, nwartandair.org)
Oregon Jamboree (Sweet Home, oregonjamboree.com)
Oregon State Fair (Salem, oregonstatefair.org): runs through Labor Day
Willamette Country Music Festival (Brownsville, willamettecountry musicfestival.com)
SEPTEMBER
Mt. Angel Oktoberfest (Mt. Angel, oktoberfest.org)
Sublimity Harvest Festival (Sublimity, sublimityharvestfest.com)
DECEMBER
Magic at The Mill at Willamette Heritage Center (Salem, magicatthemill.org)

Also, consider a visit to one of the many county fairs in the Willamette Valley. These include the counties of Benton (Corvallis), Lane (Eugene), Linn (Albany), Marion (Salem), Polk (Rickreall) and Yamhill (McMinnville). Check oregonfairs.org for dates and details.

The Oregon Garden
879 W Main St   503/874-8100, 877/674-2733
Daily: May-Sept: 9-6; Oct-April: 10-4   oregongarden.org
Nominal to moderate

Be sure to include time to admire the gardens, waterfalls, ponds and fountains at The Oregon Garden if you are planning a visit to the

Silverton area. Since its opening in 2001, more than 20 themed gardens (Northwest Garden, Silverton Market Garden, Children's Garden, Amazing Water Garden, Pet-Friendly Garden, Rose Garden, Home Demonstration Garden, Tropical House, wetlands and more) have been developed. Each season brings new vistas with blooming annuals, perennials, trees and shrubs. In addition, this is a prime venue for festivals, weddings and a full spectrum of special events on the grounds or in the J. Frank Schmidt Pavilion. Between April and October, a tram conveys visitors throughout the 80 glorious acres. **The Gordon House** (503/874-6006, thegordonhouse.org), Oregon's only Frank Lloyd Wright-designed home, was relocated to showcase at The Oregon Garden and offers tours by reservation. The design concept is "Usonian," characterized by an open floor plan, cantilevered roofs and floor-to-ceiling windows.

Oregon Garden Resort

895 W Main St   503/874-2500
Moderate   oregongardenresort.com

The Oregon Garden Resort includes a full-service, moderately-priced restaurant with tables situated to enjoy the expansive Valley views. The resort also features full-service **Moonstone Spa** and the **Fireside Lounge** which hosts live music every evening. Several Northwest-style buildings contain 103 guest rooms (some pet-friendly); all include private patios or decks and fireplace, complimentary breakfast and admission to The Oregon Garden. A seasonal outdoor pool and year-round hot tub are on the property.

Seven Brides Brewing

990 N 1st St   503/874-4677
Breakfast: Sat, Sun; Lunch, Dinner: Thurs-Sun   sevenbridesbrewing.com
Lunch: Inexpensive; Dinner: Moderate

The brewery's name comes from the seven daughters of the three partners, who realized they'd better make some dough to pay for upcoming weddings. They refined their home brew hobby and started the microbrewery that celebrated its first bottling in 2010 and created seven signature beers, one named for each of the seven young daughters. Local is something they strive for every day, from hops to beef and cheese.

Enjoy lunch and dinner at this fun brewery and tap room; unlike most breweries and pubs, they do not, nor will they ever have a deep fat fryer. Try the small plate selection with a flight of beer or wine or full meals of salads, sandwiches, burgers, fish tacos, meatloaf, steaks and other land and sea items. Breakfast items include huevos rancheros and beer as well as brown sugar pancakes. Seven Brides' beers are also sold in growlers and bottles and at select retailers; now eleven choices available.

Silver Grille

206 E Main St   503/873-8000
Dinner: Wed-Sun   silvergrille.com
Moderate and up

Chef **Jeff Nizlek** is in command of the Silver Grille, a charming and intimate contemporary bistro. His travels and experiences have honed his desire to offer fresh and savory first-class Willamette Valley cuisine. Appetizers, salads, entrees and desserts are artfully plated, each as pleasing to the eyes as to the stomach. The menu is ever-changing as Jeff incorporates the wide variety of products grown and raised in the Willamette Valley. The Forest Meadow Farm chicken breast was the best I've ever tasted. Seasonal entrees are prepared for hearty winter appetites and include vegetarian options. Overall, everything is beautifully executed and surprisingly affordable; the environment comfortable and relaxed. Also available are world-class wines from the valley's best wineries.

Silverton Inn & Suites

310 N Water St   503/873-1000
Inexpensive and up   silvertoninnandsuites.com

In 2005, **Doug DeGeorge** purchased the dated Nordic Motel; he completed a total redesign and remodel in 2006, adding an elegant two-story lobby with a massive fireplace. A stay in one of the 18 accommodations may bring a quaint European town to mind. All suites (one, two or three beds; one or two bedrooms) are outfitted with full kitchens or kitchenettes. Each room is named after a portion of Silverton's rich history. For additional glimpses of the town's history, wander through town to view the dozen or so colorful murals.

LAKESIDE

Though most of the state has endured recent drought, part of what makes our state so beautiful is its amazing multitude of rivers, lakes and reservoirs. Whether your activity of choice is boating, skiing, swimming, fishing and just lounging and picnicking dockside, the choices are boundless; choose bodies of water large or small; calm or fast moving; remote or with food and housing; with or without motorized boats. Travel Oregon (traveloregon.com) is an excellent source for a complete list of waterways and their particular features. Some of my favorites:

Crater Lake: stunning aqua lake in Klamath County; deepest lake in the Western Hemisphere; hiking trails; historic lodge

Detroit Lake: formed by the Breitenbush and Santiam rivers at Detroit Dam some 50 miles east of Salem; large campground borders lake; two swimming areas, boating and fishing

Diamond Lake: ten miles north of Crater Lake; campsites and lodge; trout fishing

Paulina Lake: a crater lake in Deschutes National Forest near La Pine; two campgrounds, cabins and a lodge offering home cooking; salmon and trout fishing

Suttle Lake: on the east side of Santiam Pass; lodge and restaurant; canoeing, hiking and fishing

Upper Klamath Lake: Oregon's largest lake by surface area, located near the California border

Wallowa Lake: a melted glacier near Joseph; campsites, cabins, chalets and resort; hiking, biking, watersports and fishing; take the tram to the top of Mt. Howard

SPRINGFIELD

McKenzie Orchards Bed & Breakfast

34694 McKenzie View Dr   541/515-8153
Moderate   mkobb.com

Get pampered in the countryside on the lower McKenzie River at this 2009 boutique bed and breakfast. Just 15 minutes from Eugene, this ADA-accessible, modern accommodation houses five guest rooms; four rooms offer tranquil river views. Wine and hors d'oeuvres are served each evening as guests regale one another with accounts of fly-fishing, bicycle touring or day trip excursions. Pampered overnighters are on the receiving end of hosts **Karen and Tom Reid**'s culinary expertise for morning breakfasts; if you'd rather stay in and enjoy the solitude, inquire about light evening bistro fare. Check with the Reids for a seat at their popular cooking school held at the inn; hands-on demonstrations (elegant but easy, French, Mexican, Italian, etc.), paired wines and a delicious dinner with fellow classmates make for a great and entertaining evening.

The Pump Cafe
710 Main St   541/726-0622
Breakfast, Lunch: Mon-Sat   Facebook
Inexpensive

Spend a little time in downtown Springfield and you'll garner a glimpse of Springfield's historic past. Colorful murals depict The Oregon Trail, turn of the century commerce, McKenzie River scenery and more. This breakfast and lunch gathering spot was previously a service station. The eclectic decor is accented with signage and artifacts befitting the former business. Although raspberry cream cheese French toast is the specialty of the house, corned beef over hashbrowns and potato pancakes are tasty, too. The lunch menu consists of sandwiches, homemade chili and soups and a variety of salads; lighter choices plus kids' and senior portions are available for breakfast or lunch. Since this is a popular spot, you may have to wait for a table; the food is good and so are the prices; a catering department handles off-site events.

ST. PAUL

French Prairie Gardens & Family Farm
17673 French Prairie Road   503/633-8445
Seasonal days and hours   fpgardens.com

The Pohlschneider family has operated this gem since 1987. Through the years it has morphed from a self-service fruit and vegetable stand into a country experience on a working farm; the store was built in 1995. Fresh produce is sold in the farm market as are homemade fruit pies, muffins, cookies, scones and coffee cakes (March to mid-December) and nursery products in the spring and summer. Fun festivals herald the first crop of strawberries, the fall harvest and other family-oriented gatherings. Mother Nature's spectacle of fragrant blooming flowers and ripe produce are part of garden dinners (local meats, produce, brews and wines) which are a big hit summer to fall; call for details and reservations.

STAYTON

Gardner House Cafe and Bed & Breakfast

633 N 3rd Ave
Cafe: Breakfast, Lunch; Tea: Tues-Sat
Inexpensive

503/769-5478
gardnerhousebnb.com

PASS THE CHEESE, PLEASE

I love cheese, and Oregon continues to gain recognition as a source for excellent cheeses. Goat's milk, blue, brie and farmstead cheese are but a few local products. **The Oregon Cheese Guild** (oregoncheese guild.org) was formed in 2006 with the purpose of promoting local cheese production. Currently 21 members represent better-known producers plus some newer to the scene: Pholia Farm, Rogue Creamery, Tillamook Cheese, Willamette Valley Cheese and others. The guild's website details member cheesemakers and their products and is an excellent source for festival events as well as retailers and restaurants featuring specific cheeses.

You'll find Stayton a charming small town not far from Silver Falls State Park, a jewel of our state park system. Proprietors **Loni and James Loftus** operate this classic Queen Anne Victorian turned into a cozy spot for breakfast, lunch or tea. Breakfast, served until 11, has plenty of egg combination plates, scones, crumpets and pancakes; your appetite determines the number you order. Salads, sandwiches, homemade soups and seasonal specials such as mac and cheese, pizzas and pot pies satisfy lunchers. Afternoon tea is also served (11 to 3, reservations required) with a delightful array of teas, fresh fruit, savory tarts, assorted finger sandwiches or scones. Talented Loni has won over 100 awards at the Oregon State Fair for her baked items. Some of those pies, cakes, cheesecakes, cookies and muffins are also served at the cafe. An overnight stay in the private cottage won't break the bank; breakfast is delivered to your room or you may opt to eat in the cafe.

TURNER

Turnaround Cafe

7760 3rd St
Breakfast, Lunch: Tues-Sun
Inexpensive

503/743-1285
Facebook

Proprietor **Nancy Walsh** acquired a loyal following with her theme dinners that she donated to charitable auctions; she always had visions of one day owning a restaurant. Her aspiration became a reality when she leased a former bank building in downtown Turner and renovated it to suit her fancy. The result is a breakfast and lunch spot with local fare, decorated with images of roosters and cows, country fabrics and furnishings, photos of historic Turner, antiques and an original Western Security Bank vault door—all with rustic charm. Breakfasts are hearty enough for a lumberman or lighter for small appetites. Muffins, coffee cakes, cinnamon rolls, biscuits, sandwich buns and pies are homemade; marionberry pie with ice cream is irresistible! Breakfast temptations include

URBAN OPENING

Urban Alley (350 Chemeketa St NE, Salem; 503/362-0736) opened late 2015 in the space that was formerly McGrath's downtown. With new floors, new seating, custom artwork and a revamped outdoor seating area, owner **John McGrath** and chef **Gregory Gilbert** highlight locally-sourced food at affordable prices. Housemade pizzas, soups, salads, sandwiches and burgers are featured; innovative small plates include jalapeno hushpuppies, fried beer-battered pickles and pork belly street tacos. Weekend brunch offers frittatas, waffles, biscuits and more. Eight Northwest craft beers are listed on tap.

buttermilk pancakes layered with pulled pork, omelets, chicken-fried steak with farmhouse sausage gravy and other fare. Quiches, hamburgers, garden or chicken club sandwiches, hot turkey sandwiches and macaroni and cheese topped with Andouille sausage are all favorites. Cold deli sandwiches, salads and milkshakes round out the menu.

Willamette Valley Vineyards

8800 Enchanted Way SE   503/588-9463, 800/344-9463
Tasting room: Daily: 11-6   wvv.com
Kitchen: Daily: 11-5:30

Entrepreneur and civic leader **Jim Bernau** not only put Oregon pinot noir on the map, but has built one of the most visible and elegant wineries in Oregon. The new Estate Tasting Room is spectacular with warm woods, sofas surrounding an indoor fire pit and comfortable seating. One tasting area is situated in front of a wood-fired oven where food pairings and cooking demonstrations are conducted. Winery chef **D.J. MacIntyre** oversees the culinary domain and has developed menus for small plates and exquisite multi-course dinners. A separate tasting room for wine club members is beautifully appointed and features a fireplace and floor-to-ceiling windows that frame breathtaking views. An outdoor terrace, underground wine library and vault are newly constructed, and two hospitality suites are available to accommodate special guests. Other tasting room locations include McMinnville and Forest Grove. Jim Bernau is a legend in the wine business.

VENETA

Our Daily Bread Restaurant

88170 Territorial Road   541/935-4921
Breakfast, Lunch: Daily; Dinner: Wed-Sun   ourdailybreadrestaurant.com
Inexpensive and up

Our Daily Bread is a suitable name for a restaurant and bakery in a renovated country church near Fern Ridge Reservoir. The dining area is especially cheery with sunlight streaming through the stained glass windows and backyard seating is perfect on a warm day. The extensive breakfast menu offers good ol' American standards: bacon, eggs, rustic red potatoes, hotcakes and more scrambles and omelet combinations than you can shake a stick at. Lunch lists a choice of soups, salads and sandwiches on housemade bread, plus wraps and specials. Steaks, chops, pastas, seafood and chicken are filling dinner entrees; Friday is prime rib night. Sweet meal-enders include caramel or bourbon bread pudding and three berry pie a la mode.

VIDA

Eagle Rock Lodge
49198 McKenzie Hwy   541/822-3630, 888/773-4333
Moderate and up   eaglerocklodge.com

Enjoy four acres of gardens and 400 feet of frontage on the McKenzie River. Fish from the backyard, take a raft trip, hike the Willamette National Forest, visit Koosah and Sahalie Falls—or just relax and enjoy the sounds of the river. Eagle Rock Lodge bed and breakfast consists of a main building with five rooms and suites and a cozy common room where guests can enjoy a good read and the wood-burning fireplace with a glass of wine and cookies. Three additional rooms are located a few steps away in the carriage house. Each unit has a small refrigerator, microwave and coffeemaker; en suite private bathrooms are supplied with fragrant toiletries. Each morning breakfast is cooked to order in the main lodge, along with fresh fruit, freshly baked scones or muffins and homemade granola.

WILSONVILLE

Abella Italian Kitchen
8309 SW Main St   503/582-1201
Lunch: Mon-Fri; Dinner: Daily   abellaitaliankitchen.com
Moderate

Start your Italian meal with a pleasant assortment of fresh soups, appetizers (gorgonzola cheesecake, bruschetta, broiled polenta) and salads (Caesar, Caprese and assorted greens). Pasta dishes prevail with tempting additions of prawns, Italian sausage, meatballs or chicken. Traditional choices include chicken piccata, marsala and parmesan; veal scallopine; steaks; fish, seafood, pizzas and calzones. Most items are served for both lunch and dinner, including an extensive list of small plates; housemade double chocolate torte is superb. Celebrate the first Thursday of each month with a five-course dinner and wine pairings from a local vineyard.

Dar Essalam
29585 SW Park Pl, Suite A   503/682-3600
Lunch: Mon-Thurs; Dinner: Mon-Sat   daressalam.org
Moderate

Born and raised in Morocco, **Abdellah Elhabbassi** immigrated to the U.S. in 1985 where he met and married his wife, **Dee**. Intent on operating a Moroccan establishment, they moved back to Morocco in 1999 to study the cuisine. Now in Wilsonville, Dee infuses fine North African spices and other exotics at Dar Essalam, which means "House of Tranquility." From the signature hummus supreme with roasted red peppers, capers, feta and black olives and served with warm pita bread to a variety of kabobs or a gyro, you won't be disappointed. Dinner offers a choice of meat tajines combined with savory, sweet or spicy options; gluten-free and vegetarian also. Interesting dessert options include the Casablanca dessert for two, buttery filo layers stuffed with fruit, dusted with powdered sugar and toasted almonds and topped with ice cream.

Oswego Grill at Wilsonville
30080 SW Boones Ferry Road   503/427-2152
(See detailed listing with Oswego Grill at Kruse Way, Lake Oswego)

WOODBURN

Al's Garden Center
1220 N Pacific Hwy   503/981-1245
Mon-Fri: 10-6; Sat: 9-6; Sun: 10-5   als-gardencenter.com

A visit to one of the Al's Garden Center locations is a springtime ritual for folks far and wide. A dream of the Bigej family, Al's is a third generation family-owned and -operated nursery business. Nursery stock prevails, but plenty of other quality merchandise is attractively presented such as planters, patio furniture and accessories, statuary, fountains, household decor and women's apparel. Al's friendly and informed helpers in Woodburn, Sherwood (16920 SW Roy Rogers Road, 503/726-1162) and Gresham (7505 SE Hogan Road, 503/491-0771) are easily spotted by their signature purple shirts. A retractable roof in Sherwood provides a covered shopping area as big as a football field; expanded greenhouse space at Al's in Gresham keeps customers dry and cozy. Satisfied shoppers return for seasonal items like Christmas trees, pumpkins, lilies and holiday gift items. Store hours vary slightly according to the season.

OSU LEADERSHIP

In his State of the University address, **Edward Ray**, 14th President of Oregon State University, stated "Excellence, innovation and leadership are three qualities that define OSU's mission. These qualities are fundamental to the university's commitment to shape the success of our state, the nation and the world's ability to address the most significant problems facing our future."

Dr. Ray is a remarkable man that many say has transformed OSU. Under his leadership, amazing things have happened, including:

- OSU's first comprehensive capital campaign raised $1.14 billion!
- Twenty-eight construction and renovation projects are possible.
- Endowment of 79 faculty positions
- Creation of 600 new scholarships serving 3,200 students
- Enrollment rose to over 30,000 students
- OSU is now the largest university in Oregon
- OSU has become an internationally recognized research University
- OSU research budget for 2014 was $285 million

Woodburn Premium Outlets

1001 Arney Road   503/981-1900
Daily   premiumoutlets.com/woodburn

This attractive 110-store outlet mall is a wildly popular shopping destination. Savings of 25 to 65% off retail draw huge crowds, especially on holiday weekends. Shoppers from the Northwest and Canada target Woodburn Premium Outlets for great deals and tax-free shopping at stores such as adidas, Ann Taylor, Bose, Coach, Columbia Sportswear, Cole Haan, Fossil, Helly Hansen, Nike, Nine West, The North Face and dozens more. Twelve buildings are bursting with bargains in family clothing, footwear and accessories, housewares, luggage, fragrances, electronics, toys and fine jewelry. Boost your shopping energy with a break at Fresca's Mexican Grill, Jamba Juice, The Pie Shop (by Willamette Valley Pie), Starbucks, Subway and other assorted eateries. It's no wonder that this is one of Oregon's top tourist attractions; shop on!

LEADERSHIP AT UO

Michael Schill began his term as the 18th President of the University of Oregon on July 1, 2015. Prior to joining the UO, President Schill served as Dean Professor of Law at the University of Chicago Law School.

In his first convocation address, being new to the university himself, President Schill could relate to all the new students. Some of his encouraging key points were:

- "Football, fun and friends are important, but don't let that be all; commit to become educated!
- Learn from each other, especially people who are not exactly like you.
- Your friends here will be your friends for life; make good friends.
- If you fall behind, don't wait too long, ask for help; we are a family.
- Today your journey is just beginning, so grab the steering wheel, find your path, take a few detours, buckle your seatbelt and enjoy the ride!"

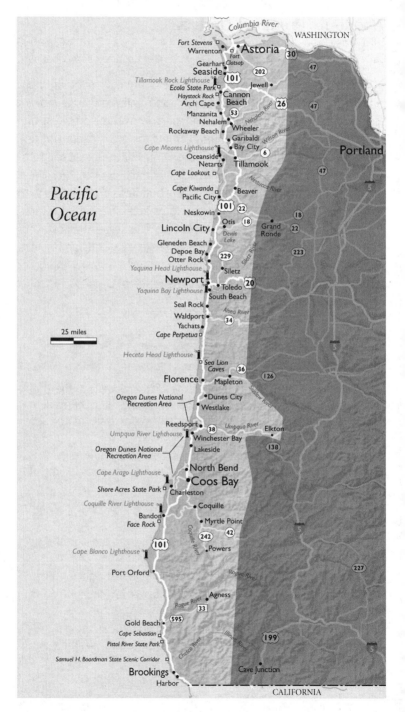

Columbia River

WASHINGTON

Fort Stevens □
Warrenton •
Astoria
30

Gearhart •
Seaside
202
47

Tillamook Rock Lighthouse •
101
Jewell •

Ecola State Park □
Haystack Rock □ Cannon
Arch Cape • Beach
26
47

Manzanita •
53

Nehalem •
Wheeler •

Rockaway Beach •
Garibaldi •

Cape Meares Lighthouse •
Bay City •
6

Oceanside •
Netarts • Tillamook

Cape Lookout □
47

Cape Kiwanda □ • Beaver
Pacific City •

101
22

Neskowin •

Otis •
18

Lincoln City •
Grand
Ronde
22

Devils
Lake

Gleneden Beach •
Depoe Bay •
229
223

Otter Rock •

Yaquina Head Lighthouse •
• Siletz

Newport
Toledo •
20

Yaquina Bay Lighthouse •
South Beach

Seal Rock •
Alsea River

Waldport •
34

Yachats •
Cape Perpetua □

Heceta Head Lighthouse •
□ Sea Lion
Caves
36
126

Florence • Mapleton

Oregon Dunes National
Recreation Area
• Dunes City
• Westlake

Reedsport •
38
Umpqua River
Elkton •

Umpqua River Lighthouse •
Winchester Bay •

Oregon Dunes National
Recreation Area
• Lakeside
138

Cape Arago Lighthouse •
• North Bend
• Coos Bay

Shore Acres State Park □ Charleston •

Coquille River Lighthouse •
• Coquille

Bandon •
Face Rock □
• Myrtle Point

242
42

Cape Blanco Lighthouse •
101
• Powers

Port Orford •

Rogue River

Agness •

Rogue River
33

Gold Beach •
595

Cape Sebastian □
Pistol River State Park □

Samuel H. Boardman State Scenic Corridor □

Brookings •
Cave Junction •
199

Harbor

CALIFORNIA

Portland

*Pacific
Ocean*

25 miles

Oregon Coast

AGNESS

Cougar Lane Lodge

04219 Agness Road   541/247-7233
Moderate   cougarlane.com

Some 32 miles inland from Gold Beach is an outdoor enthusiast's escape. **Bill McNair** and sons **Scott and Nic** purchased this lodge in August 2013 and began a major renovation project; six lodge rooms were overhauled in the process. A log cabin theme was created for the bar and dining room where they serve excellent smoked, slow-cooked ribs, pulled pork, chicken and beef brisket, accompanying homemade sides as well as locally-produced microbrews; enjoy scenic river views from the deck. The lodge is a central hub of activity for fishermen and rafters finishing their three-day white water float trips; it is also a welcome lunch stop for round trip jet boat excursions. Snacks and last minute supplies are sold at the convenient general store. Backing up a bit, the name McNair should ring a bell. Bill and sons are at the helm of **Jerry's Rogue Jets and**

Mail Boats in Gold Beach; he has spent much of his life on the Rogue River.

Singing Springs Resort

34501 Agness Illahe Road
Lodge: Seasonal
Inexpensive

541/247-6162, 877/330-3777
singingspringsresort.com

It is a given that the Rogue River is spectacular any time of the year! Consider Singing Springs Resort for a true Oregon getaway. You can drive (about an hour northeast of Gold Beach), but it's more fun to take a commercial jet boat from Gold Beach. Country cottages are clean and comfortable, accommodate two to four guests and are available throughout the year. The lodge is open between May and mid-October by the day, week or month. Continental breakfast is included with an overnight stay and a lunch buffet and sandwiches are also available. The all-you-can-eat dinner buffet and salad bar (July and August) features Southern fried chicken, house-smoked ribs, turkey, brats, barbecued pork loin, freshly-baked biscuits, fresh fruits and vegetables from the garden and all the trimmings. Meals in the off-season are optional with prior arrangement. Plan ahead if you want to book a fishing guide.

ARCH CAPE

Arch Cape Inn & Retreat

31970 E Ocean Lane
Moderate to very expensive

503/436-2800, 800/436-2848
archcapeinn.com

This romantic chateau is perfect for adult couples celebrating special occasions and is sure to elicit plenty of oohs and aahs. The inn is well-appointed, service is extremely gracious and the experience nearly magical. Nine rooms and one suite have private baths, European-style furnishings, soft pillows, fine linens and Aveda bath products. Relaxing, oversized soaking or Jacuzzi tubs and gas fireplaces in most rooms enhance this get-away-from-it-all location with ocean and garden views. Overnight stays include a three-course gourmet breakfast with locally foraged ingredients and fresh-from-the-kitchen-garden produce and herbs masterfully woven into an ever-changing menu. Other pleasant touches are afternoon wine and light appetizers and in-room refreshments. You'll want to plan a return visit even before you depart.

ASTORIA

Astoria Column

2199 Coxcomb Dr   503/325-2963
Mon-Fri: 9-5:30; Sat, Sun: 9-5   astoriacolumn.org

Put one foot in front of the other, take a few deep breaths, and before long you have climbed the 164-step spiral staircase up to the observation deck of the Astoria Column where the rewards are magnificent views of the Columbia River, the Pacific Ocean, rivers, forests and the community. Kids get a kick out of launching balsa wood gliders (available in the gift shop) from the 125-foot tall tower. The exterior depicts 14 early Oregon events (such as Captain Robert Gray's discovery of the Columbia River, Lewis and Clark's wintering over at Fort Clatsop and John Jacob Astor's fur trading company's arrival in 1811). These events are depicted via murals which spiral the length of the column. The nonprofit Friends of Astoria Column look after the column's maintenance and were behind a major restoration project in 1995 and more recently, a granite plaza, lighting and replacing the staircase. Can you imagine what the Astoria Column was like when it was erected in 1926?

Baked Alaska

1 12th St   503/325-7414
Lunch, Dinner: Daily   bakedak.com
Moderate

Jennifer and Chris Holen oversee this full-service lunch and dinner house where all tables are placed to capture a view of the Columbia River. Soups and clam chowder are homemade; eclectic choices make up the lunch menu: sandwiches, burgers, pastas and entree salads based on fish, seafood and meats as the main ingredients. Appetizers are primarily from the ocean; crab hush puppies and pancetta-wrapped wild prawns are always good. Ranch and ocean choices and the chef's tasting menu are offered. And for dessert, Baked Alaska (a smaller version is named Half Baked Alaska) or a seasonal sweet. There's more: a fully-stocked lounge and private dining rooms for groups. A new addition to the remodeled space includes a brick-oven pizzeria.

Blue Scorcher Bakery & Cafe

1493 Duane St   503/338-7473
Daily: 8-5   bluescorcher.com
Inexpensive

Artisan breads, almond bear claws, scones, other pastries and handcrafted seasonal and organic foods are the bread and butter at this bakery. Fresh, quality ingredients make the difference; eggs, produce, honey, flowers and coffee are from local suppliers. Families come for healthy breakfasts (heartier choices on weekends) and lunches of seasonally-driven soups, salads, pizzas, calzones and sandwiches made on Scorcher bread. This worker-owned cooperative is fierce about creating top-shelf meals, breads and pastries in a relaxed setting with no white tablecloths in sight. A great spot for afternoon tea!

Bridgewater Bistro

20 Basin St   503/325-6777
Lunch: Mon-Sat; Dinner: Daily; Brunch: Sun   bridgewaterbistro.com
Moderate

Under the Astoria-Megler Bridge, this is a fabulous venue with stunning river views. You can feast upon small bites, salads and seafood dishes (wild local salmon, local steamer clams, seafood cakes of the day or pan-fried Willapa Bay oysters). If you're not in the mood for fish, the steaks, pork and fowl preparations may be more to your liking. Add a housemade soup or salad to make for a tasty dinner. Sunday brunch offers a bit of everything good such as eggs and oysters, hash, seafood cakes, smoked tomato mac and cheese, sandwiches and burgers (over 90% of the menus are gluten-free).

Cannery Pier Hotel & Spa

10 Basin St   503/325-4996, 888/325-4996
Moderate to expensive   cannerypierhotel.com

Situated on 100-year-old pilings and jutting out into the mighty Columbia, this hotel was once the Union Fisherman's Cooperative Packing Company. The 38 rooms and eight suites have hardwood floors, private balconies, gas fireplaces and in-room mini-fridges, microwaves and dining tables. With a nod to the area's Scandinavian heritage and fishing industry, the complimentary continental breakfast features Finnish delicacies; Oregon wines, cheeses and smoked salmon are served each evening. If you need a lift around town, you may be chauffeured in a classic car or head out on your own to explore the area on one of the hotel's vintage loaner bikes. Other amenities include a hot tub, sauna, exercise room, day spa and library. For the ultimate experience, book the Pilot House penthouse (two bedrooms, jetted tub, guest bath, full kitchen, living and dining

SHOWCASING OREGON

Charged with the responsibility of encouraging Oregon residents and visitors to explore the wonders of our state, the **Oregon Tourism Commission** (800/547-7842) is hard at work. The nine dedicated board members appointed by the Governor with very capable CEO, **Todd Davidson**, and his staff do this with exceptional expertise and dedication. The commission has won a number of national awards for its professionalism and effectiveness. An annual hardcopy publication (*Travel Oregon*) and the website (traveloregon.com) provide a wealth of information on all aspects of our state's many attractions and advantages. Order travel guides, trip planning kits and maps for your next adventure. Three e-newsletters (general, outdoors and culinary) are produced by the commission; subscribe at the website or by phone. Having served on the commission for a number of years (chair, 1996-2001), I can wholeheartedly attest to the standard of information and help provided.

rooms and two decks). Pet packages include treats and necessities to care for your canine travel companion.

The Cellar on 10th
1004 Marine Dr   503/325-6600
Tues-Sat: 10-5:30   thecellaron10th.com

Over 4,500 bottles of local, domestic and imported fine wines and champagnes are in stock in this historic perfect-for-wine underground shop; more than 70% of the libations are from the Northwest. Proprietor **Mike Wallis** will help pick just the wine you want. Also find wine-related linens and table pieces, international gourmet foods, spices, sea salts, stemware and accessories. Wine tastings, Saturdays between 1 and 4, feature a new winery, varietal or wine region each week. The shop remains open when cruise ships are in port.

Clemente's Cafe & Public House
175 14th St   503/325-1067
Lunch, Dinner: Tues-Sun   Facebook
Moderate

For fresh and local meats and seafood, Clemente's is a sure bet. Now located in the historic Pilot Station Building, owners **Lisa and Gordon Clement** change the menu seasonally. A sampling of choices includes fish and chips, cioppino, raw bar selections, organic beef (steaks or burgers) and handmade pasta dishes; all sauces and soups are homemade.

Columbia River Maritime Museum
1792 Marine Dr   503/325-2323
Daily: 9:30-5   crmm.org
Inexpensive to moderate

Land at this museum for fascinating exhibitions of Northwest maritime artifacts and collections that preserve the rich maritime heritage of the Columbia River region. View the Pilot Boat *Peacock*, the Lightship *Columbia* (kids especially enjoy roaming the officers' quarters, mess deck, radio room and galley), other vessels, nautical equipment, historical memorabilia and interactive displays spread among six galleries and the Great Hall. The Barbey Maritime Center is situated in the beautifully restored Astoria Railroad Depot at the east end of the property. The center focuses on maritime-related demonstrations, workshops and classes on wooden boat building, wood carving, bronze casting and tool making. Allow plenty of time to meander between the exhibits. This is said to be the largest collection of Pacific Northwest maritime artifacts in the country.

Drina Daisy

915 Commercial St   503/338-2912
Lunch, Dinner: Wed-Sun   drinadaisy.com
Moderate

Lovers of ethnic food will enjoy comfort food with an Old World twist at this Bosnian restaurant. The third-generation Bosnian chef presents flavors that are very Euro-Mediterranean with cabbage rolls and goulash and the like. Many entrees are slow-cooked and braised to perfection and served with fresh pickled vegetables and tasty breads. Dishes are savory but not too spicy, traditional baklava is pleasingly sweet. Drina Daisy is derived from the name of a southern Bosnia river (the location of the chef's prior restaurant) and Daisy is the owner's mother.

Fort George Brewing & Public House

1483 Duane St   503/325-7468
Lunch, Dinner: Daily   fortgeorgebrewery.com
Moderate

Founded in 1811 as a principal fur trading post, Fort George (named after King George III) was Astoria's original settlement site. There's been a lot of water (literally!) under the bridge since then, and today, dozens of craft beers from pale ales to stouts are produced in this renovated building. Step into the Lovell Taproom for good pub grub or upstairs for casual fare and calzones and pizzas from the woodstove pizza oven. Inquire about their occasional brewer's dinners ($65) which pair craft beer and epic cuisine (seafood, Indian and more); reservation only.

Grandview Bed & Breakfast

1574 Grand Ave   503/325-0000, 800/488-3250
Inexpensive to moderate   grandviewbedandbreakfast.com

Stay at the Grandview, a unique Victorian mansion with nine attractive, individually decorated and affordable rooms; all but one have private baths. A few rooms connect to make two-bedroom suites. Delicious breakfast is served each morning in the Bullet Turret with views of the river and numerous Astoria landmarks. The home is located in a hilly area full of picturesque historic homes.

Home Baking Co.

2845 Marine Dr   503/325-4631
Tues-Sat: 6-5   astoriacinnamontoast.com

The Tilander family provides Astoria with authentic Finnish baked goods since 1910. Third generation, **Kathy and Jim Tilander** continue to use traditional family recipes for breads, doughnuts, pastries, pies, cakes, apple fritters, prune tarts, cookies and dozens more baked goods. Holiday spreads are extra special with their oh-so-good Scandinavian holiday breads. For a taste from the past, try their famous cinnamon toast (Korpus). Its popularity dates back to Finland in the 1800s and also became a staple for Astorians and local fishing fleets because of the long shelf life. Sweet coffee bread is toasted, liberally sprinkled with cinnamon and sugar and packed in two-pound boxes. Enjoy any of these sweets and coffee at the bakery or to go; online orders, too.

Hotel Elliott

357 12th St   877/378-1924
Inexpensive and up   hotelelliott.com

Hotel Elliott is a boutique hotel with turn-of-the-century elegance but modern conveniences in the 32 rooms and suites. Designer bathrooms feature heated tile floors and plush terry robes. Signature beds are extra comfy and furnished with goose down pillows and custom duvet covers; up-do-date technologies are standard amenities. Additional luxuries await in the suites: custom-mantled gas fireplaces, cedar-lined closets, handcrafted cabinetry and Jacuzzi tubs (varies according to suite). The Presidential Suite is fit for a king: two stories with private access to the rooftop terrace, fully-furnished kitchen, living and dining rooms, two bedrooms and views of the city and river. Complimentary breakfast is offered in the expanded lobby and a wine bar is upstairs. Dining and shopping are steps away from the front door.

In the Boudoir

1004 Commercial St   503/325-4400
Daily: June-Sept; Mon-Sat: Oct-May   intheboudoirs.com

This specialty store focuses on bedrooms and luxurious appointments. Attractive displays feature romantic, whimsical and practical bedding, towels, pillows, throws, rugs, furniture, wall decor and accessories. The colorful selection also includes baby bedding and cribs, men's and women's toiletries and gift items for every day and special occasions.

Josephson's Smokehouse & Specialty Seafood

106 Marine Dr   503/325-2190, 800/722-3474
Mon-Fri: 9-5:30; Sat: 9:30-5:30; Sun: 10-5   josephsons.com

For four generations and over 90 years, Josephson's has been specializing in seafood. Stop in for fish and seafood that has been smoked, canned or made into jerky. The deli offers lunch fare of chowders, salmon burgers and smoked seafood dishes; eat inside, on the deck or pack your choices into a basket or cooler for a picnic. The premium products are made from #1 grade seafood and natural ingredients and are free of preservatives, dyes and unhealthy additives. Likely you've encountered their products in leading retailers or read about them in numerous magazines and major newspapers. They do a whale of an online business and ship the best of the Northwest worldwide; catalogs available.

Old Town Framing Company

1287 Commercial St   503/325-5221
Mon-Fri: 9:30-5:30; Sat: 10-5   Facebook

Dulcye Taylor's frame shop is not just for a fine showing of frames, but also for the outstanding collection of greeting cards — everyday,

AROUND THE CAMPFIRE

What a great way to end your day at the beach — sitting around the campfire, listening to ocean waves and reminiscing about the day's activities. Be aware of any city and state ordinances (800/551-6949, oregonstateparks.org) before starting a fire, and keep in mind these safety tips. In general, small recreational beach fires are allowed in the ocean shore recreation area if they are located in the open dry sands, downwind of and below beach grass and the driftwood line. No fires are allowed in dunes or beach log accumulations. Fire pits should be no larger than six feet in diameter and two feet deep. Never leave your fire unattended, and extinguish it before leaving the area. Now bring on the s'mores!

all-occasion and appropriately inappropriate. Although they specialize in custom framing, a nice selection of ready-made frames and local and regional artists' limited edition prints and photography are in stock. Old Town Framing participates in downtown Astoria's 2nd Saturday Art Walk, a popular event featuring refreshments, entertainment and interesting exhibits.

Oregon Film Museum

732 Duane St   503/325-2203
Daily: Hours vary
oregonfilmmuseum.com
Nominal

Oregon movie buffs will enjoy a visit to this museum in the old Clatsop County Jail (1914-1976). The museum celebrates the art and legacy of films and film-making in Oregon. A hallway of famous quotes, movie props and movie memorabilia from various movies with Oregon ties are displayed. You'll learn the ins and outs of making a major motion picture and create your own short film clip using green screens, lighting and cameras.

Pilot House

1 14th St   503/289-9926, 888/683-7987
Expensive   astoriapilothouse.com

An elegant three-bedroom vacation home is available on Pier 14 upstairs (no elevator) from the Columbia River Pilots station.

This location gives a catbird seat to the pilots who masterfully guide ocean-bound or arriving ships right outside your windows all day long. Guests will appreciate the state-of-the-art electronic access and quality of the furnishings; many are maritime artifacts. Up to eight adults are accommodated in the spacious quarters that include three bedrooms, three bathrooms, a complete kitchen, living and dining areas and gas fireplaces in all bedrooms and the living area. Master bedroom guests enjoy a private balcony and bathroom Jacuzzi tub. Rates vary according to season and length of stay and are adjusted for couple-only occupancy. Operating seasonally, the Riverfront Trolley stop is right outside the front door.

Silver Salmon Grille

1105 Commercial St   503/338-6640
Lunch, Dinner: Daily   silversalmongrille.com
Moderate

The Fisher Building has seen restaurants come and go since it was built in 1924. Today, salmon reigns at **Laurie and Jeff Martin**'s restaurant. The lounge's antique bar (acquired in the 1950s) is a remnant of the Thiel Brothers restaurant operation at this location. The elaborate 130-year-old beauty is constructed of Scottish cherry wood that was shipped around Cape Horn in the 1880s. As the story goes, its first Astoria home was in Anna Bays Social Club, a house of ill repute in this fishing town. Now in a more refined setting, it is the lounge's centerpiece. Joining salmon dishes on the lunch menu are halibut fish and chips, Willapa Bay oyster stew, a variety of sandwiches (San Francisco melt: turkey, bacon, tomato, avocado, onions and cheese on sourdough bread, dipped in egg and grilled), soups and clam chowder. A number of salmon entrees headline the dinner selections plus halibut (topped with Dungeness crab, cheese and chives), more seafood, steaks, pastas and chicken. Lighter appetites will appreciate specialty salads (tropical prawn, seafood Caesar or Cobb, smoked salmon spinach) for lunch or dinner; also low-carb and vegetarian entrees. The fine dining is matched with an impressive selection of fine wines and choices from the saloon. An assortment of mouthwatering sweets is presented on the dessert tray.

Supple Rockers

1542 Grand Ave   503/791-8237
Mon-Fri: 8-5 by appointment   supplerockers.com

If you or family members are passionate about baseball, a unique, custom rocking chair from Supple Rockers may be a fine addition to your home or the man-cave. Made with six Marucci or genuine Louisville Slugger bats and laser engraved with "ticket stub" backs, each rocker is one of a kind. Seats are made with premium leather and hand-sewn baseball stitch detail. Choose from dark or natural white ash bats; light or dark brown, black, red or white seats and dark brown, tan, black or red stitching. **Kim and Dan Supple** take great pride in their family-owned Oregon business which they recently moved into larger quarters.

T. Paul's Urban Cafe

1119 Commercial St   503/338-5133
Lunch, Dinner: Mon-Sat   tpaulsurbancafe.com
Moderate

Two diverse menus distinguish the T. Paul venues. The Urban Cafe's menu offers salads, sandwiches, quesadillas, pastas and beer and wine. Down the street and around the corner, **T. Paul's Supper Club** (503/325-2545, tpaulssupperclub.com) serves seafood plus pastas, chicken, steaks and all-natural beef half-pound burgers. Entree-size salads are creative and make a meal on their own. A full bar with beer, wine and cocktails adds to the supper club ambience. Both restaurants feature live music every weekend. T. Paul's is also known for fabulous homemade desserts, many are from grandma's tried-and-true recipes.

BANDON

Alloro Wine Bar & Restaurant

375 2nd St SE   541/347-1850
Seasonal days and hours   allorowinebar.com
Moderate to expensive

Chef **Jeremy Buck** and wine steward **Lian Schmidt** honed their restaurant experiences in Florence, Italy. The wine list pays homage to Northwest and Italian wines with several available by the glass. Fish stew, braised lamb shank and grilled salmon are made from local seafood and meats, fresh seasonal produce and imported specialties. From the appetizer menu, choose from antipasto, oysters on the half shell, salads and soups. Pasta dishes also feature fresh seafood, vegetables and herbs; a hearty New York steak preparation is always an option. Call ahead for seasonal hours and reservations.

B Home Teak and Outdoor Living
49667 Hwy 101   541/347-4410
Tues-Sat: 8-4:30   bhome-bandon.com

Want to dress up your yard, deck or patio? Here you'll find well-made teak tables and chairs, bar stools, benches and loungers for your outdoor spaces. Give your bathroom a luxurious spa feel with teak shower stools and bathroom accessories as well as custom-made cushions. Teak wood is ideal for the wet and humid Oregon coast as it is low maintenance and becomes more beautiful as it weathers; the longevity of teak is 70-plus years.

Bandon Dunes Golf Resort
57744 Round Lake Dr   541/347-4380
Daily   bandondunesgolf.com

Visionary entrepreneur and golf enthusiast, **Mike Keiser** made his fortune in the Midwest in recycled paper and greeting cards. Playing golf around the world and especially in Scotland, Mike was inspired when he came to the Oregon Coast and found a wee bit of the Old Country on Oregon's south coast near Bandon. Thus, Bandon Dunes was born on the shelf of the Pacific Ocean. (That's the short version; never mind that it took several years of dedication to the project and untold millions of dollars; the rest of the story is that Mike Keiser put Oregon and Oregon golf on the world map while giving a huge boost to the local and statewide economy in terms of both jobs and tourism dollars.) Along with the best architects and experts in links golf, Mike added the most capable GM he could find in **Hank Hickox** who had already made his mark at several resort properties. Bandon Dunes offers five 18-hole courses (Bandon Dunes,

Pacific Dunes, Bandon Trails, Old Macdonald, Bandon Preserve), each unique and challenging. Food and drink are served in several unique restaurants; fine Northwest cuisine and exquisite wines, casual lounges, a Scottish-style pub and day-long casual dining (hours vary by season). Comfortable, luxurious lodge, inn and cottage accommodations are designed for singles, couples and foursomes (rates vary). Resort amenities include shuttle service between lodging, courses, restaurants and lounges; a business center in the lodge; fitness center; well-stocked pro shops and daily golf clinics. This is a fantastic golf experience.

Devon's Boutique

92 2nd Street   541/347-8092
Daily: 10-5   devonsboutique.com

Chic resort wear is the focus at this charming Old Town shop. Look for unique investment pieces in beach casual plus special occasion finery. Owner **Devon Matsuda** hand knits scarves in luscious color combinations that are warm and stylish; also quality handknit sweaters and other women's attire (many made from bamboo or other sustainable materials).

NORTH OF THE BORDER

For a moment I am crossing the Columbia River from Astoria to mention **The Depot Restaurant** (depotrestaurantdining. com) where casual meets fine dining. Set in a century-plus-old train station, in Seaview, Washington, you'll be greeted warmly. Owner/chef **Michael Lalewicz** presents interesting small plates like Thai calamari and other delicacies from the international menu. Of course you'll find fresh local oysters for which this area is famous. Braised lamb shank, Peruvian mango sea scallops and Mediterranean prawns are among the entrees; all are exceptionally well-prepared. Wines and beers also share global origins. Take it from your author, a wandering foodie, you will find great food and service to match at this out-of-state dining destination.

The Loft

315 1st St SE   541/329-0535
Dinner: Thurs-Sun   theloftofbandon.com
Moderate

For stunning views and casual fine dining, head to the upper level of the High Dock building in Old Town. Not surprisingly, this coastal dinner house features seafood, but not exclusively; all meals are built around seasonally available fresh bounty. Plates on the changing menu are beautifully presented and attractively garnished. Try the crab bruschetta appetizer and the sweet potato bread pudding if they are available. The 12-layer chocolate hazelnut praline dobos torte is made in-house like most of the offerings.

Lord Bennett's

1695 Beach Loop Dr   541/347-3663
Dinner: Daily; Brunch: Sun   lordbennett.com
Expensive

Lord Bennett's has been owned and operated by chef **Rich Iverson** for 26 years; locals and tourists keep coming back for wonderful steaks and seafood that are cooked to perfection. Delicious pasta dishes may be prepared with or without crab, scallops and prawns. Appetizers are mainly of the ocean-going variety; soups and salads are fresh and made with healthy ingredients. Sunday brunch features items such as sweet potato pancakes, eggs Benedict, salmon hash, wild mushroom hash and egg platters. The location affords magnificent views of Face Rock, sunsets and the crashing Pacific below the parking lot. (Banquet facilities; live music on weekend evenings.)

Misty Meadows Jam and Jelly Products

48053 Hwy 101   541/347-2575, 888/795-1719
Daily   gotjam.com

Jam lovers will find just about any flavor to top your morning toast. At this family-owned and -operated farm, second generation **Traci and Mike Keller** offer marmalades, syrups, jellies, fruit butters, no-sugar-added items, seedless offerings, super honey, pepper jellies, barbecue sauces and salsas. Most all products are Oregon-grown and have been since they began business in 1971. Some of the interesting or hard-to-find products include tayberry, wild huckleberry, salal and chokecherry jams and local cranberry jam and syrups. Retail activity is in a large building next to the familiar roadside stand; phone, mail and Internet orders are also welcome.

Tony's Crab Shack & Seafood Grill
155 1st St   541/347-2875
Lunch, Dinner: Daily   tonyscrabshack.com
Moderate

Owner **Tony Roszkowski** takes good care of customers at his restaurant and next-door **Port O' Call** bait and tackle shop. Crab is the main attraction on the menu — whole with drawn butter and in crab cakes, sandwiches, pasta, salad and cocktails. Shrimp and fish tacos are superb; worth noting is the lack of a deep-fat fryer in this establishment. Salmon is smoked on-site and delicious in sandwiches and salads. Speaking of fresh — Tony rents crab rings for folks to catch their own (cleaning and cooking available) from Weber's Pier or other local hot crabbing spots. Port O' Call also carries fishing essentials — rods, licenses, tackle and bait. In case you get skunked, Tony always has fresh ocean fare on the menu.

BAY CITY

The Fish Peddler at Pacific Oyster
5150 Oyster Dr   503/377-2323
Daily: Hours vary   pacseafood.com

At this division of Pacific Seafood, nearly 10,000 pounds of oysters are processed weekdays. The oyster shucking process is interesting to watch; it involves brute force, finesse and a certain twist of the wrist before triple washing and sorting. The retail counter and restaurant are open year-round. Nestled on Tillamook Bay, this picturesque setting has picnic tables available for outdoor dining. Inside, diners will find ocean-fresh dishes like cioppino, fish and chips, crab Louis salad, clam chowder (made in-house), shrimp, steamer clams, sandwiches, entree plates and oyster shooters from the retail counter. If it swims nearby, you're likely to find it at this visitor-friendly operation.

Tillamook Country Smoker
8250 Warren Ave   503/377-2222, 800/325-2220
Daily: 9-5   tcsjerky.com

The county of Tillamook is famous for not only cheese and ice cream, but also for jerky and other meats hot out of Tillamook Country Smoker. From humble beginnings more than 50 years ago, **Art Crossley** started selling jerky and smoked meat sticks from his small meat market. Today, the third-generation business produces thousands of pounds of meat snacks that are sold in the store alongside nuts, sausages and other goodies. All of these items and gift packs, including a military care package, are available on the website.

BROOKINGS

Beachfront RV Park
16035 Boat Basin Road   541/469-5867
Inexpensive   beachfrontrvpark.com

If your family likes RV camping, this Port of Brookings-Harbor facility offers parking on the beach, a rarity on our state's coastline. Spaces are available year round, daily or weekly; reservations accepted. RVers have a choice of pull-through or back-in spots, ocean or river views and partial or full hook-ups; river view area is dry camping with no hookups. Tent sites are also available for those who wish to rough it.

Oxenfrē Public House
631 Chetco Ave   541/813-1985
Lunch: Fri, Sat; Dinner: Daily   oxenpub.com
Moderate to moderately expensive

Brookings has an excellent gastropub! It's not surprising that the warm and inviting Oxenfrē Public House is very busy; ownership is on the ball and the menu categories are outstanding (including inexpensive snacks). The best snacks are Bavarian pretzel bites with pub cheese, mustard and raw honey and Rogue blue cheese walnut mousse served in a Mason jar. The fried chicken and Belgian waffle sandwich and braised short rib tacos were tempting, but I settled on the Oxpub Wagyu beef burger on ciabatta roll with seared pork belly, cheese and fries. To top it all off, Belgian waffle s'mores were good and gooey! A late night snack menu is available for those arriving after regular dinner hours. There are no fewer than eight brews on tap along with a selection of wines, bottled beers and from-scratch cocktails. Live music is featured weekly and can be found on their events page or via Facebook.

Pancho's Restaurante Y Cantina
1136 Chetco Ave   541/469-6531
Lunch, Dinner: Daily   Facebook
Moderate

Pancho's is the place to go in this north-of-the-border town for south-of-the-border fare. Start with an ice-cold margarita (an excellent selection of tequilas), choose your favorite flavor (classic, strawberry or exotic) and munch on Pancho's Salsa Rubio and chips. Authentic dishes are homemade from family recipes using quality, fresh ingredients (no lard). A nice selection of chicken, seafood, vegetarian, beef and pork dishes and combinations is offered.

Whaleshead Beach Resort
19921 Whaleshead Road   541/469-7446, 800/943-4325
Cabins: Inexpensive to moderate   whalesheadresort.com
Restaurant: Breakfast, Lunch, Dinner: Daily
Moderate $ $ $

This is a unique stay. Cottages and cabins accommodate two to ten guests and have forest or ocean views; each unit is privately owned (amenities and furnishings vary). RVers enjoy terraced pads with concrete or cedar decks, restrooms, showers and utilities; a laundromat and market are within the confines of the resort. Whaleshead Beach is accessed through a 700-foot tunnel, and the

Traveling with your pet? Try these pet-friendly spots for a meal or lodging:

Fairfield Inn & Suites (2014 W 7th St, The Dalles; 541/769-0753): feeding mat, bowl, treats and a "Pet in Room" sign for the door

Klondike Restaurant & Bar (71 Cowlitz, Old Town in St. Helens; 503/366-2634): water dish and treats

Lucky Labrador Brew Pub (915 SE Hawthorne Blvd, Portland; 503/236-3555): patio seating plus a dedicated section of the restaurant

Ocean Breeze Motel (85165 Hwy 101, Florence; 855/201-7819): two extra sheets for sleeping on the bed, plus fresh towels

The Ocean Lodge (2864 S Pacific St, Cannon Beach; 503/436-2241): treats, feeding bowl, sheet and towel; outside shower, too!

Open Door Wine Bar (303 W Hood St, Sisters; 541/549-6076): water dish and an extra chair

Oxford Hotel (10 Minnesota Ave, Bend; 844/204-3860): pet bed, travel bowl and treats, plus a map of trails and parks for owners

Tin Shed Garden Cafe (1438 NE Alberta St, Portland; 503/288-6966): a waitlist that includes dogs plus a doggie menu

Redwood National Park is just some 20 miles down the highway in California.

CANNON BEACH

Bistro Restaurant
263 N Hemlock St   503/436-2661
Dinner: Daily (Wed-Sun in winter)   Facebook
Moderate

You'll need to venture off the beaten sidewalk for this cozy, romantic restaurant. The brick walkway and patio are utterly charming, especially when abloom with flowers. A savory salad of organic greens, pears, walnuts and blue cheese is the perfect prelude to deliciously prepared fresh seafood and beef entrees. The signature dish, seafood stew, has been a staple on the menu for nearly 30 years. Reservations are accepted, although not necessary in this wee little cottage turned regional-American fare restaurant. The Bistro was rebuilt in 2013 following a devastating fire the year prior; an outdoor courtyard seating area was created in the rebuilding process.

Bronze Coast Gallery

224 N Hemlock St, Suite 2   503/436-1055
Daily: 10-6   bronzecoastgallery.com

This gallery is among the best in Cannon Beach, where art is big. Owner **Kim Barnett** operated an Eastern Oregon art foundry prior to opening this premier establishment and possesses an in-depth knowledge of the bronze casting process. Original paintings, limited edition bronze sculptures and *giclée* (with high-quality ink jet printer) reproductions are exhibited by over 40 regional, national and international artists. Frequent citywide art events and festivals occur throughout the year.

Bruce's Candy Kitchen

256 N Hemlock St   503/436-2641
Daily: 10-5   brucescandy.com

Some four decades ago, Vicky Hawkins, an Englishwoman who was the editor of the *Cannon Beach Gazette*, asked the late Bruce Haskell whether he might be able to make the peppermint Bah Humbug candies she joyfully remembered from her childhood in England. Bruce's now mixes more than 200 pounds of this delicious seasonal (autumn and winter) treat. Family-owned and –operated since 1963, the fourth generation continues Cannon Beach's sweet tradition with salt water taffy (30 flavors, regular and sugar-free), hand-dipped chocolates (60 varieties) and assorted brittles, popcorns, caramels, hard candies and other favorites. Who can resist a purchase at this store with the distinctive clickity-clack of the taffy cutting and wrapping machine and aroma of homemade confections?

Cannon Beach Book Company

130 N Hemlock St, Suite 2   503/436-1301
Daily: 10-6 (weekends and seasonally till 8)   Facebook

This is one of the better independent bookstores remaining in the state. If you like whodunits, there are plenty; latest *New York Times* best sellers, check here first; children's bedtime stories, a wonderful assortment and well-loved classics, you'll find them here, too. In essence, all types of books are in stock or can be specially ordered and quickly delivered. Other quality merchandise includes unique greeting cards, journals, sassy reading glasses, eco-friendly reusable bags, book lights and art supplies so you can release your inner artist at the beach.

Cannon Beach Hardware and Public House

1235 S Hemlock St   503/436-4086
Store: Thurs-Tues: Hours vary   cannonbeachhardware.com
Pub: Lunch, Dinner: Thurs-Tues
Moderate

This hardware store (aka the Screw & Brew) is the epitome of full service. Whether you need plumbing or electrical supplies, yard gear or most any do-it-yourself tools, you can find them here. And get this; they claim to be the singular hardware store to serve microbrews, wine and liquor! The sports bar side of the biz has fish and chips, burgers and other pub fare; they also smoke their own pork for pulled pork sandwiches and brine and smoke their own pastrami. (Be careful, you could be waylaid from those home projects by the four big screen TVs and free popcorn and peanuts.) Whether you need hardware or not, stop by for a casual pick-me-up when you're at the beach.

Cannon Beach Hotel

1116 S Hemlock St   503/436-1392
Inexpensive and up   cannonbeachhotellodgings.com

Since 1914, this hotel has offered lodging in midtown Cannon Beach. Now, a century later, the classically elegant New England-style hotel is totally refurbished. In addition, furniture is custom designed, linens and bedding are luxurious, and the artwork is original. This weathered beauty, one block from the ocean, has a cozy lobby with fireplace that sets the tone for a romantic getaway (no children, pets or smoking). Each of the ten guestrooms is impeccably furnished, has a private bathroom and may contain a fireplace, four-poster bed or claw-foot tub. An expanded continental breakfast includes frittatas, hash brown casserole and granola (all made in-house), pastries, yogurt and more (morning mimosas) and is included in the nightly rate. Inside the hotel, **Cannon Beach Café** is a Parisian-style eatery; open seasonally (March-Nov).

Cannon Beach Spa

232 N Spruce St   503/436-8772, 888/577-8772
Seasonal: Days and hours vary   cannonbeachspa.com

After a hike in Ecola or Oswald West state parks, book an appointment and pamper yourself at this luxurious spa or slip next door to the decadent **Chocolate Café** (503/436-4331, cannonbeachchocolatecafe. com). The spa has been in town for 17 years and offers a variety of massage, hydrotherapy, skin-care and foot treatments. Total packages include seaweed, volcanic clay and aromatherapy applications to rejuvenate the body and soul. Treat yourself at the Chocolate Café dedicated to exquisite Moonstruck Chocolate and other candies from France, Belgium, Switzerland and Ghana. An over-the-top shake is made from melted chocolate — oh my! Desserts, hot chocolate and French press coffee are equally tempting; even the cafe's walls are a rich chocolate brown. Your body and your tastebuds will thank you for stopping by these indulgent shops.

Castaways Restaurant & Tiki Bar

316 Fir St   503/436-8777
Dinner: Wed-Sun   Facebook
Moderately expensive

For international-fusion type food and tiki drinks, this is a highly popular venue. The place is comfortable, the service is unpretentious, and the platters are tasty. Chef **Josh Tuckman** offers Thai satay chicken combined with Jamaican jerk chicken served with spicy and unusual sauces. The honey-orange coconut prawns served with a sweet chili dipping sauce are another appetizer favorite. Crab fritters and Ahi tuna, plus homemade seafood chowder and a variety of salads are popular for light eaters. Dinner platters include a delicious Jamaican pork chop and a very different house mac and cheese with chicken breast, sausage, mushrooms and peppers, and yes, some cheese in the mixings. You won't go wrong with the thirst-quenching drinks.

Center Diamond

1065 S Hemlock St
Daily: 10-5

503/436-0833
centerdiamond.com

Another gem in this laid-back community is a store chock-full of fabrics, patterns, books and gifts especially for quilters and textile artists. The large selection of fabrics includes seashore, maritime and Asian designs, batiks and other colorful prints and solids. Beautiful ready-made wall hangings and quilts are a source of inspiration, and workshops and classes will help you create your own keepsake.

DID YOU KNOW...

... Saddle Mountain is the highest point in the Coast Range. Experienced hikers can trek a challenging trail to the top of the mountain; colorful spring wildflowers, too.

... Haystack Rock off Cannon Beach is 235 feet high and is the third largest coastal monolith in the world.

Driftwood Restaurant & Lounge

179 N Hemlock St
Lunch, Dinner: Daily
Moderate

503/436-2439
driftwoodcannonbeach.com

For over 70 years, visitors have returned time and again to the Driftwood for dependable service and good food. Ward off a chilly day with homemade clam chowder served in a sourdough bread bowl or opt for entree salads, burgers and sandwiches. Steaks are hand-cut, tender and a complete dinner with a choice of sides. Smaller portioned entrees, appetizers and homemade marionberry pies are also offered.

Claim a spot on the massive front patio for lunch or dinner; you never know who will stroll past while you enjoy libations and a tasty repast.

EVOO Cannon Beach

188 S Hemlock St   503/436-8555, 877/436-3866
Days and hours vary   evoo.biz

Extra virgin olive oil is the central player in dinner shows and private events at EVOO. During the dinner show, guests relax in the open kitchen/dining room watching as chefs prepare several courses and share recipes, techniques and wine pairing tips. Hands-on shows include the culinary basics of artisan breadmaking, crepes, culinary fundamentals, omelets, pasta, pizza and more. Shows end with students eating a full meal of the delicious results. Reservations required.

Fruffels

140 S Hemlock St   503/436-4160
Daily: Seasonal hours   fruffels.com

Fruffels is best described as a boutique department store. For this community, it means a store with quality gifts and home accessories plus complimentary gift wrapping and personal shopping services. No matter what your decorating taste, you're sure to find furniture, lighting, rugs and linens to furnish or accessorize one room or a whole house with unique tableware, tabletop items and glassware. Co-owners **Tony Lawler** and **David Kiedrowski** provide complete residential and corporate design services, room makeovers and landscape design. Luxurious bath and body products, scented candles and other tastefully selected items are thoughtful gifts.

The Irish Table

1235 S Hemlock St   503/436-0708
Dinner: Fri-Tues   theirishtablerestaurant.com
Moderate

Come early to this casual restaurant where **Crystal and Sean Corbin** preside. Enter through **Sleepy Monk Coffee Roasters** (503/436-

2796) for seating at a large convivial table in the center of the dining venue (the Irish table), at smaller tables around the room or in the coffeehouse. The menu changes frequently with a selection of soups, salads or cheeses for appetizers. Irish stew (lamb and vegetables) is offered, as well as a vegetarian shepherd's pie with wild mushrooms, a seafood dish and meat platter. My favorites are the chicken pastie (tender chicken and veggies in a buttery pastry with a creamy mushroom sauce) and delicious corned beef with potatoes and cabbage accompanied by warm Irish soda bread. Trifles, scones with homemade lemon curd and Guinness ice cream sandwiches stand out on the dessert menu. Servers are attentive and the menu has unusual appeal.

Newmans at 988
988 S Hemlock St   503/436-1151
Dinner: Daily (Wed-Sun in winter)   newmansat988.com
Moderate to expensive

Many a return diner has made Newmans their go-to place for French-Italian fare. Husband-and-wife team **Sandy and John Newman** share restaurant duties; on most days John is in the kitchen and Sandy minds the front of the tiny house with room for about 30 diners. White table linens, fresh roses and classy dinner music set the tone for simple elegance. This gourmet eatery offers a three- or four-course chef's menu nightly, or order from exquisite a la carte selections (including vegan and gluten-free). With so many folks visiting this charming community, especially on weekends, it is a good idea to make reservations; also check for seasonal hours. A few of my favorites are lobster ravioli appetizers, marinated rack of lamb and an assortment of fine cheeses. John is a top-rated chef who works wonders in limited space!

The Ocean Lodge
2864 S Pacific St   503/436-2241, 888/777-4047
Moderate to expensive   theoceanlodge.com

The Ocean Lodge is a fabulous destination for romantic getaways, family vacations or a small retreat. Developers/owners **Mike Clark,**

Tom Drumheller and **Patrick Nofield**'s vision for a 1940s-style beach resort is right on the mark. True to the name, this oceanfront property of 37 studios and suites in the lodge (plus eight more adjacent to the lodge) is just feet away from a long stretch of sandy beach and familiar Haystack Rock is directly off shore. The gorgeous lodge is warm, welcoming and staffed by the friendliest, most helpful team on the north coast. A crackling fire in the lobby's river rock wood-burning fireplace warms up chilly days. Stacks of books are scattered throughout the lodge, in the library and around informal seating areas encouraging guests to enjoy a quiet respite. The delicious, complimentary breakfast buffet is upstairs; hot beverages and cookies are always available in the lobby. Oregon artist Andy Nichols' breakfast room chandelier depicting orange and blue tentacles and shells are spectacular. Other glass pieces and local artwork are displayed around the lodge. Bathrooms are luxurious; guest accommodations are tastefully furnished with gas fireplaces, balconies, microwaves and snack refrigerators. Family-friendly at The Ocean Lodge means a warm welcome for the four-pawed member, too.

Pizza a' fetta

231 N Hemlock St   503/436-0333
Lunch, Dinner: Daily   pizza-a-fetta.com
Inexpensive

Pizza a' fetta only uses the finest seasonal ingredients and offers Oregon and Italian wines, microbrews, pizzas, salads, appetizers and much more. Roma tomato sauce is cooked for three hours and fermented an additional 12; the pizza dough is made fresh daily, then hand tossed, just how owner **James Faurentino**'s grandmother made it. The pizza ranks in the nation's top 50 for its original methods of preparation. Next door, **Bella Espresso** (503/436-2595, bella-espresso.com) offers air-roasted Arabica coffee, gourmet desserts, pastries, Panini sandwiches, fine wines, beer and fresh fruit smoothies. You will be transported back in time with its frescos, paintings and bronzes.

HOW SWEET IT IS!

It is well-known fact that I am a chocoholic, so it wouldn't do not to mention some of Oregon's sweet players. You will find quality chocolate products around the state and nation from these fine purveyors.

Branson's Chocolates (Ashland, 541/488-7493, bransons chocolates.com)

Brigittine Monks (Amity, 503/835-8080, brigittine.org)

Candy Basket (Portland, 503/666-2000, candybasketinc.com)

Cary's of Oregon (Grants Pass, 888/822-9300, carysoforegon.com)

Chocolate Café (Cannon Beach, 503/436-4331, cannonbeach chocolatecafe.com)

Chocolates by Bernard (Lake Oswego, 888/829-6800, bernardc chocolates.com)

Enchanté (Milwaukie, 503/654-4846, enchantechocolatier.com)

Euphoria Chocolate Company (Eugene, 541/344-4605, euphoria chocolate.com)

Extreme Chocolates (Salem, 503/581-6099, extremechocolates. com)

Goody's (Bend, 541/385-7085, goodyschocolates.com)

Indulge Sweets (Seal Rock, 541/563-2766, indulgesweetsfudge. com)

Ladybug Chocolates (Canby, 503/263-3335, canbychocolates. com)

Lillie Belle Farms (Central Point, 888/899-2022, lilliebellefarms. com)

Moonstruck (Portland, 800/557-6666, moonstruckchocolate.com)

Pacific Hazelnut Farms & Candy Factory (Aurora, 503/678-2755, pacifichazelnut.com)

Puddin' River Chocolates (Canby, 866/802-2708, puddinriver chocolates.com)

The Sycamore Tree (Baker City, 541/523-4840, sycamoregifts. com)

Tamani Chocolates (McMinnville, 503/298-9427, tamanichoco lates.com)

Woodblock Chocolate (Portland, 503/477-5262, woodblock chocolate. com)

Sleepy Monk Coffee Roasters

1235 S Hemlock St   503/436-2796
Fri-Mon: 8-4; Tues: 8-2   sleepymonkcoffee.com
Inexpensive

Indulge in a superb cup of coffee at this organic tasting room. Beans are roasted on-site and also sold by the bag (served at area restaurants and hotels, too). Come evening, the adjacent restaurant, **The Irish Table**, uses the Monk's space for additional seating.

Stephanie Inn

2740 S Pacific St   503/436-2221, 800/633-3466
Expensive   stephanieinn.com

Not only does Stephanie Inn have all the elements necessary for a really "luxe" vacation, but it does it with a big smile. Guests enjoy a host of complimentary amenities including an afternoon wine and beer reception and the chef's breakfast buffet (Benedicts, homemade granola, morning-fresh baked goods and more). The guest rooms and suites, luxuriously appointed and designed with privacy and relaxation in mind, feature wet bars with refreshments and large bathrooms (including Jacuzzis and oversized towels). On-site massage services are available in two beautiful massage suites. A classy dining room serving excellent Northwest-inspired cuisine (moderate) is open nightly; reservations are required. The menu is irresistible; choose the multi-course *prix-fixe* option available with wine pairing or a la carte entrees such as filet mignon, Dungeness crab cakes, excellent appetizers and tempting desserts. Haystack Rock and sunset views from the hotel grounds are spectacular; Stephanie Inn is a first-class venue.

The Surfsand Resort

148 W Gower St   503/436-2274, 800/547-6100
Moderate   surfsand.com

Location, location, location! This full-service resort is steps away from Haystack Rock, adjacent to the **Wayfarer Restaurant and Lounge** and on the edge of Hemlock Street's eclectic, artsy shops, restaurants and galleries. Views are incomparable at the Surfsand

Resort. Comfortable guest rooms are contemporary and appointed with deluxe bath amenities, Tempur-Pedic beds, gas fireplaces and modern technologies. Cabana service, ice cream socials, weenie roasts and kids' club activities are offered seasonally. Optional special packages are created with a host of extra goodies for beach bonfires, romance, celebrations and kids' birthday parties. Take a dip in the heated indoor swimming pool, play on the beach, relax, fly a kite or go for a bicycle or horseback ride (rentals nearby); the choices are seemingly endless.

Tom's Fish & Chips

240 N Hemlock St   503/436-4301
Lunch, Dinner: Daily   tomscannonbeach.com
Inexpensive to moderate

Family-friendly dining is a little brighter in Cannon Beach with the addition of Tom's Fish & Chips. Yes, there is a Tom; actually there's two! **Tom Drumheller** is a local hospitality impresario with the likes of The Ocean Lodge in his portfolio and his partner on this project is **Tom Krueger**. They make for a great team at this nautical themed restaurant. Fish baskets are prepared with artic cod, prawns, clams, salmon or halibut; fresh fish is cut and breaded each morning. Other choices include Caesar salad (add shrimp or blackened salmon for a delicious option), New England clam chowder and shrimp cocktails; classic burgers, four draft beers and other thirst-quenchers round out the affordable menu. Large glass floats hang from the ceiling and a wall mural depicts pirates in search of plunder.

Wayfarer Restaurant & Lounge

1190 Pacific Dr   503/436-1108
Breakfast, Lunch, Dinner: Daily   wayfarer-restaurant.com
Moderate to expensive

Choose buttermilk pancakes or Dungeness crab cakes Benedict for morning meals or the Dungeness crab mac and cheese (with Beecher's Flagship cheddar) for lunch. A full dinner menu offers clams, fresh fish, housemade wild forest mushroom ravioli and tender filet mignon. Starters (heavy on seafood options) make fine meals on the lighter side for lunch or dinner. Sit in the main dining room or bar and enjoy the view.

CHARLESTON

Portside Restaurant
63383 Kingfisher Dr   541/888-5544
Lunch, Dinner: Daily   portsidebythebay.com
Moderate

The selection is wide and varied at this fishing port dinner house: steak any way you please, fresh catch (broiled, fried, poached, grilled), chicken specialties, satisfying pastas and smaller portions for youngsters and oldsters. There are plenty of appealing appetizers including pickled herring, salmon with capers, deep-fried bar bites and homemade daily soups. An outdoor garden patio and solarium are alternatives to the dining room.

CLOVERDALE

Sandlake Country Inn
8505 Galloway Road   503/965-6745
Moderate   sandlakecountryinn.com

The "Old Allen Place" farmhouse near Pacific City was constructed of red fir bridge timbers around 1900. It is now on the Oregon Historic Registry and is also a green lodging facility. Choose from three very comfortable suites and a private brookside guest cottage. All rooms have whirlpool tubs, refrigerators, fireplaces (wood, gas or electric) and private decks; each room is tastefully decorated in a different theme. Coffee, tea and a four-course breakfast are delivered to guest rooms each morning. The menu varies, but may include blackberry brûlée, baked or fresh fruit, hot egg dishes, crepes, roasted potatoes, meats and freshly-baked pastries and breads. This is a small, quiet, relaxing retreat (no pets; children accommodated only in the cottage). All-inclusive small weddings and elopements are available.

COOS BAY

Benetti's Italian Restaurant

260 S Broadway   541/267-6066
Lunch: Mon-Fri; Dinner: Daily   benettis.com
Moderate

Try **Tricia and Joe Benetti**'s first-class establishment for great Italian cuisine featuring dishes his grandmother used to make. The dinner house overlooks the boardwalk where diners can enjoy the comings and goings of ships, people and pets. Wine and cocktails are served in the upstairs dining room or downstairs in the full-service lounge. Popular dinner entrees include calzone, fettuccini alfredo, steaks and outstanding spaghetti; daily specials and half-and-half platters are also enticing. It's hard not to fill up at the start with all-you-can-eat soup, salad and wonderful garlic bread.

OREGON BEACONS

Eleven beautiful lighthouses dot Oregon's scenic coast; most have been restored and some are still navigational aids. While several are decommissioned, these iconic Oregon pillars were built to last, warning ship captains of imminent dangers in the midst of wild and wooly weather and are a testament to our state's marine history. Most are open to the public, and Heceta Head offers a B&B opportunity. From north to south:

Tillamook Rock (Cannon Beach)
Cape Meares (Tillamook)
Yaquina Head (Newport)
Yaquina Bay (Newport)
Cleft of the Rock (Yachats, private)
Heceta Head (Florence)
Umpqua River (Reedsport)
Cape Arago (Charleston)
Coquille River (Bandon)
Cape Blanco (Port Orford)
Pelican Bay (Brookings, private)

Oregon Connection

1125 S 1st St
Mon-Sat: 9:30-5

541/267-7804, 800/255-5318
oregonconnection.com

Known for years as the House of Myrtlewood, the current name more accurately reflects the mix of Oregon goods: myrtlewood products, women's apparel and accessories, gourmet food items and fudge. The wood of the myrtlewood tree is treasured for unique colors, grains and burls manifested in gorgeous bowls, trays, desk accessories, weather stations, one-of-a-kind tables and decorative accessories and gifts. The Wooden Touch Putter has been tried by some of the best golfers in our state, and reports are that it really does facilitate more accurate putting. Objects made from logs are cut, dried and turned on-site from the impressive stack of logs outside the building. Complimentary factory tours are open to the public. This is one of the oldest continuously-working myrtlewood factories in the area, now owned and operated by a nonprofit agency serving the disabled.

HOLIDAY LIGHTS AND MORE

A fun holiday event is the annual **Holiday Lights at Shore Acres State Park** (89039 Cape Arago Hwy, Coos Bay; 541/888-3732; shoreacres.net). Seven acres of the park, plus gardens, paths and the Garden House come alive with more than 300,000 lights, illuminated sculptures and holiday trees during the entire month of December. The Friends of Shore Acres organize entertainment, refreshments and activities. This magnificent park was once the estate of timber baron Louis Simpson. It has nearly 750 acres of gardens, ponds, trails to the beach and an observation building with a history of the estate. The park is open throughout the year 8 a.m. till dusk and is a popular spot for whale watching, storm watching and picnicking.

Sharkbite's Seafood Cafe

240 S Broadway
Lunch, Dinner: Mon-Sat
Moderate

541/269-7475
Facebook

This is one shark bite you don't want to avoid. Tacos, more specifically, fish tacos, are the specialty of the house at Sharkbite's

Seafood. Two large corn tortillas are brimming with cod, shrimp or halibut and dressed with cabbage, onions, Jack cheese, avocados and either salsa or tartar sauce. Baskets and sandwiches also feature ocean fare with house-cut French fries or beer-battered onion rings; landlubbers may prefer grilled burgers or chicken sandwiches. Kids are welcome at the casual, surf-themed cafe and are provided with a kid-specific menu. A full bar with signature mixed drinks, beers and a nightly happy hour encourage conversations that center around the best surfing waters on the southern Oregon coast and shark sightings!

DEPOE BAY

The Channel House
35 Ellingson St   541/765-2140, 800/447-2140
Moderate to expensive   channelhouse.com

This prime location overlooks the ocean and Depoe Bay channel where boats continuously enter and leave the harbor. The intimate contemporary inn has 16 beautiful rooms and suites with Tempur-Pedic mattresses, gas fireplaces and Jacuzzis on the oceanfront decks. A natural color palate and understated elegant furnishings create a peaceful ambience sure to wash stress away. Select from wine, champagne or romantic packages (a bottle of wine or champagne, etched glasses); in-room massage service by appointment. Join fellow guests each morning in the dining room for a complimentary continental breakfast before exploring the central coast.

Gracie's Sea Hag Restaurant and Lounge
58 N Hwy 101   541/765-2734
Breakfast, Lunch, Dinner: Daily   theseahag.com
Moderate and up

Founded in 1963 by Gracie Strom, this is one of the central coast's favorite seafood restaurants and lounges. Current owners **Clary and Jerome Grant** continue Gracie's welcoming hospitality, and tunes are still being played on the liquor bottles. Hand-crafted recipes dominate the menu, even at breakfast with shrimp Neptune. The appetizers (seared ahi tuna) and mouthwatering seafood salads are well-presented and famous, award-winning clam chowder is creamy, thick and swimming with chunks of clam. Bouillabaisse, crab and shrimp au gratin, grilled or baked oysters, whole Dungeness crab, USDA Choice steaks and much more are available at dinner. There is live music year round in the lounge at this Depoe Bay classic!

Restaurant Beck
2345 S Hwy 101   541/765-3220
(See detailed listing with Whale Cove Inn)

Thai Bay
250 SE Hwy 101   541/765-2497
Lunch, Dinner: Thurs-Tues   Facebook
Inexpensive to moderate

Big flavors are served in this small restaurant. Appetizers, curries and noodle dishes are particularly delicious. Thai cuisine can be somewhat spicy; not to worry if you prefer less heat as the spice level can be adjusted accordingly between mild and extra hot. Service is very pleasant, the restaurant is spotless and the owners are super friendly.

Tidal Raves Seafood Grill
279 NW Hwy 101   541/765-2995
Lunch, Dinner: Daily   tidalraves.com
Moderate

Since its opening in 1990, the hallmarks of Tidal Raves have been consistently good seafood dishes and outstanding service. The menu features tasty starters, housemade soups (clam or smoked salmon chowder, spinach oyster bisque, black bean or Manhattan-style shrimp), classic seafood salads, enticing entrees and more. A sampling of the menu includes udon noodles with seared sea scallops; crab casserole; mixed platter of shrimp, mahi mahi and oysters; pasta with seafood and choice of sauce; and red curry barbecued shrimp. The menu is beefed-up at lunch with sandwiches (snapper po' boy or smoked pork loin) and grilled ribeye steak at dinner. Arrive early as the place is always packed.

Tradewinds Charters

118 Hwy 101   541/765-2345, 800/445-8730
Prices vary   tradewindscharters.com

Depoe Bay carries the title of Whale Watching Capital of the Oregon Coast with prime time viewing December through January and March through May during annual migrations. Excursions are informative and fun for the family (practice shouting "Thar she blows!" beforehand); one- and two-hour trips available. Tradewinds is the oldest charter company on the West Coast and offers a variety of fishing trips (bottom, salmon, tuna, halibut). Some excursions include setting crab pots along the way and vary between four hours and a full day.

Whale Cove Inn

2345 S Hwy 101   541/765-4300, 800/628-3409
Expensive   whalecoveinn.com

This is a very special, sumptuous bed and breakfast inn! Guests enjoy fantastic vistas of the Pacific Ocean from private balconies. This property includes seven signature suites, plus a three-bedroom premier suite and features walk-in showers, patios with hot tubs and continental breakfast. Classy in-house **Restaurant Beck** (541/765-3220, restaurantbeck.com) competes neck and neck with the amazing view. The evening's gourmet fare might be pork belly, halibut, pork brisket or some such local, in-season preparation. For a special occasion, splurge on the five- or seven-course tasting menu for your entire party.

ELSIE

Camp 18 Restaurant

42362 Hwy 26   503/755-1818, 800/874-1810
Breakfast, Lunch, Dinner: Daily   camp18restaurant.com
Moderate

If you're on the way to or from the north coast along Highway 26, you've probably spotted this roadside compound at milepost 18. The impressive log cabin restaurant and adjacent **Old Time Logging Museum** are the dreams of **Gordon Smith** who built the place in the early 1970s and still operates it with the help of next-generation family. The hand-carved double-door entry is made of 4½-inch thick old-growth fir; the massive fireplaces are fashioned from 50 tons of local rock and the 85-foot ridge pole in the central dining room weighs in at 25 tons and contains 5,600 board feet of lumber. The plates match in scale, piled high with comfort food for logger-type appetites for breakfast, lunch and dinner. You'll pick up some logging lingo from the menu headings; for example, choker setters, riggin' boss and hot deck. If your sweet tooth needs a fix, the gigantic homemade cinnamon rolls are just the thing!

FLORENCE

1285 Restobar

1285 Bay St   541/902-8338
Lunch, Dinner: Daily   1285restobar.com
Moderate

San Francisco-style Italian cuisine is served at this family-friendly trattoria in Old Town. Select a table inside or on the relaxing outside patio (seasonal). Pizza and pasta are the mainstays, even better when made with San Marzano tomatoes or locally-made sweet Italian sausage. If you're not in the mood for Italian fare, grilled meats and seafood are an option. The selection of early dinner specials changes weekly and prime rib is served every Wednesday.

BJ's Ice Cream Parlor

1441 Bay St   541/902-7828
2930 Hwy 101   541/997-7286
Daily: 10-10   Facebook

Most communities have a local ice cream parlor; Florence has two. One location is in Old Town, a delightful stop for a dish or cone while you're wandering around the waterfront. The second location (also the ice cream-making locale) is on the north end of town, an easy turn off Highway 101 for a quick pick-me-up when you're on the road. Scoops are 14.2% butterfat, come in 48 hard-to-resist flavors

Florence

R CLAM CHOWDER

A visit to the Oregon coast just isn't complete without a steaming, hot bowl of clam chowder. Perhaps my first "go to" for this treat would be **Gracie's Sea Hag Restaurant and Lounge** (58 N Hwy 101, Depoe Bay, 541/765-2734). Other worthy choices:

Baked Alaska (1 12th St, Astoria; 503/325-7414)

Bay House (5911 SW Hwy 101, Lincoln City; 541/996-3222)

Bell Buoy of Seaside (1800 S Roosevelt Dr, Seaside; 503/738-6357)

Bridgewater Ocean Fresh Fish House (1297 Bay St, Florence; 541/997-1133)

Cafe on Hawk Creek (4505 Salem Ave, Neskowin; 503/392-4400)

Canyon Way Bookstore & Restaurant (1216 Canyon Way, Newport; 541/265-8319)

Driftwood Restaurant & Lounge (179 N Hemlock St, Cannon Beach; 503/436-2439)

Firehouse Grill (841 Broadway St, Seaside; 503/717-5502)

The Fish Peddler at Pacific Oyster (5150 Oyster Dr, Bay City; 503/377-2323)

Fishtails Cafe (3101 Ferry Slip Road, Newport; 541/867-6002)

Josephson's Smokehouse (106 Marine Dr, Astoria; 503/325-2190)

Luna Sea Fish House and Village Fishmonger (153 NW Hwy 101, Yachats; 541/547-4794)

Mo's (195 Warren Way, Cannon Beach; 503/436-1111; 860 SW 51st St, Lincoln City; 541/996-2535; 122 1st St, Otter Rock; 541/765-2442; 622 SW Bay Blvd, Newport; 541/265-2979; 1436 Bay St, Florence; 541/997-2185)

Norma's Seafood & Steak (20 N Columbia, Seaside; 503/738-4331)

Ona Restaurant and Lounge (131 Hwy 101 N, Yachats; 541/547-6627)

Pelican Pub & Brewery (33180 Cape Kiwanda Dr, Pacific City; 503/965-7007)

Rising Star Cafe (92 Rorvik St, Wheeler; 503/368-3990)

Spinners Seafood, Steak & Chophouse (29430 Ellensburg Ave, Gold Beach; 541/247-5160)

Sportsmen's Cannery & Smokehouse (182 Bayfront Loop, Winchester Bay; 541/271-3293; offered in summer only)

Tidal Raves Seafood Grill (279 NW Hwy 101, Depoe Bay; 541/765-2995)

Tom's Fish & Chips (240 N Hemlock St, Cannon Beach; 503/436-4301)

Tony's Crab Shack & Seafood Grill (155 1st St SE, Bandon; 541/347-2875)

(plus yogurt and sugar-free ice cream) and are also used in refreshing floats and malts.

Bridgewater Ocean Fresh Fish House and Zebra Bar

1297 Bay St   541/997-1133
Lunch, Dinner: Wed-Mon   bridgewaterfishhouse.com
Moderate

The establishment's name is a mouthful and that's what you'll get at this Old Town eclectic dining house. Eclectic more in decor than menu, the African-themed bar with zebra-striped chairs is a fun setting. Seafood is definitely the order of the day, though "land" options are available, too. Choosing becomes a bit problematic with chowder, cioppino, crab and salmon cakes, mussels, clams, fish and chips, various fish entrees and seafood sides, red meat and fowl menu items; vegan and vegetarian options, too.

Driftwood Shores Resort & Conference Center

84416 1st Ave   541/997-8263, 800/422-5091
Moderate to very expensive   driftwoodshores.com

Uninterrupted sandy beaches are the main attraction at this hotel — the only oceanfront hotel in the Florence area. All rooms have oceanfront views and a balcony, deck or patio. Most guest rooms contain a full kitchen; mini-refrigerators and microwaves are furnished in standard rooms. **Surfside**, the moderately priced on-site restaurant, is open daily for breakfast, lunch and dinner. This is casual fine dining with plenty of local and classic choices at each meal. If you are hankering for beef, garlic- and rosemary-roasted prime rib is served on Friday evenings. Steaks, meatloaf, pork, chicken and lamb dishes are always offered. Event and banquet rooms with full-service catering are also available.

Edwin K Bed & Breakfast

1155 Bay St   541/997-8360, 800/833-9465
Moderate   edwink.com

Area pioneer William Kyle built this 1914 Sears Craftsman home. It is now a charming bed and breakfast accented with fine furnishings and antiques; there are six guest rooms with private bathrooms in the main building. A separate apartment with a full kitchen and living room accommodates up to four guests (breakfast on your own). **Laurie and Marv VandeStreek** prepare and serve a five-course gourmet breakfast to house guests in the dining room.

Kitchen Klutter
1258 Bay St   541/997-6060
Daily: 9:30-5:30   Facebook

This well-arranged shop features kitchen gadgets, tableware and items to turn your home kitchen into a gourmet showplace. Bath products, gifts and other fun and unique items round out the appealing merchandise.

La Pomodori Ristorante
1415 7th St   541/902-2525
Lunch: Tues-Fri; Dinner: Tues-Sat   lapomodori.com
Moderate

You can't go wrong at this fine Italian restaurant. Start with the garlic onion cheese bread as you peruse the expansive menu. Pasta dishes include prawns, seafood, pork, chicken, sausage, Italian vegetables and rich cream or tomato sauces. Ribeye steaks are well-seasoned; other meats and seafood are grilled or prepared as picattas, scaloppinis, marsalas or with special sauces and ingredients. Appetizing sandwiches (Cubano, baked pastrami), soups, hearty salads and specials are served at lunch. Reservations accepted.

Lighthouse Inn
155 Hwy 101   Pets   541/997-3221, 866/997-3221
Inexpensive   lighthouseinn-florence.com

You'll find good value and friendly hosts at the Lighthouse Inn. While there have been sales and renovations to this property over time, the inn has been one family or another's venture since the 1930s (originally the Hotel Ragan). What endures is the location in the heart of town. Choose your accommodation (all non-smoking) from basic rooms to a family suite with kitchenette, games and other creature comforts. Speaking of creatures, some rooms are pet-friendly.

Little Brown Hen Cafe

435 Hwy 101
Breakfast, Lunch: Daily
Inexpensive

541/902-2449
Facebook

   Newly remodeled and voted by locals as serving the best breakfasts for miles around, the Little Brown Hen continues to do a bang-up job. Pop in for breakfast anytime. There's no skimping on biscuits and gravy, many egg incarnations, pancakes, Belgian waffles and French toast of several varieties. Lunchtime brings clam chowder, chili and other soups, salads, seafood dishes, burgers and moist pressure-fried (broasted) chicken. Tasty hand-sliced potatoes, covered with a secret seasoned-flour mixture and then deep fried, are referred to as "chirps."

ELK IN SIGHT

Elk viewing has become very popular, and resident Roosevelt elk (also called Wapiti and Olympic elk) can be seen year round in the coastal and Cascade ranges of the Pacific Northwest. There are certain times and places where viewing is better. Perhaps the best month is September, when bulls are bugling and breaking brush with their antlers to impress cows and intimidate their rivals. Morning and evening are the best viewing times. Several viewing areas offer ideal opportunities to observe Oregon elk (ouroregoncoast.com):

Dean Creek Elk Viewing Area: About three miles east of Reedsport, view a herd (at times over 120 head) of Roosevelt elk and other mammals, birds and carnivores. Look for wildlife in marshes and meadows; good interpretive center.

Jewell Meadows Wildlife Area: This one is tucked in the Fishhawk Creek Valley of the coast range, next to the town of Jewell and along a mile-long stretch of Highway 202. Open pastures offer views of some 200 elk.

Lovejoy's Restaurant & Tea Room

195 Nopal St

Tues-Sat: 11-2

Inexpensive to moderate

541/902-0502

lovejoysrestaurant.com

If it's an English-style meal that you desire, try Lovejoy's. For lunch, they offer English pub food like bangers and mash, Cornish pasties, savory sausage rolls, stuffed Dover sole, homemade soups, salads (pear, walnut and blue cheese is excellent), sandwiches and specials. The Royal Tea is a three-course affair with salads, a choice of delectable tea sandwiches (cucumber and cream cheese, bay shrimp and more), scones with Double Devon clotted cream, a petite dessert and your choice of tea. The gift shop is the source for tea (25 kinds), unique tea pots and tea accessories. Hannah and Heather are the amiable mother/daughter team tending to customers; reservations are suggested.

Maple Street Grille

165 Maple St

Lunch, Dinner: Tues-Sat

Moderate

541/997-9811

maplestreetgrille.com

Locals frequent this house with its great service and well-prepared food. The eclectic menu incorporates a few tropical-influenced items on the menu; Maui Wowie chopped salad includes pineapple and bacon with fresh salad ingredients and a PuPu platter includes skewers and lettuce wraps. A changing selection of small plates, salads and homemade soups are yummy. Other favorites include pot roast dinner, burgers, sandwiches and tantalizing pasta dishes. Owner **Elizabeth Stenke** oversees the Maple Street experience.

Sand Master Park

5351 Hwy 101

Seasonal hours

541/997-6006

sandmasterpark.com

For a super memorable ride on the famous Florence dunes, grab a sandboard. If need be, instruction, equipment rental and sales are offered. The only requirements for the thrill of a glide down the hill or hitting the jump ramps are your feet and the desire for fun. The park offers more activities (March through December) sand sculpting, dune buggy tours, themed gardens, games and RV parking.

The Waterfront Depot Restaurant

1252 Bay St
Dinner: Daily
Moderate

541/902-9100
thewaterfrontdepot.com

In a picturesque building that once housed the Mapleton train depot, this unpretentious restaurant has delicious offerings. The informal blackboard menu is appealing and the well-worn wood floors and cozy bar enhance the ambience. Seafood dishes shine, especially oyster Madrid and crab-encrusted halibut. You won't pay a fortune, and you will be treated to freshly-baked garlic French bread. Located on the Siuslaw River — delightful!

GARIBALDI

Garibaldi House Inn & Suites

502 Garibaldi Ave
Inexpensive to moderate

503/322-3338, 877/322-6489
garibaldihouseinn.com

When you're fishing, crabbing, clamming, whale watching, kayaking and such in the area, Garibaldi House can serve as a great place to drop anchor. The 49 rooms and suites are professionally run as a B&B rather than a motel, and offer hearty breakfasts and personal attention to customers' whims. An indoor heated pool, whirlpool, sauna and fitness center will add "ahhhh" to your coastal home away from home. Cookies and coffee, local cheeses and meats, popcorn and other snacks are available 24/7. This is a hidden gem on the north coast!

Pirate's Cove Restaurant

14170 Hwy 101 N
Breakfast: Wed-Sun; Lunch, Dinner: Daily
Moderate to expensive

503/322-2092
piratesonline.biz

The restaurant is situated to view fishing boats on Tillamook Bay, many laden with fresh catch. Perhaps your seafood dinner was on this morning's boat. Pirate's Cove is known for superb oyster stew; dinners and sandwiches are served with a choice of the stew, creamy clam chowder or salad. Steaks are excellent with the option of adding crab, seafood or other toppers. Lunch includes specials from the sea, burgers, sandwiches and salads, with plenty of appetizer choices for lunch or dinner. Breakfast Benedicts and omelets are utterly delightful when made with crab, lobster or prawns. Dressed up pancakes, waffles, egg dishes and hearty biscuits and gravy should keep your motor running for several hours; take time to enjoy a second cup of coffee by the beautiful bay.

GEARHART

Gearhart Grocery
599 Pacific Way
Mon-Sat: 9-6 (Daily in summer)

503/738-7312
gearhartgrocerycatering.com

For more than half of a century, this building has been a community fixture in one form or another. The current full-service grocery store stocks a smattering of everyday necessities and has evolved to become a gourmet market. A wide selection of homemade salads and sandwiches, healthy snacks, natural foods, fresh local choice meats (cut to your preference), homemade pies, fresh produce and a fine assortment of wine and other beverages are stocked. The catering side of the operation handles everything from a casual affair at the beach to an intimate wedding or family gathering. Choices are many and are customized to meet customers' requirements.

Gearhart Ocean Inn
67 N Cottage Ave
Moderate

503/738-7373
gearhartoceaninn.com

A former motor court is now a boutique lodging property with a dozen tastefully restored attached cottages converted into king and queen studio units and one- and two-bedroom suites. Rooms are light and charming and outfitted with gas Franklin stoves, well-equipped kitchenettes or kitchens, luxury linens, modern electronics and über comfortable furniture and beds. Locally-roasted coffee, herbal tea and use of books, DVDs, magazines, cruiser bikes, kites, clam-digging equipment and beach towels are complimentary to guests. The private backyard is designed for relaxation; lodgers may choose to sprawl on Adirondack chairs or warm themselves around the fire pit, and kids have plenty of room to romp. An outdoor gas grill and picnic tables are handy for cookouts. Don your walking shoes and stroll along the historic Ridge Path which offers up-front views of the dunes and Gearhart's historic homes. Well-mannered canines are also welcome; several rooms accommodate dogs and their masters.

Natural Nook Flower Shop

738 Pacific Way   503/738-5332
Seasonal days and hours   seasidenaturalnook.com

Irresistible specialty gifts are tucked here and there into eye-catching displays at this European-style flower shop brimming with plants, blooms and nifty accouterments to outfit any home or beach bungalow. Colorful seasonal flowers, vegetable plants, shrubs and decorative and useful garden art and accessories spill out onto the decks, raised beds and pathways. Each visually appealing vignette can be replicated in your yard or on your deck.

Pacific Crest Cottage

726 Pacific Way   503/738-6560
July-Sept: Daily; Oct-June: Wed-Mon (hours vary)   Facebook

This delightful bungalow is chock-full of large and small antiques, pillows, soaps and lotions, dishes and whatnots at all price points. Owner **Joy Sigler** is quick to welcome her customers and recommend uses for some of the more unusual items. On your way in, you can't miss the cast stone garden seating and decorative outdoor pieces. Authentic Japanese floats are available in sizes from two inches to 20 inches in diameter.

Pacific Way Bakery & Cafe

601 Pacific Way   503/738-0245
Bakery: Thurs-Mon   pacificwaybakery-cafe.com
Cafe: Lunch, Dinner: Thurs-Mon
Moderate

When I was young, my family would spend summertime in Gearhart. We would leave our Portland environs for the low-key, charming, quaint coastal village and embark upon a summer filled with family, friends and activities. The season would start as soon as the school year was finished and end on Labor Day. Gearhart has retained its charm and draws visitors year round. **Lisa and John Allen**'s main street cafe/bakery is a favorite place to eat. Irresistible pizzas are built on handmade crusts. Traditional Italian pies are prepared on a tomato sauce base; Thai chicken, island ham and other varieties are made with specially flavored sauces. Homemade soups, sandwiches and entrees are served at lunch. Dinner starts with a basket of freshly-baked breads and features pizza and full meals from the seasonally-changing menu; ribeye steak, ravioli and lighter fare are a few examples. The cafe's desserts, of course, are fresh from the bakery where they also bake cookies, pastries, savories and assorted breads.

GLENEDEN BEACH

Cavalier Beachfront Condominiums

325 NW Lancer St   541/764-2352, 888/454-0880
Moderate   cavaliercondos.com

Families will love these spacious units with two bedrooms, two baths, fully-equipped kitchens, large living rooms with wood-burning fireplaces and open oceanfront decks. The 1,300-square-foot units are right on the coastline with easy beach access, covered parking, heated indoor swimming pool, two saunas and recreation room with pool and Ping-Pong tables. The large, exceptionally clean beach area gives families lots of room to run and build bonfires and sandcastles.

Salishan Spa & Golf Resort

7760 Hwy 101 N   541/764-2371, 800/452-2300
Moderate to expensive   salishan.com

From the time the lodge at Salishan opened, I have been a frequent guest and great fan of this beautiful property. Founder John Gray sold the resort in 1996, and since then it has survived several reincarnations. Sadly, at the moment it is in need of some tender loving care. The 205

KITE FLYING

The Oregon beaches are certainly a great place for kite flying. Specialty kite shops dot the coastline offering hundreds of colorful kites: traditional, box, sport, trick and soft kites. There are also spinners, banners, flags and streamers of every imaginable design; great fun just to browse.

CANNON BEACH
Kite Factory (307 Fir St, 503/436-0839)
Once Upon a Breeze (240 N Spruce St, 503/436-1112)

LINCOLN CITY
Northwest Winds Kites & Toys (130 SE Hwy 101, 541/994-1004)
Winddriven (1529 NW Hwy 101, 541/996-5483)

NEWPORT
The Kite Company (407 SW Hwy 101, 541/265-2004)

SEASIDE
The Kite Shop (Carousel Mall, 300 Broadway St, 503/739-7016)
Northwest Winds Kites & Toys (19 Broadway St, 503/738-6338)

A number of coastal kite festivals are hosted during the year. You can watch kite-flying experts at the summer and fall kite festivals in Lincoln City. Held in Lincoln City on the beach at the D-River Wayside, the two-day weekend festivals include kite flying demonstrations by experts, free kids' kite-making and some of the most colorful "big" kites in the world! In southern Oregon, Brookings hosts a kite festival the third weekend in July (southernoregonkitefestival.com). The two-day event welcomes some of the world's renowned kite fliers and makers; activities include kite-flying demonstrations and kite-making.

rooms and suites are spread among 21 buildings; many overlook the golf course and forested areas from balconies and patios. Rooms are well appointed, reflecting natural northwest elements with cozy seating areas for winter storm watching. For dinner, the signature dining room offers magnificent views of Siletz Bay and Salishan Spit to go along with fresh seafood and wines from the impressive wine cellars; steaks are also available. The Sun Room starts the day with hearty and light breakfasts and serves lunch and dinner in a family-friendly setting. At the clubhouse, **The Grill** satisfies golfers' appetites with breakfasts, sandwiches, soups, salads and appetizers. A stunning spa, with an array of health and pampering services, is situated on the estuary's edge.

Side Door Café and Eden Hall

6675 Gleneden Beach Loop Road
Lunch, Dinner: Wed-Mon
Moderate

541/764-3825
sidedoorcafe.com

Come with a big appetite; the portions are humongous! **Brooke Price** is a very hands-on person at her popular restaurant, working the floor, supervising the kitchen and making sure that her large facilities at the old Gleneden Brick and Tile Factory are kept in A-1 order. The evening menu features seafood salads and entrees (ribeye steak with oysters, fish, seafood, pork medallions) and also offers a great selection of pastas, quiches, steaks and several vegetarian items. Lunch soups, salads and quesadillas may also be ordered for dinner. Service is pleasant and informed. Adjacent to the cafe, **Eden Hall** (541/764-3826, edenhall.com) is a 200-seat venue for live music and theater as well as private parties, exhibits and weddings (check website for schedule and prices).

GOLD BEACH

Ev's Hi-Tech Auto and Towing/Chevron

29719 Ellensburg Ave
Daily

541/247-7525
evshitechautoandtowing.com

"May I clean your windshield? Check the tires and the oil?" All of this without a prompt? Seems unlikely these days, but when you're motoring through Curry County, fill 'er up at Ev's where courteous assistance is always provided. Additional work includes towing, recovery, lock-out, jumpstart, snow and beach recovery services for autos, RVs and motorcycles. This place is a model for all service stations.

Gold Beach Books
29707 Ellensburg Ave   541/247-2495
Daily: Seasonal hours   oregoncoastbooks.com

You never know what you'll find in a large book shop and **Ted Watkins**' store is no exception. The inventory in the state's second largest bookstore encompasses well over 75,000 new and used books in every category. You're sure to find the latest tome from your favorite authors, classics, self-improvement and how-to books, travel guides and great reads. The Showroom Collection features first edition works, autographed books and rare collectibles. Frequent cultural events highlight local authors, artists, musicians and poets. Swing on by for specialty coffee and baked goods from the coffeehouse.

Indian Creek Cafe
94682 Jerrys Flat Road   541/247-0680
Breakfast, Lunch: Daily   Facebook
Inexpensive

Located at the convergence of Indian Creek and the Rogue River, this small eatery just happens to serve great breakfasts and steaming hot coffee. It's not fancy, but you'll find pancakes and waffles with fruits, berries or pecans and fluffy omelets with hash browns or fried grits. Burgers and sandwiches (served with fries and baked beans, slaw or potato salad), soups, salads and chili are satisfying lunch choices. Enjoy the outdoor deck as weather allows.

Jerry's Rogue Jets and Mail Boats
29985 Harbor Way   541/247-4571, 800/451-3645
Seasonal   roguejets.com
Prices vary

Back in 1895, the only way to deliver mail and freight to communities up the Rogue River was by mail boat. Now, over a century later, a 64-mile trip follows the same route with your jet boat pilot delivering historical tidbits and lore along the way. Go a bit farther and take the exhilarating 80-mile whitewater round-trip excursion. Spend an unforgettable day when you travel 104 miles up and back to the wild section of the Rogue and Blossom Bar Rapids to experience the rugged wilderness and class II to III rapids. Trips include rest stops and lunch (separately priced). Take in abundant wildlife, lodges, breathtaking scenery and be wowed by your pilot's stories, skills and knowledge. Jerry's also transports guests to lodges along the river. Daily departures from May 1 to October 15; museum and gift shop open all year. This is another must-do Oregon adventure.

Nor'Wester Steak & Seafood

10 Harbor Way   541/247-2333
Dinner: Daily   norwesterseafood.com
Moderate

Enjoy harbor sights from the upstairs dining room; there is always activity — boats, seagulls, occasional harbor seals, fishermen and romantic sunsets. This fine dining house serves fresh local catch (as available) in appetizers, chowder, salads and generously portioned entrees, combinations and pastas. Steaks, chops and chicken dishes are equally delicious; add prawns or oysters to a sirloin steak to create a land and sea platter. There is also a full bar, beer and wine selections and menu offerings for the younger set.

Rogue River Lodge at Snag Patch

94966 North Bank Rogue Road   541/247-0101
Inexpensive to expensive   rogueriverlodge.com

Seasonal autumn leaves, ever-changing views of the Rogue River, osprey, falcons, wildlife, gardens and forests form a backdrop to the Rogue River Lodge at Snag Patch. The intimate lodge is perched above the river and is made up of eight units; six suites have river views and two rooms are secluded with views of the creek. A light breakfast is set out each morning in the main building or delivered to guests' rooms upon request. Suite retreats are cozy with gas parlor stoves, sitting rooms and kitchen facilities; most have a private deck with a hot tub.

The spacious Eagle House Suite has three bedrooms, two bathrooms, a full kitchen and outdoor gas grill. A recent overhaul updated the property inside and out, kept the rustic ambience and added modern touches; television and Wi-Fi are standard in each unit.

Spinners Seafood, Steak & Chophouse

29430 Ellensburg Ave   541/247-5160
Dinner: Daily   spinnersrestaurant.com
Moderate

The large, often-full parking lot is your first clue; Gold Beach has a number of good dining spots and Spinners falls into that category. Salads are fresh and entree salads are, indeed, a full meal, especially with the addition of chicken, prawns or oysters. Big burgers (including buffalo) and chicken main dishes are alternatives to seafood, steaks and chops. Seafood specialties may include scampi-style sea scallops, lobster, fresh salmon roasted in leeks or a seafood choice combined with pasta. The dessert menu lists several varieties of pies, cakes and pastries — all homemade and delicious. You won't go away hungry!

Tu Tu' Tun Lodge

96550 North Bank Rogue Road   541/247-6664, 800/864-6357
Moderately expensive   tututun.com

Tu Tu' Tun Lodge has been one of my favorite R&R destinations for many years. This resort is under the very capable management of owner **Kyle Ringer** whose friendly ease and hospitality acumen have made this an award-winning abode. When you go (and you should!), you'll be greeted as a friend as you enter this magical boutique river house, one of the best in the nation. The lodge's immaculate accommodations encompass two houses, two generous suites and 16 rooms, all gorgeously appointed and include top-notch creature comforts. Fabulous breakfasts, lunches and dinners are optional (availability varies by season). I wholeheartedly recommend you experience TTT's gourmet cuisine at least once during your stay (reservations necessary). Every season brings a different perspective of the river and forest from private decks and nicely landscaped outdoor spaces. Travel magazines have named this one of the best small resorts in the world!

HEMLOCK

Bear Creek Artichokes

19659 Hwy 101
Daily: 9-close (seasonal variations)

503/398-5411
bearcreekartichokes.com

You may not have heard of the small unincorporated community of Hemlock, but you may have stopped at or driven past this 20-acre farm about 11 miles south of Tillamook and 18 miles north of Neskowin. Fresh produce (from the farm and throughout the Northwest), a gift shop, farm kitchen (scrumptious strawberry shortcake all summer), espresso drinks, greenhouse, display pond and the perennial crop of artichokes attract visitors. The market stocks preserves and gourmet goods prepared in the farm kitchen and smoked salmon artichoke dip, pesto, hummus, salsa and bruschettas. Customers know they will find fun and unusual fruits and vegetables and fresh, local crab and Netarts Bay oysters. The gorgeous handmade hanging baskets and plants will perk up any yard or porch.

LANGLOIS

Langlois Market

48444 Hwy 101
Mon-Sat: 8-6; Sun: 10-5

541/348-2476
langloismarket.com

Midway between Bandon and Port Orford is a must-stop for world famous hot dogs (some are even named after your author: Gerry's Franks). A secret mustard recipe makes these top dog among hot dog aficionados; sandwiches and burgers are also available. The market is tidy and bright with various stuffed and mounted game animals hanging on the walls and from the rafters, ostensibly keeping an eye on the merchandise. Super-friendly second-generation owner **Jake Pestana** stocks the shelves with staples, beer, local produce, snacks and local grass-fed beef from his brother's ranch. Another must stop just down the road is **The Greasy Spoon** (541/348-2514); this Pestana venture offers home-cooked breakfast and lunch offerings in a rustic, family atmosphere.

Wild Rivers Wool Factory
48443 Hwy 101   541/348-2033
Days and hours vary   wildriverswool.com

Warm hats and scarves, socks, totes, toys and accessories are fashioned in natural hues and a colorful array of bright and pastel shades by more than 60 talented consignees. These quality goods are made with locally produced fibers (sheep, alpaca, mohair and pygora goat, llama and angora rabbit). Versatile wool and wool blend felt are sold by the yard and also made into vests, handbags, bowls and wall art. Knowledgeable and novice felters, spinners, weavers, knitters and crocheters shop here for supplies and materials, including yarns sold in 101-yard skeins in bulky, worsted, sport and lace weights. A unique process wraps aromatic bars of soap with felt, which results in a long-lasting, gently exfoliating product. Sign up for classes in spinning, felting and dying fibers.

LINCOLN CITY

Barnacle Bill's Seafood Market
2174 NE Hwy 101   541/994-3022
Daily: 9:30-5   barnaclebillsseafoodmarket.com

As you pass through town, look for a plume of steam billowing out of massive crab cooking pots. The succulent crustaceans are sold whole, by pieces or picked and ready to devour. Barnacle Bill's shrimp and crab cocktails are superb and so is the service! Owners **Penny and Ron Edmunds** oversee the operation and son **Sean Edmunds** tends the smoker and turns out some of the tastiest smoked salmon around. Other fresh catch makes its way to the counter; convenient Styrofoam coolers are available to tote your delights to the beach or home. No credit cards. When in Cloverdale, check out **Barnacle Bill's Annex** (541/994-3022).

FESTIVALS & FAIRS AT THE COAST

FEBRUARY

Newport Seafood & Wine Festival (Newport, seafoodandwine. com)

APRIL

Astoria Warrenton Crab, Seafood & Wine Festival (Astoria, oldoregon.com)

Wooden Boat Show, Crab Feed, and Ducky Derby (Depoe Bay, depoebaychamber.org/event)

MAY

Azalea Festival (Brookings Harbor, ouroregoncoast.com/ brookings-harbor-guide)

JUNE

Cannon Beach Sandcastle Contest (Cannon Beach, cannonbeach. org/events)

Lincoln City Summer Kite Festival (Lincoln City, oregoncoast.org/ festivals-events)

Waldport Beachcomber Days (Waldport, waldport-chamber.com)

JULY

Curry County Fair (Gold Beach, curryfair.com)

Southern Oregon Kite Festival (Brookings, southernoregon kitefestival.com)

AUGUST

Charleston Seafood Festival (Charleston, charlestonseafood festival.com)

SEPTEMBER

Gold Beach Brew and Art Festival (Gold Beach, goldbeachbrewfest. org)

OCTOBER

Lincoln City Fall Kite Festival (Lincoln City, oregoncoast.org/ festivals-events)

North Coast Seafood Festival (Tillamook, northcoastseafood festival.com)

Bay House

5911 SW Hwy 101   541/996-3222
Dinner: Wed-Sun   thebayhouse.org
Expensive

When **Stephen Wilson** took over the venerable Bay House in 2005, he knew he faced the challenge of keeping its excellent reputation intact. He rose to the test and also added a wine bar and cocktail lounge to the 1930s building which overlooks Siletz Bay. The gourmet menu is a standout on the Oregon Coast and includes seasonal items such as butternut squash ravioli, exquisitely prepared seafood, Piedmontese beef tenderloin and other Northwest tastes. If you'd like the chef to do the decision making, you won't be disappointed with the five-course tasting menu with recommended wine pairings from a superb wine selection. Sublime desserts include crème brûlée with housemade hazelnut biscotti and berry cobbler with a scoop of fresh vanilla ice cream. The adjoining bar features small plates and a three-course, $25 locally-sourced Neighbors to Neighbors dinner menu. Periodic live music is a nice addition. Bay House is one of only two restaurants in Oregon to earn AAA's Four Diamond award!

Christmas Cottage

3305 SW Hwy 101   541/996-2230
Daily: 10-5:30   christmascottage.net

If you're looking for the perfect holiday decoration or a personalized ornament for a special gift, then a visit here may be in order. The store was established in 1974 and is the oldest Christmas store in the state continuously operating under single ownership. Although the shop is open and celebrates Christmas year round, it is a beehive of activity in the weeks leading up to the holiday. In addition to the thousands of ornaments of every theme from around the globe, there are also nutcrackers, cards, figurines and a multitude of seasonal collectibles. Owner **Barbe Jenkins-Gibson** and her personable staff handle every customer service detail offering personalization and suggestions, answering questions, processing telephone orders and wrapping gifts.

The Coho Oceanfront Lodge

1635 NW Harbor Ave   541/994-3684
Inexpensive to very expensive   thecoholodge.com

Coho Oceanfront Lodge is a few blocks off busy Highway 101. This boutique-style hotel is a winning combination of ocean views, service, price and spacious accommodations; 65 spotlessly clean rooms and suites include decks overlooking the Pacific, jetted tubs, luxurious beds, flat-screen TVs and fireplaces. Kids are sure to enjoy the unique suite created with them in mind. One room is furnished with bunk beds, a kid-size table and Wii or Play Station. Other features of the property are a heated indoor pool, sauna, Jacuzzi, on-site spa, continental breakfast and outdoor fire pits. The service-oriented Lee family and staff go out of their way to make guests feel welcome.

The Culinary Center in Lincoln City

801 SW Hwy 101, 4th floor   541/557-1125
Tues-Sat: by reservation   oregoncoast.org/culinary

Executive chef **Sharon Wiest** manages the menu of cooking demonstrations, hands-on classes and wildly popular cook-offs. Joining her are chefs who share a penchant for working with fresh bounty from Oregon's fertile land and waters. Recreational cooking sessions (pasta, seafood) may last one to three hours or all day; multi-day courses may include canning, pickling or delve into one of many ethnic cuisines.

Jennifer Sears Glass Art Studio

4821 SW Hwy 101   541/996-2569
Daily: 10-6   jennifersearsglassart.com

Unleash your artistic bent and create a glass float, paperweight, heart, starfish or bowl. Customers are paired with trained instructors to blow and twirl molten glass in a 2,200-degree "glory hole" until it takes shape. The creative process takes less than an hour, but cooling takes overnight. The artists display and sell stunning large and small glass pieces at the studio and across the street at **Volta Glass Gallery** (4830 SW Hwy 101, 541/996-7600) Wednesday through

Sunday. Reservations are a must for glassblowing activities; hours vary by season and both operations are on hiatus the first two weeks of January.

Looking Glass Inn
861 SW 51st St
Inexpensive to moderate

541/996-3996
lookingglass-inn.com

Siletz Bay and a marvelous easily-accessible beach are in the historic Taft area with restaurants and shops close at hand. This inn is mere steps from the beach with incomparable bay and ocean views. Spacious studios and suites are nonsmoking and furnished with flat-screen TVs and kitchens; one suite is outfitted with a king bed, whirlpool tub and deck. Some one- and two-bedroom suites also include a gas fireplace and living area with sofa bed. Guests receive complimentary continental breakfast each morning. Several rooms are dog-friendly; Fido is sure to enjoy chasing sticks on the beach or playing in the waves.

PREMIUM BEEF

OregonGrassFed (Langlois; 541/260-8969; oregongrassfed. com) is raising and selling 100% premium Oregon grass-fed beef; a healthier, nutritionally-balanced consumer choice. This homegrown business is tended by a descendent of the Sweet clan, one of Oregon's most well-respected families on the south coast. **Joe Pestana**, owner, pays careful attention to "clean" techniques (limited antibiotics and no hormones) in steers that make their way to market. Meats can be purchased online or at several grocery stores in Portland and on the southern coast. If you happen to find yourself midway between Bandon and Port Orford, stop at Langlois Market where brother **Jake Pestana** offers the Gerry's Franks with secret mustard recipe. These treats are also available seasonally at my Salem restaurant, Gerry Frank's Konditorei.

Macadangdangs Reefside Bar & Grill

3521 SW Hwy 101   541/614-0970
Breakfast, Lunch, Dinner: Daily   macadangdangsreefsidebarandgrill.com
Inexpensive and up

Macadangdangs — with a name like that you just know this has to be a fun place for families! The large menu has dang wings, squealer fries (with barbecued pulled pork), a Macadang burger (cheese, bacon, pulled pork and barbecue sauce), housemade soups and wonderful fresh salads. Corned beef is prepared in-house for Reuben sandwiches, and sliced ribeye steak is used for cheesesteak and French dip sandwiches; there's no skimping on fillings. Burgers and sandwiches are messy and sloppy to eat and require both hands and several napkins! The same menu is offered at lunch and dinner with nightly specials Sunday through Thursday. The bar offers microbrews, wines and cocktails with an ocean view.

Nelscott Cafe

3237 SW Hwy 101   541/994-6100
Breakfast, Lunch: Thurs-Mon   Facebook
Inexpensive

Surfers, locals and tourists have this place pegged for really good food and over-sized cups of steaming coffee or hot cocoa. Owner **Don Williams'** menu is full of enticing breakfasts and lunches. Favorites include breakfast poppers (scrambled egg-filled crisp dumplings finished with bacon and creamy gravy), a wipe-out platter, doughnut holes, beignets and weekend-only scones. Menu-staple burgers go beyond basic offerings. Try the peanut butter bacon version with hand-cut fries, chips or pickle chips (a house specialty), or one of several chicken sandwiches or wraps and delicious soups. Seating is on the main floor, loft and dog-friendly patio.

Northwest Winds Kites & Toys

130 SE Hwy 101   541/994-1004
Daily: 10-6   nwwinds.biz

Susan and David Gomberg, experienced kite fliers, have demonstrated their expertise around the country and world; their business is centered on what they love. Their store offers factory-direct pricing on a large selection of kites and supplies, wind decor, banners and other fun items. A second location is in Seaside near the turnaround (19 Broadway St, 503/738-6338); both shops are open until 7 p.m. during the summer.

MANZANITA

Awtrey House
38245 James Road   503/368-5721
Very expensive   awtreyhouse.com

Warm and contemporary, this luxurious two-bedroom bed and breakfast is a Northwest architectural beauty. Situated between Manzanita and Neahkahnie cliffs, it was designed to showcase the capricious Pacific Ocean and seven miles of sandy beach. Private terraces, sumptuous king-sized beds and an inviting living room provide front-row access to the beach and ocean. In-room amenities include complimentary beverages, espresso/coffee makers, an oversized soaking tub, overhead rain shower and modern electronics. Hosts **Peggy and Dennis Awtrey** delight in preparing a full breakfast while Dennis, a former NBA player, captivates guests with stories of his experiences with the Blazers, Sonics and other basketball teams. There is no other inn like this on the Oregon coast.

Big Wave Cafe
822 Laneda Ave   503/368-9283
Breakfast, Lunch, Dinner: Daily   oregonsbigwavecafe.com
Moderate

Carol and Brian Williams make a big deal out of breakfast! Whether you're heading out to catch the big wave or savoring alone time with newspaper in hand, you'll find just-right morning choices (available all day) of daily specials, breakfast burritos, omelets, banana bread with fresh fruit and more. When weekends roll around, out comes the waffle bar with fresh fruit toppings, whipped cream and flavored syrups. Gourmet burgers, sandwiches, wonderful specialty salads and a handful of entrees are offered at lunch. The dinner menu focuses on steaks and seafood. Desserts like marionberry pie, chocolate cake and Bananas Foster are homemade and even better with a scoop of ice cream.

Bread and Ocean

154 Laneda Ave
Breakfast, Lunch: Wed-Sun
Inexpensive

503/368-5823
breadandocean.com

This deli and bakery offers sit-down lunches serving up a variety of salads, sandwiches, deli items, baked goods, breads and desserts all while using local and organic products whenever possible. If it's before 11 a.m., energy-fueling breakfast items can be found in the deli cases with dishes like the frittata and polenta with layers of spongy grains, Tillamook cheddar cheese, scrambled eggs and smoked ham. Specialty bread schedules are found on their website listing all the week's specials. Organic grains and flours, European butter, free-range eggs, organic cinnamon and vanilla are used to create their unbelievably good breads and pastries. They also make organic multigrain, wild yeast sourdough and baguettes every day. The fun part about their deli menu is that you can make anything into a picnic lunch box for just $3.25 extra; this includes your choice of a side salad or soup and a cookie. On a nice day, enjoy patio seating or take your lunch to the beach, just steps away. The bakery fills up fast, especially in the morning when the regulars come for their hot coffee and morning pastry. Whether you are a carnivore, vegetarian or going gluten-free, they have something to satisfy your craving.

Coast Cabins

635 Laneda Ave
Moderate to very expensive

503/368-7113
coastcabins.com

There are coastal cabins, and then there are the accommodations at Coast Cabins. Six private cabins, which provide perfect escapes for those "wanting to get away from it all," are as charming as Manzanita. Units are one or two levels of varying sizes plus a modern ranch cabin.

Tranquil comfort is achieved at this Zen-like property through intimate gardens, relaxing courtyard, cozy fire pit and wooded surroundings. Amenities differ among the quarters, full or convenience kitchens, outdoor jet spas, dry sauna, steam shower and wood or gas barbecues. The spa and modern ranch cabin are the ultimate in relaxation and romance.

The Inn at Manzanita
67 Laneda Ave   503/368-6754
Moderate   innatmanzanita.com

At the end of Manzanita's main avenue of appealing shops is a delightful inn. Four buildings (two to four units per building) are nestled on beautifully landscaped grounds amid coastal pine and spruce trees. Main and cottage building amenities include queen beds, jetted spa tubs, gas fireplaces and wet bars with a refrigerator. The north building is similar, with a captain-style queen bed situated in a curtained nook. Larger units are located in the Manzanita building; some have kitchen facilities. The three-bedroom, two-bathroom penthouse is a home-away-from-home with full kitchen, partial ocean view and full amenities.

Left Coast Siesta
288 Laneda Ave   503/368-7997
Lunch, Dinner: Wed-Sun   leftcoastsiesta.com
Inexpensive

For great Mexican food with a healthy twist, check out **Lynn and Jeff Kyriss**' establishment. Serving hungry customers since 1994, Left Coast has become a traditional "first stop" for visitors returning to the area. Burritos and tacos are assembled with a choice of tortilla, chicken, pork or beef, organic refried or black beans and organic rice, plus veggies and freshly-made salsa available in three heat levels. Enchiladas are prepared with white or blue corn tortillas, one filling and topped with red or green sauce. Portions are large and tasty; kids' menu, too. Left Coast has a unique bar of 100 to 200 hot sauces (hot, hotter, hottest and grab the fire extinguisher!) to sample or purchase.

NEHALEM

Wanda's Cafe

12870 Hwy 101 N
Breakfast, Lunch: Thurs-Tues (daily in summer)
Inexpensive

503/368-8100
wandascafe.com

When you see a waiting line spilling onto the porch of a Nehalem establishment, you know you've arrived at Wanda's! Once you're seated, the quick, personal service is impressive. Wanda's specialties are big breakfasts (served all day), satisfying lunches, daily specials and a fine array of homemade pastries. Outdoor patio seating is great when Oregon's beach weather cooperates. You'll be tempted by glass cases filled with fresh and tasty goodies to take out.

NESKOWIN

Breakers Beach Houses

48060 Breakers Blvd
Moderate and up

503/392-3417
breakersoregon.com

You can't get much closer to the beach than in one of these individually-owned and -decorated townhouses. The location affords unobstructed views of glorious sunsets with long stretches of beach just yards away. Each of the ten homes is tastefully furnished and has three bedrooms and two bathrooms, a wood-burning fireplace, an ocean-facing deck and a completely outfitted kitchen. Check out the seasonal senior discounts for a really good deal.

The Cafe on Hawk Creek

4505 Salem Ave
Breakfast, Lunch, Dinner: Daily
Inexpensive to moderate

503/392-4400
cafeonhawkcreek.com

This perfectly charming cafe is located in the perfectly charming village of Neskowin. Cafe on Hawk Creek is no secret on the Oregon Coast. On any given evening, people are lined up out the door and down the sidewalk of this gourmet bistro. Owners **Genie and Frank Ulrich** have remodeled the 1982 building to make the cozy atmosphere even better. The outdoor deck is a fabulous place to gather with friends on a warm evening. The menu offers many rustic pizzas, all cooked in the wood-fired oven. Other scrumptious offerings are steaks, seafood, pastas, crisp entree salads and homemade soups;

KIDS' ACTIVITIES: THE COAST

ASTORIA
Columbia River Maritime Museum (503/325-2323, crmm.org)

FLORENCE
Oregon Dunes National Recreation Area (541/271-3611, stateparks. com/oregon_dunes)
Sea Lion Caves (541/547-3111, sealioncaves.com)

GARIBALDI
Garibaldi Maritime Museum (503/322-8411, garibaldimuseum.org): mid-March to December

GOLD BEACH
Jerry's Rogue Jets and Mail Boats (800/451-3645, roguejets.com): May to mid-October

NEWPORT
Hatfield Marine Science Center (541/867-0100, hmsc.oregonstate. edu)
Oregon Coast Aquarium (541/867-3474, aquarium.org)

PORT ORFORD
Prehistoric Gardens (541/332-4463, prehistoricgardens.com)

SEASIDE
Seaside Aquarium (503/738-6211, seasideaquarium.com)

TILLAMOOK
Tillamook Cheese Factory (503/815-1300, tillamookcheese.com)
Tillamook Forest Center (503/815-6800, tillamookforestcenter.org): March to December

WARRENTON
High Life Adventures (503/861-9875, highlife-adventures.com): reservations required

plus breads from Rockfish Bakery. There is also a wide selection of Northwest wines and brews.

Neskowin Trading Company and Beach Club Bistro

48880 Hwy 101 S   503/392-3035
Daily: 8-8 (Fri, Sat till 9)   neskowintradingcompany.com

This attractive gourmet market has become a cornerstone of the Neskowin community. Owners **Kim and Mike Herbal** have just completed a two-year remodel. As a result, they have turned a 1984 building into a welcoming village market offering necessities and gourmet delights to vacationers and local patrons. You can make your selection from the tasty sandwiches, salads, quiches, fresh-baked pastries, deli treats and espresso bar. Ask Mike for help in selecting a great bottle of Northwest wine or one from Italy, France and California; seasonal wine tastings. The latest addition to the market is the **Beach Club Bistro**. Choose from a delicious menu of foods with an international flair. Popular choices are calamari with sweet and hot Thai sauce, handmade pot stickers and fresh local fish. The Bistro received "Best of the Coast" award for clam chowder the past three years. Also of note is the art gallery and studio just behind the market where Kim shows her beautiful artwork in oils; plus watercolors, acrylics and pastels for sale by local artists.

NETARTS

The Schooner

2065 Netarts Bay Blvd   503/815-9900
Lunch, Dinner: Daily; Breakfast: Fri-Sun   theschooner.net
Moderate

The Schooner has been a Netarts fixture for over 60 years. A long table dominates the inviting dining room, and glass windbreaks shield the outdoor deck from coastal breezes. The menu leans toward local ocean and farm products and wood-fired gourmet pizzas. A recent chef's choice creation included foraged mushrooms, leeks, spinach, Fontina and Romano cheese, clams and smoked oysters from Netarts

Bay. The lounge serves classic and contemporary cocktails and area microbrews with live music on special occasions.

NEWPORT

April's at Nye Beach
749 NW 3rd St   541/265-6855
Dinner: Wed-Sun   aprilsatnyebeach.com
Moderate

April and Kent Wolcott's Northwest-fresh farm-to-fork dinner house is a longtime favorite. Their variations of Mediterranean dishes are uniformly excellent. Breads and desserts are homemade; flowers, produce and herbs are grown on the Wolcott's Buzzard Hill Farm and meats and seafood are selected for seasonal availability. That being said, a sample of offerings may include linguine with clams, chicken piccata, baseball cut sirloin or New York steak finished with gorgonzola brandy butter. Chef April assembles interesting nightly specials; Kent tends to the front of the house.

Bridie's Irish Faire
715 NW 3rd St   541/574-9366
Daily: 11-6   bridiesirishfaire.com

All things Ireland! Bridie's is a treasure trove of Irish jewelry, apparel and gifts. The shop is owner **Susan Jeanne Spencer**'s celebration of Irish traditions. She also organizes and accompanies small group pilgrimages to Ireland, Scotland and elsewhere in the world; check the website for tour dates.

Cafe Stephanie
411 NW Coast St   541/265-8082
Breakfast, Lunch: Daily   Facebook
Moderate

Hearty breakfasts are served in an unpretentious building. Quiches, waffles, burritos and delicious homemade buttermilk pancakes are on the breakfast menu and priced right; kids' breakfasts are served with a freshly-baked scone. Lunch choices include soups, chowder, salads, sandwiches (whole or half) and fish tacos. Outdoor tables expand the limited inside seating capacity; it's always a good sign when locals fill the seats!

Canyon Way Restaurant

1216 SW Canyon Way
Lunch: Mon-Sat; Dinner: Fri
Moderately expensive

541/265-8319
Facebook

Dozens of places along the coast offer crab cakes with a variety of ingredients and presentations, but none better than those served by **Roguey and Ed Doyle** at their bookstore/restaurant. These Dungeness delicacies are just the right size and consistency, containing a great deal of crab meat. Homemade soups are another customer favorite; choices may include chicken curry, mushroom, cream of roasted garlic, New England-style clam chowder or soup du jour. Oyster or shrimp po' boys, Szechuan chicken pasta or fresh spinach salad are also good. Custardy bread pudding is made with homemade bread and topped with warm caramel rum sauce; rich and unforgettable!

SPRING 2016 OPENING

Announcing a spring 2016 opening in Cannon Beach! **Public Coast Brewing Co.** (264 E 3rd St, 503/436-0285, Facebook) will occupy the space of the former Lumberyard Rotisserie & Grill. A fully-operational brewery, it will serve up tasty original craft beers and great food in a top-quality family-friendly environment. Named for Oregon's 363 miles of open, publicly-owned coastline, the brewery will reflect that spirit of inclusion, with beers that appeal to both craft and non-craft beer fans. The lineup will list house-brewed craft beer and root beer along with a good selection of other carefully selected beers on tap. A coastal Northwest-inspired menu beyond the typical pub grub will feature locally-caught fish and chips, hand-pattied beef burgers, homemade sausages and fresh salads. Quick counter service will keep things moving; other features include indoor seating (seasonal patio), a wrap-around bar and large windows that look onto the brewing process.

Captain's Reel Deep Sea Fishing

343 SW Bay Blvd   541/265-7441, 800/865-7441
Year round   captainsreel.com

Grab your fishing license, sack lunch, rain gear and sunscreen, and head to Newport's waterfront to board one of Captain's fleet (six to 26 passengers). Tackle and hot coffee are provided onboard. Depending on season and luck, you might pull in a prize halibut, albacore tuna, salmon or lingcod; squid and bottom fishing are options. Most trips offer a crab combo opportunity. Excursions range from five to 18 hours with prices varying accordingly; fish filleting is available on the dock.

Elizabeth Street Inn

232 SW Elizabeth St   541/265-9400, 877/265-9400
Moderate to expensive   elizabethstreetinn.com

Expect to be pampered at the Elizabeth Street Inn: cozy fireplaces, comfortable robes, hot breakfast buffet, private balconies and an indoor saltwater swimming pool. All rooms face the beach and some have an extra window facing north toward Yaquina Head Lighthouse. Choose from several accommodation types: queen, king or king Jacuzzi rooms and a spacious family suite; a limited number of dog-friendly rooms are also available. In addition to the complimentary breakfast, fresh cookies are set out in the lobby each evening and smoked salmon chowder is a hit on cool, off-season afternoons.

Fishtails Cafe

3101 Ferry Slip Road   541/867-6002
Breakfast, Lunch: Daily   fishtailscafe.com
Inexpensive to moderate

Plenty of fish tales are surely told at Fishtails, a local hangout that dishes up fishermen-size meals for breakfast and lunch. The house is not fancy, but you'll be welcomed warmly and the food is good; prices are easy on the wallet, too. As expected, seafood is often a feature with various egg dishes or choose pancakes, biscuits and gravy or homemade cinnamon rolls. The sauteed marionberry

French toast, though, takes the prize with lightly sweetened cream cheese stuffed between two pieces of homemade bread and topped with homemade berry sauce. Lunch also turns to seafood options, burgers, sandwiches and slumgullion (original recipe clam chowder).

Georgie's Beachside Grill

744 SW Elizabeth St   541/265-9800
Breakfast, Lunch, Dinner: Daily   georgiesbeachsidegrill.com
Inexpensive to moderately expensive

On the same property as Newport's **Hallmark Resort** (hallmarkinns. com/Newport) is Georgie's Beachside Grill, a favorite amongst locals and visitors. Georgie's combines a casual feel with a sophisticated look for an ambience to suit any mood. Like the hotel, the grill is also very family-friendly, treating your little ones with "Georgie's Money" to pick something out of the treasure chest upon leaving. The panoramic ocean views from the restaurant are a treasure in themselves. This beachside grill offers authentic northwest coastal cuisine. Menu options include dishes in their simplest form such as traditional bacon and eggs, fresh salmon and halibut, juicy steaks and burgers to more spiced up entrees like the Diablo seafood pasta. The kids' menu is one of the most expansive found in Newport. Georgie's not only offers great food, but a full bar as well, and has been voted for the best romantic evening in Newport.

Inn at Nye Beach

729 NW Coast St   541/265-2477, 800/480-2477
Moderate   innatnyebeach.com

This three-story earth-friendly oceanfront property has many innovative energy-saving alternatives. You'll even find some of the old Viking Cottage timbers recycled into the building. The 20 units offer balconies and gas fireplaces, Wi-Fi, French press coffee makers, microwaves and refrigerators. Sustainable custom furnishings, an advanced plumbing system and other conservation practices were employed during construction. A stairway provides access to Nye Beach.

COASTAL HISTORY

The **Lincoln County Historical Society** (oregoncoasthistory. org) of Newport is working to bring the history of the Oregon Coast alive. In the same building as the historical society offices, the **Burrows House Museum** (545 SW 9th St, 541/265-7509) began as a Queen Anne Victorian residence before functioning as both a boarding house and funeral parlor. It was relocated before its present tenure as a museum. Current exhibits feature "Cars: Motoring the Coast" and "Coastal Curiosities." (Thursday to Sunday, donation suggested.)

Down on the bayfront, overlooking Port Dock 5, the **Pacific Maritime & Heritage Center** (333 SE Bay Blvd, 541/265-7509) opened in 2013. This building was previously a private residence and most recently operated as Gracie's at Smuggler's Cove. It is now a museum and interactive center featuring maritime-related exhibits and arts. (Thursday to Sunday, nominal.)

La Maison Bakery & Cafe

315 SW 9th St   541/265-8812
Breakfast, Lunch: Daily   lamaisoncafe.com

The attractive green cottage sets the stage for what's inside. Fare is distinctly French: eggs Sardou, Chambord crepes, Provence omelets, croissant sandwiches and more. *Tres délicieux* gourmet desserts are presented on fused-glass plates; local, organically-grown produce and eggs are used in all dishes.

Local Ocean Seafoods

213 SE Bay Blvd   541/574-7959
Daily   localocean.net
Moderate

Seafood is always best fresh — and it's really fresh at this place. Products in the cases are tagged with specific information about the catch, the name of the boat and how and where it was caught. Only high-grade products are purchased, and the flavors show this advantage. Fish tacos, tuna kabobs, tuna wraps, plus salmon, halibut and crab are popular choices. (Only the French fries are deep-fried here.) Owner **Laura Anderson** runs a spotless restaurant with an open kitchen; as weather allows, roll-up glass doors are opened to bring the fresh ocean air into the dining area. The menu emphasizes a fine selection of seafood, including oyster shooters, steamer clams, Thai-style mussels, Dungeness crab and fishwives' stew (in a garlic and herb broth). A few non-fish options, kids' selections and homemade ice cream are also available.

Made in Oregon
342 SW Bay Blvd   541/574-9020
(See detailed listing with Made in Oregon, Portland)

Nana's Irish Pub
613 NW 3rd St   541/574-8787
Lunch, Dinner: Daily   nanasirishpub.com
Moderate

Traditional Irish fare here! Shepherd's pie, corned beef and cabbage, Irish beer-battered fish and chips and bread pudding made with Irish whiskey are the order of the day at this family friendly stop. You won't go wrong with a Bunratty Reuben or Cu Chulainn chicken sandwich, and for good measure, a few American favorites are offered, too. The outdoor patio is pleasant on warm summer days (and pet-friendly) and weekend entertainment draws a crowd. Of course, it wouldn't be a pub without stouts, lagers and ales; Nana's has imported beers on tap, wine and a full bar.

Oregon Coast Aquarium
2820 SE Ferry Slip Road   541/867-3474
Daily: 10-5 (9-6 in summer)   aquarium.org
Reasonable

Newport's aquarium is a world-class center of excellence for ocean literacy and plays an active role in conservation, education and marine animal rehabilitation efforts. The 39-acre facility features indoor and outdoor exhibits that earn the aquarium consistent recognition as one of the top ten aquariums in the country. International notoriety was earned when it hosted Keiko, the orca whale that starred in the movie *Free Willy* during his rehabilitation from 1996 to 1998. After Keiko departed for Iceland the aquarium was transformed into the iconic Passages of the Deep gallery, which features three immersed tunnels. Visitors have 360-degree views of the three marine habitats found off Oregon's shores, complete with thousands of fish and over 100 sharks. Fun and educational opportunities include seal, sea lion and giant octopus encounters, overnight stays to sleep with the sharks, private parties and more. Over 250 species call the facility home as well as various exhibits (sandy and rocky environs, sea otters, seals and sea lions, sea nettle jellies and a seabird aviary); many are hands-on. A full-service cafe offers food and beverages for visitors. Before you depart, browse the aquarium's gift shop; books, colorful posters and DVDs about the marine life, plus art, toys, clothing and ocean-themed gifts are displayed.

OSU Hatfield Marine Science Center

2030 SE Marine Science Dr   541/867-0226
Daily: 10-5 (Thurs-Mon: 10-4 in winter)   hmsc.oregonstate.edu/visitor
Free

An ocean-related educational experience awaits you and your children. The visitor center (a Coastal Ecosystem Learning Center) is the public wing of Oregon State University's Mark O. Hatfield Marine Science Center and is managed by Oregon Sea Grant. This fascinating operation is part aquarium and part ocean laboratory. Learn about "habitat snatchers," aquatic invasive species (such as Asian clams and zebra mussels) that are an environmental threat to native wildlife, tropical fish research, earthquakes, tsunamis and more. Engaging exhibits include getting up close and personal with an octopus and other live marine animals, interactive wave tanks, plus games and puzzles that demonstrate marine science concepts. Request a film to view in the auditorium and visit the well-stocked gift shop with ocean and natural science-related books, videos and the like. Check the website for feeding and event schedules.

Panini Bakery

232 NW Coast St
Daily: 7-7

541/265-5033
Facebook

What a good find for quick and casual lunches of soups, sandwiches and pizzas. Breads are out-of-this-world, especially the sourdough, and sweet and savory pastries are addicting. The pizzas are excellent and sold whole or by the slice. The Nye Beach location is on a charming street; opt for outdoor seating for tranquil coastal ambience while sipping organic coffee and munching on cookies or equally delicious baked goods. Get the bread while it is fresh!

Saffron Salmon

859 SW Bay Blvd
Lunch, Dinner: Thurs-Tues
Moderate

541/265-8921
saffronsalmon.com

Exceptional "from-scratch" cooking lends itself to exceptional entrees and desserts. Wild salmon takes a starring role in salads and entrees and in a sandwich with saffron aioli on the lunch menu. Local farms provide lamb, beef and chicken; produce is purchased at the seasonal farmers market and local fishermen supply the restaurant with in-season crab and seafood. Warm marionberry cobbler with ice cream is the signature dessert. Reservations suggested; seasonal hours in November.

Sylvia Beach Hotel

267 NW Cliff St
Moderate

541/265-5428, 888/795-8422
sylviabeachhotel.com

Sylvia Beach Hotel is the most unusual bed and breakfast. Built a century ago, it opened as the New Cliff House and later became Hotel Gilmore before current owners **Sally Ford** and **Goody Cable** and friends turned it into a novel beachside 21-room B&B with rooms furnished and named after renowned authors (Agatha Christie, Dr. Seuss, J.K. Rowling, F. Scott Fitzgerald). Room types are categorized as classic, bestseller or novel (all have private baths) and are designed for relaxation, reading and writing. No TVs, Wi-Fi, telephones or other tech conveniences here. Guests and non-guests are in for an informal and relaxed treat at **Tables of Content** where the Northwest cuisine dinner menu changes daily. The format is a bit bizarre; when dinner reservations are made, diners are asked which of four entrees they prefer (seafood, poultry, meat or vegetable). Seating is family-style with six or eight at a table; diners may enter into fun ice-breaker games to get acquainted with their tablemates. There is one seating each evening (6 p.m. during the winter and 7 p.m. on weekends, during the summer and holidays). Meals include tasty appetizers, a fresh salad, vegetable and starch with the main course, dessert and coffee or tea (beer and wine are available). Group luncheons and special occasions are accommodated.

The Whaler
155 SW Elizabeth St   541/265-9261, 800/433-9444
Moderate   whalernewport.com

The 73-room Whaler has great Pacific views from guest room balconies. Various units are equipped with fireplaces, wet bars and microwaves; all rooms offer Internet access and refrigerators. A continental breakfast is complimentary to guests with hot beverages and fresh popcorn available throughout the day. Walk along the beach, visit Nye Beach or Old Town's excellent restaurants and shops or enjoy the indoor pool, spa and exercise facility. Five comfortable three- and four-bedroom homes with ocean views are also available. Owner/host **John Clark** operates a first-class establishment and is also one of the strongest supporters of all manner of good causes on the Coast.

OCEANSIDE

Roseanna's Cafe
1490 Pacific Ave   503/842-7351
Breakfast, Lunch, Dinner: Daily   roseannascafe.com
Moderate

Roseanna's Cafe is nestled in a distinctive 1900s building with siding weathered gray by the elements. Large windows frame evening sunsets, tidal activity and Three Arch Rocks. A bowl of steaming clam chowder and homemade berry cobbler are lunch favorites, or choose from full breakfast, lunch and dinner menus and daily specials like spicy seafood pasta. Actual hours vary by season.

OTIS

Otis Cafe
1259 Salmon River Hwy   541/994-2813
Breakfast, Lunch, Dinner: Daily   otiscafe.com
Inexpensive

This, my friends, is a quintessential stop about five miles northeast of Lincoln City. The tiny, funky roadside diner is a must-visit for down-home cooking, especially breakfast. Toast is a big deal here; it is made from homemade black molasses bread. Loaves of black molasses, sourdough and pumpkin bread are available for purchase. Eggs and such are served with or without meats and with homemade hash browns (shredded baked russet potatoes). Sourdough or buttermilk pancakes and waffles are also popular; the kids' pancake version is made in the shape of a teddy bear face. With only a half-dozen small tables, be ready to wait in line; outside seating available in warmer months. Hot and cold sandwiches, burgers, soups, salads and creamy clam chowder welcome a new wave of midday diners. Soup or salad, starch, vegetables and, of course, homemade bread accompany the comfort food dinners.

OTTER ROCK

Inn at Otter Crest
301 Otter Crest Dr   541/765-2111, 800/452-2101
Inexpensive to moderate   innatottercrest.com

Decades ago, T. Harry Banfield, a major player in Portland's leadership during the mid-20th century, was among the first to build a vacation home at Otter Crest. Eventually the home was sold as Banfield spent more time as chairman of the Oregon State Highway Commission. The property was developed and continues as The Inn at Otter Crest, a vacation destination. These days some units are for rent, owned by one or more owners or have become timeshare properties. Forests, waterfalls and wildlife surround this 27-building complex with abundant attractions and activities to keep everyone occupied for days. Wall-to-wall windows and private balconies provide spectacular views from every guest room and vantage point. The on-site restaurant serves up seasonal dishes in the panoramic ocean-view dining room.

PACIFIC CITY

Ben and Jeff's Burgers and Tacos
33260 Cape Kiwanda Dr   503/483-1026
Breakfast: Sat, Sun; Lunch, Dinner: Daily   benandjeffs.com
Inexpensive

The name of this business aptly describes the menu. Burgers are juicy and tacos and burritos are filled with pork, chicken, halibut or prawns (deep fried or grilled); if you prefer fish and chips, they are also available. Delicious breakfast burritos are a new addition to the listings. In the liquid department, there are sodas, slushies, beers and margaritas. **Ben Johnson** and **Jeff Mollencop** also operate **Moment Surf Company** (503/483-1025, momentsurfco.com), a small surf shop where they rent and sell surfing and water-related beach activity gear and the latest surf-inspired clothing and accessories.

Cottages at Cape Kiwanda
33000 Cape Kiwanda Dr   503/965-7920, 866/571-0605
Expensive   yourlittlebeachtown.com

Pacific City is home to Oregon's fleet of dory fishing vessels. It is quite a sight to watch the flat-bottom boats rush the waves on the way out to fertile fishing. The Cottages at Cape Kiwanda have a catbird seat to the dory activity. This beautiful property consists of 18 two- and three-bedroom fractionally-owned cottages, also available for nightly rental. The cozy units are outfitted with inviting contemporary furnishings; master bedrooms are situated to garner ocean views.

Amenities and special features include heated bathroom floor tiles, gas fireplaces and barbecues, beachfront decks and patios, covered parking and much more. The on-site concierge is friendly and helpful in locating massage and spa services, restaurants, special activities and filling special requests.

Delicate Palate Bistro

35280 Brooten Road
Dinner: Wed-Sun
Moderate to expensive

503/965-6464, 866/567-3466
delicatepalate.com

In contrast to the rather ironic name, the bar conjures up a he-man half-pound natural burger served on ciabatta bun with housemade aioli and tomato ketchup. Other interesting choices include duck

THE HUNT IS ON

Lincoln City's glass float project, **Finders Keepers** (oregoncoast. org/finders-keepers), began in 1997 when a local artist thought it was an interesting way to launch the new millennium. The **Lincoln City Visitor and Convention Bureau** (800/452-2151, 541/996-1274) continues this promotion annually, running from mid-October to Memorial Day with brilliantly-colored, hand-crafted, signed and numbered glass floats being placed along the 7½ miles of public beach in Lincoln City, from the Roads End area to Siletz Bay area. They put out the number of floats reflected by the year — so 2,001 floats placed in 2001; 2,015 placed in 2015, etc. If you find one, you keep it!

Floats may be found during daylight hours above the high tide line and below the beach embankment. No floats will be found in or on the cliffs. Always be aware of beach safety when treasure hunting; never turn your back on the ocean! No "drops" occur during storms. Occasionally, extra pieces of glass art are hidden on the beaches for beachcombers to find. Special drops can include any combination of glass floats, sand dollars, crabs or starfish. When you find a float, call the Visitor and Convention Bureau to register your float. You will receive a certificate of authenticity and information about the artist who crafted your float.

carnitas tostados, braised baby back ribs with marionberry barbecue sauce and an apple and gorgonzola salad. Superb bistro dinner choices include Asian seafood bouillabaisse in coconut curry broth, herb-crusted halibut, New York steak, oven-roasted rack of lamb and delightful seasonal selections; irresistible desserts are made in-house. Rare vintage wines and specialty drinks are served in both the bistro and bar. **Patt and Geoff Williams, Sr.** head up the family-owned enterprise, including the 16-room **Pacific City Inn** (pacificcityinn.com) at the same location.

Inn at Cape Kiwanda

33105 Cape Kiwanda Dr   503/965-7001, 888/965-7001
Moderate to expensive   yourlittlebeachtown.com/inn

Each of the 35 rooms has a private balcony overlooking the ocean at this friendly and attractive family-oriented property. Nice touches include coffee in the lobby and guest rooms, complimentary newspapers, cozy gas fireplaces, pillow top mattresses and feather pillows, complimentary chocolates on arrival and free Wi-Fi. The Haystack Suite includes a living room, large bedroom and Jacuzzi tub with ocean view. Take a spin on one of the inn's complimentary cruiser bikes to explore this delightful coastal community.

Pelican Pub & Brewery

33180 Cape Kiwanda Dr   503/965-7007
Breakfast, Lunch, Dinner: Daily   pelicanbrewery.com
Moderate

This pub is a beehive of activity for breakfast, lunch and dinner, particularly with the on-premises brewery and dramatic beach setting — Oregon's only oceanfront brewery. A huge menu gives diners choices of everyone's favorites plus blackened salmon, cioppini, salads, gourmet pizzas, burgers and the catch of the day. Pelican's own brews complement meals and are used in the preparation of numerous dishes like pale malt-crusted salmon, Scottish-style ale cakes for breakfast and beer-a-misu for dessert. Beer pairings are a specialty and so noted on the menu. Brewmaster **Darron Welch** masterminds three five-course brewers' dinners (reservations necessary) annually.

A second location in Tillamook (1708 First St, 503/842-7007) offers a smaller, simpler menu and abbreviated hours; the tap room overlooks the brewery.

PORT ORFORD

Hawthorne Gallery

517 Jefferson St   541/366-2266
Daily: 11-5 (closed Tues in winter)   hawthornegallery.com
Restaurant: Lunch, Dinner: Daily; Brunch: Sun
Moderately expensive to expensive (restaurant); Expensive (lodging)

Opening in 2010, the Hawthorne Gallery has become a destination for art lovers and collectors around the world. With over 30 artists, ten being from the Hawthorne family, expect to view an amazing, eclectic mix of glass, sculpture, paintings, furniture and more. Walk through the sculpture garden and into **Redfish** (541/366-2200, redfishportorford. com), the Hawthorne's upscale restaurant, where coastal cuisine is offered for brunch, lunch and dinner. WindDownWednesdays have become a favorite event (every Wednesday from 5:30-8:30) for an evening of wine, great food and local musical talent. Above the restaurant is a unique guest suite, **Redfish Loft** (541/366-2266, redfishloft.com), where you can take in the view, soak in the huge tub or sit by the fireplace.

Wildspring Guest Habitat

92978 Cemetery Loop   866/333-9453
Expensive   wildspring.com

From its hilltop location, this overnight gem is akin to staying in a private estate. Five beautiful cabin suites and the oceanview Guest Hall are nestled on five forested acres. Amble over to the Guest Hall for a tasty morning breakfast buffet; enjoy beverages, fruit, popcorn and chocolates anytime during the day; gaze at the Pacific while soaking in the open-air, slate jetted hot tub; or arrange for spa treatments, guest bikes, hiking guides and other services. Luxurious appointments vary among the cabins; sliding doors separate the cozy living rooms from bedrooms. Furnishings include artwork, down comforters, antique and vintage pieces, oversize walk-in slate showers, massage tables, refrigerators and a flat-screen TV/DVD for movies (over 500 titles available in the Guest Hall library). No telephones, in-room cooking facilities or TV reception; however, guests are free to use a fully-equipped kitchen in the Hall. This small, eco-friendly property is a year-round destination for relaxation, picnics in the forest and walking the labyrinth.

REEDSPORT

Sugar Shack Bakery
145 N 3rd St   541/271-3514
Daily: 3 a.m. to 7 p.m. (seasonal variations)   sugarshackbakery.biz

When you're in or passing through Reedsport, stop in for coffee and a doughnut, other sugary treats or a dish of ice cream to keep you going. The Bigfoot doughnut (chocolate and maple icings with whipped cream filling) is large enough to tame Sasquatch-size cravings! All delicious cookies, scones, cakes and candies are made from scratch. More substantial offerings include breakfast sandwiches and biscuits and gravy; soups and sandwiches are served midday until closing.

Umpqua Discovery Center
409 Riverfront Way   541/271-4816
Daily: Seasonal hours   umpquadiscoverycenter.com
Reasonable

This interesting educational and cultural center with interactive, multi-sensory exhibits and programs geared to families is situated along the tidewater of the Umpqua River. The displays will take you back in time to experience life in a 1900s tidewater town, loggers' camp and salmon cannery; meet the early explorers such as Jedediah Smith and learn the culture of coastal Indian tribes. There's much to entertain and inform kids, including a 35-foot periscope in the community room for capturing 360-degree views of the surrounding area.

WHALE WATCHING

Whale watching takes place almost year-round on the Oregon Coast. Peak season for the annual gray whale migration to warmer Pacific Ocean waters off Mexico occurs from mid-December through January.

Spring watch begins in March near the end of the month and finishes in June with mothers and babies traveling north. Each migration brings some 18,000 whales close to the Oregon Coast. In summer, some 200 whales remain along our coast to feed from July to mid-November.

Oftentimes, these huge mammals can be seen from shore. Any location with an ocean view may yield whale sightings, and morning light with the sun at your back is best. First locate whale spouts with your naked eye; then focus more closely with binoculars. For an even closer view, try whale watching from a charter boat. And some people prefer the view from above — from an airplane or helicopter.

Park Rangers and volunteer staff at the **Whale Watching Center** (126 N Hwy 101, Depoe Bay; 541/765-3304) share their vast knowledge and assist in spotting whales. Winter hours are 10 a.m. to 4 p.m. Wednesday through Sunday; daily in summer.

The Whale Watching Spoken Here® program (whalespoken.org) places volunteers at great whale watching sites during "watch" weeks (the last weeks in December and in March) so they can help others spot the whales. For more than 30 years, trained volunteers have helped visitors watch whales at 24 sites along the Pacific Northwest coast; Cape Lookout State Park, Cape Kiwanda, Cape Foulweather, Devil's Punchbowl, Umpqua Lighthouse and Cape Blanco Lighthouse to name a few.

ROCKAWAY BEACH

Surfside Oceanfront Resort

101 NW 11th Ave
Inexpensive to moderate

503/355-2312, 800/243-7786
surfsideocean.com

Surfside Oceanfront Resort is family-friendly to kids and pets. The sprawling, two-story resort has rooms with one or two beds, ocean-facing decks and gas fireplaces. The expansive beach is conducive to kite-flying, beachcombing, walking, bird and whale watching and building sandcastles. If you prefer other activities, there is a heated indoor swimming pool; most rooms have kitchens equipped to prepare and serve a family meal. Fishermen take note! The large parking area offers plenty of space to park your car and boat!

Twin Rocks Motel
7925 Minnehaha St   877/355-2391
Moderate   twinrocksmotel.net

Folks have been coming to Rockaway Beach since it was incorporated as a beach resort in the early 1900s. There are seven miles of sandy beaches accessible from the motel and waysides. This property has five homey cottages, each containing a living room and two bedrooms and equipped with full kitchens, fireplaces and large outdoor decks. Three oceanfront units are directly ashore from the namesake Twin Rocks, and the other two units offer ocean views. Modern amenities include Wi-Fi and flat-screen TVs with cable. The property's location allows for hours of walking the beach, building sand castles, flying kites or playing fetch with your canine.

SEAL ROCK

Brian McEneny Woodcarving Gallery
10727 Hwy 101   541/563-2452
Daily: 10-4 (closed Mon in winter)   woodcarvinggallery.com

Ultra-talented artist and owner **Brian McEneny** creates incredible artwork using driftwood, Port Orford cedar, Manzanita roots, cypress, myrtlewood and other coastal woods. The fluidity of ocean life makes up the bulk of his menagerie, but you'll also find other animals, abstracts and Native American works. Pieces are finished to enhance distinctive wood grains. The two floors of the gallery are chock-full of Brian's small decorative pieces, driftwood tables with glass tops as well as impressive large carvings; works by other Northwest carvers and master carvers are interspersed throughout. The gallery is closed for six weeks during the winter, so best to call ahead.

SEASIDE

Bell Buoy of Seaside
1800 S Roosevelt Dr
Daily

800/529-2722
bellbuoyofseaside.com

A landmark neon bell buoy sign tops this family-owned specialty seafood store on the south end of town. Fish is purchased right off the local fishing boats and sold fresh; look for fresh Oregon Dungeness crab (whole or crabmeat only); salmon, albacore tuna, sturgeon and oysters are smoked and canned on-site. Gift boxes contain smoked and canned Oregon ocean delicacies. Enjoy clam chowder and fish and chips at their next-door restaurant (503/738-6348).

Bigfoot's Steakhouse
2427 S Roosevelt Dr
Lunch, Dinner: Daily (closed Mon in winter)
Moderate and up

503/738-7009
bigfootssteakhouse.com

Every so often there are reported sightings of the elusive and mysterious Sasquatch. There is nothing mysterious about Bigfoot's in Seaside! The home cooking appeals to Yeti-size appetites and consists of big steaks, razor clams, halibut fish and chips, burgers, from-scratch soups, pub-style eats and housemade potato chips. Food and drink choices are abundant! This is a fun, family-friendly, casual spot; the Bigfoot theme prevails, starting at the front porch where a bigger-than-life Yeti woodcarving greets one and all.

Bruce's Candy Kitchen
1111 N Roosevelt Dr
(See detailed listing with Bruce's Candy Kitchen, Cannon Beach)

503/738-7828

McKeown's Restaurant & Bar
1 N Holladay Dr
Lunch, Dinner: Wed-Sun; Breakfast: Sat, Sun
Moderate

503/738-5232
mckeownsrestaurant.com

Nancy and Dennis McKeown oversee this popular eatery that features fresh seafood and a nod to Irish palates. Offerings include lager-battered fish and chips, Irish cottage pie, bangers and mash, crab-stuffed salmon, house cioppino, steaks and burgers. Breakfast is served on the weekend as well as a Sunday buffet with various pastries, fruits, breakfast dishes, salads, meats and sweets. McKeown's adjoining **Irish Bar** is run by son **Sean Patrick McKeown** and is a fun spot for a pint, pool, darts and pub eats. Try the Dubliner potato skins or the corned beef Swiss melt.

Nonni's Italian Bistro

831 Broadway St   503/738-4264
Lunch, Dinner: Thurs-Mon   nonnisitalianbistro.com
Inexpensive to moderately expensive

Conveniently located east of the promenade, Nonni's is the best place to enjoy a quality Italian dinner in a comfortable setting. This family-owned and -operated restaurant strives to create food just like their *nonni* (the Italian name for grandma) used to make, always using the freshest ingredients. Desserts such as panna cotta with fresh berries and tiramisu are also homemade. Their spaghetti and meatballs entree is enormous; the meatballs are stuffed with fontina cheese for a more flavorful bite. The chicken piccata is another house favorite; pair it with a glass of red wine or amaretto from their full-service bar and you have yourself a topnotch Italian dinner. For a mom-and-pop style breakfast and lunch spot, visit their restaurant **Firehouse Grill** (503/717-5502, Facebook) next door.

Norma's Seafood & Steak

20 N Columbia St   503/738-4331
Lunch, Dinner: Daily   normasseaside.com
Moderate to moderately expensive

Award-winning clam chowder and accommodating service draw folks to Norma's, located a stone's throw off Broadway in downtown Seaside. Current owners **Darleen and Randy Frank** (no relation to your author) run this environmentally-conscientious operation and offer a diverse menu. There are a dozen or so seafood appetizers; oysters, crab, shrimp, clams and more are prepared raw, fried, steamed, in crab cakes and as tangy shrimp or crab cocktails. Fish and seafood entrees dominate the early bird lunch specials accompanied by fresh-baked bread and choice of green salad with bay shrimp, French fries or chowder. Dinner portions and more are available all day; the captain's platter is full of crab legs, razor clams, prawns, halibut, calamari, scallops and oysters. Create your favorite surf and turf platter by adding a choice of seafood to natural Angus beef steaks or porterhouse-cut pork chops. Pasta dishes, seafood salads, burgers and assorted sandwiches are tasty alternatives. Satisfy your sweet tooth with mocha mud pie, chocolate nut torta, chocolate layer cake, brownie sundae, housemade marionberry cobbler or apple crisp.

Osprey Café

2281 Beach Dr   503/739-7054
Breakfast, Lunch: Thurs-Tues   Facebook
Inexpensive to moderate

To fuel your family before the next round of beach activities, try Osprey Café for breakfast or lunch where the food is fresh. Meals are homemade with South and Latin American influences in addition to everyone's favorites of pancakes, omelets, sandwiches, salads, cinnamon rolls and such. Huevos rancheros and *arepas* (South American corn and cheese dumplings) are tasty and nicely presented. There is both inside and outside seating in this corner eatery located amidst hotels and vacation rentals.

Relief Pitcher

2795 S Roosevelt Dr   503/738-9801
Lunch, Dinner: Daily   Facebook
Inexpensive to moderate

The exterior doesn't have much curb-appeal and the funky interior isn't anything to write home about, but superb burgers are served here. The Grand Slam burger, a half-pound juicy beauty topped with ham, egg, Tillamook and provolone cheese, along with cole slaw or fries make up for the environs. Albacore tuna tacos, sandwiches and Reubens are also popular. Brews are available by the pitcher, glass or pint; full bar and wine offerings also. Check out the three horseshoe pits for fun!

Seaside Aquarium

200 N Prom
Daily: 9-6 (seasonal closing hours)
Nominal

503/738-6211
seasideaquarium.com

The Seaside Aquarium is privately owned and is one of the oldest aquariums on the West Coast. The 1924 building was originally a salt water bath house and pool; after major renovations, it reopened in 1937 as this quaint aquarium. As you enter, visitors are delighted by the barking of seals anticipating their fish treats; underwater and touch tanks are home to some 100 species of marine life. It is said that the first program to breed harbor seals in captivity was started here. Marine-related momentos await discovery in the small gift shop.

Seaside Mostly Hats

300 Broadway
Daily: Hours vary

503/738-4370
Facebook

This shop is one of the most complete hat stores in the state. Located in the Carousel Mall, you'll find fun and dress hats for men, women and kids at reasonable prices in a variety of fabrics, styles and sizes. Depending on the weather, pop in to buy a rain hat or a straw hat. Some of the whimsical lids are made to look like fish or embellished with characters and attention-grabbing adornments; others come with synthetic hair attached.

Tipton's

319 Broadway
Daily: Hours vary

503/738-5864
Facebook

Shopping for classy home decor and holiday items? Visit **George Tipton**'s attractive 2,500- square-foot shop; George has a discerning eye for warm Tuscan and French Country tabletop items, lamps, canisters, pictures, candles and soft goods. Don't overlook the case of delicious gourmet chocolates (once the mainstay of the business). Delightful smells, nice background music (George is also a talented musician) and appealing merchandise blend harmoniously to create a pleasant ambience.

TILLAMOOK

Blue Heron French Cheese Company

2001 Blue Heron Dr   503/842-8281, 800/275-0639
Daily: 8-8 (till 6 in winter)   blueheronoregon.com

Housed in a 1930s Dutch Colonial barn, this marvelous retail business includes a deli and tasting room with fantastic cheeses, gourmet foods and wines. Products, tasty samples and gift items are arranged throughout the store suggesting attractive entertaining possibilities. The pièce de résistance is the cheese counter featuring the famous Blue Heron Brie with a selection of other fine cheeses; free samples provided. Another popular attraction is the wine tasting bar. For a nominal fee, sample five Northwest wines from four flights. The deli features homemade soups, chowder, salads and sandwiches on freshly-baked bread. Outside, kids can get up close and pet farm animals or engage in other activities geared to the pint-size set.

Koko's Restaurant

7300 Alderbrook Road   503/842-6413
Dinner: Daily   alderbrookgolfcourse.com
Moderately expensive

The clubhouse at Alderbrook Golf Course is very attractive with soaring ceilings in the dining room and beautiful landscaping outdoors. The dinner house features an Italian menu that lists seafood alfredo, elk ragout, lemon chicken picatta and spaghetti with housemade meatballs. The house specialty is Koko's beer cheddar soup made with Oregon beer and Tillamook cheese; other starters include Caprese salad, bruschetta, calamari and spinach artichoke dip.

Latimer Quilt & Textile Center

2105 Wilson River Loop   503/842-8622
Daily: April-Oct (closed Sun, Mon in winter) latimerquiltandtextile.com
Nominal

The former Maple Leaf Schoolhouse building is home to a changing gallery, a research library and a fine gift shop where you'll find handmade items by local craftspeople, books, vintage fabrics, quilt patterns and other vintage and contemporary pieces. The nonprofit working museum opened in 1991 and showcases textiles from the mid-19th century to the present. A self-guided Tillamook County Quilt Trail celebrates the county's rural heritage using painted wooden quilt blocks on historic barns built by Swiss and German immigrants. Watch the interesting weaving and spinning demonstrations or arrange for weaving, spinning, knitting, quilting and rug-hooking instruction.

Pelican Brewery & Tap Room
1708 First St   503/842-7007
(See detailed listing with Pelican Pub & Brewery, Pacific City)

Rodeo Steak House & Grill
2015 1st St   503/842-8288
Lunch, Dinner: Daily   rodeosteakhousegrill.com
Moderate

Rodeo Steak House stakes its claim on good steaks, in particular, bacon-wrapped filets. First thing you'll notice when you enter is the fun, family-friendly, casual ambience and peanut shells strewn on the floor. The peanuts are free and the selection from the full bar is sure to wet your whistle. Many of the appetizers and entrees are prepared with a Texas influence: rodeo egg rolls are served with jalapeno jelly for dipping, grilled steak tips are listed as "road kill" and crispy critters (chicken or fish) are offered on the kids menu. There are plenty more choices including pasta dishes, generously-portioned salads and really good homemade chili. A second location is in Coos Bay (1001 N Bayshore Dr, 541/808-0644).

Tillamook Cheese Factory
4175 Hwy 101 N   503/815-1300, 800/542-7290
Daily: Seasonal hours   tillamook.com

Beginning over a hundred years ago, Tillamook County Creamery Association continues to create high-quality dairy products and outstanding cheddar cheese from the original recipe. Visitors can peer through large viewing windows on a free self-guided factory tour; interactive kiosks and informative videos about cheese making and packaging processes. Tillamook produces over a dozen varieties of cheese in loaves, sliced or shredded which are sold at the on-site Tillamook Cheese Shop and stores across the country. Every flavor of Tillamook ice cream (28 in all) is scooped into dishes and cones at the ice cream counter or used in milkshakes and sundaes; the enticing aroma of hot-off-the-griddle waffle cones permeates the retail and eating areas. Other Tillamook dairy products are featured on the Creamery Cafe menu with items such as macaroni and cheese, grilled cheese sandwiches, burgers, salads and breakfast omelets and scrambles. Before you leave, make a stop at the gift shop for souvenirs, gourmet food items and Northwest goods. Be sure to choose something from the fudge counter for munching in the car; 30 flavors and everything is delicious!

Tillamook County Pioneer Museum

2106 2nd St   503/842-4553
Tues-Sun: 10-4   tcpm.org
Nominal

This small museum has a large collection of over 48,000 artifacts and 15,000 photographs depicting the rich history of the north Oregon coast. Exhibits pertain to pioneers, Native Americans, the military, natural history and musical instruments, plus the area's industries (logging, beaches, dairy). Take note of the late Senator Mark Hatfield's superb Abraham Lincoln collection, which once graced the walls of his Washington, D.C. office.

Tillamook Forest Center

45500 Wilson River Hwy   503/815-6800, 866/930-4646
Seasonal days and hours   tillamookforestcenter.org
Free

Longtime Oregonians will remember the devastating fire in 1933 that ravaged nearly 240,000 acres of prime forest land, mostly in Tillamook County. (Smaller fires in 1939, 1945 and 1951 burned an additional 120,000 acres and are also considered part of the Tillamook Burn.) A massive reforestation effort resulted in more than 72 million Douglas fir seedlings planted in the area. An interpretive center owned and operated by the Oregon Department of Forestry is located near Jones Creek, 22 miles east of Tillamook on Highway 6. It offers fascinating, interactive exhibits along with a 40-foot tall replica of a fire lookout tower and a dramatic 250-foot-long pedestrian suspension bridge that leads to the Wilson River Trail and onto the nearby Jones Creek. A classroom, theater and interpretive trails provide educational opportunities; this is an exceptional destination for exploration, outdoor learning and free family fun.

TOLEDO

Pig Feathers BBQ
300 S Main St
Lunch, Dinner: Tues-Sun
Moderate

541/336-1833
pigfeathersbbq.com

Toledo has BBQ! Proprietor **Stu Miller** gives the award-winning ribs, burgers and prime rib a good rub-down with his hand-blended, spice concoction before they are smoked or grilled; choose from a la carte meats and housemade sides or opt for a meal of your favorite or a combination of ribs and wings. Burger lovers have a spicy assortment of offerings from which to choose. Pig Feathers also sells small-batch rubs and sauces by the bottle; sauces such as Smokey Sweet, Smokin' Wasabi and Savory Napalm (heed the warning if you have delicate taste buds) are gluten-free and descriptively named. You're sure to need a cold beverage; I recommend a pint from the adjacent **Twisted Snout Brewery and Public House** (318 S Main St; 541/336-1833; twistedsnout.com).

WHEELER

Rising Star Cafe
92 Rorvik St
Lunch: Wed, Thurs, Sat; Dinner: Wed-Sat; Brunch: Sun
Moderate

503/368-3990
risingstarcafe.net

This charming blue house is a bright spot in Wheeler where the motto is "fresh food simply prepared with style." Bountiful lunches might include fresh fish of the day, cioppino or seafood chowder, large omelets, sandwiches, pasta and rice noodle bowls and as many local vegetables as possible. Dinner menus change daily based upon current sourcing and consist of fresh seafood, pasta and at least one meat item for carnivores (vegetarians and special diets accommodated where possible). Entrees are accompanied by crisp salads and great desserts that are made daily. Reservations recommended; no credit cards.

WINCHESTER BAY

Sportsmen's Cannery & Smokehouse

182 Bayfront Loop   541/271-3293, 800/457-8048
Mon-Sat: 9-5:30 (closed Wed); Sun: 10-4   sportsmenscannery.com

At **Brian Reeves**' store, the business is catching and packaging some of the best quality seafood available. Fresh fish and seafood are caught, smoked, canned and packaged right here. The catch includes salmon, tuna, ling cod, oysters, prawns and crab; pollock roe is a special treat. In summer, if you notice the outdoor barbecue smoking, stop to enjoy fresh fish right off the grill! Pick something up at the store or arrange for overnight shipping anywhere in the country. Gift boxes also include local and gourmet seasonings, jams and preserves; the price is right!

Umpqua Oysters

723 Ork Rock Road   541/271-5684
Daily: 9-5:30 (closed Tues, Wed in winter)   umpquaoysters.com

Fresh oysters are a delicacy, especially those cultivated at the confluence of the Umpqua River and Pacific Ocean. **Cindy and Vern Simmons** operate their aquaculture farm using innovative oyster "curtains" that keep the shellfish suspended in the water, free of air and mud exposure. This method produces a cut-above quality of tasty morsels, shucked or in the shell. When you are at the retail shop, pick up perfect condiments and sauces, observe shuckers and inspectors as they process the catch and watch an informative video depicting the long-line growing system.

YACHATS

The Adobe Resort
155 Hwy 101   541/547-3141, 800/522-3623
Inexpensive and up   adoberesort.com

The Adobe has been a popular respite on this stretch of the Pacific for several decades. All guest rooms are furnished with refrigerators, microwaves and other conveniences and have views of the ocean or mountains. Suites are outfitted with king beds, Jacuzzi tubs with ocean views, electric fireplaces and other amenities. Appealing features include an indoor pool, children's pool, expansive lawn, accessible beach and tide pools, convenient pathway into town, pleasant lounge and meeting and banquet space (ideal for weddings). Seasonal hotel packages include breakfast or dinner in the award-winning ocean-view restaurant. Dinner entrees are moderately priced and deliciously prepared; same goes for early-bird dinner specials. There is a nice variety of beef, pork, fish and poultry offerings served by a friendly and efficient wait staff. This family-owned resort also welcomes canine buddies.

Earthworks Gallery
2222 Hwy 101 N   541/547-4300
Daily: 10-5   gocybervision.com/earthwork

For more than twenty years, Earthworks Gallery has been featuring some 150 Northwest artists at this same location. Talented artists represent all art mediums; fine-art pieces, sculptures, glass, baskets, clay, watercolors, jewelry and other selections, all attractively arranged.

Green Salmon Coffee and Tea House
220 Hwy 101 N   541/547-3077
Daily: 7:30-2:30   thegreensalmon.com

Next time you're in Yachats, skip the mini-mart coffee pot and instead indulge in a cup of wonderful custom-roasted coffee. If coffee is not your cup of tea, then opt for a pot of tea from the selection of teas and infusions. Fair trade and organic beans (eight seasonal selections) and teas (over 30 varieties) are sold in the retail store. Add a bit of sustenance with homemade breakfast pastries, scones and savories, hearty and delicious panini sandwiches or a smoothie, espresso or mocha drink.

Heceta Head Lighthouse Bed & Breakfast

92072 Hwy 101 S   866/547-3696
Moderate to expensive   ✗ Check it out hecetalighthouse.com

Another unique Oregon experience awaits at one of the last remaining lighthouse keeper's cottages on the Pacific Coast. This year-round bed and breakfast has a capacity for 15; four rooms have private bathrooms and two rooms share a bathroom. The cottage has been restored to its original look and appointed with warm down comforters, antique furnishings and a fully-equipped guest kitchen. A nighttime view of the lighthouse is memorable, as is the seven-course gourmet breakfast prepared by innkeeper **Steven Bursey** and his highly-trained staff. Built around 1894, the lighthouse is one of the historic highlights of our state and one of the best-preserved beacons anywhere; a full renovation was completed in 2013.

Luna Sea Fish House and Village Fishmonger

153 Hwy 101   541/547-4794
Daily: Seasonal hours   lunaseafishhouse.com
Inexpensive

Luna Sea is owned and operated by a local fisherman who also knows a thing or two about preparing the fruits of his labor. The menu is predominantly fish and seafood: chowders and slumgullion; fish (cod, halibut, salmon, tuna, scallops, oysters, clams or a combination) and chips; added to an already tasty house salad and in tacos, sandwiches and breakfast items (omelets, hash and Benedicts); the alternatives are hamburgers, veggie burgers and bean burritos. Seating is limited in the turquoise-hued restaurant and fish market which is in a complex of four businesses; call ahead for an order to go.

CULINARY GREATS

Food is a big deal in Oregon; a really big deal. The culinary scene has caught the attention of people around the country who make the trip to Oregon to partake of the fresh Northwest bounty, craft beers, wines and distilled spirits. Others bring their culinary experience with them to set up shop here. We are blessed that a number of great chefs are practicing their trade in our area; their passion is our reward! Here's just a few; there are many more.

- **Philippe Boulot** (Multnomah Athletic Club, 1849 Salmon St, Portland; themac.com): James Beard Award recipient; a recognized genius in the food world
- **Gabrielle and Greg Denton** (OX Restaurant, 2225 NE Martin Luther King Blvd, Portland; oxpdx.com): top innovators; James Beard nominees
- **Ken Forkish** (Ken's Artisan Bakery, 338 NW 21st Ave, Portland; kensartisan.com and Ken's Artisan Pizza, 304 SE 28th Ave, Portland): pastry virtuoso
- **Tim Garling** (Jackalope Grill, 750 NW Lava Road, Bend; jackalopegrill.com): Bite of Bend's Top Chef winner
- **Greg Higgins** (Higgins Restaurant and Bar, 1239 SW Broadway, Portland; higginsportland.com): James Beard Award recipient
- **John Newman** (Newmans at 988, 988 S Hemlock St, Cannon Beach; newmansat988.com): outstanding professional; James Beard Award recipient
- **Vitaly Paley** (Paley's Place, 1204 NW 21st Ave, Portland; paleysplace. net; Imperial, imperialpdx.com and Portland Penny Diner, Hotel Lucía, 410 SW Broadway, Portland; portlandpennydiner.com): a true class act; James Beard Award recipient
- **Naomi Pomeroy** (Beast, 5425 NE 30th Ave, Portland; beastpdx. com): legendary; Best Chef Northwest winner
- **Andy Ricker** (Pok Pok, 3226 SE Division St, Portland; Pok Pok Noi, 1469 NE Prescott St, Portland; pokpokpdx.com and Whiskey Soda Lounge, 3131 SE Division St, Portland; whiskeysodalounge. com): Best Chef Northwest winner
- **Allen Routt** (The Painted Lady, 201 S College St, Newberg; the paintedladyrestaurant.com and Storrs Smokehouse, 310 E 1st St, Newberg; storrssmokehouse.com): perfection personified
- **Gabriel Rucker** (Le Pigeon, 738 E Burnside St, Portland; lepigeon. com and Little Bird, 219 SW 6th Ave, Portland; littlebirdbistro. com): James Beard Award recipient

Ona Restaurant and Lounge

131 Hwy 101 N   541/547-6627
Lunch, Dinner: Daily (Dinner: Fri-Tues in winter)   onarestaurant.com
Moderate to moderately expensive

Select a table at this casual restaurant and lounge which offer views of both the mouth of the Yachats River and the ocean. The ambience is warm, the menu is sophisticated and there are ample choices on the wine list. For starters, Manila clams are steamed with a just-right mixture of garlic, butter, dry vermouth and grape tomatoes and accompanied with warm crusty bread to soak up the broth; remoulade sauce with capers adds a new dimension to always popular Dungeness crab cakes. Menu standouts include a mixed grill of Oregon seafood; Dover sole stuffed with crab and bay shrimp; meatloaf made with ground beef, lamb and pork and Angus rib eye steak served with blue cheese compound. Housemade clam chowder, soups, salads and sandwiches are lunch standbys in addition to seafood choices; grilled rockfish, fries and Asian slaw are very good for either meal. Salad dressings are made in house and blood orange vinaigrette is especially tasty.

Overleaf Lodge & Spa

The Fireside is Pet Friendly

280 Overleaf Lodge Lane   800/338-0507
Moderate and up   *NO Pets*   overleaflodge.com

All 54 lodge rooms and suites (with optional adjoining rooms) are situated to secure unobstructed ocean views. Accommodations in seven room-types may include patios (standard for first floor units), balconies or window seats, fireplaces, full kitchens and whirlpool tubs. The complimentary continental breakfast includes freshly-baked scones or muffins, a delicious main entree and homemade granola in addition to the usual fruit, cereal and beverage spread. The spa, showers, steam rooms, saunas and therapy tubs are located on the third floor; refreshing spa treatments include massages, therapeutic body care treatments and facials. Not coincidentally, seaweed is used in many of the treatments to moisturize the skin and limit the effects of aging. The neighboring sister property, **Overleaf Village** (2090 Overleaf Loop, 800/338-0507, overleafvillage.com), consists of charming cottages situated along a nature path to the ocean. These view and non-view homes are fully furnished and designed for six to 12 guests.

SeaQuest Inn Bed and Breakfast

95354 Hwy 101 S   541/547-3782, 800/341-4878
Moderate to expensive   seaquestinn.com

Stephanie Szuts and **Sherwood Heineman** are the hospitable innkeepers and chefs at this expansive inn. After previous experiences in similar venues and the restaurant business in Florida, they made the trek to Oregon to manage and turn around this property. The five luxurious guest rooms and honeymoon suite are well-appointed with a variety of desired amenities and offer private bathrooms and porches. Breakfast is a delicious two-course gourmet affair which is beautifully served and presented. Throughout the day, guests are treated to hot beverages and homemade goodies; a wine and cheese hour in The Great Room combines beautiful views, cozy spots to indulge in a good book and a fireplace for a relaxing setting. Whale watch from the large wrap-around balcony, walk the beach in search of agates and shells or hike the only rainforest in Oregon. The on-property koi pond is an impressive feature with a dock, waterfall and island. The four-acre oceanfront setting is ideal for small, intimate weddings and other special events.

A packed house at the **Pendleton Round-Up**'s Let'er Buck Room which first opened in 1958 as a private club for Pendleton Round-Up directors and their guests. It opened to the public in 1969. Although it is open for six days only during Round-Up week, it has received honors as one of the best cowboy bars in America by *America Cowboy* magazine. The entire community participates in Round-Up (pendletonroundup.com) to make it an amazing event and world-class rodeo. (Rachael Owen)

Among the autographed photographs on my office walls is **Shirley Temple**. An interesting sidebar is when I was in the Army and stationed in Los Angeles in 1943. My date, Nancy Schlesinger (a personal friend of Shirley Temple) and I double dated with Shirley and her beau; as I recall, we enjoyed an evening of dinner and dancing. (Personal photo)

Antoinette and Mark Hatfield welcomed their first child, daughter Elizabeth, who was also the first grandchild for Josephine and Vincent Kuzmanich and Dovie and Dolan Hatfield. The expectant grandparents and "honorary uncle" Gerry were anxiously awaiting news of the arrival. (Personal photo, 1959)

Built in 1914, Pittock Mansion (pittockmansion.org) is full of rich history and remarkable stories of one of Portland's first and most influential families—Georgiana and Henry Pittock. The views of Portland are magnificent! (Pittock Mansion)

Designed by David McLay Kidd, Bandon Dunes Golf Resort (bandondunesgolf. com) opened in 1999 and is a premier destination for golfers. The view from the 16th hole is breathtaking. Founder Mike Keiser is a great booster of Oregon golf and deserves credit for this outstanding property. (Wood Sabold)

Jerry's Rogue Jets (roguejets.com) operates nature-based whitewater jet boat tours on the famous Wild and Scenic Rogue River in Gold Beach and has been delivering mail to the town of Agness since 1895. The scenery is nothing short of stunning! (Jerry's Rogue Jets)

Explore the extreme forces at work along the Columbia River Bar where waves can exceed 40 feet in height during the most severe winter storms. These and other amazing exhibits are featured at the Columbia River Maritime Museum in Astoria (crmm.org), one of the great maritime attractions in the country. (Columbia River Maritime Museum)

Kam Wah Chung State Heritage Site museum was home to Ing "Doc" Hay and Lung On, late 19th century Chinese immigrants who operated a successful dry goods store, herbalist shop and import business for nearly 60 years. The building in John Day is now a National Historic Landmark. (Oregon Parks and Recreation Department)

Ashland boasts one of the nation's top outdoor Shakespearean theaters. This photo depicts a performance of *As You Like It* at the Oregon Shakespeare Festival's (osfashland.org) Allen Elizabethan Theatre. 2012 (T. Charles Erickson)

Lan Su Chinese Garden (lansugarden. org), located in the heart of downtown Portland, is an authentic Suzhou-style garden built by 65 master artisans from China. Open year round, it offers visitors a tranquil oasis and provides more than 500 programs each year, all of which are included with the cost of admission or membership. (Lan Su Garden)

The Round Barn at Pete French State Heritage Site, near Burns, was part of a cattleman's empire. The barn was designed and built around 1880 and was used to train wild horses during the long winters. The barn is included in the National Register of Historic Places. (Oregon Parks and Recreation Department)

The iconic South Falls is a 177-foot curtain of water and is part of the Trail of Ten Falls, a nationally recognized hiking trail at Silver Falls State Park just east of Silverton. Hiking behind the waterfall is a thrilling experience. (Oregon Parks and Recreation Department)

The snow-viewing lantern in front of the Portland Japanese Garden (Japanese garden.com). (Portland Japanese Garden)

MISS AMERICA 1954...EVELYN AY OF EPHRATA, PENNSYLVANIA

Meier & Frank stores staged many fashion shows; none were more popular than those featuring the reigning Miss America. Evelyn Ay, Miss America 1954, charmed customers. Throughout the years, the beautiful visiting Miss Americas were special guests at festivities in Portland and Salem including parties at your author's home, luncheons with local women and their husbands (by popular request). (Personal photo)

Timberline Lodge (timberlinelodge.com), located at the 6,000-foot level of Mt. Hood is a National Historic Landmark and considered by many to be the quintessential American ski lodge. Don't miss this year-round attraction! (Timberline Lodge)

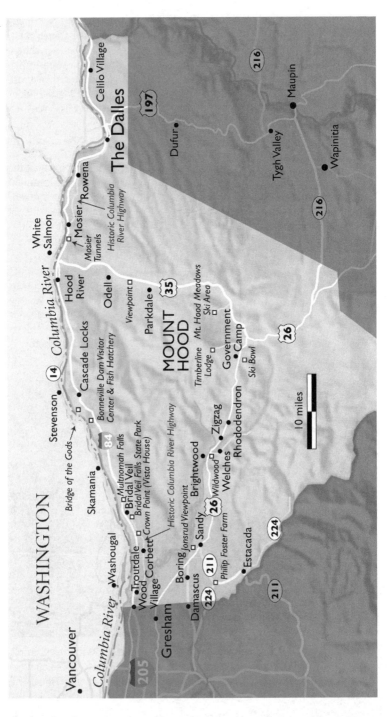

Columbia Gorge and Mt.Hood

BRIDAL VEIL

Multnomah Falls

50000 Historic Columbia River Hwy

Visitors Center: Daily: 10-5

Dining Room: Daily (days and hours vary)

Moderate to moderately expensive

503/695-2372

multnomahfallslodge.com

503/692-2376, ext 200

A stunning site at any time of the year, this is the state's number-one visited natural attraction. Multnomah Falls is Oregon's tallest waterfall and the second-highest year-round waterfall in the nation. Simon Benson donated the land and funding which led to the construction of the famed Benson Bridge; his magnanimous gesture led other private and public entities to join the project. The park was dedicated in 1915 and the lodge was completed in 1925. Albert E. Doyle (architect for the Meier & Frank Co. building in downtown Portland) designed the impressive stone and timber building, now home to a visitors center, snack and gift shops and a wonderful dining room. The cuisine in Multnomah Falls Lodge Dining Room is Northwest-inspired with fresh local ingredients; ideal for a romantic dinner for two or powering the body before or after hikes along the trail. Visitors should note that the trail is open until sunset.

CASCADE LOCKS

Bonneville Fish Hatchery

70543 NE Herman Loop   541/374-8393
Daily: Hours vary   Facebook
Free

Not surprisingly, the main attraction at this Columbia River hatchery, at the mouth of Tanner Creek, is **Herman the Sturgeon**. Herman is approaching his 76th birthday and packs 450 pounds onto his 11-foot boneless frame. The sturgeon interpretive center offers informational displays and sturgeon viewing. Guests may also walk to the rainbow trout ponds where they will see trophy-size trout, a visitor center for the spawning room and the historic Hatchery Incubation Building. The hatchery rears steelhead, Chinook and Coho Salmon. Keep your binoculars handy as birds of prey, songbirds, wading birds and waterfowl are prevalent in this area.

Columbia Gorge Sternwheeler

355 Wa Na Pa St   503/224-3900, 800/224-3901
Seasonal: May-Oct   portlandspirit.com
Expensive

Board this authentic triple-decker paddle wheeler from Marine Park for a memorable sightseeing excursion on the Columbia. There are a number of cruise options (one hour to a half-day, prices start at $27 an hour per person) to appreciate the natural beauty and historic points of interest along this section of the Columbia Gorge. Northwest cuisine is served on brunch and dinner cruises; snacks and beverages are available at the full-service bar.

HYDROPOWER

On your next trip to the Gorge, an interesting and educational stop is at one of the visitor centers of **Bonneville Lock and Dam**. The Bradford Island Visitor Center (Cascade Locks, 541/374-8820) on the Oregon side has four floors open to visitors and includes interpretive displays about hydropower, salmon migration, local history and geology. The rooftop view of the spillway is impressive. Inside, visitors can view a hydroelectric powerhouse (it's called a powerhouse for a reason!) and observe salmon and sturgeon underwater as they swim past windows in the fish ladder. Also on the Oregon side, the Navigation Lock Visitor Center (541/374-8344) tells the story of inland commercial navigation and offers views of a working lock. Cross the river to Washington Shore Visitor Center (509/427-4281) for another opportunity to see inside a working powerhouse.

East Wind Drive-In

395 Wa Na Pa St
Breakfast, Lunch, Dinner: Daily
Inexpensive

541/374-8380
Facebook

Insanely large ice cream cones here! The small soft-serve vanilla, chocolate or twist combination cone is a somewhat manageable six inches. I dare you to order the large version which is a whopping foot tall and weighs about a pound and a half! It is so precarious that it is immediately plopped into a 32-ounce paper cup. The diner also serves breakfast, burgers, fries, shakes and other drive-in type fare. Be prepared to wait in line with hungry kids and families.

CORBETT

Vista House

Crown Point, 40700 E Historic Columbia River Hwy
Nov-Feb: Sat, Sun; Mar-Oct: Daily

503/695-2240
vistahouse.com

If you drive the Historic Columbia River Highway, it takes you right to the doorstep of the Vista House. Completed in 1917, this octagonal, cliff-top structure was built as a comfort station and viewpoint.

These facilities, however, are far from typical! The restrooms are outfitted in elegant marble and mahogany with circular marble stairways leading to the lower level. An extensive 2006 restoration brought this gem back to grandeur. It houses interpretive displays of this region's rich history, a gift shop and an espresso cafe. This is one of the windiest spots in Oregon, so hang on to your hat!

GOVERNMENT CAMP

Collins Lake Resort
88149 E Creek Ridge Road
Moderate and up

800/234-6288
collinslakeresort.com

Open all year and geared for the outdoors, this resort is touted as providing luxury Chalets (four to ten people) and Grand Lodges (two or three bedrooms). Mt. Hood Skibowl owner **Kirk Hanna** is behind the master plan for this 28-acre parcel surrounded by the Mt. Hood National Forest. Snowmobiling, snowshoeing, cross-country skiing, sleigh rides, tubing and sledding are at your winter doorstep. Depart your basecamp via local shuttle buses to Skibowl, Summit Ski Area and Timberline or via car to Mt. Hood Meadows. On your return, enjoy the hot tub, heated pool or sauna or simply stretch out by the fireplace. When the snow melts, you may opt to explore the network of interpretive trails eventually leading to the village. Guests receive VIP discounts for outdoor recreation including three major ski areas and the **Mt. Hood Adventure Park** (mthoodadventure.com) at Skibowl.

The Glacier Haus Bistro
8817 E Government Camp Loop Road
Seasonal
Inexpensive to moderate

503/272-3471
glacierhaus.com

This family-owned and -operated restaurant serves authentic European comfort food made from fresh ingredients. Classic European dishes listed are wiener schnitzel, Hungarian beef goulash and sauerbraten. Other notable items include their homemade pizzas, sandwiches, salads, cakes and pies. These folks have a full-service bar and accept reservations as well as catering requests. The best part is, it's just down the street from Mt. Hood!

Huckleberry Inn

88611 E Government Camp Loop   503/272-3325
Daily: 24 hours   huckleberry-inn.com
Cafe: Inexpensive to moderate
Lodging: Moderate

Huckleberry hotcakes for dinner or at midnight? No problem, Huckleberry Inn is open all hours of the day and night and the full menu is served all day. Since 1966 this family restaurant has been a welcoming stop for folks looking for family-friendly dining in Government Camp. During ski season and holiday weekends, the Huckleberry Inn offers a steak and seafood menu in its cozy, candlelit steakhouse. Fuel up for outdoor activities with a giant maple bar or fresh doughnut; better yet, treat yourself to a refreshing huckleberry milkshake or a slice of delicious homemade huckleberry pie, a la mode, of course. On-premise lodging includes 17 standard and deluxe rooms and a two-bedroom suite with a kitchen and bunk room (sleeps 14).

Mt. Hood Cultural Center & Museum

88900 E Hwy 26   503/272-3301
Daily: 9-5   mthoodmuseum.org
Free (donations accepted)

Did you know that Government Camp was an encampment in 1849 for a detachment of the U.S. Mounted Rifles on their way to Fort Vancouver from Fort Leavenworth, Kansas? The descriptive name has stayed with this community as it grew first into a summer resort followed by a year-round destination. Today the multi-faceted Mt. Hood Cultural Center & Museum is a repository for Mt. Hood-related collections. Exhibits include natural history, the U.S. Forest Service and management of the Mt. Hood National Forest (including a 1920s ranger's office), artifacts from the Barlow Road section of the Oregon Trail and history of the exploration and development of the area. There is also a fascinating assortment of winter and mountain sports equipment and clothing used since the introduction of winter sports on Mt. Hood in the early 1900s. A gallery features fine arts and artworks by local artists; many pieces are available for sale. An interesting sidebar: my cousin, the late Jack Meier of the Mt. Hood Development Association, was a guiding force behind the construction of Timberline Lodge in the 1930s.

Mt. Hood Skibowl

87000 E Hwy 26   503/272-3206
Seasonal   skibowl.com
Fees vary by activity

Good family fun can be found on a visit to one of Oregon's best year-round resorts. Almost 1,000 acres of snow-covered topography affords alpine skiing (including the largest night-skiing terrain in the country), snowboarding, snowshoeing, cross-country skiing, sleigh rides, snowmobiling, day and cosmic tubing plus much more. Return in the summer to experience the **Mt. Hood Adventure Park** (mthoodadventure.com) when it comes to life with over 20 mild to extreme attractions for all ages, including the alpine slide, scenic sky chair, bungee tower, zip line, Indy carts, batting cages, rock climbing wall, miniature and disc golf and mountain biking. The casual eateries offer welcome and satisfying breathers. This destination is awesome any time of the year!

Ratskeller Alpine Bar & Pizzeria

88335 E Government Camp Loop   503/272-3635
Lunch, Dinner: Daily   ratskellerpizzeria.com
Moderate

Here's another winning combination on the mountain: a historic mountain town restaurant/pub with giant high-definition screens showing the big games, huge beer selection and super pizzas. Highly recommended dishes include The Rat combo pizza (pepperoni, sausage, salami, mushrooms, onions and black olives); fresh, local grass-fed beef burgers (gigantic) and build-your-own pizzas, calzones and stromboli. Satisfying food and beverages are served fireside in winter and outdoors in good weather; family-friendly until 11 p.m. General manager **Ryan Hora** leads his fun-loving, ski-town staff in providing superior service.

HOOD RIVER

Apple Valley Country Store

2363 Tucker Road
Seasonal

541/386-1971
applevalleystore.com

Make a trip to this small store for a taste of Oregon's world-famous fruit. Start with a thick milkshake and wander the store to choose among jams, jellies, butters, syrups, sauces and pie fillings; all made on-site. Mustards, mixes and sugar-free options are also available. Scratch pies are a mainstay, and don't forget to add Tillamook ice cream on top. Further up the road in Parkdale, **Apple Valley BBQ Restaurant and Catering** (4956 Baseline Dr, 541/352-3554) specializes in modestly-priced smoked pork ribs, pulled pork and prime rib dinners on Friday and Saturday. Hours are 11 to 8, Wednesday through Sunday. The meats are smoked with local fruit woods, complemented by side dishes of pear cole slaw and apple-cider baked beans.

BLOSSOM FEST

Hood River County celebrates the arrival of spring in style with April's three-week annual **Hood River Blossom Fest** (hoodriver.org/blossom-fest). The Hood River Valley spans the north slope of Mt. Hood to the south shore of the Columbia River Gorge and is dotted with an abundance of pear, cherry and apple orchards. This translates into acres and acres of beautiful pink and white fruit blossoms along the Valley roads. Visitors to the area will want to drive the world-famous scenic Fruit Loop; enjoy 35 miles through the beautiful Upper Valley filled with farmstands, wineries, alpaca farms, lavender fields, gift stores, orchards, forests and unparalleled scenery.

Bigfoot Lodge B&B Enchanted Forest

1819 Cascade Ave
Moderate

541/399-4222
bigfoot-lodge.com

Views of Mt. Hood, the Hood River Valley and wildlife are just part of the allure of this 5,000-square-foot custom-built, hand-hewn log lodge near Mt. Hood. Each of the four guest rooms is outfitted with quality furnishings: the John Wayne cowboy room is rustic with Pendleton decor and the Mt. Hood room with Native American accents can accommodate up to four guests. All the rooms are warm and inviting. The lodge is situated on 64 private acres on the edge of the Mt. Hood Wilderness (directions provided with reservation) with plenty of room to hike, bike, trail ride, snowshoe or cross-country ski; five major ski resorts are a short drive away. Experience the scenery on a draft horse-drawn wagon ride, pulled by resident Percheron horses Ike and Tina, or simply enjoy the hosts' hospitality and the incomparable setting. A hearty four-course organic breakfast is prepared each morning.

Boda's Kitchen

404 Oak St   541/386-9876
Lunch, Dinner: Daily   bodaskitchen.com
Moderate

Sandwiches from gourmet delis are innovative, often inspired by fresh, local ingredients and more often than not, more than a mouthful. Such is the case with creations from Boda's Kitchen. A tasty sampling includes a Cubano panini on housemade focaccia bread, stuffed with rotisserie-cooked pork loin, ham and cheese; an Italian favorite consists of salami, provolone, roasted red peppers and basil aioli wrapped in a spinach tortilla and a turkey masterpiece features house-roasted turkey breast, cranberry chutney, greens and cheese on house focaccia. Pickles made in-house accompany each sandwich; daily specials and wholesome soups and salads are also available. Boxed lunches are a specialty and include a sandwich, chips and jumbo cookie.

Celilo Restaurant and Bar

16 Oak St   541/386-5710
Lunch, Dinner: Daily   celilorestaurant.com
Moderate

Local, organic and sustainable are the by-words at contemporary Celilo where great healthy foods are crafted. From the ever-changing menu, a bowl of housemade soup or hazelnut and blue cheese salad are tasty starters for lunch or dinner. A varied selection of lunchtime sandwiches is accompanied by organic mixed greens or fries. For dinner, beef, fish, pasta, poultry and pork options are expertly and creatively prepared to showcase the regional bounty; occasional wine dinners masterfully pair outstanding Northwest wines with Celilo's best menus. Dessert showcases local fruits that are superb in delicious sorbets, tarts and cakes, or you may prefer a cheese course with regional touches. Busy chef **Ben Stenn** also conducts popular cooking classes.

Columbia Cliff Villas

3880 Westcliff Dr   866/912-8366
Moderate and up   columbiacliffvillas.com

This fabulous setting and layout are ideal for retreats, romantic getaways and family gatherings. A stay here yields ultra-comfortable digs and magnificent river and mountain views. Thirty-seven luxury rooms and suites rest above a 208-foot waterfall. Accommodations in this condominium hotel incorporate everything from European-style hotel rooms up to one- and three-bedroom adjoining villa and penthouse suites. Amenities vary by room and may include private decks (some look straight down the cliffs to the Columbia River), gas fireplaces, marble and tile walk-in showers, soaking tubs and gourmet kitchens.

Columbia Gorge Hotel

4000 Westcliff Dr   541/386-5566, 800/345-1921
Moderate to expensive   columbiagorgehotel.com

The opulent Columbia Gorge Hotel opened in 1921 as a haven for guests traveling by steamboat. Highway promoter Simon Benson purchased the hotel in 1920 with dreams of grandeur to reward motorists journeying along the Columbia Gorge Scenic Highway. The hotel was home away from home to such distinguished guests as Presidents Franklin Roosevelt and Calvin Coolidge and film legends Myrna Loy, Jane Powell and Rudolph Valentino. Through the years it fell in and out of prosperity, at one time functioning as a retirement home. Fortunately, a major restoration project propelled the hotel back to its stately beauty. There are 40 luxurious guest rooms furnished with either brass or canopy beds, all with views of the Gorge or vibrant manicured gardens. It is truly a romantic, restful destination. Diners at **Simon's Cliff House** have much to enjoy, starting with the magnificent view. There are plenty of breakfast choices, and soups, salads and hot or cold specialty sandwiches make a fine lunch, especially when served with the house sweet potato fries. Dinner starts with housemade herb garlic bread, followed by appetizers and gourmet entrees fit for screen legends. The pièce de résistance is the Sunday brunch; seven courses beginning with champagne, progressing through the pastry chef's special scones, a granola and yogurt parfait, seasonal fruit, an assortment of cheeses, a choice of chef's entrees and culminating with coffee, pastries and petit desserts. Fabulous!

Full Sail Brewing

506 Columbia St   541/386-2247
Lunch, Dinner: Daily   fullsailbrewing.com
Moderate

Full Sail Brewing operates a brewery, tasting room and pub in a building that formerly housed the Diamond Fruit Company. The cannery is gone, but the site is still bustling with dozens of skilled brewery specialists working full speed ahead at this independent enterprise crafting award-winning beers. Free brewery tours are conducted each afternoon between 1 and 4. Brewery products are often used in the bill of fare. A slow-roasted steak sandwich with sauteed onions, bell peppers, melted cheese and Amber Ale au jus (served on the side); grilled Mt. Shadow bratwurst over bacon and apple Session-cured sauerkraut topped with braised shallots and Session Black mustard sauce; salads and Session lager battered salmon fish and chips are served all day. Satisfying sweet-tooth tamers include Imperial Stout brownies and ice cream and Session Black Lager floats. The panorama from the rooftop deck across the Columbia to the Washington side of the Gorge is awesome, making this a great stop to unwind and savor brews and views.

G. Williker's Toy Shoppe

202 Oak St   541/387-2229
Mon-Sat: 10-6; Sun: 10-5   gwtoyshoppe.com

I recall spending many hours as a youngster wandering the toy department in my family's department store, eyeing the newest colorful toys and games. To this day, I check out toy stores on my travels. Every inch of this delightful shop is stocked with toys of every kind. There are plush animals, puzzles and games, small items for stocking stuffers, an entire wall of Lego products, chemistry sets, doll houses (and dolls), books and a bit of everything else. The merchandise mix includes the latest finds, nostalgic favorites and an irresistible candy counter.

The Gorge White House

2265 Hwy 35   541/386-2828
Seasonal   thegorgewhitehouse.com

This attraction is truly an event as it offers so many things to do. Once a private residence and still surrounded by orchards, this Dutch Colonial Revival landmark offers five acres of cut flower fields and u-pick fruit, local wine, hard cider and beer tasting, local fruit sales, a farm fresh gourmet food cart, local artwork, gifts and more. A historic home serves as the wine tasting room, while the converted original shop building houses the attractively displayed farmstand and beer and cider room. It is a spectacular venue for reunions, weddings and such, especially with Mt. Hood, Mt. Adams and fields of flowers abloom in the background.

Hood River Lavender Farm

3801 Straight Hill Road   541/354-9917
Seasonal   hoodriverlavender.com

Finding calmness in your busy everyday life can be difficult. Here's a suggestion: surrounded yourself with fragrant lavender fields on the volcanic slopes with mountain views. In the month of July, they hold a **Lavender Daze Festival** (lavenderfarms.net) which features arts, crafts, food and wine vendors, massages, face painting and live music; whether you visit them at festival time or pass through at another time, pick up some high quality organic lavender essential oil, it is known to help physical and emotional stress. The retail farm not only grows 75 varieties of lavender available for picking seasonally, but they also use lavender in crafts and products that are offered for sale at the farm and online.

Hood River Vineyards and Winery

4693 Westwood Dr   541/386-3772
Daily: 11-5 (Jun-Oct);   hoodrivervineyardsandwinery.com
Thurs-Mon: 11-5 (Nov-May)

Wineries and craft breweries are more than plentiful. It would take more than a weekend to take in the vast variety, but tasting rooms, brew pubs and most restaurants include these local beverages on their menus. Founded in 1981, this winery is the Gorge's oldest and specializes mainly in estate grown red, white and fruit wines; ports and sherry, too.

Mount Hood Railroad

110 Railroad Ave   541/386-3556, 800/872-4661
Seasonal   mthoodrr.com
Expensive

For more than 100 years, this train has chugged through the picturesque Hood River Valley. Depending on the season, rail excursions depart from the Mount Hood Railroad depot for Parkdale near the base of Mt. Hood. Murder mystery dinners and re-enacted train robberies are popular special events. Kids anxiously await the *Polar Express* excursion to the "North Pole" in November and December. The round-trip journey re-creates the *Polar Express* storyline and includes hot cocoa, treats and a visit from Santa Claus. Food and beverages are available on all trips; call for information about Sunday champagne brunch.

Oak Street Hotel

610 Oak St   541/386-3845
Moderate   oakstreethotel.com

The Oak Street Hotel is a nine-room boutique hotel, centrally located and within walking distance to fine dining and shopping. The comfortable 1909 home has been adapted to include en suite bathrooms in each of the unique guest rooms. Privacy may be an issue for some guests as some rooms have plush draperies in lieu of doors to separate the facilities from the sleeping area. Rooms may have views of the Columbia River, courtyard or Oak Street; some have a private entrance or are dog-friendly. Sweet or savory pie is standard fare for breakfast; fruits, eggs, vegetables and herbs are fresh from the family's farm. Oak Street Hotel also offers vacation home rentals of varying sizes; check the website for mention of **Gorge Escape Vacation Homes**.

VIEW FROM A LOOKOUT

For a unique getaway experience, former U.S. Forest Service fire lookouts and cabins (firelookout.org/lookout-rentals) are available for seasonal (and low-budget) campouts. Amenities (bathrooms, cooking facilities, running water) vary by location, so be sure to read descriptions carefully before renting; most are remote and require packing in your gear. Here's a sampling of locations, all offering amazing views:

- **Aspen Cabin**, Fremont-Winema National Forest
- **Bald Butte Lookout**, Fremont-Winema National Forest
- **Clear Lake Cabin Lookout**, Mt. Hood National Forest
- **Drake Peak Lookout**, Fremont National Forest
- **Fall Mountain Lookout**, Malheur National Forest
- **Fivemile Butte Lookout**, Mt. Hood
- **Flag Point Lookout**, Mt. Hood National Forest
- **Green Ridge Lookout**, Deschutes National Forest
- **Indian Ridge Lookout**, Willamette National Forest
- **Pickett Butte Lookout**, Umpqua National Forest
- **Snow Camp Lookout**, Rogue River-Siskiyou National Forest

The Pines Tasting Room

202 Cascade Ave, Suite B   541/993-8301
Daily: Hours vary   thepinesvineyard.com

Lonnie Wright, owner of The Pines 1852 in The Dalles, has been working and expanding the century-old vine zinfandel since 1982. Originally planted by an Italian immigrant, the vineyard has consistently yielded high-quality wine grapes. The tasting room offers boutique wines in a comfortable space with a large cherry wood bar, bistro seating and living room area. A giant garage door rolls up in fair weather for indoor/outdoor tasting. Guests needing overnight accommodations can rent **The Pines Cottage** (5450 Mill Creek Road, The Dalles, 541/993-8300) in the peaceful surroundings of the vineyard estate just up the highway in The Dalles. Rent the entire cottage (three bedrooms and a shared bath, kitchen and living areas) or individual bedrooms.

Riverside

1108 E Marina Dr   541/386-4410
Breakfast, Lunch, Dinner: Daily   riversidehoodriver.com
Inexpensive to moderately expensive

As Hood River's only waterfront restaurant, hungry travelers will find Riverside quite pleasant. and are practically guaranteed a good view. Panoramic scenes of the Columbia River are offered from the dining room, lounge and from the outdoor patio and deck. But aside from the fantastic views, Chef **Mark DeResta** cooks up some of the best food Hood River has to offer; locally-sourced Northwest cuisine is served with an Italian flair. Signature breakfast items include a housemade cinnamon roll (a Sunday special), corned beef hash and stuffed French toast. The lunch menu includes a variety of handmade soups, salads, sandwiches and entrees such as fish and chips, liver and onions and baked pasta. Dinner spans a mix of similar items along with some of the best braised short ribs around, unique pasta creations, stuffed chicken and burgers. **Cebu** lounge offers the complete menu along with free weekend entertainment (check the entertainment calendar online), big screen TVs for sports fans, a delicious happy hour menu, a full-service bar and an award-winning wine list; close to 40 local wines. All of this and more can be found at the **Best Western Plus Hood River Inn** (541/386-2200, hoodriverinn.com), with no other hotel in the area offering such a complete combination of amenities. For guests at the Inn, Riverside's breakfast is included in most circumstances!

Romuls West

315 Oak St   541/436-4444
Lunch, Dinner: Daily   romuls.com
Moderate

Romul and Lillie Grivov are experienced restaurateurs; they operated another restaurant by the same name for a dozen years before opening a new location in Hood River. Tantalizing aromas from slow-cooked Pommodoro and Bolognese sauces permeate the restaurant and hint at the Italian/Mediterranean cuisine. Cooked-to-order dishes such as eggplant parmigiana, veal piccata and lemon caper chicken may take a while to prepare, but are worth the wait. Chef Romul turns out homemade meatballs, pastas, gelato, desserts and the best robust lasagna. People travel to this house specifically for the scrumptious layers of sausage, mushrooms, olives and roasted red pepper sauce; daily specials are composed to feature seasonal ingredients from the land and sea. Patio seating is available in warmer months.

The Ruddy Duck

504 Oak St   541/386-5050
Mon-Sat: 9-6; Sun: 10-6   ruddyduckstore.com

This 1893 two-story house hosts a family-run mini-department store. You'll find high quality, trendsetting casual attire; men's, women's and kids' clothing and shoes. Just-right accessories finish the look; sunglasses, scarves, headwear, bags and jewelry. Many items are acquired from the proprietor's trips around the globe. Merchandise reflects the Gorge lifestyle and is sold at affordable prices. After shopping, or just because, relax on the lawn with a cone or fresh huckleberry shake from next-door enterprise, **Mike's Ice Cream** (541/386-6260, mikesicecream.com). This sister operation is open seasonally and serves Prince Pückler's gourmet ice cream.

HISTORIC COLUMBIA RIVER HIGHWAY

One of the most beautiful roads in the world is located right here in Oregon, and the amazing fact is that you can drive the **Historic Columbia River Highway** (columbiariverhighway.com) in just one day. Late spring may be the best time to visit as crowds are down and Oregon's vegetation is lush.

From Portland, drive Highway 84 East until you come to the Historic Columbia River Highway 30 turnoff. You will pass through beautiful wine country; in Cascade Locks look for the enchanting **Bridge of the Gods**. Next you will see a series of imposing waterfalls: **Horsetail Falls** and **Multnomah Falls**, the second tallest natural falls in the nation. The **Tunnel of Trees** will wrap its arms around you as you pass under its branches. Don't miss **Crown Point** with its incredible view and photo opportunity. Make a rest stop at beautiful **Vista House** before continuing on to the town of Corbett. At this point you have a choice of returning to Portland via Highway 84 West or taking another scenic drive around Mt. Hood to visit historic **Timberline Lodge**.

The highway through the Columbia Gorge has often been called The King of Roads. Governor **Julius Meier** (my great uncle) led the Columbia River Highway Association in building the Columbia River Highway from Portland to Astoria (1912-1915), and later from Portland to The Dalles (1913-1922.) Family members say Uncle Julius oversaw and crawled every square inch of the projected highway.

Julius loved the Gorge and built his summer estate **Menucha** on a windy bluff, 700 feet above the Columbia River. Josiah Painter farmed the land in 1873, and in 1914 Julius Meier purchased the property from the Painter family. Julius named the land Menucha which in Hebrew means waters of refreshment. The lovely home was designed by Herman Brookman in a Northwest style of architecture. It was the Meier family summer estate during the 1920s and 1930s; it was a charming showplace. Meier & Frank company picnics were hosted there, as well as two U.S. Presidents, Franklin Roosevelt and Herbert Hoover. The property was sold in 1950 to the First Presbyterian Church for use as a retreat center.

Visitors often came to see Uncle Julius; with a peephole in his private bathroom medicine cabinet, he looked into the living area at waiting guests to see if he wanted to receive them or not! That opening is still there.

Sakura Ridge

5601 York Hill Dr   541/386-2636
Moderate and up   sakuraridge.com

Ready for a night out of town? Here's a secluded bed and breakfast at the end of a short gravel road six miles outside of Hood River. **Deanna and John Joyer** practice organic farming on a 93-acre working farm: pears, berries, chickens, sheep, honey bees and raised beds which contain Deanna's vegetable and flower gardens. Guests may opt to participate in the farm experience or be an "armchair farmer" while settled into an Adirondack chair to admire the fruits of someone else's labors. Three of the five guest rooms offer spectacular views of Mt. Hood from private patios; other rooms provide views of the valley or orchard. The Northwest-style accommodations are well-appointed and very comfortable with rural peacefulness replacing urban street traffic sounds. Sakura Ridge specializes in preparing the farm's organic fresh abundance for breakfast and will accommodate special diet requirements upon prior request. Other options include ploughman's platter, picnic basket, cooking classes or an opportunity in the summer to work the bees with John; advance arrangement and additional costs apply. A two-night minimum is imposed April through October.

Silverado Jewelry Gallery

310 Oak St   541/386-7069
Mon-Sat: 10-6; Sun: 10-5   silveradogallery.com

The works of nearly 100 artisans are shown in this inviting gallery; outstanding local talent plus a carefully curated selection of handmade jewelry from some of the most famous and sought-after jewelry artists in the world. Designs are traditional and contemporary, casual and elegant and are handcrafted using gems, jewels, pearls and turquoise. Their aim is to provide customers the best and most exclusive handmade jewelry; by the looks of the colorful eye candy, I'd agree. It's a great place to buy a gift or indulge yourself.

Simon's Cliff House

4000 Westcliff Dr   541/386-5566
(See detailed listing with Columbia Gorge Hotel)

Solstice Wood Fire Café & Bar

501 Portway Ave   541/436-0800
Lunch, Dinner: Daily (summer); Wed-Mon (winter) solsticewoodfirecafe.com
Moderate

In 2013, Solstice Wood Fire Café & Bar moved to a beautiful location in Hood River across from the waterfront. In prior years, the Washington location had what was considered one of the 50 best pies in the country, the Country Girl Cherry pizza; a unique combination of cherries from the Columbia River Gorge region paired with chorizo sausage and goat cheese, topped off with a dash of rosemary and thyme. It's no wonder it won over the editors of the *Food Network Magazine*. Talk about inventive! This husband-and-wife team strongly believes in sourcing food from local farmers, ranchers and purveyors to bring customer's good organic food at a fair price. They too are allergy-friendly and offer gluten-free, vegan and vegetarian options. Although pizza is their specialty, they have a full menu consisting of small plates, salads such as the Siragusa pear salad, gluten-free seasonal soups and pastas/entrees including the grilled Chinook salmon. It doesn't end there, they have a full bar with culinary-inspired cocktails, rotating local microbrews, hard cider and a house wine to enjoy in the cafe or outside on the outdoor patio seating. Owners **Suzanne and Aaron Baumhackl** have created a family-friendly environment with a special menu and play area for kids.

Stonehedge Gardens

3405 Wine Country Ave   541/386-3940
Dinner: Daily   stonehedgeweddings.com
Moderate and up

This charming dinner house is situated on seven acres of spectacular gardens and terraces. Indoors, a fireplace, cozy tables and wood-paneled walls create a romantic setting. The alfresco site is a popular wedding venue; the ceremonial area is cleverly framed with heart-shaped shrubbery. **Shawna and Mike Caldwell**'s gourmet menu features delicious specials such as authentic French onion soup, halibut and rack of lamb. Regular menu offerings include such tempting plates as a garlic mushroom dish, Thai-style crab cakes, spicy peanut chicken, steak Diane, wild salmon and pork scaloppini.

Gluten-free gourmet entrees, housemade dinner rolls, stocks and sauces are also specialties. For dessert, try the flaming bread pudding topped with crème brûlée and served tableside.

Western Antique Aeroplane & Automobile Museum

1600 Air Museum Road   541/308-1600
Daily: 9-5   waaamuseum.org
Reasonable

This fascinating museum houses one of the largest collections of flying antique airplanes and operating antique automobiles in the country. It showcases over 300 working planes, cars, motorcycles, military jeeps and tractors. Volunteers are always tinkering on engines, polishing chrome and ensuring that the collection is in functioning order. For added enjoyment, plan a visit on the second Saturday of the month when proud drivers take the antique cars out for a spin (weather permitting) offering rides between 10:30 a.m. and 2 p.m. Allow plenty of time to partake in the monthly cookout and view the demonstrations.

BEST OPENING AWARD

It's official! **Escape Lodging Company**'s **Fairfield Inn & Suites The Dalles** (2014 W 7th St, The Dalles; 541/769-0753) was awarded "Best Opening" property by Marriott International for 2014-2015. This was their first Marriott endeavor as an independent boutique hotel developer. What an honor for Escape Lodging Company and The Dalles Fairfield team under general manager **Troy Crowe**. The prestigious award was given to only four hotels out of more than 200 new properties. Well done!

MOSIER

Three Sleeps Vineyard B&B

1600 Carroll Road   541/478-0143, 541/490-5404
Moderate   threesleepsvineyardbandb.com

Enjoy a welcoming evening taste of Dominio IV wine (dominiowines. com) with owners **Liz and Glenn Bartholomew** at their manicured environs. The accommodation overlooks the Dominio Estate Vineyard and Mt. Adams in the distance; take a vineyard tour if you'd like. Choose from either a king or queen room, each with a private entrance and bath and a patio where world-class views are yours; arrangements for in-room massages are gladly made. The B&B name originates from the Lewis & Clark expedition when explorers asked how far it was to the ocean. Native Americans replied, "Three sleeps."

MT. HOOD

Mt. Hood Meadows
14040 Hwy 35   503/337-2222
Seasonal   skihood.com

Locals call it "Meadows;" the premier ski area on the mountain, with 2,777 vertical feet, 2,150 skiable acres, 11 lifts and the widest variety of skiing for all abilities from beginner to expert. When conditions cooperate, powder hounds will appreciate Heather Canyon, which can offer wonderful deep-powder experiences. The location on the southeast flank of the mountain is sunnier and more wind-protected than the south-facing slope, resulting in broader and more diverse downhill opportunities. As a day area so close to Portland (90 driving minutes away), weekends and school vacations can bring huge crowds; consider a mid-week visit. Energizing and delicious dining options in the South and North lodges include sit-down service at the **Alpenstube Restaurant** and **Vertical Restaurant and Sports Bar** and two quick, casual eateries. On the slopes, **Mazot** serves bistro fare at 6,000 feet and utterly awe-inspiring views. Additional services incorporate ski and snowboard schools and Nordic and demo centers.

Mt. Hood Organic Farm
7130 Smullin Dr   541/352-7492, 541/352-7123
Seasonal   mthoodorganicfarms.com

Apples and pears fresh from the orchard are the specialty of Mt. Hood Organic Farms, where crops are organically and biodynamically grown. This was the first farm in the Hood River Valley to receive full organic certification and is the only organic orchard in the valley that is open to the public. **Brady and John Jacobson** raise over a million pounds of apples and pears each year. All total, there are some 60 varieties to choose from; the selection varies as orchards mature and they are replaced with new stock. Only fruits from their 210-acre farm are sold at the packinghouse farmstand. Ask about their hard cider in European-champagne style, an up-and coming product. The farm is also a popular destination for a picturesque wedding, with farm-to-table wedding dinners; the gardens, architecture and incredible views are worth the drive.

PARKDALE

Apple Valley BBQ Restaurant and Catering
4956 Baseline Dr   541/352-3554
(See detailed listing with Apple Valley Country Store, Hood River)

Old Parkdale Inn Bed & Breakfast
4932 Baseline Dr   541/352-5551
Moderate   hoodriverlodging.com

Three guest rooms reflect Oregon's state symbols: Meadowlark, Douglas fir and Chinook; the latter two are suites with separate living rooms. All are furnished with queen beds and private baths, flat-screen televisions, microwaves, refrigerators and Internet access. Breakfasts feature famous Hood River fruits and produce, served in the dining room or delivered to your room. The deck or picturesque gardens are tranquil morning coffee venues. The innkeepers have created several packages ranging from romantic seclusion to outdoor adventures.

RHODODENDRON

A Majestic Mountain Retreat
Lolo Pass Road   503/686-8080
Expensive and up   amajesticmountainretreat.com

This secluded three-story log home has all the creature comforts: plush towels and robes, 600 thread-count bed linens, a game room, fully-equipped kitchen (serving up to 24 people), dining and sitting area, individual iPod systems in each room, hot tub and a handcrafted two-story wood-burning fireplace. Two luxurious master king suites with en suite bathrooms and two queen bedrooms (one with a bunk bed, too) are strategically arranged in the home for maximum privacy. Custom touches are everywhere including the powder room's sink basin which is carved from a local boulder and cradled in a small tree. Mt. Hood, restaurants and year-round outdoor activities are only minutes away. (The exact address will be given upon reserving the retreat.) Owner **Becca Niday**'s handmade chocolate truffles are to die for!

Mt. Hood Roasters
73451 E Hwy 26   503/622-6574
Daily: 8-5   mthoodroasters.com

As you enter Mt. Hood Roasters you are sure to be energized by the aroma of their air-roasted coffee. The business is passionate about quality over quantity, always using 100% Arabica coffee beans. Coffee is handcrafted on site and each 10-pound batch of coffee is guaranteed to be gourmet, rich in flavor and smooth in taste. Mt. Hood Roasters is a quaint shop with a table or two outdoors to enjoy a pastry with your afternoon coffee. Call ahead for a possible staff tour of the facility. Their great reputation has allowed them to distribute gourmet coffee to restaurants, professional offices and other retail operations; remember them when searching for a gift for the coffee lover in your life. Coffee is available for purchase in-store and online; customize your purchase with a private label, picture or logo.

Zigzag Mountain Cafe
70171 E Hwy 26   503/622-7681
Daily: Breakfast, Lunch   Facebook
Inexpensive

Many travelers making a trek to Mt. Hood, stop regularly at the rustic Zigzag Mountain Cafe. The cafe cooks up feel-good favorites at breakfast and lunch; housemade biscuits and jam are popular as

OREGON GOVERNOR JULIUS MEIER

Julius Meier was the third child of Aaron and Jeannette Meier. He graduated from University of Oregon Law School in 1895 and practiced law for four years until he went into the family retail business. Legend has it that a sign painter was putting Julius' name on the office door and asked his middle initial. Julius said he didn't have one. The painter insisted that every lawyer of substance had a middle initial, so Julius suggested an "L." It was Julius L. Meier from then on.

Julius married Grace Rose Mayer of San Francisco, on Christmas Day, 1901. With a smile, Julius told everyone it was the only day he was allowed off from the Meier & Frank store! They had three children Jean, Elsa and Julius Jr. (Jack).

Julius spent 30 years involved in civic affairs. In 1930, when friend George W. Joseph died while running for governor of Oregon, Julius was recruited to enter the race as an Independent candidate. He won 55% of the total vote, more than the Republican and Democratic candidates combined. His overwhelming victory reflected his support (and that of the public) for hydropower development. Julius was the only Independent to be elected Governor of Oregon and one of two Jewish governors of Oregon.

Among Meier's accomplishments as governor were the formation of the Oregon Liquor Control Commission, Oregon State Police and the State Unemployment Commission. Julius used his business experience to help the State of Oregon navigate through the financial problems of the Great Depression.

After one term (1931-1935), Julius was encouraged to run again; however, because of ill health, he retired to his lovely Menucha estate where he passed away in 1937.

*(Excerpted from **Oregon's Own Gerry Frank**, with permission from author Jan Boutin.)*

are the comforting chicken noodle soup, stew and chili. Take a seat on the mezzanine, the tables overlooking the forest and Bear Creek or near the large stone fireplace with hot cocoa in hand.

SANDY

Calamity Jane's Hamburger Parlor
42015 SE Hwy 26   503/668-7817
Lunch, Dinner: Daily   calamity-janes.com
Moderate

The Western façade is appropriate for this calorie-laden emporium named for the famous 19th century frontierswoman. Many a hungry skier and hiker have eaten here on their way to and from the Mt. Hood area. The restaurant's burgers (over 50 different fabrications) are nothing to sneeze at, claiming to be award-winning, world renowned. Other comfort foods are on the menu: pot roast, chicken in various embodiments, fish and chips, sandwiches and "pizza" burgers — all in large portions.

The Hidden Woods Bed & Breakfast
19380 E Summertime Dr   503/622-5754
Moderate   thehiddenwoods.com

Guests here will spend a memorable night (or longer) in a private two-bedroom log cabin with rustic charm and modern conveniences. The setting (ten miles east of Sandy) sets the mood for relaxation with beautiful gardens to stroll, a trail to the nearby Sandy River, a contemplative trout pond and a deck with a hot tub and fire pit. Come evening, hunker down and unwind in front of the living room's rock fireplace and prepare your favorite dinner or snacks in the well-appointed kitchen. A splendid breakfast is served in the hosts' log home just a short walk from the guest cabin. (Cash or checks only; no children under eight years of age; no pets.)

Joe's Donut Shop
39230 Pioneer Blvd   503/668-7215
Mon-Fri: 4 a.m.-5 p.m.; Sat, Sun: 5-5   joes-donuts.com

Can you say doughnuts? On the way up to the mountain, stop in at this old-time hangout for a bracing cup of coffee to accompany the freshest apple fritters, maple bars and scrumptious doughnuts (the same doughnut production technology since 1974). Weekend customers often find themselves choosing from baked pastries like strudels, filled croissants, Danish and turnovers. Look for the recognizable red and white block front building, a local landmark.

Rainbow Trout Farm

52560 E Sylvan Dr   503/622-5223
Mar-Oct: Daily   rainbowtroutfarm.com
Inexpensive and up

For a fishing excursion that guarantees a sure-bet catch, visit this Sandy trout farm. It's "pay" fishing in any of the ten ponds spread over 30 wooded and landscaped acres; no license is required. The catch charge is based upon fish size (up to two-foot lunkers) and pool; the bigger the fish, the more you pay. A hospitality room includes a full kitchen and barbecue set up; bring side dishes and fry up the fresh catch. Poles and tackle are provided or bring your own; staff will gladly clean your catch or do it yourself. This place is a great venue for company outings, birthday parties or field trips; wheelchair accessible.

Sandy Salmon Bed & Breakfast Lodge

61661 E Hwy 26   503/622-6699
Expensive   sandysalmon.com

This 6,000-square-foot log building sits on a bluff some 60 feet above the confluence of the Sandy and Salmon rivers. Choose from four guest rooms with private bathrooms, including two with a Jacuzzi tub that could serve as a romantic bridal suite; other suites have outdoor decks and all feature native Oregon woods. The beautiful lodge hideaway also offers hearty breakfasts and plenty of recreation, including games around the comfortable stone fireplace, a theater room with a large 73-inch TV screen and a handcrafted pool table. Artistic wood carvings, a koi pond, waterfall and massive antler chandelier enhance the interior of the lodge's ambience. The vistas around this five-acre setting are breathtaking and enjoyed from the relaxing decks or while fishing, rafting, hiking, mountain biking and skiing — all nearby.

Tollgate Inn Restaurant & Bakery

38100 Hwy 26	503/668-8456
Breakfast, Lunch, Dinner: Daily	visittollgate.com
Moderate	
Bakery: Daily	503/826-1009

The menu selection is large and portions are satisfying. Breakfast classics are built around three eggs and sided with hash browns, home fries, toast, pancakes or fruit; omelets are prepared with six eggs and meats, cheese, vegetables and all the trimmings. It is a great place for Sunday breakfast any time of the year! The sandwich choices include burgers (nine variations) and a tasty assortment of BLTs, tuna and turkey melts, clubs, Reubens and an eight-ounce New York steak fully-loaded on a homemade hoagie roll. Specialties like pot roast, chicken-fried steak, liver and onions and favorites such as chicken pot pie, roasted turkey dinner and grilled pork chops are on the dinner menu as well as char-broiled steaks and prime rib (Thursday through Saturday). This is home-style cooking in a homey atmosphere complete with a big stone fireplace to warm your bones after a trek through the snow. Their next-door, made-from-scratch bakery turns out copious quantities of breads, pastries, cakes, pies, muffins and cookies to go along with freshly-made soups, sandwiches and espresso drinks; the irresistible baked goods are also served in the restaurant. Pick a treat (bear claw, cannoli or seasonal fruit pie) to pack along to your destination as well as a jar of jam or jelly from the gift shop.

THE DALLES

Baldwin Saloon

205 Court St	541/296-5666
Lunch, Dinner: Mon-Sat	baldwinsaloon.com
Moderate	

Originally opened in 1876, the business at this saloon was primarily provided by railroad and Columbia River activity. The building has morphed through many entrepreneurial uses, and in 1991 **Tracy and Mark Linebarger** purchased and restored it, adding a pleasant outdoor patio. Now it's a great place to browse the acquired antiques and artwork while enjoying lunch or dinner. The large and varied menu of soups, salads, sandwiches, burgers, seafood, steaks and pasta dishes is fresh and homemade. Standouts are the French onion soup topped with Gruyere cheese and old-fashioned bread pudding with blueberries and whipped cream.

Big Jim's Drive-In

2938 E 2nd St   541/298-5051
Lunch, Dinner: Daily   bigjimsdrivein.com
Inexpensive

Big Jim's has been the spot in The Dalles for great tasting burgers, fresh fruit milkshakes, fantastic fish and chips, chicken strips and huge salads made fresh daily. Hungry burger lovers have lots of flavors and sizes from which to choose as well as other sandwiches and dozens of hard ice cream concoctions to quell hunger pangs. This local landmark offers inside dining, an enjoyable fresh-air patio during nice weather and drive-through service; call-in orders are welcome.

OUTLET SHOPPING

Quality merchandise at impressive discounts (25% to 65% from retail prices) is available at these Oregon outlet centers. Special events and coupon books (also offered online) afford even deeper savings.

Bend Factory Stores (63100 S Hwy 97, Bend; 541/382-4736; bendfactorystores.com): 19 stores, good savings

Columbia Gorge Premium Outlets (450 NW 257th Way, Troutdale; 503/669-8060; premiumoutlets.com/columbiagorge): 38 stores, minutes from Portland

Seaside Factory Outlets (1111 N Roosevelt Dr, Seaside; 503/717-1603; seasideoutlets.com): 26 stores, Nike and Pendleton outlets

Tanger Outlet of Lincoln City (1500 SE East Devils Lake Road, Lincoln City; 541/996-5000; tangeroutlet.com/lincolncity): 58 well-known shops, plenty of parking

Woodburn Premium Outlets (1001 Arney Road, Woodburn; 503/981-1900; premiumoutlets.com/woodburn): 116 stores and services, attractive buildings

Celilo Inn

3550 E 2nd St   541/769-0001
Inexpensive and up   celiloinn.com

From its hillside perch, this updated circa-1950 motel provides wondrous views. Accommodations range from a deluxe family suite (with both queen- and king-size beds), king suites, junior king rooms and queen rooms (non-view rooms). Ease into your stay with a complimentary glass of local wine at check in; a carefully selected menu of Gorge wines are for sale in the lobby. Morning pastries, granola and fruit are presented early mornings and a 24-hour coffee bar satisfies caffeine cravings. An outdoor patio with fire pit, fitness facility with a view, seasonal outdoor pool and wine tasting packages are nice additions to this property.

The Columbia Gorge Discovery Center and Wasco County Historical Museum

5000 Discovery Dr   541/296-8600
Daily: 9-5   gorgediscovery.org
Nominal

Have you ever wondered how the Gorge was formed? Check out the Ice Age exhibit when you begin your journey through this beautiful museum adjacent to the Columbia River. Interactive displays depict the past; live birds of prey are featured in the center's raptor program. Learn how this area was shaped and influenced by early inhabitants, the Lewis and Clark expedition and settlers along the Oregon Trail. Catch a glimpse of Wasco County in a re-created setting. The award-winning building and location are magnificent, surrounded by phenomenal vistas, trails, a pond and overlooks; don't miss the nature walk.

Cousins Country Inn

2114 W 6th St   541/298-5161, 800/848-9378
Inexpensive to moderate   cousinscountryinn.com

One look at this welcoming complex beckons travelers to stop in for a meal or overnight respite. All of the rooms are outfitted with a refrigerator, microwave, DVD player and coffeemaker; a seasonal outdoor pool and hot tub are on-site. In addition to 97 deluxe accommodations, eight rooms are enhanced with large showers (three showerheads), fireplaces, patios, balconies and sundecks. Feel free to dip into the large jar of homemade cookies at the front desk where you can request a complimentary pass to The Dalles Fitness Club. An expansive menu of wonderful comfort food is a few steps away all day, every day at **Cousins Restaurant & Saloon** (cousinsthedalles.com). Generous portions of homemade chicken pot pie, loaded chicken salad, old-fashioned meatloaf, pot roast sandwiches and fresh, gigantic cinnamon rolls are sure to please anyone in your party. Breakfast is served all day; a fun saloon menu of appetizers and libations satisfies the of-age group. As the name implies, this is a family-friendly place. The proprietor is Escape Lodging.

Fort Dalles Museum

500 W 15th St   541/296-4547
Daily: 10-5 (Mar-Oct); Fri-Sun: 10-5(Nov-Feb)   fortdallesmuseum.org
Nominal

This is one of Oregon's oldest history museums, housed in the former Surgeon's Quarters of Fort Dalles, a U.S. Army outpost from 1850 to 1860. The museum was founded in 1905 with collections dating back to that time, as well as new additions on display. Early furniture, Native American artifacts, clothing, kitchen items, cookware, books and photographs of the area's people and places are spread throughout the two-story building. Saddles and guns are displayed in an upstairs bedroom. Over 30 antique wagons and vehicles are housed in two buildings on the property; a stage coach, mail wagon, horse-drawn hearses, surreys, buses, road-building equipment and early automobiles are among the collection of items with local connections. The Anderson Homestead was relocated from nearby Pleasant Ridge to property across the street from the main museum; the log home, granary and two-story barn were restored to original condition. Admission includes a welcome and orientation to the complex; peruse the museum and grounds at your own pace.

NOTEWORTHY STOPS ON
THE WASHINGTON SIDE

Visitors take note: there are many "don't miss" attractions on the Washington side of the Columbia River, within minutes of Oregon. Some of these engaging sights are along the historic **Lewis & Clark Trail** (lewisandclark.com).

The natural **Bonneville Hot Springs Resort & Spa** (509/427-7767, bonnevilleresort.com) is just up the Gorge from Portland. The geothermal water was originally enjoyed by Native Americans for medicinal purposes. Today you can take advantage of the same healing and relaxing properties in the upscale spa and lodge facility; add hiking, biking, windsurfing or play a round on the minigolf course; on-site fine dining won't disappoint.

Joining iconic Oregon destination resorts such as Salishan and Sunriver, **Skamania Lodge** (866/399-7980, skamania.com) is just a hop, skip and jump from Bonneville. Just across the Bridge of the Gods at Cascade Locks, 254 Cascadian-style rooms offer river and mountain views, along with golf, horseback riding, spa and valuable R&R time away from it all. The Cascade Dining Room is a favorite special-occasion and brunch destination.

As you make your way farther east (from I-84, cross the Sam Hill Memorial Bridge at Biggs Junction), **Maryhill Winery** (877/627-9445, maryhillwinery.com), the **Maryhill Museum of Art** (509/773-3733, maryhillmuseum.org) and the **Stonehenge Memorial** associated with the museum are worth your time. **Samuel Hill** originally built the museum structure as his grand home and named it Maryhill after his wife, Mary. Hill built the Stonehenge replica as a monument to heroism and peace, honoring WW I servicemen of Klickitat County, Washington. The Columbia Gorge Highway, known now as I-84, is attributed to Hill's advocacy to build a great highway so that the world can realize the magnificence and grandeur of the Columbia River Gorge. **Vicki and Craig Leuthold** established the Maryhill Winery in 1999, now a destination for fine wines, picnicking and world-class summertime concerts in the 4,000-seat amphitheater.

Extending from the Columbia River and up the hills several miles on the north side of Highway 14 is **Beacon Rock State Park** (509/427-8265, parks.wa.gov/474/Beacon-Rock). It is named for Beacon Rock, a distinctive basalt monolith and unique landmark documented and so-named by the Lewis and Clark Expedition. While camping   →

NOTEWORTHY STOPS ON THE WASHINGTON SIDE, CONTINUED

← is available April through October, it is mainly a day-use park offering a full range of outdoor recreation. Paddling, fishing and boating are popular river activities. Hikers will find trails ranging from quite easy to strenuous; the switchback trail up Beacon Rock itself is well traveled and rewards you with stunning Columbia River Gorge views. Some trails are open to mountain biking and horseback riding. Rock climbers, after registering, are allowed on part of Beacon Rock.

Just off Highway 14 in the small town of Stevenson, the **Columbia Gorge Interpretive Center Museum** (509/427-8211, columbiagorge. org) features human and natural history of the Gorge. Exhibits and artifacts illuminate ancient and traditional Native American life on the Columbia River and includes pictographs, stone tools and baskets. The huge fish wheel, logging equipment and railroad machinery provide a fascinating look at the region's early industry.

Sacajawea State Park (506/545-2361, stateparks.com/sacajawea) is a 284-acre Washington State Park located at the joining of the Snake and Columbia rivers in the city of Pasco. The Lewis and Clark Expedition camped at this location on October 16, 1805. The park bears the name of the Shoshone woman Sacagawea who was an active member of the expedition and who was married to French-Canadian interpreter and explorer Toussaint Charbonneau. The park's **Sacajawea Interpretive Center** features exhibits about both her and the Lewis and Clark Expedition. Park activities include hiking, boating, fishing, swimming, waterskiing, birdwatching, interpretive programs, wildlife viewing and horseshoes. Of note for cyclists, the **Sacagawea Heritage Trail** is a 23-mile paved trail that begins at the park and connects Pasco, Kennewick and Richland (the Tri-Cities) in Washington.

Momma Jane's Pancake House

900 W 6th St   541/296-6611
Breakfast, lunch: Daily   Facebook
Inexpensive

This pancake house serves breakfasts sure to please the heartiest of eaters. Omelets and scrambles are filled with delicious cheese combinations, breakfast meats and vegetables and are served with a choice of hash browns, home fries or fruit and toast, biscuits and gravy or all-you-can-eat pancakes. Specialty pancakes are filled with fruits, berries, nuts and other good things; squirrel pancakes feature sliced almonds and homemade honey-cream cheese topping. Other options include fruit crepes, cinnamon roll French toast (made with housemade cinnamon rolls), Benedicts and waffles. At lunch, burgers and favorite hot and cold sandwiches are just as tasty and are accompanied by fries, cottage cheese, soup, salad or homemade potato salad. Filling hot roast beef or turkey sandwiches are served with mashed potatoes and gravy plus soup or salad. Hot lunches include meatloaf, chicken strips, beer-battered fish filets and country fried steak with all the trimmings, including homemade cornbread.

Nichols Art Glass
912 W 6th St   541/296-2143
Wed-Sun: 10-6   nicholsartglass.com

Artist and entrepreneur **Andy Nichols** found his artistic dream niche in hot glass work and opened his gallery in 2007. You've likely seen his signature salmon, pumpkin and cherry pieces and other glasswork in galleries and installations throughout the Northwest. He produces unique pieces in his 2,700-square-foot studio, incorporating a wine barrel, barge or other unexpected element; custom orders welcome. The comfortable gallery contains colorful and interesting displays; an open viewing area gives onlookers the opportunity to see Andy and associates in action. Classes in glass blowing and art glass are offered throughout the year.

Petite Provence of the Gorge
408 E 2nd St   541/506-0037
(See detailed listing with Petite Provence, Portland)

The Pines Cottage
The Pines 1852
5450 Mill Creek Road   541/993-8300
(See detailed listing with The Pines Tasting Room, Hood River)

Sunshine Mill Artisan Plaza and Winery

901 E 2nd St   541/298-8900, ext 1
Seasonal   sunshinemill.com

The Sunshine Mill has been a towering landmark in The Dalles for over a century and previously milled wheat for the Sunshine Biscuit Company. That industry is just a memory, but the setting is alive with mechanisms, artifacts and contrivances from that business. The new name describes the campus' newest use. Quenett and Copa Di Vino wines are produced on-site by local vintners **Molli and James Martin** and are featured in the tasting room; specialty appetizers are available. Good use is made of the property's boiler house, warehouse and open spaces. An outdoor amphitheater is a delightful place to sip wine in the sunshine at the Sunshine Mill. Check the events schedule for occasional closures for private functions.

TIMBERLINE

Timberline Lodge

27500 E Timberline Road   503/272-3311, 800/547-1406
Moderate and up   timberlinelodge.com

Mt. Hood is one of our state's most beloved and visited all-season attractions! Whether you ski, take a hike, enjoy a fabulous meal in the splendid dining room, spend the night or enjoy a day trip to Timberline Lodge, you won't be disappointed. The lodge was dedicated in 1937, a project of the Works Progress Administration (WPA), and is furnished with incredible handmade furnishings and hand-painted artwork, centered by a massive wood-burning stone fireplace. The **Cascade Dining Room** (503/272-3104) continues to serve first-class alpine cuisine in this National Historic Landmark. Tantalizing buffet offerings can be enjoyed for breakfast and lunch. Dinner offers a full service menu; reservations required. Oregon produce and products are highlighted with entrees such as alder-smoked and grilled ribeye with black truffle butter, braised lamb shank, chicken and a Northwest artisan cheese selection. Lighter fare is served at the lodge's other lounges and eateries. Overnighters will find cozy lodge rooms outfitted with handmade furnishings, modern necessities and wood-burning fireplaces in some rooms. Chalet rooms (outfitted with bunks to accommodate two, six or eight guests; shared bathrooms) are an option for groups and families. A larger chalet room, with private bath, sleeps ten. **Silcox Hut**, a hand-crafted stone and timber cabin, is situated farther up the mountain at 7,000 feet and offers groups of 12 to 24 unique lodging, dinner, breakfast and round-trip transportation from the lodge. An extra special indulgence at this restored rustic beauty is the winemaker's dinner series featuring Oregon vineyards, six-course gourmet fare and unforgettable snowmobile transportation between the lodge and hut. The ski area and lift network appeal to beginning and intermediate skiers. Palmer Snowfield offers summer skiing above the tree line, although much of the hill is reserved for summer racing camps; mountain biking and hiking, too.

TROUTDALE

Caswell Gallery

255 E Columbia River Hwy   503/492-2473
Tues-Sat: 10-5:30; Mon: by appointment   ripcaswell.com

Rip Caswell's path to full-time sculpting has been an interesting one. Caswell studied animal anatomy in detail and was named best taxidermist in the nation in 1991. He went on to study human anatomy, and the rest is history. His bronze pieces include the National Monument of Admiral Chester Nimitz at Pearl Harbor, the magnificent larger-than-life-size former Governor Tom McCall at Salem's Riverfront Park, two life-size elk at the High Desert Museum near Bend, an Iraq war memorial in Madras, an entryway monument in Tualatin and other installations around the country. The artist's studio and gallery are also featured in Troutdale's monthly First Friday Art Walk.

Ristorante Di Pompello

177 E Historic Columbia River Hwy   503/667-2480
Breakfast: Tues-Sun; Lunch, Dinner: Daily   dipompello.com
Inexpensive to moderate

Ristorante Di Pompello is a delightful Italian family restaurant in picturesque Troutdale under the direction of **Ruby and Saul**

HOTELS OF YESTERYEAR

Renovated hotels of yesteryear still roll out the welcome mat for visitors all around the state. Check the websites for the interesting history of these lodgings. Some accommodations are more rustic than others.

ASHLAND
Ashland Springs Hotel (ashlandspringshotel.com)
Peerless Hotel (peerlesshotel.com)

ASTORIA
Hotel Elliott (hotelelliott.com)

BAKER CITY
Geiser Grand Hotel (geisergrand.com)

CAVE JUNCTION
The Chateau at the Oregon Caves (oregoncaveschateau.com)

CONDON
Hotel Condon (hotelcondon.com)

DUFUR
Balch Hotel (balchhotel.com)

HOOD RIVER
Columbia Gorge Hotel (columbiagorgehotel.com)

JACKSONVILLE
Jacksonville Inn (jacksonvilleinn.com)

McMINNVILLE
Hotel Oregon (mcmenamins.com/8-hotel-oregon-history)

MITCHELL
The Oregon Hotel (theoregonhotel.net)

PORTLAND
The Benson Hotel (bensonhotel.com)
The Heathman Hotel (heathmanhotel.com)

PRAIRIE CITY
Historic Hotel Prairie (hotelprairie.com)

PROSPECT
Prospect Historic Hotel (prospecthotel.com)

TIMBERLINE
Timberline Lodge (timberlinelodge.com)

WHEELER
Old Wheeler Hotel (oldwheelerhotel.com)

There are others, including **Portland's Embassy Suites** (embassysuites.hilton.com) where the historic Multnomah Hotel was formerly located.

Pompeyo. Classic pasta dishes such as ravioli marinara, garlicky fettuccini alfredo and layered lasagna are delicious dinner options or choose from chicken basil tortellini, gnocchi alle bistecca, chicken parmesan and other robust dinners. Tiger prawns alle lobster sauce, Tuscan salmon and more scampi entrees are also enticing. The lunch menu has a full array of salads, sandwiches, Italian entrees, pasta, fish and seafood choices. Roman pan-fried lamb stewed in red wine, Milanese pork with a light mushroom sauce and seafood risotto are standouts. Breakfast is available most mornings with the usual

KIDS' ACTIVITIES: IN AND AROUND TOWN

BRIDAL VEIL
Multnomah Falls (503/695-2372, oregon.com/attractions/multno mah_falls)

CASCADE LOCKS
Bonneville Lock and Dam (541/374-8820, nwp.usace.army.mil/ locations/bonneville.asp)
Sternwheeler Columbia Gorge (541/374-8427, portofcascadelocks. org/sternwheeler.htm): seasonal

CORBETT
Vista House (503/695-2240, vistahouse.com)

GOVERNMENT CAMP
Mt. Hood Meadows Ski Resort (503/337-2222, skihood.com)
Mt. Hood Skibowl & Adventure Park (503/272-3206, skibowl.com)

HOOD RIVER
Hood River WaterPlay (541/386-9463, hoodriverwaterplay.com)
Mount Hood Railroad (541/386-3556, mthoodrr.com)

THE DALLES
The Columbia Gorge Discovery Center (541/296-8600, gorge discovery.org)

TIMBERLINE
Timberline Lodge & Ski Area (503/272-3311, timberlinelodge.com)

TROUTDALE
The Rail Depot Museum (503/661-2164, troutdalehistory.org/ the-rail-depot)

items: bacon, eggs, potatoes, pancakes, French toast, chicken-fried steak and such. Local artist Rip Caswell's bronze trout statues flank the signage which reads "Troutdale, Gateway to the Gorge." Just down the street is Troutdale's illuminated Centennial Arch.

Riverview Restaurant

29311 SE Stark St   503/661-3663
Dinner: Tues-Sun   yoshidariverview.com
Moderate

Linda and Junki Yoshida's romantic dinner house along the Sandy River was meticulously designed to capture the area's natural beauty; inside, original artwork from their private collection is displayed. The Northwest cuisine showcases game dishes (seasonally available), fresh seafood, steaks and chicken punctuated with Asian influences. The lounge has daily happy hour specials and plenty of good eats including Mr. Yoshida's Teriyaki Bowl, sandwiches, salads and bar favorites. Diners are often entertained with local musical talent.

Shirley's Tippy Canoe

28242 E Columbia River Hwy   503/492-2220
Breakfast, Lunch, Dinner: Daily   shirleysfood.com
Moderate to moderately expensive

Here's an enjoyable restaurant with an attractive outdoor dining spot. The menu is large and portions are plentiful. Breakfast consists of egg dishes with, among the usual offerings, housemade Italian or Polish sausage; corned beef hash; omelets with everything imaginable and freshly-squeezed juices. Sandwiches prevail on the lunch menu and are especially filling with freshly-cut French fries. Hungry beef lovers may opt for the 60-ounce ribeye or New York steak; other choices include fresh seafood, meat and pasta entrees. Jams, soups, salad dressings, sauces and desserts are homemade from old-fashioned recipes; try the Sloppy Sally cake (named for the process). Most every Friday and Saturday night, the Tippy has live music, or cozy up to the outside fire pits where blues and jazz liven up summer Sundays.

Tad's Chicken 'n Dumplins

1325 E Historic Columbia River Hwy   503/666-5337
Dinner: Daily   tadschicdump.com
Moderate

Every time I dine on chicken and dumplings, I am reminded of long-ago family dinners. While Tad's is known for this stick-to-your-ribs dish, crispy fried chicken and chicken liver dinners have also enticed folks here for many years. You may also deviate to seafood, beef (liver and onions, too) and pasta entrees plus hearty salads. Dinners include a relish tray, soup or salad, bread and home-style green beans. A trip to Tad's merits a Sunday drive on this scenic highway along the Sandy River.

Troutdale General Store

289 E Historic Columbia River Hwy   503/492-7912
Mon-Fri: 8-5; Sat, Sun: 9-5   troutdalegeneralstore.com

You'll be taken back to a simpler time when you visit this store in the heart of town. Browse through 8,500 square feet of nostalgic toys, decor and souvenirs or stop in for an inexpensive breakfast or lunch of biscuits and gravy, a Cajun meatloaf sandwich or a splurge from the ice cream counter. Weekends offer piping-hot smoked salmon chowder, a meal in itself, or pair it with a great sandwich.

WELCHES

Barlow Trail Roadhouse

69580 E Hwy 26   503/622-1662
Breakfast, Lunch, Dinner: Daily   barlowtrailroadhouse.com
Inexpensive and up

Home-style cooking has been the mainstay at this historic 1926 log cabin which originally served as a general store and later became an inn. The name is derived from the famous Oregon Trail namesake toll road (circa 1846), constructed by Sam Barlow. For a hearty morning start, dig into mountain toast — Texas toast dipped in pancake batter, oats and frosted flakes, then deep fried. Chicken-fried steak with all the accompaniments, homemade chicken cordon bleu sandwich and "the best burger on the mountain" are favorites at this rustic roadhouse.

The Rendezvous Grill and Tap Room

67149 E Hwy 26   503/622-6837
Lunch, Dinner: Daily   thevousgrill.com
Moderate to moderately expensive

"Vous Grill" as it is affectionately called by regulars, has been a mainstay in Welches since 1995. Owners **Susie and Tom Anderson** present fresh, innovative dishes in a casual, inviting eatery. Menu selections are made to order with good options of hearty soups, salads and interesting sandwiches (grilled brie, bacon and apple) for lunch. Well-prepared fish, seafood, beef and pork dinner entrees are complemented with seasonal vegetables that are given gourmet treatment. Specialty pasta entrees, on-request gluten-free breads and housemade ice cream round out the appealing menu. Chef's three-course dinner ($28) is offered on Monday and Tuesday nights.

The Resort at the Mountain

69010 E Fairway Ave   503/622-3101, 877/439-6774
Moderate to expensive   theresort.com

Located on what was Oregon's first golf resort in 1928, The Resort at the Mountain is an outstanding northwest destination resort. Two golf courses (Foxglove Nine and Thistle Nine) joined Pine Cone Nine, this region's oldest; each offers a distinct golfing challenge. Rooms, suites and large villas provide comfortable lodging options for couples or groups. The year-round restaurant, **Altitude** (altituderestaurant.com), is conveniently located near guest quarters and serves Northwest farm-to-table cuisine throughout the day. Room service and additional casual eating venues are seasonally open in the spring and summer. A short trail leads to the activity center, spa, putting green, playground and more. This is a great getaway locale with leisure interests geared toward families: tennis, outdoor swimming pool (enclosed and heated seasonally), volleyball, bicycles, croquet, lawn bowling and badminton areas and rentals. Mountain sports and other activities are close by.

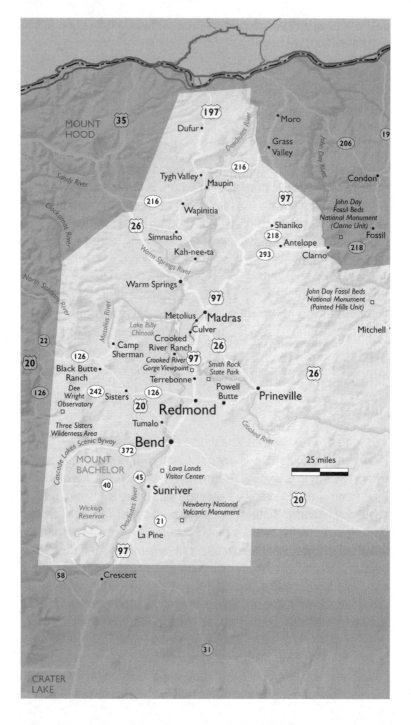

Central Oregon

BEND

Ariana

1304 NW Galveston Ave
Dinner: Tues-Sat
Expensive

541/330-5539
arianarestaurantbend.com

This is a beautiful choice for exceptional upscale dining and professional service where a relaxed atmosphere in a Craftsman bungalow is the order of the day. The European bistro menu has ever-changing Mediterranean flair with such items as a spicy calamari appetizer, roasted beet salad, Spanish paella, grilled quail and an assortment of meat and seafood entrees. I heartily recommend the chocolate cake dessert, although the artisanal cheese plate comes in a close second. Outside, the patio will pique diners' appreciation for summer days.

The Blacksmith Restaurant

211 NW Greenwood Ave   541/318-0588
Dinner: Daily   bendblacksmith.com
Moderate

This is a well-known Bend staple under the culinary direction of Bryan Chang, where your tastes will not be disappointed in the historic Pierson's Blacksmith Shop. Distinctive, bold cuisine is featured at this steakhouse, bar and lounge. Stone and brick walls, a copper bar top, subtle lighting and leather upholstery create a casually-elegant ambience with cozy seating areas. The sophisticated comfort food meals are attractively plated with delicious accompaniments. "The Tomahawk" 24-ounce bone-in ribeye steak is a customer favorite! Other not-to-be-missed dishes are cider-brined pork chops, decadent mac and cheese sides, shrimp and grits and crab corn dogs. Local, natural, dry-aged steaks are prepared in exquisite sauces or served simply. Desserts are to die for, especially the show-stopping Fostered bananas split, prepared tableside.

Brickhouse

5 NW Minnesota Ave   541/728-0334
(See detailed listing with Brickhouse, Redmond)

Cascade Culinary Institute

2555 NW Campus Village Way   541/318-3780
Lunch, Dinner: Wed-Fri   cascadeculinary.com, elevationbend.com
Inexpensive to moderate

Central Oregon Community College operates a state-of-the-art training ground for chefs and food service workers where students get a taste for running a fine-dining restaurant. At **Elevation** (877/541-2433), fine-dining lunch options include a choice of appetizer, seasonal entree and decadent dessert. Ingredients may include house-cured bacon and meats, locally sourced bounty and other quality components in preparations rivaling the area's better restaurants. A typical dine-in lunch menu may feature crawfish au gratin with house-smoked tasso ham and white cheddar cheese. The take-out menu might include ale and stone-ground corn tortilla-battered halibut, a contemporary version of Cobb salad and a house hamburger garnished with caramelized onion jam. Appetizer servings of smoked salmon beignets followed by New York strip steaks, miso-glazed ling cod or braised lamb shanks, may be the evening's selections. Reservations are suggested and small groups (40 to 80 people) may reserve the space for a three-course *prix-fixe* dinner. Culinary classes are presented through the community learning program.

Deschutes Brewery & Public House

1044 NW Bond St   541/382-9242
Lunch, Dinner: Daily   deschutesbrewery.com
Moderate to moderately expensive

This über-fun Public House is a great place to unwind after an outdoor day in Deschutes County. There are plenty of food choices including sausages and brewery pretzels with white Tillamook cheddar cheese and Black Butte Porter stone-ground mustard. The Brewmaster and Italian chop are a couple of the fresh salad choices, hearty enough for a meal. Tasty wings, bar snacks, sandwiches (barbecued chicken and bacon), burgers and satisfying entrees (boar meatloaf) are easily washed down with one of the dozen and a half year-round and seasonal brews and ales (also liberally used in menu items). While at the brewery, purchase a keg to go or fill a growler; bottled selections are sold at retailers.

Desperado

330 SW Powerhouse Dr, Suite 120   541/749-9980 (both stores)
Shoes &... by desperado   desperadoboutique.com
330 SW Powerhouse Dr, Suite 125
Mon-Sat: 10-8; Sun: 11-6

Desperado and its new shoe and accessory boutique, located in Bend's historic Old Mill District, are perfect stops for topnotch Western clothing with a mix of Bohemian charm. These boutiques offer clothing, boots, jewelry, gifts and home decor from top Western couture designers — like Ryan Michael, Johnny Was, Double D Ranchwear, Tasha Polizzi, Minnetonka and world-renowned bootmakers Old Gringo and Liberty Boot. Owner **Joanne Sunnarborg** has created an eclectic array of Americana, Native American and Western-influenced fashion appropriate for every day, special occasion and anytime in between.

Dudley's Bookshop Cafe

135 NW Minnesota Ave   541/749-2010
Daily: Hours vary   dudleysbookshopcafe.com

Dudley's has become a community center of green recycling as a secondhand bookstore offering some 30,000 volumes. There are also new books by local authors as well as local artwork. The small first-floor cafe area serves local coffee, tea and baked goods in a living room atmosphere. You'll find local musicians here on most Friday evenings along with interesting weekly and monthly events.

Elk Lake Resort

60000 Century Dr   541/480-7378
Inexpensive to expensive   elklakeresort.net

Central Oregon offers some of Oregon's finest skiing, winter hiking and mountain relaxation. For a wintertime family treat, park your vehicle at Dutchman Flats and ski, snowmobile or take the Sno-Cat to the resort. Cabins and homes are most appealing; they are outfitted with kitchens, bathrooms and other necessities and accommodate up to ten guests. Three heated camping cabins are rustic with no power, bathrooms, water or amenities. The year-round lodge functions as the activity hub with a store, equipment rentals (summer and winter sports) and dining room.

Greg's Grill

395 SW Powerhouse Dr   541/382-2200
Lunch, Dinner: Daily   gregsgrill.com
Moderately expensive

This Northwest lodge-themed restaurant in the Old Mill District is one of the most innovative and charming places to dine. Relaxing views of the lazy Deschutes River and landscaped outdoor areas are framed by the floor-to-ceiling windows heightened by the soaring natural wood ceiling. Greg's could be called a steakhouse, but also offers flame-grilled burgers, sandwiches, chicken, seafood and healthy salads and soups for lunch and dinner. The grill also features handcrafted cocktails, gluten-free hard ciders, liqueurs, bottled beer and draft beer selections. Dessert options include locally-made ice cream, locally-sourced artisan gelato, housemade cobbler and the indisputably-decadent chocolate indulgence.

High Desert Museum

59800 S Hwy 97   541/382-4754
Daily: Winter: 10-4; Summer: 9-5   highdesertmuseum.org
Reasonable

Located four miles south of Bend, this museum highlights the natural and cultural resources of the High Desert. Meet raptors, porcupines, lynx, fox, otter and more live animals in natural habitat settings and in fun, educational programs. Kids love to explore the nature trails on 135 forested acres and learn through hands-on activities. Indoor and outdoor exhibitions feature historical characters portrayed live at a re-created 1880s town, working homestead ranch and a 100-year-old sawmill. Collections of High Desert historic artifacts and Western art are outstanding. Additional features include guided tours, play spaces for young kids, a cafe and Silver Sage Trading (the museum store). Parking is plentiful and convenient for tour buses, RVs and autos; the complex is ADA accessible. Picnic areas are provided, but beware, chipmunks and squirrels may be brazen in their quest for your picnic goods!

STARGAZING

With its elevation, pitch-dark surroundings and crystal clear air, Sunriver is perfect for stargazing (weather permitting). At the **Oregon Observatory** (57245 River Road, Sunriver; 541/598-4406; oregonobservatory.org) there are many telescopes, from Tele Vue refractors to a 30-inch Newtonian. Witness a meteor shower, view faraway galaxies, nebulae and deep space binary stars; even safe solar viewing. Check ahead for viewing hours; nominal charge.

The Hillside Inn

1744 NW 12th St   541/389-9660
Moderate   bendhillsideinn.com

This unique lodging offers an urban setting with a convenient location close to bustling downtown. Proprietor **Annie Goldner**'s inn features a pond, waterfall and a nearby hot tub, perfect for unwinding after a busy day. Breakfasts are especially nice, healthy and flexible to address special dietary issues. Newly constructed in 1999, this is not an antique-filled country inn; it is light and bright with contemporary furnishings and modern conveniences. The balcony suite overlooks the patio and pond while the ground-floor studio suite is complete with a fully-equipped kitchen and dining area, ideal for longer stays. Comforting amenities include silky robes, Turkish towels and luxury soaps and lotions. Shops, a park, bike trails and downtown are easily accessible within a mile.

Ida's Cupcake Cafe

1314 NW Galveston Ave   541/383-2345
Daily: 10-5 (Sun till 4)
1155 SW Division St, A-7   541/678-5057
Mon-Sat: 10-6   idascupcakecafe.com

Thank you, Ida, for appealing to my insatiable sweet tooth! I could be here all day contemplating the perfect combination of cake and frosting flavors, about 80 in all, not counting the seasonal or rotating flavors. Request your favorite pairing or choose from pre-frosted regular size "kidcakes" or twice-the-size gourmet cupcakes. Special occasions are more distinct with these beautiful uniquely decorated treats. Other party-worthy options are personalized bundt cakes, small layer cakes and mini-cupcakes — just about bite size. There are also a few gluten-free cupcake flavors as well as a gluten-, egg- and dairy-free cupcake. Visitors to Redmond can taste their treats at a third location (738 SW Highland, 541/548-8164).

Jackson's Corner

845 NW Delaware Ave	541/647-2198
1500 NE Cushing Dr	541/382-1751
Breakfast, Lunch, Dinner: Daily	jacksonscornerbend.com
Moderate	

If you're away from home and have a hankering for home cooking, you'll want to make note of Jackson's Corner. Basics include breakfast eggs and go-with dishes, housemade biscuits with gravy and brioche French toast. Pizzas, sandwiches and salads are offered at lunch and dinner; seasonally available ingredients determine the menu particulars. Pasta is made in-house for dinner and paired with tasty sauces and other ingredients. If you're in the mood for a hamburger, you'll need to wait for the weekly burger night (Wednesday eastside, Thursday westside) which features a six-ounce natural beef patty on a brioche bun topped with fresh-made aioli and just-right trimmings and fixings.

Joolz

916 NW Wall St	541/388-5094
Dinner: Daily	joolzbend.com
Inexpensive to moderately expensive	

Blend the Middle East with the Wild West at Joolz, serving Eastern Mediterranean cuisine with Central Oregon influences. Small plate options include vegetarian stuffed grape leaves, pan-seared unripened cheese with a wonderful savory concoction, sauce-laden elk served over hummus, salads and other unique plates. Dinner choices consist of ribeye steak seasoned with a housemade blend of spices, chili made with braised organic elk, chicken kabobs accompanied by a wicked garlic sauce, seasonal fish and seafood along with burgers made with longhorn beef, elk or ground lamb. For something different, try a warm sandwich made with ground falafel. Wines are as eclectic as the menu with labels from around the world; cocktails are exotic and may contain sagebrush-infused spirits. Overall, this is the ultimate stop for Meza plates, flatbread pizzas and all things Mediterranean.

Kanpai Sushi & Saké Bar
990 NW Newport Ave   541/388-4636
Dinner: Daily   kanpai-bend.com
Moderate

Look to this westside restaurant for satisfying sushi and Pan-Asian cuisine prepared with French techniques. Guests are assured that only locally-sourced, fresh, natural, hormone- and antibiotic-free meats and produce are used whenever possible; and a good-size takeout list includes Nigiri and seared filet mignon. Talented instructors show diners how delicious Kanpai dishes are created and assist neophytes in selecting items from the ample menu including the area's largest selection of imported Japanese saké and beer (a full bar and wine, too). Kanpai!

Lone Crow Bungalow
937 NW Wall St   541/383-2992
Mon-Sat: 10-6; Sun: 11-5   lonecrowbungalow.com

Don't miss Lone Crow Bungalow for a wonderful selection of quality handcrafted home goods made in America and from around the world. Featured items for your nest include pottery, clocks, dinnerware, artisan candles, garden accents, textiles and rugs, jewelry, lighting and much more. The staff at this beautiful shop is talented, helpful and creative.

McKay Cottage Restaurant
62910 O.B. Riley Road, #340   541/383-2697
Breakfast, Lunch: Daily   themckaycottage.com
Inexpensive to moderate

Enjoy award-winning comfort food breakfasts and lunches with a creative twist: Baja chicken hash stack, stuffed croissant French toast, Smith Rock "Benny" (a change-up on the usual eggs Benedict), mahi fish tacos, homemade soups, salads and sandwiches. Cinnamon rolls, pecan sticky buns, plump muffins, scones and a variety of desserts are made daily from scratch. Depending upon the weather, choose indoor seating next to the warm fireplace or pleasant outdoor seating on the lawn.

Mt. Bachelor

13000 SW Century Dr   800/829-2442
Seasonal   mtbachelor.com

Mt. Bachelor is the tallest (elevation 9,065 feet) resort peak in the Cascade Range covering 3,365 feet of vertical drop from summit to base. It is one of the few peaks in the world that affords skiing the entire mountain 360 degrees off the top. Grab a trail map before you venture out; there is a network of 12 lifts (quads, triples and tubing) and 88 runs. Guests of all ages and levels of experience will find their Eden on the mountain from Dilly-Dally Alley for youngsters to the double black diamond extreme territory on the backside of the mountain for proficient skiers. Four lodges are conveniently placed on the mountain to refresh skiers, 'boarders, 'tubers, 'shoers and snow enthusiasts with food and drink. Other services include lessons; retail, rental and tuning shops; a demo center; childcare; guide service; sled dog rides; cross country skiing and snowshoe tours. Just in case, Bend Memorial Clinic Urgent Care has an outpost in the ski patrol building. For an entirely different perspective, head to the mountain in summer for activities including the newly-introduced mountain bike park, disc golf, spectacular vistas from scenic lift rides and sunset gourmet dinners at mid-mountain Pine Marten Lodge.

Next Level Burger

70 SW Century Dr, #120   541/306-6778
Lunch, Dinner: Daily; Breakfast: Sat, Sun   nextlevelburger.com
Inexpensive

Husband-and-wife owners, **Cierra and Matt de Gruyter**, have re-invented the all-American burger. They have created a 100% plant-based burger, and it's delicious. Being true health advocates, they simply wanted a place where they could have a healthy burger with a side of fries and a shake, so they created it. Much of the menu is housemade, organic and non-GMO produce bought locally. Their heart-healthy, cholesterol-free menu is sure to please anyone dieting or just trying to live a healthier life. Besides burgers, menu options include salads, hot dogs and sandwiches. Don't live in town? Visit their newest location in Portland (4121 SE Hawthorne Blvd, 503/719-7058).

The Oxford Hotel

10 NW Minnesota Ave   541/382-8436, 877/440-8436
Moderate   oxfordhotelbend.com

This 59-suite, four-diamond boutique hotel is dedicated to sustainable hospitality. The Oxford Hotel has all the amenities of a top-drawer hotel, combined with "green" bedding, selections from a pillow menu, plush bathrobes, premium organic toiletries, in-room French press coffee service, room service and a state-of-the-art fitness center. Cruiser bicycles (summer only) are complimentary to guests. Airport shuttle and pet-friendly rooms are available; a nominal fee includes a size-appropriate bed for your canine, house-made treats and more. Three squares a day of "urban-organic" cuisine are available on the lower level at **10 Below Restaurant and Lounge**. Offerings change to capture the essence of the seasons. Sophisticated, contemporary luxury is a stunning addition to historic downtown.

Pilot Butte Drive-In Restaurant

917 NE Greenwood Ave   541/382-2972
320 SW Century Dr, Suite 410   541/323-3272
Daily: 7-7   pilotbuttedrivein.com
Inexpensive

A local and visitor favorite since 1983, Pilot Butte Drive-In has earned a reputation for quality food and big portions. Burgers are just the way I like them: flavorful hand-pattied ground chuck, juicy and requiring several napkins. Variations to the basic burger are created with the addition of bacon, cheese, mushrooms, jalapenos, ham, guacamole, roasted garlic or a combo of the aforementioned fixings. The Pilot Butte burger is 18 ounces of beef; quite a mouthful! Plain or seasoned fries or onion rings and a float, freeze, shake or malt from the fountain complete the meal. Breakfast orders are also generously portioned.

GREAT FISHING IN CENTRAL OREGON

Crane Prairie Reservoir (42 miles from Bend): Here you will find amazing views and great boat fishing for trout, rainbow trout, brook trout, largemouth bass and kokanee. Boat rentals and other services are available, but little bank access for fishing. Rock Creek Campground is nearby with better bank access and good fishing.

Wickiup Reservoir (About 43 miles from LaPine): Fishing here is a little more challenging, but you can catch Kokanee, brown trout, rainbow trout and largemouth bass. It is best to fish from a boat. Look for Reservoir Campground if you plan to camp. Nearby Wickiup Butte offers camping and some bank fishing near the dam.

Davis Lake (55 miles from Crescent): This one is loaded with plenty of trout and bass; fly-fishing only lake. Camping available at Lava Flow Campground and East Davis Campground; unimproved boat launch at Lava Flow.

Sparks Lake (25 miles from Bend): The shallow lake has beautiful scenery and good fishing. The day use area is an excellent spot for a canoe or small boat.

Devil's Lake (28 miles from Bend): Perfect for families, this small lake has a day use area and hike-in tent camping only. With lots of bank access, kids can catch rainbow trout and brook trout.

Big Cultus Lake (47 miles out of Sunriver): This is a popular location for fishing, boating, swimming and picnicking. A day use area, boat rentals and other services are available at Cultus Lake Resort (541/408-1560). Several campgrounds are nearby.

East Lake (located in Newberry Volcanic National Monument, 42 miles from LaPine): A good fly-fishing lake; the best fishing is from a boat at East Lake. Open in early June, boat rentals and other services are available at East Lake Resort (541/536-2230) and nearby camping.

Paulina Lake (42 miles from LaPine, in Newberry Volcanic National Monument): This is your chance to catch a trophy brown trout. The site offers great photo opportunities as well as camping, boat rentals and other services at Paulina Lake Lodge (541/536-2240).

Suttle Lake (36 miles from Sisters): The lake is famous for their kokanee and brown trout. Here you have bank access from a trail that encircles the lake; great for kids.

Lava Lake (39 miles from Bend): Take your camera for great shots of Mt. Bachelor and South Sister. The trout fishing is usually excellent. Boat rentals and many services are available at Lava Lake Lodge (541/382-9443). Camping is available at Lava Lake Campground. Right next door is Little Lava Lake (39 miles from Bend) which is the headwaters of the Deschutes River; rainbow trout and brook trout are plentiful. Enjoy this lake for fishing, boating (small boats only), float tubing and swimming.

(Information from Oregon Department of Fish and Wildlife, dfw.state.or.us/resources/fishing)

Pine Ridge Inn

1200 SW Mt. Bachelor Dr   541/389-6137
Moderate to expensive   pineridgeinn.com

Perched above the Deschutes River Canyon is a boutique hotel over-looking the river, Farewell Bend Park and the Old Mill District. The location and superb views can't be beat! All 20 suites are furnished with gas fireplaces, private patios, plush king beds and mini-fridges. Overnight stays include complimentary hot breakfast, an afternoon glass of wine or locally-made beer and fresh-baked cookies upon arrival. The well-tended property is beautiful; suites are spacious and relaxing, perfect for an R&R getaway.

Pine Tavern Restaurant

967 NW Brooks St   541/382-5581
Lunch, Dinner: Daily   pinetavern.com
Moderate

Founded in 1936, the Pine Tavern has faithfully served Bend and its timber industry workers and their families, soldiers from Camp Abbot and tourists. The building overlooks picturesque Mirror Pond and has morphed through the years to accommodate additional customers and modern facilities. Two gigantic Ponderosa pine trees are enclosed in the Garden Room, and the patio and garden remain an important part of the ambience. The menu features both classic and eclectic choices prepared with Northwest ingredients, daily lunch specials, pastas and steak dinners. Signature scones with honey butter are like manna from heaven; this is a traditional Central Oregon dining excursion.

Pronghorn

65600 Pronghorn Club Dr   866/320-5024
Expensive   pronghornresort.com

Pronghorn is a superior getaway for golfers and non-golfers. Exquisite lodging includes 48 lodge units situated on the 18th hole of the Jack Nicklaus Signature Course. Junior suites consist of one bedroom and bathroom. Spacious two-, three- and four-bedroom units are furnished with gourmet kitchens, a home theater system and other technology, private patios and original art work. Personal concierge services (pre-stocked groceries, local activities, dining) are also available. All guests have access to the clubhouse, restaurants, fitness facility, sports courts and pools; shuttle service is available to Roberts Field-Redmond Municipal Airport. The Jack Nicklaus golf course is open to the public while the Tom Fazio Championship Course is restricted to club members. The resort dining venue, **Chanterelle**, boasts a dramatic floor-to-ceiling fireplace with impeccable panoramic views of the Cascades. **Cascada** is a comfortable, relaxing spot to capture the sunset or watch a game on TV. Order a Bloody Mary with breakfast or a signature cocktail and appetizers (baked brie, pot stickers, wild mushroom tortellini) later in the day. Burgers, pork tacos and the like are available all day; the dinner menu shines with New York steak, seafood, lamb and other outstanding entrees. Another casual eatery for family-friendly, lighter fare and full bar, **Trailhead Grill**, is nestled in the heart of Pronghorn; inside and patio seating. This property is ideal for weddings, corporate retreats, special events and, of course, golf tournaments.

The Riverhouse

3075 N 97 Business   541/389-3111, 866/453-4480

Moderate and up   riverhouse.com

This resort, with adjacent 18-hole golf course and convention center, is located on the Deschutes River. It is also within easy walking distance to Sawyer Park, shops, boutiques and restaurants. Updated guest accommodations range from oversized rooms with one queen bed to fully-furnished executive suites and kitchen, family and spa suites. Amenities in the 220 guest rooms include current electronics and connection necessities, refrigerators and microwaves; the full, hot breakfast is complimentary. There's plenty to do: relax at the indoor and outdoor pools, spas and saunas; play billiards, shuffleboard or tennis; work out in the exercise room or go for a walk on the scenic riverside walking trail. Enjoy magnificent scenery and casual fine dining for lunch and dinner at **Crossings at the Riverhouse**, with some of the best steaks in town; room service is available to guests. Crossings hosts free monthly wine and beer tasting events; the lounge has 18 Bend beers on tap.

The Sparrow Bakery

50 SE Scott St   541/330-6321
Mon-Sat: 7-2; Sun: 8-2
2748 NW Crossing Dr, #110   541/647-2323
Mon-Fri: 7-5; Sun: 7-3   thesparrowbakery.com
Inexpensive

Owners **Whitney Keatman** and **Jessica Keatman** specialize in rich French pastries and bountiful fresh salads. Their Ocean Roll (hand-rolled croissant dough filled with sugar, vanilla and cardamom) is a popular treat; c'est magnifique! Ask any repeat customer and they will heap accolades on other croissants, tarts, breads, cookies and breakfast sandwiches. Chicken waldorf, croque monsieur or Monte Cristo sandwiches and savory quiches are very satisfying. These bakeries, with super lattes, are warm, cozy and friendly, just as a bakery should be.

Spork

937 NW Newport Ave   541/390-0946
Lunch, Dinner: Daily   sporkbend.com
Inexpensive to moderate

This 50-seat restaurant began as an Airstream chow cart. Its continuing success stems from the globally-inspired healthy menu which incorporates flavors of Asia, Mexico and elsewhere. Beef, pork, chicken, catfish and tofu are the main ingredients in rice bowls, tacos, salads, sandwiches, small plates and more. If you prefer gluten-free or vegan choices, there are plenty of those options, too. Your mouth will go wild when you eat the grilled vegetable coconut green curry dish or one of the daily chalkboard specials. In later hours, great cocktails and a fun happy hour are two more reasons to visit!

Tetherow

61240 Skyline Ranch Road   877/298-2582, 541/388-2582
Moderate to expensive   tetherow.com

After a full day of fun, whether it includes tours of the local breweries, biking the 300 miles of available trails or exploring the great outdoors, nothing beats a comfortable bed. Tetherow Lodges is Bend's newest world-class resort. This 50-room boutique hotel brings you the best of both worlds: the most spectacular views in the area with the feeling of being secluded, plus the convenience of being seven minutes from shops, restaurants and entertainment. Opening in 2014, all rooms feature gas fireplaces, flat-screen TVs, soaking tubs and terraces with views that make it hard to leave your room. Luxurious finishes fill the rooms as well as locally crafted coffee, tea and chocolate — they had me at chocolate. For golf enthusiasts, it's off with your coat and out with the clubs at the resort's award-winning golf course, voted number 54 on *Golf Digest*'s "Top 100 Greatest Courses" of 2015 and created by the same course architect who designed Bandon Dunes. Aside from the golf course, the development also includes two restaurants and homesites; pets are welcome and an outside doggie bath is available. Light fare is served in **The Row** (open daily at 11 a.m., closing hours vary), a family-friendly pub where American and Scottish-inspired items such as bangers and mash, braised elk shepherd's pie, fish and chips, sandwiches, salads and mini-corndogs (which are actually bangers) are on the menu. **Tetherow Grill** is open all day, and among the usual breakfast offerings are buttermilk biscuits with maple sausage gravy, stuffed crepes and Benedicts made with duck confit, crab cakes, Portobello mushrooms or Black Forest ham. Dinners are served a la carte or as *prix-fixe* meals and feature pork, duck, beef, fish and more with delectable sauces, sides and preparations to satisfy every palate. Service and presentation are superb! The Grill opens at 7 a.m. and remains open through dinner.

Tim Garling's Jackalope Grill

750 NW Lava Road, Suite 139   541/318-8435
Dinner: Daily   jackalopegrill.com
Moderately expensive

French/Northwest cuisine is featured at this upscale, fine-dining establishment where local art accents the walls. Ease into dinner with an order of escargot a la bourguignonne served in a delectable garlic and shallot broth or Dungeness crab-stuffed mushroom caps. The menu includes game entrees (medallions of elk are superb), schnitzels, fish, charbroiled ribeye steak, osso bucco prepared with pork and other delicious items from local ingredients. A variety of delectable desserts, such as crème brûlée, are fresh from the kitchen. Outside dining is available in the summer. Chef **Tim Garling**'s award-winning restaurant is the result of culinary training in Paris and a very successful restaurant venture in Utah. He teaches culinary classes at Central Oregon Community College.

Trattoria Sbandati
1444 NW College Way   541/306-6825
Dinner: Tues-Sat   trattoriasbandati.com
Expensive

Upscale Italian cuisine in Bend translates into a visit to Trattoria Sbandati. Chef **Juri Sbandati** is from Tuscany and has earned a much-deserved reputation for authentic, cooked-to-order dishes that are superb. For instance, meatballs are made from Juri's family recipe, served with delightful tomato sauce and a side of sauteed spinach. Handmade tagliatelle will surely melt in your mouth. Other entrees are made with pork, beef, veal or fish. This dinner house is warm and inviting and service is professional.

The Victorian Cafe
1404 NW Galveston Ave   541/382-6411
Breakfast, Lunch: Daily   victoriancafebend.com
Moderate

For locals, see you at "The Vic" means The Victorian Cafe, a Central Oregon institution for great breakfasts in a fun environment with commendable service. Traditional breakfast fare morphed into gourmet cuisine with the arrival of proprietor **John Nolan** in 2002. His reinvented menu offers about 20 descriptively-named omelets (the Green Hornet includes spinach, asparagus, jalapenos, scallions and avocados), eggs Benedict (Cuban ham, mango and black beans make up the Caribbean version) and potato specialties like the Apollonius (linguica sausage, artichoke hearts, spinach, kalamata olives, red peppers and feta cheese). Legendary Bloody Marys and "ManMosas" (crafted with The Vic's private label champagne) put this full-service bar on the radar. About a dozen sandwiches (as a wrap or on bread), burgers and fresh salads entice the lunch crowd. The Vic is so popular, you may find yourself settling into an outside bench as you wait for your table.

Wanderlust Tours

61535 S Hwy 97   541/389-8359, 800/962-2862
Prices vary   wanderlusttours.com

For a really cool experience in the Bend area, how about a visit to a high desert lava cave? Half-day tours take visitors beneath the area's desert floor. In winter, this outfit does a series of extraordinary experiences including snowshoeing by the light of a full moon and bonfires on the snow. Professional naturalist guides accompany groups; delicious desserts and warm drinks are added treats. For the 21 and older generation, hop on Wanderlust's Bend Brew Bus for a rollicking tour of four local craft breweries. The Local Pour jaunt includes beer, cider, wine and spirit stops; samples are a part of the package. Other tours involve canoeing, kayaking, GPS Eco-challenge, volcano sightseeing, evening tours and special events; guides, transportation and appropriate equipment are furnished. Bring the wee ones and grandma; certain activities can be modified for the whole family!

Zydeco Kitchen & Cocktails

919 NW Bond St   541/312-2899
Lunch: Mon-Fri; Dinner: Daily   zydecokitchen.com
Moderately expensive

The hands-down favorite at this classy Cajun place is barbecue shrimp served with a Southern grits cake. The Southwest Louisiana-inspired fare features étouffée; shrimp po' boy; artichoke and corn fritters and shrimp, Andouille and crawfish jambalaya. Other standouts are Acadian flatbread (you choose the toppings), Mama G's steak salad (avocado, tomato, chopped egg and blue cheese), sandwiches, pot pie and seasonal preparations made from scratch using fresh, quality ingredients. The Creole food is super and the atmosphere loads of fun; your toes will be a tappin'!

CAMP SHERMAN

House on Metolius

541/595-6620
Expensive   metolius.com

Retreat. Relax. Rewind. Renew. This privately owned 200-acre estate on the Metolius River dates back over a century, looks to the Mt. Jefferson and Three Finger Jack mountain peaks and is surrounded on all sides by the Deschutes National Forest which offers impressive hiking, fishing, birdwatching, biking and skiing. Choose from the rustic, upscale Main Lodge (eight guest rooms); Reidun's Cabin (one or two units); or one of the other four cabins (Eleanor's, Ponderosa, Gorge, Power House) for a special recreational weekend, wedding, business conference or other occasion. Accommodations are available year-round. This is a gated locale; specific directions will be given upon reservation. Fishermen, take note: there is private and exclusive fly-fishing access on both banks of the Metolius River.

GELATO EXTRAORDINAIRE

Bontà is the all-natural gelato handcraft of **Juli and Jeff Labhart**. Inspired in part by a year-long world trip, and wanting to showcase local products, their ice cream is a denser, more flavorful creation. Nearly twenty rich and creamy offerings: salted chocolate, pistachio, roasted strawberry, coconut lime, Theo dark chocolate, vanilla bourbon pecan and peanut butter with chocolate fudge. Now you can get your scoop at their downtown Bend storefront, **Bontà** (920 NW Bond St, Suite 108; 541/306-6606; bontagelato. com); the shop is actually on Minnesota Avenue, just west of the Oxford Hotel. A growing list of specialty markets and food stores (New Seasons, Whole Foods, Roth's Fresh Markets, Food 4 Less and more) offer the premium treat by the pint; select Oregon restaurants (Gerry Frank's Konditorei, Greg's Grill, Jackson's Corner, Latigo, Spork and others) also serve the signature and seasonal tastes by the bowl or scoop.

Kokanee Cafe

25545 SW Forest Service Road   541/595-6420
Dinner: May - mid-Oct   kokaneecafe.com
Inexpensive to expensive

Tantalizing gourmet fare turns up in the most unexpected places around our state. Kokanee Cafe, northwest of Sisters in Jefferson County, is just such a place. For over two decades, this rustic dinner house has served Northwest cuisine in a relaxing setting amid tall pine trees and the Metolius River. Steak and seafood entrees dominate the menu along with game meats, lamb, pasta and vegetarian dishes. A recent menu highlighted fennel-braised wild boar appetizers smoked with injera, an eight-ounce beef tenderloin with sunchoke mashed potatoes and a double-cut pork chop with wild mushroom bread pudding. Dishes are made with fresh, local, seasonal ingredients; the Anderson Valley Ranch lamb chop with pancetta and crispy polenta is a favorite. Regionally-named and -influenced desserts include campfire tart (dark chocolate, graham crackers, toasted marshmallows and candied pine sugar), layered flourless chocolate cake with Oregon berries and buttercream as well as housemade ice cream and sorbet. Flavors are sensational and plates are artistically presented! The full bar features a seasonal rotation of beers, cocktails made with local spirits and an eclectic wine list. Family-owned and -operated, the cafe is open May to mid-October (weekends only early and late in the season and daily during the busy summer months); doors open at 5 p.m. and close when the last customers say good night. Best to call ahead for weekend reservations and for directions to this out-of-the-way restaurant.

DIAMOND LAKE

Diamond Lake Resort

350 Resort Dr   541/793-3333
Inexpensive and up   diamondlake.net

Five miles north of Crater Lake National Park is a resort with a variety of lodging choices: motel rooms, studio units, cabins (modern or rustic) and a Jacuzzi suite. Rates vary by season, lodging type and features. The resort's restaurant is open to guests and the public throughout the year for breakfast, lunch and dinner; herb-crusted prime rib is featured on Friday and Saturday nights. There is always a full slate of seasonal activities. The store and marina are the rental centers for fishing, patio, paddle and bumper boats; kayaks; canoes and other recreational equipment. By the way, access roads are kept clear when the snow falls for snow tubing, snowboarding, snowcat skiing, cross country skiing, snowshoeing and snowmobiling at Mt. Bailey located ten miles west of Diamond Lake.

DUFUR

Balch Hotel
40 S Heimrich St   541/467-2277
Seasonal   balchhotel.com
Inexpensive to moderate

This area boasts 300 days of sunshine a year! The hotel was built in 1907 by rancher Charles P. Balch and the 1908 opening ads offered rooms for as little as 50 cents, promoting the fact that there was hot and cold running water in every room. Now the 18 rooms (five with private bathrooms) and one suite with en suite bathroom offer modern conveniences and still maintain comfortable prices. Gracious innkeepers **Josiah Dean** and **Claire Sierra** will start you on a day of exploring museums, wineries or cycling the back roads with a full gourmet breakfast and homemade goodies. You won't find an elevator, televisions or telephones, but there are cookies and special malty hot cocoa.

LA PINE

Paulina Lake Lodge
22440 Paulina Lake Road   541/536-2240
Moderate to expensive   paulinalakelodge.com

Adventurous Oregon travelers shouldn't miss this rustic lodge on the shores of Paulina Lake (23 miles south of Bend on Highway 97, then 12 miles east on Road 21) deep in the Deschutes National Forest.

BEST FOR SNOWSHOEING

Snowshoeing is one of the cheapest winter recreations; all you need are snowshoes (rent for $10 a day) and an Oregon Sno-Park permit ($25 for the season, $9 for three days, $4 daily). Permits can be acquired at DMV locations and sporting goods stores, allowing access to trails off plowed roads. Check road conditions before leaving; dial 511 in Oregon for 24-hour road reports. Come prepared, buddy-up and chat with local rangers before leaving. Look for maps at the trailheads; some locations offer warming yurts open to the public. Three suggested routes for the Bend area:

Edison Butte Sno-Park (19 miles west of Bend on the Cascade Lakes Highway): several scenic trail options of moderate lengths or a loop trail with two warming shelters; views of Mt. Bachelor; contact Bend-Fort Rock Ranger District Office (541/383-4000)

Ten Mile Sno-Park (24 miles south of Bend on Highway 97): Ponderosa Rim Trail from Ten Mile Sno-Park follows Paulina Creek; gentle climb with views of Paulina Lake; contact Bend-Fort Rock Ranger District Office (541/383-4000)

Three Creeks Sno-Park (11 miles south of Sisters): access to 14 miles of trails; Three Creeks Lake to Snow Creek involves an 11-mile, 1,300-foot climb; contact Sisters Ranger District Office (541/549-7700)

Depending on the season, enjoy fishing, boating, swimming, snowmobiling, hiking and more. There are 200 miles of groomed snowmobile trails. Vintage cabins are equipped with bathrooms, linens, firewood and kitchenware. Moderately priced, hearty full lunches and dinners are served in the 1929 log lodge; the famous prime rib dinner is a Saturday night staple on the home cooking menu. A general store (summer only) is convenient for fishing licenses, food, clothing, equipment rentals, gas and oil, beer and groceries. This area's history is an interesting read.

Paulina Plunge

53750 Hwy 97   541/389-0562, 800/296-0562
Daily: May 1-Sept 15   paulinaplunge.com

Take the plunge, the Paulina Plunge, for an all-downhill mountain biking adventure from Central Oregon's Newberry National Volcanic

Monument. You'll drop more than 2,500 vertical feet on four 1½ mile segments and stop at up to six pristine waterfalls (two are natural waterslides where you can cool down and play). A couple of lively hikes are required to reach the falls, but they're easily achievable for tots to seniors. Experienced guides lead the charge and along the way impart insight into the local history, geology and archeology. A few details: catch a shuttle at Sunriver Resort for a 25-minute ride to the gathering spot. Bike, helmet and day pack are included in the price. There's plenty of fine print; call or check the website for the minutiae and pricing.

MADRAS

Geno's Italian Grill
212 SW 4th St   541/475-6048
Lunch, Dinner: Tues-Sun; Breakfast: Sun   genositaliangrill.net
Moderate

Madras for "authentic" Italian food? Yes, that and more at Geno's where the extensive menu features ingredients that are fresh and local as much as possible. The casual fare encompasses meat cannelloni, steaks, chicken, chops, assorted calzones, pasta dishes, gourmet and traditional pizzas and hearty hero sandwiches. Sunday breakfast leans toward traditional choices of omelets and pancakes, plus skillets. Special attention is paid to providing great service and food.

MAUPIN

Deschutes Canyon Fly Shop
599 S Hwy 197   541/395-2565
Mon-Sat: 8-5 (Sun till 1)   flyfishingdeschutes.com

John Smeraglio, fisherman and owner of this fly shop and guide service, shares his love of angling and the outdoors with others. John and his team teach the finer art of casting flies, offer customized guided float and non-float tours and stock high-quality brand name gear. They also share information on river conditions, fishing reports and fish counts. Throughout the year, look for seasonal product demos, clinics, lessons and more. Their customer-friendly motto is: "We guide; you fish!"

Imperial River Co.

304 Bakeoven Road   541/395-2404, 800/395-3903
Lodging: Inexpensive to moderate   deschutesriver.com
Restaurant (seasonal hours): Moderate

When hardworking entrepreneurs **Susie and Rob Miles** purchased this whitewater rafting and lodging operation in 2001 they added a full-service restaurant, quiet bar, 45-seat conference room, courtyard with fire pit, sand volleyball court, additional guest rooms and a photo shop to take digital pictures of everyone rafting this stretch of the Deschutes River. All 25 guest rooms have names and Oregon themes appropriate to the area, are well-appointed and include wader dryers. Try to plan your stay to coincide with restaurant hours (open daily in the summer and winter weekends). Angus beef and lamb are sourced from nearby Imperial Stock Ranch; chicken, fish, sandwiches and desserts are also good. Well-trained personnel, guided whitewater rafting, great photo ops, superb fishing, guided upland bird hunting plus more are available.

POWELL BUTTE

Brasada Ranch

16986 SW Brasada Ranch Road   541/526-6865, 888/322-6592
Moderate to very expensive   brasada.com

Just east of Bend, this high desert getaway offers all the beauty of the Oregon Trail, but with modern luxuries you might expect from an award-winning resort. Brasada Ranch was named *Conde Nast Traveler's* "Best Resort in the Pacific Northwest" in 2014 and 2015. Stay in an intimate Ranch House Suite ideal for couples or a one- to four-bedroom Sage Canyon Cabin for families. In addition to lodging, the welcoming **Ranch House** (541/526-6870) restaurant offers full-service, family-friendly dining for breakfast, lunch and dinner year-round; plus outside seating on the wrap-around deck. The 17,000-square-foot athletic center has an indoor lap pool, two outdoor pools and a waterslide. Take advantage of the full workout facility and complimentary fitness classes while children stay entertained in The Hideout. The semi-private Peter Jacobsen-designed 18-hole **Brasada Canyons Golf Course** (541/504-4421) is limited to members and resort guests. The full-service spa is open to the public and affords clients (and one additional guest) entrance into the athletic club pools. Biking and hiking trails, horseback riding, whitewater rafting and fishing are easily accessible on the 1,800-acre property. Fine dining at the **Range Restaurant and Bar** (541/426-6862) opens to a panoramic view of the Cascades and is a perfect vantage point for a stunning sunset show. The changing menu is innovative, yet down-to-earth; most importantly, fresh, local ingredients are used to a large extent for this farm-to-fork experience.

PRINEVILLE

Bellavista Bed & Breakfast

5070 SE Paulina Hwy   541/416-2400
Inexpensive   bellavistab-b.com

For fabulous 180-degree views of the Three Sisters and the Cascades, try this hilltop bed and breakfast accented with furnishings from **Fulvia and Ben Guyger**'s Tuscan home. They will make you feel right at ease with two comfy bedrooms with bathrooms. The signature gourmet breakfast served on the sun deck or upper gazebo consists of orange-glazed sausage and apricot kabobs, eggs and fruit. The gracious hosts, unbeatable scenery and European elegance produce a memorable stay anytime of the year. (Credit cards not accepted.)

HOMETOWN THEATER

It seems that talent is everywhere in Oregon, from the large venues of Portland's **Keller Auditorium** (auditoriumportland.com) and the **Hult Center** (hultcenter.org) in Eugene to Ashland's highly-acclaimed **Oregon Shakespeare Festival** (osfashland.org) and Jacksonville's **Britt Festivals** (brittfest.org). Let's not forget small-theater settings (oregon.com/state/info/theatre.htm), many of which have survived and thrived through hometown commitment.

ASHLAND
Oregon Cabaret Theatre (oregoncabaret.com)
ASTORIA
Liberty Theater (liberty-theater.org)
BEND
2nd Street Theater (2ndstreettheater.com)
CANNON BEACH
Coaster Theatre Playhouse (coastertheatre.com)
CORVALLIS
Majestic Theatre (majestic.org)
COTTAGE GROVE
Cottage Theater (cottagetheater.org)
ELGIN
Elgin Opera House (elginoperahouse.com)
EUGENE
The Very Little Theatre (thevlt.com)
KLAMATH FALLS
Ross Ragland Theater (rrtheater.org)
LAKE OSWEGO
Lakewood Center for The Arts (lakewood-center.org)
MEDFORD
Craterian Ginger Rogers Theater (craterian.org)
PORTLAND
Oregon Children's Theatre (octc.org)
SALEM
Historic Elsinore Theatre (elsinoretheatre.com)
Pentacle Theatre (pentacletheatre.org)
THE DALLES
The Theatre Company of The Dalles (thetheatrecompany.org)

REDMOND

Brickhouse

412 SW 6th St   541/526-1782
Dinner: Tues-Sat   brickhouseco.com
Moderate

One of Redmond's best restaurants is the casual fine dining Brickhouse. In addition to natural, hormone-free steaks you'll find crab, lobster, ahi tuna, fresh Alaskan salmon and halibut, white prawns and bivalves. Chops, chicken and pasta dishes, soups and nice meal-size salads are equally tasty choices. Cobbler a la mode is housemade as are other desserts and savory sauces. In downtown Bend, a sister Brickhouse has moved to the Firehall Building (5 NW Minnesota Ave, 541/728-0334) and is open nightly for dinner.

Diego's Spirited Kitchen

447 SW 6th St   541/316-2002
Lunch, Dinner: Daily   Facebook
Moderate

Diego's is crowded, lively and serves up great Mexican cuisine. Start with guacamole made tableside; it doesn't get any fresher! Although you may be tempted to make a meal of guacamole, chips and a margarita or two, pace yourself. Excellent dinner choices include pork osso buco, pork fajitas, carne asada and gulf shrimp dishes. Service is friendly, portions are generous and there are plenty of menu options to satisfy south-of-the-border cravings.

Eagle Crest Resort

1522 Cline Falls Road   855/682-4786, 541/923-2453
Lodge: Inexpensive to moderate   eagle-crest.com
Vacation rentals: Moderate to expensive

Nestled against the magnificent Cascade Mountains with Deschutes River frontage, the fully renovated Eagle Crest Resort is truly an all-season oasis. Summer months invite you to venture out and experience the best recreation in the region. The **Stables at Eagle**

Crest Resort provide everything from pony rides to multi-hour trail rides. Located on 1,700 acres in high desert, this is the ultimate golfer's paradise with two championship golf courses, including a putting course and a challenge course. At the Ridge Sports center, one of three on-site sports centers, adults can choose to be lulled into bliss by professional spa therapists at **The Spa at Eagle Crest** with a variety of pampering options or take a fitness class while kids play at the outdoor Splash Park. This family-fun resort also features indoor and outdoor pools, bike rentals to explore over 11 miles of trails and they even welcome your four-legged friends. Winter months bring a new experience to your stay with the colorful holiday lights celebration known as Starfest, running from Thanksgiving to New Years with a mile long exhibit. If marveling at the lights doesn't get you in the spirit, the holiday carolers, weekend horse-drawn wagon rides and cowboy Santa will! As far as dining goes, enjoy breakfast at **Aerie Cafe** where kids under 12 eat free; lunch at **Greenside Cafe** or **Silverleaf Cafe** where you can enjoy fresh sandwiches, wraps, burgers and a variety of snacks; and dinner and drinks at **Niblick and Greene's** serving an array of entrees including seafood, chicken, beef and pasta. Enjoy all of these amenities for yourself with a stay at one of their spacious 100 guestrooms or choose to stay at the two-, three- or four-bedroom vacation rentals.

Ida's Cupcake Cafe
738 SW Highland Ave   541/548-8164
(See detailed listing with Ida's Cupcake Cafe, Bend)

Pig & Pound Public House
427 SW 8th St   541/526-1697
Lunch: Sat, Sun; Dinner: Mon-Sat   Facebook
Inexpensive and up

What do you get when a native Brit moves to Central Oregon? An English pub, of course. This cozy corner establishment is bent on preparing food from scratch with local products and serving a changing selection of local beers and hard ciders. Be sure to order the beer-battered onion rings; they are superb. I took a liking to bangers and mash while I was a student in England and owner **Paul Mercer** does an admirable job with his version of housemade sausage spiced with fennel and apple. Other common pub fare includes fish and chips, steak and ale pot pie and a half pork/half beef burger named the Oink and Boink. The menu is seasonal with hearty dishes in winter and lighter choices in summer. Chocolate Pig is the featured dessert; think of it as the classic Ding Dong treat on steroids!

Tate and Tate Catering

1205 SW Indian Ave   541/548-2512
Mon-Fri: 9-5:30; Sat: 9-4
2755 NW Crossing Dr, Suite 109, Bend   541/706-9317
Mon-Fri: 10-6   tateandtatecatering.com

Stop in at either location for a grab-and-go (not your typical fast food) lunch or dinner; order in (nominal delivery fee) or place your phone or e-order the day prior (before 5 p.m.). Choose from multiple soups, salads, land and sea entrees and desserts. "Special value pack-ages" with eats such as casseroles, cabbage rolls, spaghetti and meat-balls or three cheese pasta are ideal for now or to stow in the freezer. **Barbara and George Tate** are available to cater any event, from office lunches to full-service affairs; voted Best Caterer in Central Oregon for five years running.

SISTERS

Angeline's Bakery & Cafe

121 W Main St   541/549-9122
Daily: 6:30-6 (winter till 4)   angelinesbakery.com

Start your morning coffee routine with muffins, scones, cinna-mon rolls, coffee cakes and bagels. All of these temptations, breads, cookies, brownies and more are handcrafted each day. Creative sal-ads, homemade soups, wraps, polenta pizza and specials make tasty lunchtime choices. Many of the items are vegan, gluten-free, agave-sweetened and/or dairy-free in response to the dietary demands of health-conscious people; a strong emphasis is placed on raw foods and green smoothies. You can also find these flavorful baked products at small health food stores and coffee shops in Central Oregon. Angeline's white rice bread makes super sandwiches.

Aspen Lakes Golf Course
16900 Aspen Lakes Dr   541/549-4653
Golf Shop: Daily: 6:30 a.m.-dusk   aspenlakes.com

Aspen Lakes Golf Course began as an ongoing Cyrus family project in 1987 with the first nine holes completed in 1996 and the second in 2000. Natural elements were incorporated into the design and red cinders from the Cyrus property were crushed to fill the sand traps creating signature red sand bunkers. Restaurants operate seasonally; **Brand 33** (541/549-3663) features Northwest cuisine, a mix of land and sea platters with fresh fruits and vegetables for dinner and Sunday brunch. Sandwiches, burgers, appetizers, pizza and entrees are offered at **The Frog Pond** (541/549-3663), the casual bar and lunch option. It is clear why Aspen Lakes is on many golfers "must play" list when visiting Central Oregon. Golf boards are a fun alternative to riding in a cart; they feel similar to boarding or surfing.

Black Butte Ranch
13899 Bishops Cap   541/595-1252, 866/901-2961
Moderate and up   blackbutteranch.com

With magnificent Central Oregon field and mountain vistas, the Black Butte Ranch setting is one of the most dramatic in the state. All manner of activities are available, including two 18-hole golf courses, tennis courts, swimming pools, 18 miles of bike paths, horseback riding, canoeing, fishing, snowshoeing, cross country skiing and nearby winter skiing at Hoodoo Ski Area. In the early 1900s, the area was the home of the Black Butte Land and Livestock Co.; later the summer home of Howard Morgan and his family, members of the pioneer Portland Corbett dynasty. The 1,280 acres were then sold to Brooks-Scanlon Lumber firm; now homeowners own and oversee the property's management. **The Lodge Restaurant** is popular with residents, vacationers and those who simply come to enjoy dining in this rustic but upscale atmosphere.

FIVE BEST HIKES

GREEN LAKES AND SPARKS LAKE

Local and visiting hikers love this lake area hike. The spectacular 8.4-mile round-trip hike, often called an Oregon classic trek, is located in Three Sisters Wilderness area and is easily reached by the Cascade Lakes Highway. Remember, fires are illegal and camping is in designated sites only. For a shorter trek, just hike across the highway to Sparks Lake. It is one of the most beautiful spots to photograph with Mt. Bachelor, South Sister and Broken Top in view.

Open: Green Lakes, mid-July to October; Sparks Lake, late June to November

Directions: From Bend, travel 26.2 miles west on Cascade Lakes Highway 46. Turn left at pointers for Sparks Lake on Forest Road 4600 and 400 and follow to lakeshore. Turn right at a large sign for Green Lakes Trailhead.

SMITH ROCK STATE PARK

This hike is considered the best overall hike when snow makes the trails into the Three Sisters inaccessible. The huge, orange-tower rocks are thought to be 30 million years old and have become the center of popular sport rock climbing. The moderately difficult four-mile hike through the center of the park begins at the trailhead; cross Crooked River Bridge, then take on the toughest section "Misery Ridge Trail" which climbs up to 700 feet and offers amazing viewpoints. Pass by Monkey Face and follow Mesa Verde to River Trail to finish the loop.

Open: Year-round

Directions: A 36-minute drive from Bend; follow Highway 97 north 22 miles to the small town of Terrebonne. From the town, simply follow the signs.

BLACK BUTTE

If you have driven from Salem to Sisters on Highway 20, you've probably noticed a massive black cone in the distance. Seeing the huge, dark mountain, it is hard to believe that the summit is easier to reach than it might look. From the upper trailhead, the hike is

4.4 miles round-trip; at the summit you have reached 1,500 feet. Your reward is an incredible panorama of the Cascades and two historic fire lookouts.

Open: July to October

Directions: From Sisters, head 6.3 miles northwest on Highway 20. Turn north onto Forest Service Road 11 for 3.9 miles, then west on FFS Road 1110 for 5.5 miles to Black Butte Trailhead.

TUMALO FALLS

The locals in Bend enjoy this 97-foot waterfall because it is just outside of town. A short walk will bring you past the waterfall, but if you continue to the top of the falls you will find a wonderful trail system to Double Falls and Upper Falls. This is just a 3.8-mile hike; if you want a longer moderate hike, complete the entire seven-mile loop.

Open: June to October

Directions: From Bend, follow Skyliners Road ten miles west and veer left past a yellow gate onto Forest Road 4603 to the road's end and the parking area for Tumalo Falls.

LAVA RIVER CAVE

Just south of Bend you can explore the inside of a lava tube on the Newberry National Volcanic Monument. This is a self-guided, mile-long subterranean trail; a $5 fee or a Northwest Forest Pass is required. Headlamps can be rented from the Forest Service for $5. Dress warmly as cave temperatures are in the 40s.

Open: Hours and days vary seasonally; best to call ahead. (Lava Lands Visitor Center, 541/593-2421)

Directions: From Bend, travel south on Highway 97 to Exit 151/Cottonwood Road. Turn left after exiting and proceed through underpass following signs to Lava River Cave. The cave is one mile down the road on your left.

(Adapted from Urness, Zach (June 2015). Best Overall Hikes in Bend. Statesman Journal)

Clearwater Gallery and Framing & The Open Door

303 W Hood Ave   541/549-4994
Gallery: Daily   theclearwatergallery.com
Bistro: Lunch, Dinner: Mon-Sat

DID YOU KNOW...

...**Pilot Butte**, a cinder cone volcano, exists within the city limits of Bend. Bend is one of four cities in the United States to have a volcano within its boundaries. The 114 acres of **Pilot Butte State Scenic Viewpoint** (800/551-6949) are a Bend icon. Pilot Butte itself is a popular hiking destination with two trails to the summit; rising nearly 500 feet above the surrounding plains, a scenic road winds up and around the cone. From the top the entire city of Bend is visible, as well as several major Cascade peaks; most prominent are the Three Sisters, Broken Top and Mt. Bachelor which are located about 20 miles to the west.

Food, wine, art and music are all under one roof at this social and cultural gathering spot. When owners **Julia and Dan Rickards** remodeled the building for the gallery and framing business they created a cozy space for a bistro, cocktails and a wine bar. The inventory of fine arts, sculptures, pottery, woodworks and Dan's wildlife and landscape paintings is ever-changing. Works by over a dozen artists, mainly from the Northwest, are also displayed throughout the pine-paneled rooms. Daily specials at the The Open Door bistro include satisfying homemade soups and pasta entrees. One of the best features is the outdoor courtyard; bask in the sunshine and enjoy food and drink with regular live entertainment and other fun weekly events. Days and hours change in the winter months.

Depot Cafe

250 W Cascade Ave   541/549-2572
Daily: 8-8 (Wed-Sun: 8-8 in winter)   sistersdepot.com
Inexpensive to moderate

No matter the time of year, the town of Sisters sees a steady flow of traffic. It's long been a popular break for folks driving over the mountains on Highway 20 to walk the Western-style main street and peruse the shops, restaurants and boutiques. This rustic cafe makes everything from scratch with an emphasis on local ingredients. With that in mind, breakfasts are large and inexpensive; so are the excellent lunchtime turkey club and other sandwiches. Dinner specials change weekly and may feature short ribs, steaks, salmon, beef pot pie, prawn fettucini or chicken parmesan; beer, wine and cocktails are also at hand. Bread is homemade and you will want to save room for a delicious piece of pie (also homemade). Be sure to look up when you're inside to catch a glimpse of an electric train that continually chugs along an overhead track. The beautiful outdoor patio is restful in summer.

FivePine Lodge and Conference Center

1021 Desperado Trail   541/549-5900, 866/974-5900
Moderate to expensive   fivepinelodge.com

The FivePine Lodge caters to business groups who want five-star facilities in a small community. The state-of-the-art meeting facility also doubles as an intimate wedding, party and family reunion scene. Forget the briefcases and laptops and the luxurious accommodations become attractive for romantic stays; distractions are at a minimum. There are 24 cabins and eight lodge rooms outfitted with Amish-built hardwood furniture, tubs filled by a ceiling waterfall, gas fireplaces and large plasma screen TVs. Bookings include complimentary deluxe continental morning breakfast and hosted evening wine and craft beer reception. Borrow a free cruiser bicycle (seasonal) or play in the outdoor heated pool. The campus encompasses **Sisters Athletic Club** (541/549-6878, sistersathleticclub.com), where guests can take advantage of pursuing personal health and wellness; **Shibui Spa** (541/549-6164, shibuispa.com) for pampering treatments; and other food and entertainment venues. One could only hope to be snowed in over a long weekend.

Hoodoo Ski Area

Hwy 20   541/822-3799
Seasonal   skihoodoo.com

At the summit of Santiam Pass is Central Oregon's original ski area. Skiers, sledders, 'boarders, 'tubers and snowbikers are all accommodated on beginning and expert runs at this family-friendly butte where the average snowbase is 10 to 15 feet. First-timers to Hoodoo will find convenient lessons and equipment rentals. Part of Hoodoo's appeal is its proximity to the mid-Willamette Valley, affordability as compared to the larger ski locales, deep powder, 32 groomed runs and night skiing. There are over 800 acres of terrain, five lifts, a full-service lodge and the Autobahn Tubing Park with multiple runs (free tubes and cable tube tow with ticket purchase).

BEND'S OLD MILL DISTRICT

The **Old Mill District** (450 SW Powerhouse Dr, Bend; 541/312-0131; theoldmill.com) is Bend's premier shopping location, featuring local and regional brands as well as nationwide chains. The property formerly housed two competing lumber mills (Shevlin-Hixon Lumber and Brooks-Scanlon Lumber). At their peak the mills were two of the largest pine sawmills in the world, employing more than 2,000 workers each. Now this 270-acre parcel along the Deschutes River is a mixed-use area known for its shops, galleries and restaurants. Elements of some of the original buildings, including the area's three signature smokestacks, have been maintained. Over 40 stores include well-known national names like American Eagle, Banana Republic, Buckle, Chico's, Gap, J. Jill, REI and Victoria's Secret; additionally there are local shops like Confluence Fly Shop, Desperado and Ginger's Kitchenware. Refuel at one of over a dozen restaurants and food shops or indulge in wine tasting at Naked Winery.

Other features of the Mill include canoe and bike rentals; a national casting course; sand volleyball courts; an off-leash dog park; and a network of trails maintained by Bend Parks and Recreation, complete with historical and memorial plaques. The Les Schwab Amphitheater hosts numerous concerts and events, including Bend Brew Fest. Regal Cinemas, IMAX and two topnotch hotels (Hilton Garden Inn and Hampton Inn & Suites) are conveniently located within the district.

Latigo

370 E Cascade Ave   541/633-5748
Dinner: Daily   latigosisters.com
Moderate to expensive

Western cuisine does not mean barbecue at newly-constructed Latigo. **Tim Christman** is executive chef and his wife **Sucy** is the general manager of their rustically elegant, fine dining establishment. This is not Tim's first rodeo either, with over 25 years' experience at a variety of venues! Most recently Tim honed his craft in Hawaii to develop Latigo's upscale ranch-to-table style utilizing fresh, high-quality ingredients. The menu changes daily to feature regional, natural and organic wild game, beef, seafood, poultry and pork in a la carte choices and a four-course *prix-fixe* dinner. A recent sampling of the fare included rack of lamb with roasted butternut squash puree, pan-roasted duck breast with apricot-almond wild rice, swordfish with Hawaiian salsa and filet mignon. Flavors are bold and accompaniments are very tasty, oftentimes incorporating figs, beets, mushrooms and the like in interesting combinations. Appetizers and salads are equally delicious and wine pairings are suggested. Reservations are recommended at this upscale ranch!

Long Hollow Ranch

71105 Holmes Road   541/923-1901
Seasonal: March-Oct   lhranch.com
Moderate

If you're looking for a guest ranch experience you'll find it at this historic Oregon ranch. With a history as a working ranch that goes back over a century, Long Hollow offers guest activities associated with producing hay, running cattle and operating a large ranch. Choose from three guest rooms and a cottage, each offering different themes and daily or weekly stays. The ranch operates on the American plan, which includes home-cooked meals, lodging and many other things you might want to do, including horseback riding, fishing, whitewater rafting, cookouts, games, reading, playing the piano or mingling with other guests and ranch hands. History comes alive in the redesigned ranch that was once headquarters of the Black Butte Land and Livestock Company; remnants of the old ways are still evident. Check the website for pricing, restrictions and additional information.

Sisters Bakery

251 E Cascade Ave   541/549-0361
Daily: 5-5   sistersbakery.com

Sisters Bakery is a great place to discover! The glass case is chock-full of decadent pastries and eclairs, brownies, cookies, muffins, scones, breads, pies and cobblers all made from scratch and baked fresh daily. You will also find cheese sticks and marionberry biscuits (made with whole berries), artisan and sandwich breads, as well as soups and coffee drinks. Beautifully decorated cakes are created from a menu of several cake, filling and icing flavors. Handmade, all-butter croissants are out of the oven by 7 every morning and filled with sweet or savory ingredients for breakfast-on-the-run. The list of tempting delights is mighty long and everything is delish!

Sisters Drug and Gift

211 E Cascade Ave   541/549-6221
Daily: Hours vary   pillboxinc.com

Aspirin to afghans, calamine lotion to candles; you get the picture! Ladies can spend hours perusing the fabulous gift department — a destination in itself. Shop for the latest totes from Vera Bradley, collectibles, kitchen necessities and accessories from the well-stocked Cook's Nook, Oregon-based food products, great home accessories, jewelry and one-of-a-kind gifts. There is a great selection of Baggalini travel products including handbags, luggage and a variety of travel accessory bags. The drug section will tend to your health needs with over-the-counter medications, prescription service and flu vaccines for residents and visitors alike. This classy, unique store may become your favorite boutique in Sisters.

KIDS' ACTIVITIES: CENTRAL OREGON

BEND

Cascade Indoor Sports (541/330-1183, cascadeindoorsports.com)
Deschutes Historical Museum (541/389-1813, deschuteshistory.org)
High Desert Museum (541/382-4754, highdesertmuseum.org)
Mt. Bachelor Ski Resort (800/829-2442, mtbachelor.com)
Sun Mountain Fun Center (541/382-6161, sunmountainfun.com)
Wanderlust Tours (800/962-2862, wanderlusttours.com)

SANTIAM PASS

Hoodoo Ski Area (541/822-3799, skihoodoo.com)

SISTERS

Sisters Rodeo (541/549-0121, sistersrodeo.com)

SUNRIVER

Oregon Observatory (541/598-4406, oregonobservatory.org)
Sunriver Nature Center (541/593-4442, sunrivernaturecenter.org)

WARM SPRINGS

The Museum at Warm Springs (541/553-3331, museumatwarmsprings.org)

Slick's Que Co.

442 E Hood Ave   541/549-4227
Lunch, Dinner: Wed-Sun (fall)   slicksqueco.com
Inexpensive to moderate

Previously located in Bend, but now back in Sisters, Slick's Que Co. is the ultimate spot for authentic pit barbecue cooked low and slow over split wood. The lineup includes pulled pork, brisket (and delicious burnt ends), smoked turkey breast, baby back ribs, chicken and sausage. Create your favorite combination plate with one meat and a side or two; build a platter with two to four meats and enough sides to satisfy one very hungry diner or a family. Takeout meal kits include meats, hot and cold sides, corn bread and plenty of sauce on the side. You can't go wrong with New Orleans-style bread pudding for dessert. Pitmaster

Roy Slicker readily shares his secrets and techniques at in-house barbecue classes; he is a recognized expert in this arena and serves as the president of the National Barbecue Association.

Sno Cap Drive In

380 W Cascade Ave   541/549-6151
Lunch, Dinner: Daily   Facebook
Inexpensive

A central Oregon tradition is a treat at this tiny burger and ice cream joint which showcases the fast food of yesteryear: thick ice cream shakes and tasty burgers and fries. There are over 25 flavors of homemade hard ice cream, delicious in shakes and sundaes. If you can't decide on just one, combine flavors to make your favorite combination. The menu lists several burgers, corn dogs and assorted basket meal options; no wonder there always seems to be a line at the window!

VINTAGE AIRCRAFT COLLECTIONS

You won't have a problem spotting the **Tillamook Air Museum** (6030 Hangar Road, Tillamook; 503/842-1130; tillamookair.com) just south of town. It's huge! To be exact, it is 1,072 feet long, 192 feet tall and 296 feet wide and was built in 1942 to house military blimps used in World War II. Watch a short video chronicling the site's history and visit the Helium Room where the airships were filled; elsewhere on the property, get a close-up look at aircraft and helicopters. WWII medals, gear, military uniforms and photographs are also displayed. Open 9 a.m. to 5 p.m. daily; nominal admission fee.

In 2015 the **Erickson Aircraft Collection** was moved from Tillamook to a brand new facility at the **Oregon Air Museum** (2408 NW Berg Dr, Madras; 541/460-5065; ericksoncollection.com). This assembly of rare, vintage fighter planes (most still in flying condition) includes famous models such as the Wildcat, Thunderbolt, Corsair, Focke-Wulf 190, P-38 Lightning and P-51 Mustang. Tour this collection at the Madras Municipal Airpark, 9 a.m. to 5 p.m. Thursday through Monday; nominal admission fee.

SUNRIVER

Garrison's Fishing Guide Services
56820 Venture Lane   541/593-8394, 541/410-8374
Prices vary   garrisonguide.com

This is Central Oregon's only year-round guide service for both fly and spin fishing. John Garrison and his expert guides provide the knowledge and fishing gear to reel in the big ones from the best lakes and rivers in Central Oregon. Fish for Kokanee, mackinaw or rainbow, brook, lake and bull trout; you can keep or release your catch. Fishing trips are suitable for families (imagine the excitement of your youngster landing their first fish) as well as serious anglers; competitively priced. Garrison uses 24-foot pontoon boats with space for kids to roam about; only one fishing party of up to six guests is booked per boat.

Sunriver Resort
17600 Center Dr   541/593-1000, 866/930-2687
Prices vary   sunriver-resort.com

In 1965, Portland developers John D. Gray and Donald V. McCallum embarked on building this planned resort and residential community on property that once served as Camp Abbot, a WWII Army Corps of Engineers training facility. Through the following years, the natural environment has remained protected while attaining the reputation as a casual yet luxurious destination for families, conferences and special events. River Lodge and Lodge Village guestrooms and suites are within walking distance to the main lodge, Great Hall and other meeting spaces. Accommodations include free Wi-Fi, stone gas fireplace, a private deck and access to the **Sage Springs Club and Spa**. Homes and condos are also available for rent. Resort amenities and activities are scattered throughout the enclave: equipment rentals, bike paths, six restaurants (varying fare, seasonal operating hours), retail shops, horse stables, four golf courses and a putting course, private airport and marina,. The SHARC (Sunriver Homeowners Aquatic & Recreation Center) is open to all guests at a discounted rate. The lodge restaurant is open year-round for breakfast and lunch (seasonal dinner service) and the cozy pub is open from 11 a.m. until closing.

WARM SPRINGS

Kah-Nee-Ta Resort and Spa
6823 Hwy 8   541/553-1112, 800/554-4786
Moderate to expensive   kahneeta.com

This resort, located along the Warm Springs River, offers a fun destination for the entire family. The village is the hub of recreational activities. Enjoy the mineral hot springs fed Olympic-size pool with water slides, mini golf, Spa Wanapine, basketball and volleyball courts or horse stables. Lodging options range from village suites, RV parking spaces and tipis. Additional rooms are in the lodge (a half mile away, complimentary shuttle service), which also contains the convention center, restaurants and another pool. **Indian Head Casino** (indianhead-gaming.com) is located 13 miles down the road with expanded gaming areas and restaurants. The area boasts 300 days of sunshine a year.

The Museum at Warm Springs
2189 Hwy 26   541/553-3331
Daily: Seasonal hours   museumatwarmsprings.org
Nominal

Collections and exhibitions of Pacific Northwest Native American ceremonial clothing, masks and ritual implements as well as baskets, beadwork, paintings, photographs and sculptures are featured at this beautiful museum on the Warm Springs Indian Reservation. Artifacts are displayed in permanent and changing exhibits; interactive exhibits come alive with colorful visuals and authentic audio recordings; a small amphitheater is outside. The museum, built in 1993 (Oregon's first tribal museum), is dedicated to preserving, advancing and sharing the cultural, traditional and artistic heritage of the Confederated Tribes of Warm Springs. The interpretive Twanat Trail is a quarter-mile trail with educational displays about the area's animals, birds, plants, water creatures, geology and history.

NOTES

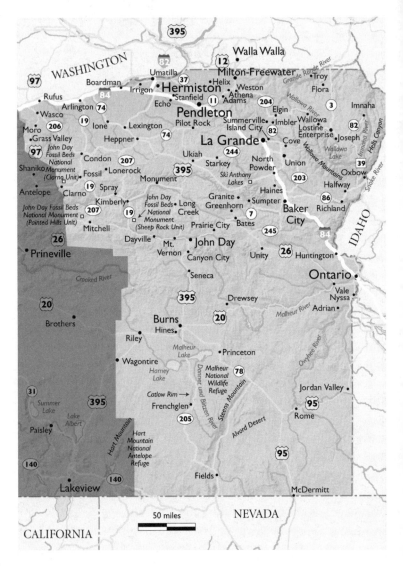

Eastern Oregon

BAKER CITY

Baker Heritage Museum

2480 Grove St
Seasonal: March-Oct
Nominal

541/523-9308
bakerheritagemuseum.com

Baker City was once the third-largest city in Oregon and fastest-growing community in the West. Housed in the city's former natatorium, this building helps preserve the area's eclectic chronicles. Along with many artifacts, the Cavin-Warfel Collection of rocks, fossils and minerals, begun in the 1930s as a hobby of two Baker City sisters who continued their passion for 45 years, is housed here; the Wyatt Family Collection is an assemblage of some 2,000 agates, jasper and other rocks and gems. The **Adler House Museum** (2305 Main St, 541/523-9308) is also managed by the Baker Heritage Museum. Mr. Adler, a low-key gent, was very successful in the magazine distribution business and became a major benefactor to nearly every local cause. A lifelong bachelor, Leo died in 1993 at the age of 98 and left his $20 million fortune to his beloved community. His Italianate home (circa 1889) has been restored to its glory days with period wallpaper, original furniture, artwork and light fixtures.

Barley Brown's Brew Pub

2190 Main St   541/523-4266
Mon-Sat: 4-10   barleybrowns.com
Moderate

Providing "small batch handcrafted beer, good food, good company, good times" is the basis of **Tyler Brown**'s mainstay eatery where you'll find plenty of comfort food along with award-winning beer to wash it down. Standout dinners include a one-pound rack of baby back ribs, shrimp and alligator pasta, steaks, salads and pub grub; a few menu items are available at the tap house. A production brewery and tap house are across the street and feature 44 of Barley Brown's beers. Not unlike the iconic *Cheers* television show, everyone is likely to know your name; or get to know it should you venture in more than a time or two.

DID YOU KNOW...

...Deadman Creek in Wallowa County was named by James Dale, a sheepherder who said he might just as well be dead as to be in such a lonesome place (1890).

...Kettle Creek in Wallowa County was named following a pack-horse that bucked its pack off and jammed the kettle beyond use; the kettle lay in the water for many years afterward and the rest is history.

Bella Main Street Market

2023 Main St   541/523-7490
Daily: Hours vary   bellabakercity.com

Check out the impressive selection of groceries plus gourmet foods, fine wines, kitchenware, gifts and good java drinks from the unique espresso bar (a massive 18-foot long, two-inch thick slab of slate). The shelves hold local and organic staples and, an extensive selection of cheese and salami and handmade pastries from **Sweet Wife Baking** (541/403-6628, sweetwifebaking.com). Many of the gourmet foodstuffs are Baker City exclusives; gather up an assortment to include in a personalized gift (choose a basket, beautiful platter or whatever strikes your fancy) appropriate for any occasion. Kitchen necessities and accessories of all sizes and prices are great go-withs; gadgets, serveware, dishes and special treasures to spiff up your kitchen, dining room or pantry.

Charley's Ice Cream Parlor
2101 Main St, Suite 101   541/524-9307
Daily (seasonal)   Facebook
Inexpensive

"Let's go to Charley's!" This familiar phrase leads locals to Basche-Sage Place at the corner of Main and Broadway. Stop in for a treat from early in the day until late into the evening and choose from a multitude of ice cream flavors, hot dogs, candies, espressos and homemade soups, salads and sandwiches.

Earth & Vine Wine Bar and Art Gallery
2001 Washington Ave   541/523-1687
Breakfast: Sat, Sun; Lunch, Dinner: Tues-Sun   Facebook

Visit this charming restaurant, wine bar and art gallery for a "taste" of Baker City. You'll be impressed with talented local artists' showings and fine wines at reasonable prices. The menu offers good choices for lunch or dinner — homemade soups, sandwiches, salads, pizzas and pasta dishes. Brunch specials include delicious homemade crepes and Benedicts with locally-roasted coffee and enticing desserts served all day. The gallery occasionally hosts live music performances.

Geiser Grand Hotel
1996 Main St   541/523-1889, 888/434-7374
Inexpensive to expensive   geisergrand.com

Barbara and Dwight Sidway undertook an unbelievable project in 1993 to restore this grande dame back to life, a restoration that has garnered prestigious awards. This historic landmark, first opened in 1889, is an architectural jewel and appealing with ornate mahogany, gleaming brass, crystal chandeliers in every room and leaded stained glass. Spend a memorable night in the grand Cupola Suite where you will enjoy impressive mountain views from your bed and luxuriate in the large, well-appointed bathroom. Other accommodations are also tastefully decorated and outfitted with amenities. Belly up to the mahogany bar in the **1889 Cafe** for sundown libations or dinner and enjoy local musicians and other entertainment. The classy **Palm Court** restaurant is surrounded by a mahogany balcony and basks under a stained glass ceiling. Fine dining entrees include meats, fish and seafood, in-house smoked meats and decadent homemade desserts. Create a memory with your children by visiting on a Saturday during the holiday months for special events and horse-drawn sleigh rides; a two-story Christmas tree and Victorian high tea as well.

Inland Cafe

2715 10th St   541/523-9041
Breakfast, Lunch, Dinner: Daily   Facebook
Inexpensive to moderate

Inland Cafe is endorsed by ranchers and loggers for stick-to-your-ribs meals. Popular dinners include traditional Angus roast beef, roasted turkey, steaks, liver and onions and a one-pound chicken-fried steak; prime rib is offered on Friday and Saturday evenings. You're likely to find folks queued up for breakfast, especially giant homemade cinnamon rolls, and substantial lunches. Not to worry though if you have a small appetite; there are senior meals, as well as lighter menu options.

The Sycamore Tree

2108 Main St   541/523-4840
Mon-Sat: 10-6   sycamoregifts.com

You will easily wrap up your gift list and please any recipient with fudge, elegant gifts, home decor, religious items or a piece from the art gallery featuring local artists. Attractive vignettes showcase the merchandise and suggest eye-appealing arrangements. If you have a sweet tooth, make a beeline to the fudge counter for morsels of

FESTIVALS & FAIRS IN EASTERN OREGON

JUNE

Elgin Riverfest (Elgin, visitelginoregon.com)

Wallowa Valley Festival of Arts (Joseph, wallowavalleyarts.org)

JULY

Chief Joseph Days (Joseph, chiefjosephdays.org)

Hells Canyon Motorcycle Rally (Baker City, hellscanyonrally.com)

Miners Jubilee (Baker City, minersjubilee.com)

North Powder Huckleberry Festival (North Powder, visiteastern
oregon.com)

AUGUST

Bronze, Blues & Brews (Joseph, bronzebluesbrews.com)

Cove Cherry and Arts Festival (Cove, coveoregon.org/cherry-fair)

Music in the Meadow (Sumpter, musicinthemeadow.wordpress.com)

SEPTEMBER

Alpenfest (Joseph/Wallowa Lake, oregonalpenfest.blogspot.com)

Hells Canyon Mule Days (Enterprise, hellscanyonmuledays.com)

Rollin' on the River (Boardman, visiteasternoregon.com)

OCTOBER

Haines Harvest Festival (Haines, visiteasternoregon.com)

Check oregonfairs.org for dates and details of county fairs in Eastern
Oregon.

chocolate sensations or other interesting flavor variations, all made
in the store by hand with quality ingredients.

BATES

Boulder Creek Ranch

72585 Middle Fork Lane   541/421-3031
Moderate   bouldercreekranch.net

Journey to Blue Mountain country for the rare opportunity to stay
in an authentic Basque sheepherder's wagon. Sheepherders and
their camps were a common sight in the 1800s, and now this ranch

brings the Old West back to the forefront with this unique idea. The canvas-covered wagon has a full-size bed and offers a table with bench seating. Amenities? No power, no running water, no phone, no television — that's the point! Coupled with the authentic wagon, however, is a one-bedroom guest cabin immediately next door. With the cabin's modern-day facilities (bath, kitchen, woodstove), perhaps mom and dad will stay there and let the kids have a private adventure in the wagon (available only in summer months). Provisions are supplied to prepare a full ranch breakfast before you head out to explore the property or help with ranch chores.

BOARDMAN

River Lodge and Grill

6 Marine Dr
Lodging: Inexpensive
Restaurant: Breakfast, Lunch, Dinner: Daily
Moderate

541/481-6800, 888/988-2009
riverlodgeandgrill.com

Don't make the mistake of missing Boardman; it is definitely worth the detour from I-84. River Lodge and Grill offers affordable lodging along the Columbia River in a log and river-stone complex in rooms that are tidy, clean and well-appointed. The riverside rooms and restaurant overlook the private rocky beach. You'll get good quality, comfort food meals at the family-friendly lodge-style restaurant where the menu changes seasonally. Special hunting, fishing and golf packages combine accommodations with local activities.

BURNS

Crystal Crane Hot Springs

59315 Hwy 78
Inexpensive to moderate

541/493-2312
cranehotsprings.com

Resting your head in the middle of nowhere is fun and a great way to better understand our diverse state. This is just such a quaint, atypical place where more adventurous travelers can spend the night in their tent, use the available RV hookups or the 26-foot tipi (seasonally) with soaking tub. More comfortable digs include one of the establishment's four rustic cabins or a room in Sage Inn (mostly shared bathrooms), a three-bedroom apartment and a three-bedroom home. Enjoy the great outdoors from the warm geothermal spring-fed pond or private soaking tubs in The Bathhouse, which also offers showers and restrooms; a nominal fee is charged for day use (daily 9-9). The Commons Room is the social center and has kitchen facilities for guests to use.

RJ's Restaurant
Hwy 20 E at Hwy 395   541/573-6346
Breakfast, Lunch, Dinner: Daily
Inexpensive

Proclaiming "anything you want, any time of the day," **Sonja and Bob McDannel** have run this quality operation for four decades. The menu includes more than a dozen milkshake flavors, salad bar, hamburgers, popcorn shrimp, baked potatoes and a kids' menu. Burgers are accompanied with a hearty portion of fries (don't miss the super Swiss cheese and mushroom burger); breakfast is available throughout the day. There's plenty of parking for big rigs and oversize RVs at this Southeastern Oregon junction.

CANYON CITY

Oxbow Trade Company
303 S Canyon City Blvd   541/575-2911
Days and hours vary; call for appointment   oxbowwagonsandcoaches.com

In this high-tech day and age, horse-drawn vehicles are an anomaly. However, owners **Mary and Jim Jensen** buy and restore these conveyances for aficionados like themselves. In addition to other utility and pleasure vehicles they sell high quality carriages, wagons, chuck wagons, sleighs, carts and an occasional hearse at fair prices. They also carry Amish-made harnesses, parts and accessories such as sleigh bells, cast iron horse heads, gears, lamps, western decor items, antiques and necessary accessories. Visitors are welcome, but call ahead to make sure someone is minding the shop; frequent auctions and shows are always a pull to add to their stock and locate hard-to-find pieces for customers.

CONDON

Hotel Condon
202 S Main St
Moderate

541/384-4624, 800/201-6706
hotelcondon.com

Condon is located in the high plateau county seat of Gilliam County. Although this historic hotel was built in 1920, it has all of the amenities you would expect in a 21st century hotel, while retaining the original period charm. The 18 guest rooms and private bathrooms are individually decorated. A complimentary wine and cheese reception is served every afternoon and a continental breakfast is served each morning. There are monthly weekend specials from September through May and the dining room and Sage Lounge

BRONZE SCULPTURES

It's hard to believe that Joseph was once a sleepy mountain town; it has become a major arts mecca. Dozens of art galleries and studios now fill formerly empty storefronts along Main Street as scores of professional artists and craftspeople have moved to the area. This movement began when **Valley Bronze** (18 Main St, Joseph; 541/432-7445; valleybronze.com) opened their foundry in the 1980s. They began casting the sculptures of some of the country's foremost artists and now have worldwide recognition for castings of the highest quality. Tours of the factory and foundry show creations sculpted in wax, formed into molds and then cast using molten metals. At **Joseph Gallery**, just half a mile away from the foundry, a magnificent sampling of artworks (mostly bronze) are displayed; it is also the starting point for foundry tours offered May through October. You will be in awe of the beauty (and size) of their creations.

are available to rent for special occasions (catering options are available). The hotel is conveniently situated for day trips to the John Day Fossil Beds and Paleontology Center and the new Cottonwood Canyon State Park located on the John Day River. Condon hosts special events throughout the year including Robert Burns Festival; the Tumbleweed Basketball Tournament; the fabulous 4th of July celebration featuring a classic small town parade, Soap Box Derby and Tricycle Races; and a Fall Festival. The region offers year-round fishing, bike riding, hiking and seasonal hunting. Condon also has a seasonal farmer's market, golf course, movie theater and summer community swimming pool.

DAYVILLE

Thomas Condon Paleontology Center
John Day Fossil Beds National Monument
Hwy 19, 9 miles north of Dayville   541/987-2333
Hours vary   nps.gov/joda
Free

The Thomas Condon Paleontology Center serves as a visitor center for the Sheep Rock Unit. See over 500 fossils in the museum and marvel at the giant murals depicting life in Eastern Oregon before it became a sagebrush desert. There are an additional 50,000 fossils stored in the collection room where cutting edge research goes on year-round. All fossils on display were found in the John Day Fossil Beds; look for rhino, giraffe-deer, camels, horses, bear-dogs, oreodonts and entelodonts, but no dinosaurs. The park's headquarters are in the James Cant 1917 homestead dwelling; its history is an interesting story. Venture a bit farther to see two other components of this national monument: **Painted Hills Unit** (Hwy 26, 9 miles northwest of Mitchell) and **Clarno Unit** (Hwy 218, 20 miles west of Fossil); the colorful formations attract visitors from around the world. Don't even think about digging for fossils on these properties; instead, head to the town of Fossil where collecting is available to the public behind the high school (wheelercounty-oregon.com/fossils.html).

DIAMOND

Hotel Diamond
49130 Main St   541/493-1898
Seasonal: April-Dec   historichoteldiamond.com
Inexpensive

With the Steens Mountain, the Malheur National Wildlife Refuge and Kiger Gorge in the Alvord Desert as backdrops, the area beckons to a wide variety of travelers. Hotel breakfasts, lunches and family-style dinners are available daily, and you'll enjoy comfortable digs with tasteful antique furnishings making you feel at home; the screened porch is a favorite guest congregating place. There are eight rooms, some shared baths and the easy price includes breakfast. During the off-season, the hotel, with kitchen privileges, is available to groups. If you are a passerby, drop in to **Frazier's**, behind the hotel, for lunch Tuesday through Saturday.

ENTERPRISE

Arrowhead Ranch Cabins
64745 Pine Tree Road   541/426-6420
Seasonal: May-Oct   arrowheadranchcabins.com
Moderate

Whether you are staying a few days or longer, this updated ranch with modern conveniences could provide just the right retreat. You can throw a horseshoe or two, bicycle the local country roads, meander the walking paths and observe the abundant flora and fauna. The one-bedroom Ruby Peak cabin provides 800 square feet of living, bed and bath space that accommodates up to four people. The white clapboard Wagon House cabin is slightly larger. Both vintage knotty-pine paneled cabins have full-service kitchens, overstuffed chairs, first-rate bed linens and down comforters making "camping" here first-class. The stately white peg-constructed barn (circa 1888) has been a favorite feature of the Wallowa County Barn Tour. Board your horse for $10 a day; you provide feed unless pasture is available (no other

OLD WEST SCENIC HIGHWAY

Drive your car or pedal your bike on the 174-mile **Old West Scenic Bikeway** loop. Locals say there are no bad views in Eastern Oregon as you travel through this rugged piece of the Old West. The route is spectacular enough to be designated an Oregon Scenic Highway. You will travel through rich ponderosa pine forests, scenic rivers, abundant wildlife, hot springs and fossil beds. The drive begins and ends at the city of John Day, the biggest town on the loop. Here you can stop by the **Kam Wah Chung State Park** (541/575-0028), a heritage site preserving the legacy of Chinese who lived and worked here. If you are a fisherman visit the North Fork of the John Day River where the salmon run. You may see the horses of Murderer's Creek nearby; they coexist with mule deer, elk, bighorn sheep, bears and other small forest animals; watch for their piles on the road. Next, head east on Highway 26 through picturesque Prairie City where you can view bald eagles high in the trees; visitors have viewed up to 11 bald eagles at one time. Turnoff at Austin Junction; these are real rural back roads as you pass through the friendly little towns of Long Creek, Monument and Kimberly before heading south to the **John Day Fossil Beds National Monument** (541/987-2333). The fossil museum is a must-see stop; it is one of the top three paleontology sites in the world. Next, you can reconnect with Highway 26 back to John Day, through Dayville and Mt. Vernon. Look for Strawberry Mountain Wilderness from the covered wagon wayside and the amazing Painted Hills; you'll know them when you see them!

pets or smoking). A secluded open-air fire pit is the perfect setting for star-gazing. Guests are treated to a box of handcrafted truffles from their **Arrowhead Chocolates** (100 N Main St, 541/432-2871) operation in Joseph.

Barking Mad Farm and Country Bed & Breakfast

65156 Powers Road
Moderate

541/886-0171
barkingmadfarm.com

If you'd like time away from the kids, you'll love a stay with **Emily and Rob Klavins** in their restored farmhouse. The working farm setting couldn't be more idyllic; grazing buffalo, alpine vistas, tranquil grounds and a short drive to Joseph and Wallowa Lake and local brew pubs. Guest rooms are spacious, well-appointed and afford glorious views. You're in for a treat each morning with gourmet breakfasts featuring local farm-fresh ingredients served on the wrap-around porch with an uninterrupted view of the Eagle Cap. Whether you spend your day shopping in Joseph, exploring the backcountry or just reading a book, unwind each night watching the sun set with a glass of wine around a crackling campfire. With backgrounds in outdoor education and sustainability, the Klavins are living their dream to share the natural beauty of an oft-overlooked, world-class corner of the state with visitors from around the world.

Enterprise House Bed & Breakfast

508 1st South St   541/426-4238
Moderate   enterprisehousebnb.com

This circa-1910 Colonial Revival mansion is minutes from Joseph and Wallowa Lake. Relaxation beckons as guests approach the beautifully restored home, resplendent with white picket fence, a porch swing, stained glass, ornate woodwork and nostalgic wood-frame screen doors. Choose from three guest rooms and two suites with private baths. Proprietors **Judy and Jack Burgoyne** start each day with an impressive breakfast buffet of organic and locally grown products.

Lear's Pub & Grill

111 W Main St   541/426-3300
Breakfast, Lunch, Dinner: Daily   learspubandgrill.com
Moderate

Dishing up three squares daily, husband and wife team **Cathi and Steve Lear** also serve up a side of lively banter between themselves and customers. Chef Steve serves local products with an emphasis on Angus beef; check the chalkboard for daily specials. Don't miss hearty breakfasts consisting of Kahlua French toast, huervos rancheros or meat and egg pair-ups; bodacious burgers or real corned beef brisket Reuben sandwiches for lunch or dinner and great steak dinners. To go with your meal or just because, wet your whistle with local microbrews or your favorite drink from the full bar. You'll get your money's worth in good prices and quality food.

RimRock Inn
83471 Lewiston Hwy   541/828-7769, 888/440-4161
Inexpensive to moderate   rimrockinnor.com

The RimRock Inn is about 34 miles north of Enterprise. The summer season officially opens Memorial Day weekend and runs through the end of September. Lodging includes five tipis which sleep one to six people; futons with mattresses, bedding, towels, organic amenities, fire pits with wood available and battery-powered lighting are provided. Water, restrooms and showers are nearby. The Eagle's Aerie Loft apartment is above the inn and has all the comforts of home including original art, antiques, western-style furnishings and a bathroom outfitted with an original claw-foot tub. Accommodations include an expanded continental buffet breakfast at the inn. If you prefer, there are tent sites for roughing it; also an RV park. Dining options include a beautiful dining room for dinner (reservations required) or enjoy your meal and the magnificent view from the deck; small plates available after 3. Fresh, local, organic fare is served and almost everything is made from scratch. This experience is also described as "glamping on the edge" (glamorous camping on the edge of Joseph Creek Canyon in Wallowa County).

Terminal Gravity Brewing and Public House
803 SE School St   541/426-3000
Seasonal: Sun, Mon: 11-9; Wed-Sat: 11-10   terminalgravitybrewing.com
Inexpensive to moderate

Pub grub reigns supreme at this home of extensive beer-making. Order a pale ale, ESG (extra special golden), IPA, porter, stout or other brewed delight (also sold in many supermarkets) to go along with family dining favorites. A sample of menu items includes nachos and other starters, beer mac and cheese, salads, burgers (buffalo and locally-raised grass-fed beef), sandwiches and pastas. Picnic tables, shaded by aspens, are liberally spread around the grounds; a refreshing stop all the way around.

MAJOR OREGON DISASTERS

A number of major disasters have affected our state; among them:

1903 — Heppner Flash Flood

A strong thunderstorm with extremely heavy rain created severe flash flooding along Willow Creek running through Heppner's town center. One-third of the city structures were swept away in a few short minutes, drowning 250 people.

1910 — Langlois Fire

The entire business district of Langlois, in Curry County, was wiped out by a fire that started in a livery stable, largely due to dry weather. Only a blacksmith shop and a soft-drink stand remained in the business area. (Langlois was also known then as Dairyville, and it was the first town on the stage line from Bandon to Curry County.)

1917 — Sumpter Fire

A fire of an unknown cause erupted in the cook's quarters of the Capital Hotel. Upon discovery, the room was totally engulfed in flames and spread to the adjacent buildings. All effort to contain the fire was futile. In no time several structures were totally aflame, even the streets were on fire, breaching the fire hoses and spreading the destruction. Nearly 100 hundred buildings in 12 city blocks were completely destroyed. There was no loss of life, but with hard rock mining winding down, it marked the end for the once thriving town.

1918 — Swine Flu Pandemic

An influenza pandemic swept the world, including the West Coast. Despite efforts for quarantine, at its height, some 400 new cases were reported daily. Twenty thousand people became ill of which, 2,000 Portlanders died.

1922 — Astoria Fire

The business district of Astoria was destroyed, hundreds left homeless and property loss estimated at $15 million. The cause was a fire that started in a restaurant and firemen resorted to dynamiting in a vain effort to stop the inferno.

1933 — Tillamook Burn (and 1939, 1945, 1951)

A fire ignited during a logging operation in the Coast Range and within two days, flames spread to 40,000 acres. Dry, strong east winds fanned the flames to a quarter of a million acres, burning huge, ancient stands of old growth Douglas fir. The front of the fire was 18 miles long, and Oregon beaches had ash and cinders two feet deep for a 30-mile stretch. Over 13 billion board feet of timber was lost. Devastation by these fires helped bring about legislation for reforestation and improved forest practices.

1936 – Bandon Forest Fire

On September 26, 1936, a fire burned several miles of forest east of Bandon. But a sudden shift in the wind drove the flames swiftly westward. Ignited by the forest fire, the town's abundant gorse (noxious weed with yellow blooms) became engulfed in flames. Bandon's entire commercial district was destroyed. The total loss stated at the time was $3 million, with 11 fatalities.

1948 – Vanport Flood

The second largest city in Oregon in 1948, Vanport was located between Portland and the Columbia River. It was the largest public housing project in the nation at the time. The town was destroyed when a 200-foot section of the dike holding back the Columbia River collapsed during a flood. Occurring at 4 p.m. on May 30th, the city was underwater by nightfall, leaving inhabitants homeless and 15 dead.

1950 – January Snowstorms

Three massive snowstorms, with little time in between and accompanied by high winds, created chaos. A severe sleet storm followed the snow, then freezing rain, generating broken and fallen trees, highway mayhem and downed power lines. Hundreds of motorists were stranded in the Columbia River Gorge. Record January snowfall totals (in inches) include: Albany (54), Astoria (39), Corvallis (52), Portland and Salem (32) and Tillamook (19).

1959 – Roseburg Blast

The accidental detonation of 6½ tons of explosive material destroyed all buildings within a 12 city-block area. A truck loaded with dynamite and nitro carbo nitrate was parked overnight in front of the Garretsen Building waiting for delivery the next morning; that night the building caught fire and the explosive-laden truck remained unnoticed until moments before it detonated. Fourteen people were killed and another 125 injured. City damages were estimated at $10 to $12 million.

1962 – Columbus Day Windstorm

This quintessential Pacific Northwest windstorm killed 38

people and did $170 to $200 million in damage. Wind gusts reached 116 m.p.h. in downtown Portland. Cities lost power for two to three weeks and 50,000 dwellings were damaged; agriculture and livestock took a devastating blow. In comparison, it's been noted that the amount of trees lost to this storm was nearly 15 times more than the 1980 eruption of Mt. St. Helens.

1964 – Southern Oregon Flood

With over eight inches of rain in five days in the Medford area, the Rogue River quickly rose to flood stage, washing away houses, roads and bridges and killing 12 people. A new gas line across the river at Gold Hill was washed out, cutting service. Highways throughout the state were closed as high water and slides crippled travel and communications. It was a bleak Christmas for thousands of flooded-out Oregonians.

1996 – Willamette Valley Flood

Combined by four days of heavy rain, extended periods of bitter cold, low level snow packs and additional downpours, ground became saturated and runoffs flooded major rivers. Floods spread beyond the Willamette Valley to the Oregon Coast and the Cascade Mountains. Eight people died and nearly every Oregon county received a disaster declaration. Region-wide damage estimates exceeded $1 billion.

2007 – Vernonia Flooding

Heavy storms that impacted the Pacific Northwest flooded Rock Creek and the Nehalem River, washing out roads, destroying homes, cars and the communications infrastructure in the town of Vernonia. Hundreds of people had to be rescued and evacuated.

FIELDS

Fields Station

22276 Fields Dr   541/495-2275
Daily: Hours vary   thefieldsstation.com
Inexpensive

Fields is a small unincorporated community 112 miles south of Burns taking Highway 205 (the highway becomes a county road, Catlow Valley Road, at the Roaring Springs Ranch). Nothing is more refreshing on a hot summer day along the dusty road than a huge milkshake or malt, made by hand the old-fashioned way and served in a frosty steel cup. The cafe is famous for its burgers; a half-pounder with chili or a double bacon cheeseburger. Breakfasts are equally satisfying and large. A most welcome sight for motorists running on fumes is one of the few gas pumps in the area; they also pump diesel and propane. If you're looking for a place to call it a night, there are guest rooms, or you may prefer to stay in the Old Hotel which rents as a single unit; RVers are accommodated in the adjacent facility. The store is the center of the community and stocks groceries, toiletries, necessary auto supplies, ice-cold beer (micros and domestic cans), other beverages and snacks; it contains a unique USPS Post Office and Oregon's smallest OLCC liquor store (with a full range of "snake bite medicine"). The epitome of Oregon's high desert is Steens Mountain for fishing, hunting and spectacular hiking and camping; be mindful of dangerous sudden weather changes.

FOSSIL

Fossil General Mercantile
555 Main St   541/763-4617
Mon-Sat: 8-7 (till 6 in winter); Sun: 8-5

Readily known as "The Merc," this store has been reincarnated several times since its 1883 opening, yet still retains the feel of yesteryear. To those who live, work and play miles from city shopping opportunities it's a godsend for fabrics, clothing, groceries and sundry items.

Wilson Ranches Retreat Bed & Breakfast
15809 Butte Creek Road   541/763-2227, 866/763-2227
Year round   wilsonranchesretreat.com
Inexpensive to moderate

The pioneer ancestors of fifth-generation **Nancy and Phil Wilson** settled in Wheeler and Gilliam counties, choosing one of the most picturesque areas in Eastern Oregon for their homestead. For an authentic Western retreat, book accommodations at this 9,000-acre working cattle and dude ranch. Up to 20 guests are housed in the 1910 Sears Roebuck Ranch House; each of the six pristine ranch-style guest rooms, some with private baths and fireplaces, is uniquely decorated. There is plenty to do with multiple scenic horseback riding trails, fishing, birding, hiking, mountain biking and, of course, the John Day Fossil Beds National Monument. While Nancy and Phil regale visitors with tales of family history, a hearty full-course ranch-style breakfast is served in preparation for a memorable day in the beautiful Butte Creek Valley. Guests are invited to grill their own steaks and burgers for dinner. Rooms are outfitted with amenities befitting a nice hotel and guests have access to a movie library, books, games, TV/DVD and cowboy

KIDS' ACTIVITIES: EASTERN OREGON

BAKER CITY
National Historic Oregon Trail Interpretive Center (541/523-1843, oregontrail.blm.gov)
BOARDMAN
SAGE Center (541/481-7243, visitsage.com)
DAYVILLE
Thomas Condon Paleontology Center (541/987-2333, nps.gov/joda)
JOSEPH
Wallowa Lake State Park (541/432-4185, oregonstateparks.org)
Wallowa Lake Tramway (541/432-5331 in summer, 503/781-4321 in winter, wallowalaketramway.com): seasonal
LA GRANDE
Eagle Cap Excursion Train (541/963-9000, eaglecaptrainrides.com)
NORTH POWDER
Anthony Lakes Mountain Resort (541/856-3277, anthonylakes.com)
ONTARIO
Four Rivers Cultural Center and Museum (541/889-8191, 4rcc.com)
PENDLETON
Happy Canyon Indian Pageant and Wild West Show (541/276-2553, happycanyon.com)
Pendleton Round-Up (541/276-2553, pendletonroundup.com)
PRINCETON
Malheur National Wildlife Refuge (541/493-2612, fws.gov/malheur)

gear (boots, hats and saddle bags). Turn your stay into an occasion with optional activities, flowers, chocolates or other thoughtful touches.

FRENCHGLEN

Frenchglen Hotel
39184 Hwy 205   541/493-2825
Mid-March-Nov   frenchglenhotel.com
Inexpensive to moderate

When you want to go to Oregon's outback, but camping isn't your cup of tea, make a reservation at this historic State Heritage Site at the base of Steens Mountain. Guest rooms are rustic and restrooms are down the hall. Breakfast, lunch and dinner are served in the dining room; dinners by reservation. The name stems from Peter French's 1800s cattle operation financed by Californian Dr. Hugh Glenn; thus, the French-Glenn Livestock Company. Commonly referred to as the P Ranch, it was once the largest spread for miles around, if not statewide (30,000 to 45,000 cattle, 3,000 horses and mules on 140,000 acres). French, unfortunately, met his demise in 1897 during a squatter's squabble when the illegal settler shot him.

HAINES

Haines Steak House
910 Front St   541/856-3639
Dinner: Wed-Mon   hainessteakhouse.com
Moderate

For Old West-style dinners, set your sights on the building with a chuck wagon above the entrance. This family-owned, Western-themed steakhouse has long been known for large portions of prime rib, steaks and extensive seafood offerings; there are also options for petite appetites or young buckaroos. Start with the chuck wagon salad bar of fresh fixin's, homemade salads, chili, baked beans and cowboy bread. Folks from all over the world venture off the beaten track for dinner here; opening hours vary.

HALFWAY

Cornucopia Lodge

Queen Mine Road   541/742-4500, 800/742-6115
Inexpensive to moderate   cornucopialodge.com

Miners working the gold strike in the northeastern Oregon town of Cornucopia in the 1800s may have wished for accommodations such as those at Cornucopia Lodge in the Eagle Cap Wilderness. The lodge's guest room and common areas are tastefully appointed with comfortable furniture; five one and two bedroom cabins (four to six people) are just as appealing. There are plenty of activities for every season: trail riding, hiking, fishing, hunting and snowmobiling. Choose a mount from their stable of horses for a guided trail ride in spectacular country (no riding experience necessary) or trailer your own horses to the property and take a guided or unguided excursion. After a day at play, hearty home-cooked dinners of roast pork loin, steak, chicken and more are served family style in the classy dining room. Breakfast is also served family style and lunches consist of soup, sandwiches and salads or request a sack lunch to take outdoors. Come winter, the snow piles up making this area a destination for snowshoers and snowmobilers who park at the bottom of the hill and sled in. The remote lodge is accessible by paved and gravel road.

Inn at Clear Creek Farm

Clear Creek Road   541/742-2238
Moderate   clearcreekinn.com

When you want a place to really get away from it all, head to the northeast corner of our diverse state. This renovated farmhouse offers unique quarters near the Oregon Trail, halfway to the top of Eagle Cap. Five rooms and one family suite (all with private baths) are decorated a la turn-of-the-century. The full country breakfast is a relaxing affair, even more so watching deer and wild turkeys graze outside the dining room window. Seasonal fresh-from-the-orchard apples and pears are a special treat and the hosts are mindful of dietary needs (prior notification, please). You're smack dab in the middle of a working cattle ranch, surrounded by wildlife, trails, orchards and other delights. If fishing is on the agenda, there are bass- and trout-filled ponds, not to mention the Snake River running through nearby Hells Canyon and Brownlee Reservoir. Horseback riding, waterskiing, canoeing, bicycle tours, llama pack trips, day hikes and ranch chores are great activities during nice weather. With four feet of snow during the winter months, cross-country skiers and snowmobilers will think they're in seventh heaven (snowmobile rental available in-house). This gorgeous home is ideal for family getaways.

JOHN DAY

Kam Wah Chung State Heritage Site

125 NW Canton St   541/575-2800
May-Oct: Daily: 9-5   oregonstateparks.org/park_8.php
Free

This unusual museum has roots back to the late 1800s when it became a social and religious center for the area's Chinese immigrants working the gold strikes. The building's seven rooms served as living quarters to Doc Hay and Lung On as well as their places of business. Hay was a medical practitioner specializing in herbal medicine and On was a merchant, labor contractor and immigration assistant. After a century of little notice, the building was deteriorating and the collections begged for preservation. In 2002, Oregon's then-First Lady **Mary Oberst** chaired the successful Kam Wah Chung capital campaign. As a result, an interpretive center and museum exhibitions chronicle the Chinese culture in Grant County. Thousands of interesting items from On's general store, Hay's medical supplies and furnishings used by the proprietors are on display. Entrance to the historic Kam Wah Chung building departs from the interpretive center, by guided tour only.

The Snaffle Bit Dinner House

830 S Canyon Blvd   541/575-2426
Dinner: Tues-Sat; Lunch: Thurs, Fri   Facebook
Inexpensive to moderately expensive

The Snaffle Bit Dinner House declares "where there's smoke

there's fire and where there's fire, there's usually steak." Yes, there certainly are steaks along with ribs, seafood and chicken. Coppercricket is an eight-ounce top sirloin laden with bay shrimp, scallops, asparagus and mushrooms. For a mere $5, add prawns, scampi or a quarter rack of barbecue ribs to sirloin, tenderloin or ribeye steaks. Choose two filling sides and you have a substantial meal. Burgers are hand-pattied and served with soup, salad or fries; all are $10 or less. The diverse menu includes baked spuds with

HISTORY STOPS

DeWitt Museum & Sumpter Valley Railway Depot (425 S Main St, Prairie City; 541/820-3330; prairiecityoregon.com) is open Wednesday through Sunday mid-May to mid-October and provides exhibits of the logging, freight and passenger railroad in the original depot building. The Sumpter Valley Railway transported freight and passengers between Prairie City and Baker City until 1933. The museum houses Oregon's most significant collection of narrow gauge railroad artifacts and historic documents and each exhibit area focuses on a specific topic of history. The depot's current collection includes many photographs of life along the rail line, visual depictions of some of the spectacular wrecks on this steep and dangerous section of the railroad, various lanterns, lights and physical artifacts collected along the line itself. The second floor of the depot provided living quarters for the station agent and today features antiques and memorabilia from the local area and the Dewitt family, arranged much as it might have appeared while the agent's family occupied the quarters.

Named for the four rivers that converge in the western Treasure Valley, **Four Rivers Cultural Center and Museum** (676 SW 5th Ave, Ontario; 541/889-8191; 4rcc.com) represents the flow of people of varied ancestry — American Indian, Basque, European, Hispanic and Japanese — that made this area so culturally diverse. Visitors enter an orientation theater and move through the exhibit gallery with audio dialogue. Exhibits include the arrival of cattlemen and the railroad to the area, as well as internment camps and the various cultures of the community. The Harano Gallery is an amazing exhibit gallery. The facility also includes a Performing Arts Theater for community drama and musical productions.

lots of extras, salads loaded with plenty of good additions and a smattering of pasta and Mexican dishes, appetizers and chicken and fish baskets. This is a dining gem in John Day; reservations suggested.

JOSEPH

Beecrowbee
1 S Main St   541/432-0158
Daily: 10:30-5   beecrowbee.com

Do you want to soothe winter-damaged skin? Try Oregon products from this outfit that handcrafts its bath and body items that not only lead to beautiful, healthy skin, but also nurture the spirit and mind. Beecrowbee sells mild soaps with different scents; lotion bars made with shea butter and various oils; bath soak blended with natural salts; plus their own blended essential oils for bath and body. The product line is complemented with five varieties of high-quality teas, soy wax candles and home decor. All these items and more are sold in their retail shop and online.

Bronze Antler Bed & Breakfast
309 S Main St   541/432-0230
Inexpensive to expensive   bronzeantler.com

Look to the Bronze Antler B&B as your home away from home when visiting scenic Wallowa County. Hosts **Heather Tyreman** and **Bill Finney** provide attentive service so you can go about exploring the area. Full breakfasts feature fresh fruits and savory or sweet entrees with accommodations for those on special diets. Coffee and tea are brewing early each morning for before-breakfast walkers. Amenity-loaded bathrooms adjoin the three second-floor guest rooms. The ground floor suite features modern Asian styling, private entrance and a bathroom more akin to a private spa. Three outdoor garden spaces expand the gathering areas on the property with a bocce ball court, water features and perennial gardens.

HIKE WITH A LLAMA

Since 1985, **Wallowa Llamas** (541/742-2961, wallowallamas. com) has conducted guided tours of small groups into the state's largest wilderness area, the Eagle Cap. Here, at the southern edge of Eastern Oregon's spectacular Wallowa Mountains, amid towering peaks, glacier-sculpted valleys and sparkling mountain streams, llamas carry the amenities, unburdening hikers to experience an ease and luxury normally not available to back country travelers in such rugged environs. **Louise and Raz Rasmussen** offer trips of three to five days and varying degrees of difficulty. Delicious meals are prepared in the great outdoors and enjoyed amid breathtaking scenery.

Mad Mary & Co.

5 S Main St   541/432-0547
Daily   madmaryandcompany.com

Mary Wolfe's successful shop is a boon for residents and tourists looking for just the right gift. Mad Mary's is home base for toys, jewelry, gourmet food, home and garden accessories, a year-round selection of Christmas items and more. Across from the retail area is the 1950s-era soda fountain (with old time rock and roll tunes) for malts, milkshakes, sundaes (made to perfection), other creamy concoctions and good ol' hand-dipped ice cream. Mary invites you to stop in for "everything fun and fattening!"

Mutiny Brewing Company

600 N Main St   541/432-5274
Lunch, Dinner: Wed-Sun (seasonal variations)   mutinybrewing.com
Inexpensive

When you're in Joseph, check out Main Street's Mutiny Brewing Company for pub food with an attitude. You'll encounter burgers made with local grass-fed beef and dressed with bacon, caramelized onions and all the rest; wraps; sandwiches and fish tacos. Nice additions to the menu include rice bowls, Asian noodles with chicken satay and salads loaded with all sorts of goodies. The beverage specialty of the house is Ssswheat, a light wheat beer with citrus flavors. When the weather calls for it, enjoy the outdoor patio featuring stunning views of the Wallowa Mountains that lean over Joseph on every side.

Vali's Alpine Restaurant

59811 Wallowa Lake Hwy
Dinner: April, May: Sat, Sun;
Memorial Day-Labor Day: Wed-Sun
Moderate

541/432-5691
valisrestaurant.com

Family-owned Vali's has been Wallowa County's place for authentic Hungarian food since 1974. One entree is prepared for dinners (seatings at 5 and 7) and may include cabbage rolls, goulash, chicken paprika, schnitzel or grilled ribeye steak; a different entree special is prepared each Friday. *Langos* (Hungarian fry bread), sweet and sour cabbage and späetzle are almost as tasty as the entrees. Desserts such as homemade apple strudel, Black Forest cake, rum ice cream cake and exquisite seasonal goodies are extra special. The selection of beers, wines and cocktails is impressive. Near-famous homemade doughnuts are fresh on weekends between 9 a.m. and 11 a.m. (they frequently sell out early) or purchase European-style cold cuts at the summer-only takeout deli counter. Dinner reservations required; no credit cards.

Wallowa Lake Lodge

60060 Wallowa Lake Hwy
Seasonal
Inexpensive to moderate

541/432-9821
wallowalake.com

A trip to this gem in "Little Switzerland" offers a family adventure that will not soon be forgotten. This cozy retreat was built in the early 1920s and included an amusement park, bowling alley, dance hall, outdoor movie theater, horse-drawn carousel and other services accessed by boat across the lake. Much has changed, but not the laid-back atmosphere and stunning views of the sparkling lake and Wallowa Mountains. Lodging options are all different and rustic; no in-room telephones or televisions (no pets or smoking either). The lodge's 22 rooms are seasonally available May through mid-October, as is the lodge's restaurant. In the off-season, the lodge hosts conferences and group events. Eight cabins are open year round; all are fully furnished, most have wood-burning fireplaces. When you go, be sure to ride the **Wallowa Lake Tramway** (wallowalaketramway.com) to the summit of Mt. Howard (May-Oct); a convenient cafe serves casual food and drink on the alpine patio; the views are breathtaking. Wear hiking shoes and bring a jacket if you want to explore or walk down the mountain; there are plenty of hiking opportunities nearby, including Aneroid Lake.

LA GRANDE

The Potter's Gift House & Gallery
1601 6th St   541/963-5351
Mon-Sat: 10-6; Sun: 11-4   thepottershousegallery.com

Judy and Bob Jensen work from a 120-year-old Victorian beauty that functions as their home, gallery and gift boutique. Each day you'll find Bob at the potter's wheel creating raku and decorative and functional stoneware pieces, all lead-free and safe for use in the microwave, oven and dishwasher. The Bob Jensen warmer would make a unique and thoughtful gift for your favorite cook or special order a full set of dinnerware. If you're crafty, schedule time to participate in making and firing a raku pot of your own design. Alongside Bob's raku in the gallery are sculptures, ceramics, prints, jewelry and photography by 20 or so local artists and craftsmen. A fine selection of boutique gifts includes candles, regional gourmet foods, collectible figurines and cottage, Western and lodge decor items.

Ten Depot Street
10 Depot St   541/963-8766
Dinner: Mon-Sat   tendepotstreet.com
Moderate

This corner brick building houses a casual, yet upscale dinner house. Lamb meatballs with Jamaican dipping sauce, house specialty smoked salmon paté or a tasty combination of bites are beyond run-of-the-mill appetizers. Daily soups are homemade and taco and Thai entree salads are prepared with a choice of chicken or beef. Enjoy prime rib, generously portioned steaks and other meats, sandwiches, seafood and pasta. Lentil pecan burgers, pasta with pesto and vegetarian dinners are pleasant choices for non-meat eaters. Tuesday and Thursday evenings offer live music; be sure to check out the turn-of-the-century bar.

LOSTINE

Lostine Tavern

125 Hwy 82
Lunch, Dinner: Wed-Sun
Inexpensive to moderate

541/569-2246
lostine-tavern.com

Affectionately dubbed the LT, Lostine Tavern has been a community gathering place since it was established as the town tavern in the 1940s. **Lisa Armstrong-Roepke** and **Peter Ferré** run the 51-seat restaurant and bar housed in a renovated historic building. Menu items are based on locally-sourced seasonal ingredients; options consist of appetizers, hearty salads, deli and grilled sandwiches and burgers with fries, as well as a deli case for picnic items. Nightly dinner specials like the bubbling macaroni and cheese topped with breadcrumbs and the smoked barbecue chicken with cheddar scallion corn bread are home-style and served in cast-iron skillets. The full-service bar features rotating taps of regional microbrews, cask wines from Walla Walla and delicious custom cocktails. Whether you are on the way to Oregon's magnificent Wallowa Mountains or simply driving through, this is a must-stop!

MILTON-FREEWATER

Blue Mountain Cider Company

235 E Broadway Ave
Daily: 11-5

541/938-5575
drinkcider.com

This friends-and-family business started in a garage and now sports industry awards displayed in the historic Watermill Building tasting room. Pressed apples are grown locally — and not just any apple, but varieties with high tannin content (winesap, pippen, winter banana) to give the best "zing" to the fermentation. The company has a signature method of adding fresh juice with a bit of carbonation prior to bottling, producing a unique and thirst-quenching result. Unusual custom rose ciders with added real juices (cranberry, cherry, raspberry, pomegranate, peach) are also available.

NORTH POWDER

Anthony Lakes Mountain Resort
47500 Anthony Lake Hwy   541/856-3277
Seasonal   anthonylakes.com

Far from the megalopolis and subject to snowpack, Anthony Lakes offers great family ski adventures on uncrowded runs that usually start in mid-November. At 8,000 feet you'll find light, dry snow, perfect for powder lovers, groomed cross-country trails, snowboard terrain and SnoCat tours to the back side of the mountain. Certified instructors are adept at teaching the entire family. Start or end your day at the lodge with breakfast or lunch in the cafeteria or gather in **Starbottle Saloon** for a hot toddy and more fun times.

ONTARIO

Four Rivers Cultural Center and Museum
676 SW 5th Ave   541/889-8191
Mon-Fri: 9-5; Sat: 10-5   4rcc.com
Nominal

Named for the four rivers that converge in the western Treasure Valley, Four Rivers Cultural Center and Museum represents the flow of people of varied ancestry (American Indian, Basque, European, Hispanic and Japanese) that made this area so culturally diverse. Visitors enter an orientation theater and move through the exhibit gallery with audio dialogue. Exhibits include the arrival of cattlemen and the railroad to the area, as well as internment camps and the various cultures of the community. The **Harano Gallery** is an amazing exhibit gallery.

Mackey's Steakhouse & Pub
111 SW 1st St   541/889-3678
Lunch, Dinner: Daily   mackeysonline.com
Moderate

Honoring their Irish heritage, **Angie and Shawn Grove** named this establishment after their grandfather, Thomas Mackey Grove. Irish fare

WHERE WILD HORSES ROAM

Wild horses still thrive in Oregon; over 1,000 wild mustangs roam within eight Herd Management Areas (Palomino Buttes, Kiger, Warm Springs, South Steens, Heath Creek/Sheepshead, Alvord-Tule Springs, Riddle Mountain and Stinkingwater) of the Bureau of Land Management in the Burns district. Check the district's web for specific information about each herd and management area (blm.gov/or/district/burns). These areas offer great opportunities for viewing the beautiful animals and their habitat; bring your binoculars and be patient. While not easily seen, Rocky Mountain elk, mule deer, mountain lion, bighorn sheep and pronghorn antelope also make this corner of Southeastern Oregon their home. You may even witness the amazing, breathtaking antics of raptors as they soar and dive in the high mountain wind currents.

starts with Dublin potato skins (famous Malheur russets, no doubt), Guinness on tap and Killian's Irish Red. Traditional dinner fare includes Guinness-glazed chicken, chicken with Jameson Irish Whiskey sauce, bangers and mash and shepherd's pie. Other options include steaks with the Mackey's traditional Irish rub, fish and seafood, sandwiches, daily fresh soups and salads. Bring the whole family for dining upstairs or on the patio; the downstairs pub is for the 21-and-over crowd.

OXBOW

Hells Canyon Adventures
4200 Hells Canyon Road   541/785-3352, 800/422-3568
April-Dec   hellscanyonadventures.com
Lodging: Moderate

Come prepared to explore a remote location; Hells Canyon is North America's deepest river gorge, carved by the Snake River on the Oregon/Idaho border and includes 215,000 acres of designated wilderness area. Jet boat tours provide dramatically different views of the north and south ends of the canyon — whitewater rapids and sheer rock walls or calm water and wide open terrain. Seasonal day and multi-day packages include jet boat adventures, fishing charters, shuttles and lodging.

Charters are available for steelhead, sturgeon, bass and trout fishing — great family outings. While camping under the stars is a romantic notion, if you're more attuned to a soft bed, try their lodge overlooking the reservoir. Breakfast is included (and lunch on some tours); however, the closest restaurants for lunch or dinner are at least ten miles down the road. GPS or other mapping programs could inevitably lead you astray; best to check the website or call for complete directions.

PENDLETON

Hamley & Co.

30 SE Court Ave   541/278-1100, ext. 1
Mon-Thurs: 9-6; Fri, Sat: 9-8; Sun: 11-5   hamleyco.com

Beginning in England, generations of the Hamley family passed on the trade of saddle and leather craftsmanship. William Hamley brought his family to America in 1840; after several moves, son J.J. Hamley settled in Pendleton to set up shop in the same building that Hamley's occupies today. **Parley Pearce** and **Blair Woodfield** acquired ownership a century later (2005) to revitalize the store to its original glory, and then some. Expect outstanding selections of magnificent leather kits, belts, chaps, saddlery and tack; ranch and fashion apparel for the whole family; hats; silver jewelry, belt buckles and accessories and western gifts for the person or home. Custom saddles are made on site, true works of art and proudly used by generations of equestrians. Service is undeniably topnotch! During Round-Up week, the store is bursting with cowboys, cowgirls and rodeo fans looking to freshen up wardrobes or garner a professional cowboy's autograph. The mezzanine level accommodates one of the best collections of Western art that I've seen anywhere. The company's legacy of community support continues today and the Hamley name is synonymous with the Pendleton Round-Up.

Hamley Steak House

8 SE Court Ave   541/278-1100, ext. 2
Dinner: Daily   hamleysteakhouse.com
Expensive

Wranglers, Pendleton Whisky and dinner at Hamley Steak House!

That, my friends, is the embodiment of an evening in Pendleton. Hamley & Co. entrepreneurs **Parley Pearce** and **Blair Woodfield** have created a superb atmosphere for traditional, hearty ranch cooking and a not-to-be-missed saloon (open at 4 p.m. daily). The melt-in-your-mouth 14-ounce ribeye steak is bar none. Pop's pot roast and mom's meatloaf head the list of other home-cooking comfort food along with lamb chops, chicken and gravy and mac and cheese. Soups are homemade and sandwiches are more than a mouthful. Check out the surroundings for an original 18th-century bar, authentic tin ceilings, Old West artifacts and faultless local craftsmanship. Sandwiched between the Western store and steakhouse, **Hamley Cafe** is a great quick stop for lunchtime soups, salads and sandwiches or coffee and pastries anytime. You'll be treated Western-style right with delicious food and faultless service. Every Friday and Saturday during summer months, free concerts are featured on the grassy area in front of the steakhouse. Look for the outdoor stage and seating area.

Montana Peaks Hat Co.

24 SW Court Ave	541/215-1400
Mon, Tues, Fri, Sat	montanapeaks.net

Western wear is *de rigueur* for spectators, locals and cowboys at the Pendleton Round-Up, and this popular retailer is dedicated to Western head gear. The array of felt hats would have pleased John Wayne, Tom Mix or Hopalong Cassidy; in fact, hat styles are named for these legendary characters. These folks shine when it comes to custom handmade cowboy hats — individualized by shape, fit, color and accessories. Best to call ahead if you're making a special trip to Montana Peaks; the owners practice random acts of kindness and take random days off.

The Pendleton Coffee Bean and Bistro

241 S Main St	541/379-3663
Breakfast, Lunch, Dinner: Tues-Sat	Facebook
Inexpensive to moderate	

Since 2004, the community has known this bistro as the PCB. Unfortunately, in 2007 the establishment burned down and it took eight years of missing her business until the owner, **Paula Dirks**, decided to rebuild and reopen. As of March 2015, Paula is at it again and still roasting her own coffees and serving up an all-American cuisine. She now has a full menu and a full-service bar. Menu items include a variety of healthy, sweet and savory options with desserts and pastries housemade by Paula herself; the banana bread is a must-try as it is baked fresh daily. The occasional lunch special of hand-dipped, housemade corn dogs sparked my interest in particular! Staple items include steaks and fresh seafood although options are plentiful. The bar offers a selection of fine wines, beer and award-winning cocktails.

Pendleton Round-Up

Office: 1114 SW Court Ave   541/276-2553
Stadium: 1205 SW Court Ave   pendletonroundup.com
Price varies by event

Let 'er Buck! That famous slogan and the saddle bronc rider astride a bucking bronc symbolize over 100 years of Pendleton's rodeo competition. This community comes alive the second full week each September for the Round-Up; schools close, businesses adjust hours, restaurants and saloons are packed and every possible lodging alternative is occupied to accommodate the thousands of competitors and spectators from around the country and world who descend upon Pendleton for an authentic taste of the Old West. Not only is lodging scarce (schoolyards serve as nearly endless camping and RV parking sites), but performances (especially Friday and Saturday afternoon) play to sell-out crowds; make arrangements well ahead of time. Afternoon rodeos allow time for evening performances of the Happy Canyon Indian Pageant and Wild West Show and for entertainment and frivolity along Main Street (blocked off to vehicular traffic). Don't miss the Friday morning Westward Ho! Parade, Cowboy Breakfasts in Stillman Park, working tipi village or a visit to the Let 'er Buck Room (you must see this) under the grandstands. The prestigious Round-Up Association has received accolades for achievements over the last century. The community is richer in many arenas for the dedication and good works of the rodeo's nearly 1,000 hardworking volunteers (Happy Canyon draws about 600 volunteers). This is one of my favorite annual events, best seen from a seat behind the bucking chutes.

Pendleton Underground Tours

37 SW Emigrant Ave
541/276-0730
Tours: Seasonal hours
pendletonundergroundtours.org
Reasonable

The influence of bootlegging, gambling, prostitution and Chinese inhabitants at the turn of the 19th century in Eastern Oregon is unknown to many. A walking tour through what was once the red light district entertains and informs tourists with character re-enactments and interesting tales of legal and illegal businesses and activities; one of the stops, Cozy Rooms, is a former brothel. Trained guides lead the curious (age six and over) along sidewalks, through tunnels and into historic buildings for a glimpse into a side of Pendleton not necessarily found in history books.

RIDING THE RAILS

Joseph Branch Railriders (541/910-0089, jbrailriders.com) offers a unique experience riding the rails on a bike-like contraption. Amazing views of the Wallowa Mountains and lush meadows, cottonwood and pine trees of the Wallowa Valley are seen from the vantage point of an unused rail line. The track from Joseph to Enterprise was once used to transport lumber, cattle and grain to the Grand Ronde Valley and beyond. The guided trip is 12 miles round trip; there is a 26-mile option for the more adventurous. Don't worry, a power assist is available as needed. Reservations encouraged.

Pendleton Woolen Mills

1307 SE Court Pl
Mon-Sat: 8-6; Sun: 9-5

541/276-6911
pendleton-usa.com

In retail, nothing says quality and craftsmanship like Pendleton, weaving world-class woolen fabrics for blankets and apparel under six generations of Bishop family leadership. The company's heritage in Eastern Oregon began in 1909. Indian trade blankets were the genesis and the tradition of vivid colors and intricate patterns continues today in the same mill opened by the Bishop brothers. Take a free informative tour (offered four times daily). The shop is stocked with selections of familiar designs as well as commemorative blankets and throws, apparel for the family, home decor and gifts.

There are currently seven production facilities and 75 retail stores for Pendleton goods.

Plateau Restaurant
46510 Wildhorse Blvd   541/966-1610
(See detailed listing with Wildhorse Resort & Casino)

Prodigal Son Brewery & Pub
230 SE Court Ave   541/276-6090
Lunch, Dinner: Tues-Sun   prodigalsonbrewery.com
Moderate

Good beer, good food and good vibes are the basic elements at Pendleton's first craft brewery smack dab in the middle of town. Ales, porters, stouts, hefs and seasonal brews are always on tap. Traditional pub fare, soups, salads and daily specials are made from scratch and the menu changes to incorporate seasonal regional ingredients. You'll want to save room for delicious whoopie pie or chocolate and hazelnut tart laced with whiskey for dessert. The family-friendly restaurant resides in a great old building with a children's room that features board games, a library and toys. The noise level certainly adds to the buzz!

Roosters
1515 Southgate   541/966-1100
Breakfast, Lunch, Dinner: Daily   roostersdining.com
Inexpensive

This house is something to crow about! Family-owned and -operated, the Code family runs this farm-themed restaurant where platters are meant for hearty breakfast (served until 3 p.m.) appetites. You'll find all the usual breakfast items, plus wonderful "corn field" French toast (egg-battered and rolled in cornflake crumbs, then grilled), that will surely fuel anyone for the better part of a day. Lunch and dinner offers comfort-food soups, salads, sandwiches, burgers, pastas, seafood and meats. Rooster noodle soup is made with fresh, hand-rolled noodles; they even roast the peppers and tomatoes used in their homemade salsa. With such high standards of quality, it's no wonder Roosters is so popular with locals and visitors alike.

GHOST TOWNS

The state of Oregon is covered with long-abandoned ghost towns that are now in the process of returning to nature. These abandoned communities are historic locations where fur traders and Oregon pioneers once traveled. If you are a historian or photographer, you'll want to visit at least one of these once-thriving mountain towns. Complete with sagging porches, rusty hinges, broken windows and caved-in roofs, these weathered ghost towns are scattered across Oregon's northeastern gold country. Oregon is reported to have more ghost towns (ghosttowns.com, ghosttownsinoregon.com) than any other state, including these:

Ashwood: 32 miles northeast of Madras; sheep and cattle country; named for its volcanic ash deposits

Auburn: ten miles southwest of Baker City and accessible by four-wheel drive road; 5,000 people once came here for gold; a marker and cemetery are all that remain

Bourne: seven miles north of Sumpter; mining ghost town with a few remaining buildings

Boyd: nine miles southeast of The Dalles; town established in gold rush days; a few abandoned homes, outbuildings and dilapidated wooden grain elevator remain

Canyon City: two miles south of John Day on highway 395; 10,000 some miners came to this major gold discovery site; presently 700 residents

Flora: north of Joseph and Enterprise on Highway 3; good photo ops

Granite: 15 miles northwest of Sumpter; once productive gold operations; mining camp of Greenhorn; about a dozen people still live here

Shaniko: most well-known ghost town in Oregon; eight miles north of Antelope on U.S. 97; town established for wool trade; recent population just under 40

Sumpter: gold rush town located in Baker County; some 200 people still live here; the Black Market building is a center for ghost town-loving tourists

Whitney: 14 miles southwest of Sumpter; old logging town on the railroad line; remaining buildings include a sawmill

Sundown Grill & Bar-B-Q

223 SE 4th St   541/276-8500
Lunch: Mon-Fri; Dinner: Mon-Sat; Brunch: Sun   Facebook
Moderate

In the historic Raley House, **Raphael Hoffman** has created fun and affordable dining. While you're perusing the menu, nibble on smoked chicken nachos or cowboy caviar, which is also a tasty accompaniment to steaks and seafood. Other choices include beef brisket, sausage and ribs from the smokehouse, entree salads and several burgers and dogs. For a unique Eastern Oregon taste experience, you may want to try the smoked rattlesnake and rabbit sausage dog!

Virgil's at Cimmiyotti's

137 S Main St   541/276-7711
Dinner: Tues-Sat   virgilsatcimmiyottis.com
Moderate and up

Jennifer Keeton pays tribute to her father in the restaurant's name, originally opened by Anne and Paul Cimmiyotti in 1959. Restorations included attention to the original red velvet wallpaper, black leather booths and crystal chandeliers. The original menu featured steak with a side of spaghetti and while that tradition continues, hand-cut Certified Angus ribeye steak is also a house favorite. Although beef takes center stage, seafood, chicken, vegetarian and Italian dishes round out the menu. Housemade chocolate toffee torte and lemon mousse are superb desserts; the bar stays open until midnight on weekends.

Wildhorse Resort & Casino

46510 Wildhorse Blvd   541/278-2274, 800/654-9453
Lodging: Inexpensive to expensive   wildhorseresort.com
Restaurant: Moderately expensive to expensive

Wildhorse Resort is a recognizable landmark as Eastern Oregon's tallest building. Rooms and suites in the ten-story hotel tower are comfortably furnished and attractively priced. Good restaurants, a nearby golf course, RV park, tipi village and various gaming opportunities make this a popular destination. **Plateau Restaurant** (541/966-1610) features farm-to-table dinners with local ingredients best exemplified in the Pendleton Whisky steak. Plateau is on the upper floor of the casino, where you'll not only enjoy one of the best Kobe beef burgers (white cheddar cheese, mushrooms, shallot ketchup, frizzled onions and hand-cut French fries) in the state, but also sweeping views of the Blue Mountains. Northwest wines, beers and special dining events are worth noting. A sports bar, 24-hour cafe and buffet satisfy casual diners. What else to do? Take in a current flick at the five-screen Cineplex, turn the kiddos loose in the children's entertainment center or head across the parking lot to **Tamástslikt Cultural Institute** (541/966-9748; tamastslikt.org) for 10,000 years of living history.

Working Girls Hotel
17 SW Emigrant Ave   541/276-0730
Inexpensive   pendletonundergroundtours.org

For a real Old West experience, stay in one of the hotel's four guest rooms or one suite operated by **Pendleton Underground Tours**. Through **Pam Severe**'s meticulous renovation 20 some years ago, the Victorian decor, hardwood floors, 18-foot ceilings and exposed brick walls remain. The circa-1890 hotel has 21st-century indulgences (like heat and air conditioning); baths are extra large. Open year round; no children or pets. In case you're wondering, yes, this was once one of Pendleton's 18 "boarding houses" (bordellos).

PRAIRIE CITY

Historic Hotel Prairie
112 Front St   541/820-4800
Inexpensive to moderate   hotelprairie.com

If you head cross-country on Oregon's designated Journey through Time Scenic Byway, Prairie City is a likely stop. Guests are welcomed into nine rooms, including one full suite with kitchen. Two rooms can create a suite effect; all rooms offer private baths. Built in 1910, the hotel has gone through several transformations, serving various business ventures from 1980 to 2005. In 2005 the current owners stepped in to create a cozy destination hotel and greeted their first guests three years later. Photos of local families, the area and bygone mining, ranching and logging line the walls. Since this is a popular route for bicyclists, the hotel offers secure bicycle storage, packed lunches and catered group meals. Garden seating and a beer and wine bar appeal to everyone.

Oxbow Restaurant & Saloon

128 W Front St   541/820-4544
Lunch, Dinner: Tues-Sun   prairiecityoregon.com
Moderate

Located in an old-west style building, **Carol and Phil Bopp** serve burgers, sandwiches, steaks, seafood and such for lunch and dinner. Do not miss the specialty of the house: Carol's homemade pies, made fresh daily and served with a scoop of hard ice cream. The original condition, antique bar (circa 1879) is quite a conversation piece where full-service drink options and a large selection of beers and microbrews are poured.

Riverside School House Bed & Breakfast

28076 N River Road   541/820-4731
Moderate   riversideschoolhouse.com

Original chalkboards with a personalized message greet guests as they enter this former one-room schoolhouse. The unusual resting place offers two suites with separate entrances and private baths; rooms are comfortable with classy furnishings. Innkeeper **Judy Jacobs** delivers the morning's bountiful gourmet breakfast at the appointed time with ample suggestions for a day full of local activities. Located on a working cattle ranch, visitors are treated to seasonal opportunities for great hiking, fishing, cycling, snowmobiling, cross-country skiing or horseback riding. Peaceful surrounds include the John Day River meandering through the property, abundant wildlife and vistas of the Strawberry Mountain Range.

RUFUS

Bob's Texas T-Bone

101 E 1st St
Breakfast, Lunch, Dinner: Daily
Moderate

541/739-2559
Facebook

The Baunach family has owned a familiar establishment in Rufus (midway between Portland and Pendleton with easy access off I-84) for more than 40 years; first as Frosty's, a local tavern. Long hours make Bob's a convenient dining stop for travelers and Gorge dwellers. Portions are generous, the salad bar items are fresh and the menu showcases hand-cut steaks, freshly-ground hamburger, family-recipe sausages, smoked chicken and ribs and seasonal Columbia River salmon. Weekend dinners feature prime rib. Daily lunch specials, homemade soups, hearty sandwiches and burgers give midday diners plenty to choose from including breakfast any time of the day.

SUMPTER

Sumpter Valley Railroad

211 Austin St
Weekends and major holidays
Prices vary

541/894-2268, 866/894-2268
sumptervalleyrailroad.org

With the march of progress, the narrow gauge Sumpter Valley Railroad that once helped haul ore, lumber, freight and passengers met its demise. Thankfully, a dedicated group of volunteers revived this great iron horse ensuring that the whistle of a steam train continues to echo through this scenic valley. Volunteers are still the mainstay of this organization. Since July 4, 1976, the railroad has provided nostalgic weekend and holiday excursions through the rugged countryside. The approximate five-mile route from McEwen to the town of Sumpter ends at a reproduction of the original passenger station; stations are located in McEwen and Sumpter. Along the way, restored historic equipment and artifacts from around the country are on display. A trip on the Sumpter Valley Railroad is a fun and affordable activity for the whole family.

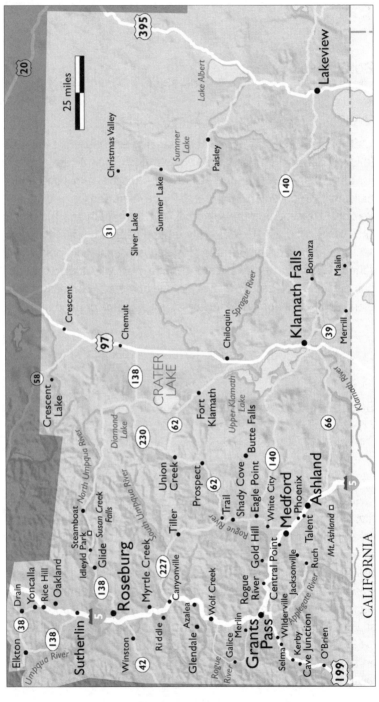

Southern Oregon

ASHLAND

A Midsummer's Dream Bed & Breakfast

496 Beach St
Moderate

541/552-0605, 877/376-8800
amidsummer.com

In a quiet neighborhood within walking distance to downtown, this classy 1901 Victorian is a fine special occasion getaway. You will be welcomed into your home away from home in a beautifully landscaped setting, with king-size beds and large private bathrooms. A spa tub and soft-as-silk robes, fireplace and wonderful linens add to the pampering. Relax in the common area, which includes a game room (and the only television on the property) with library, wet bar and tea service. **Lisa Beach** is the consummate host, offering gourmet breakfasts and anything else within her grasp.

Amuse

15 N 1st St   541/488-9000
Dinner: Seasonal   amuserestaurant.com
Moderately expensive

Chefs/owners **Jamie North** and **Erik Brown** have impressive culinary backgrounds, and it shows! North made original wedding cakes in Napa Valley and was a pastry cook at the legendary French Laundry restaurant; Brown also cooked at Napa Valley restaurants. The Northwest/French menu reflects their talents and utilizes fresh, seasonal ingredients. Green garlic soup or crispy veal sweetbreads with sunchokes, pistachio puree, black mushrooms and smoked bacon are representative of starters. Flavorful seafood, steaks and roasted game hens are paired with wonderful relishes, butters, fresh produce and palate-pleasing accompaniments. By all means, order the beignets with crème anglaise and heirloom berry jam if they are offered — exquisite! This intimate, elegant restaurant has great service and a delightful summer patio (perfect for pre-theater dining).

Ashland Creek Inn

70 Water St   541/482-3315
Moderate to expensive   ashlandcreekinn.com

This ten-suite boutique hotel is nestled into a private park-like setting; stunning blue shutters and awnings embellish the façade. Each suite is luxuriously decorated to commemorate an international area (Edinburgh, Marrakech, Normandy, Canton, Taos, Devon, Caribe, Matsu, Siena, Copenhagen) visited by owner **Graham Sheldon**. Beautiful, über-comfortable rooms have a private entrance, balcony overlooking gurgling Ashland Creek and kitchen or kitchenette. Antiques, original artwork and jetted tubs vary among the units. Relax on the inn's deck and terraced gardens for breakfast or an afternoon glass of wine. Breakfast is a multi-course gourmet production and is served in the elegant dining room or alfresco. The location is handy to downtown shops, restaurants, nightlife and theaters.

Ashland Springs Hotel

212 E Main St

541/488-1700, 888/795-4545

Lodging: Moderate

ashlandspringshotel.com

Restaurant: Moderate

Listed on the National Register of Historic Places, this hotel exudes charm and elegance. Built as Lithia Hotel in 1925 and later named the Mark Antony, it was restored to grandeur in 2000 by owners **Becky and Doug Neuman**. One look at the illuminated marquee and curved windows from the bygone era, and guests know that great care was given to the renovation. Guests are beckoned to a palm-filled conservatory and English garden featuring a wrought-iron gazebo and old-fashioned rosebushes. All 70 eclectically furnished and tastefully appointed guest rooms offer comfort and charm not found in modern hotels. Free parking and continental breakfast are included in the rates. For breakfast, lunch or dinner, on-site **Larks Home Kitchen Cuisine** (541/488-5558, larksrestaurant.com) serves farm-to-table gourmet comfort food made from scratch with local organic components, housemade charcuterie and artisan cheeses. The chef is a master at showcasing Oregon wines and splendid local, seasonal ingredients. Dishes such as homemade meatloaf, hearty soups and fresh Pacific Northwest seafood are popular; the pastry chef's creations are divine! Nature-inspired **Waterstone Spa** (541/488-0325, waterstonespa.com) is also part of this downtown resort and offers a full-service rejuvenating and beautifying menu. A variety of thoughtfully developed packages may include tickets to the Varsity Movie Theatre, the Oregon Shakespeare Festival, Oregon Chocolate Festival or wine tasting at local wineries.

Beasy's on the Creek

51 Water St

541/488-5009

Dinner: Tues-Sat

beasysonthecreek.com

Moderate

No matter the season, Beasy's capitalizes on its picturesque setting. Big windows and a big red fireplace frame the outdoor deck, creek and trees which provide welcome shade to outside diners. This dinner house features steaks, seafood, chicken and several pasta entrees, all with Texas-Mediterranean influences. Several dishes can be spiced up Inca Inca style with the addition of a sauce made with fresh jalapenos, garlic and lime juice. Entrees include a choice of salad or housemade gumbo; add salmon, prawns, crab or chicken to a salad to make it a meal.

Callahan's Mountain Lodge
7100 Old Hwy 99 S   541/482-1299, 800/286-0507
Lodging: Moderate to expensive   callahanslodge.com
Restaurant: Moderate

Established in 1947, Callahan's is a full-service restaurant and lodge that has become a Southern Oregon landmark. The picturesque setting is tucked into a wooded canyon ten minutes south of Ashland, just below Mt. Ashland Ski Resort and the Pacific Crest Trail. Nineteen guest rooms are furnished with corner jetted tubs, wood-burning fireplaces and terraces with rockers to while away the afternoon. Lodge amenities include a wine and gift shop, game room, horseshoe pit, rock waterfall features and unscheduled sideshows starring native wildlife. The lodge restaurant is a destination for breakfast, lunch and dinner. Start the day with basic to fancy egg dishes served with fruit and lodge-made pastries; or opt for crepes and pancakes. House-cut fries go well with lunch wraps and sandwiches. "Western mountain lodge" dinner entrees are sourced from pastures, freshwater and saltwater and are served with a signature hazelnut pear vinaigrette house salad and artisan bread. For a different dessert, try the baked banana split. Callahan's is open 365 days a year with nightly live music at dinner. This beautiful location is a favorite of brides and grooms and ideal for gatherings for up to 150 guests.

Country Willows Bed & Breakfast Inn
1313 Clay St   541/488-1590, 800/945-5697
Moderate   countrywillowsinn.com

This charmer has all the atmosphere of bygone days, but with comfortable, modern facilities. The original farmhouse was built more than a century ago and is now in its third decade as a B&B. Features include two-course gourmet breakfasts, top-grade bed linens and magnificent views. Mt. Ashland skiing, hiking and biking trails, theaters and wineries are close at hand. Four guest rooms are in the main house; four comfortable suites and a standard room with private porch are located in the renovated barn behind the house. A separate cottage has queen and twin beds, wet bar and private patio. Bicycles, a heated outdoor swimming pool and croquet and lawn bocce equipment are accessible in warm weather. Comfy seating is spread throughout the property, by the willow tree, in the den or sunroom and on the porch; enjoy a cookie and cup of tea — on the house, of course.

Cowslip's Belle B&B and Boutique Vacation Rentals

159 N Main St   541/488-2901, 800/888-6819
B&B: June-mid-Sept; Vacation Rentals: Year round   cowslip.com
B&B: Moderate to expensive; Vacation Rentals: Inexpensive to moderate

Lush gardens surround Cowslip's Belle B&B and Boutique Vacation Rentals making for a beautiful, aromatic and relaxing stay just a few blocks off Ashland's beaten path. Fragrant flowers, gurgling waterfalls, patios and foot bridges, a koi pond and seasonal flowering trees and plants provide a delightful background to the property; most rooms overlook the manicured gardens. The private Rosebud Suite is situated at the rear of the main house; the carriage house is comprised of four rooms and suites, each with a private outside entrance. All tastefully appointed accommodations sleep one to three guests and include en suite bathrooms and outdoor seating areas; varying amenities include full kitchens or kitchenettes, gas fireplaces, spa tubs and laundry facilities. B&B guests are welcomed with a tray of sherry and biscotti upon arrival and guests have the option of taking full breakfast in the dining room with fellow travelers or fending for themselves elsewhere.

Green Springs Inn & Cabins

11470 Hwy 66   541/890-6435
Moderate   greenspringsinn.com

A relaxed atmosphere awaits at this retreat about 25 minutes east of Ashland. Amenities in the eight lodge rooms may include

Jacuzzi tubs, private decks and a fireplace. You can also choose from nine cabins, mainly powered by solar energy, that sleep up to six. Each is furnished with a Jacuzzi tub, fully-equipped kitchen, wood-burning stove, gas grill and large deck. The inn serves three square meals a day from a menu of great selections. For Tesla, Volt and other electric car travelers, Green Springs Inn offers a free Level II charging station.

Larks Home Kitchen Cuisine
212 E Main St   541/488-5558
(See detailed listing with Ashland Springs Hotel)

Lithia Springs Resort
2165 W Jackson Road   541/482-7128, 800/482-7128
Moderate and up   lithiaspringsresort.com

This property is home to a serene, spa-like resort with a beautiful outdoor pool and fitness room. Nearly 40 bungalows, studios and suites with contemporary furnishings in soothing tones are situated around a courtyard on four acres of gardens and mineral springs; for privacy, request the water tower suite overlooking the resort. The springs, once considered holy water by the Native Americans, are purported to restore and heal the body; in-room soaking tubs provide tranquil environs to enjoy those properties. The charming bungalows sleep up to four guests and are furnished with a small kitchenette. An overnight stay includes a complimentary hot breakfast in the breakfast room and afternoon tea and cookies. On-site spa services are provided a la carte or combined with lodging for romantic and relaxing packages. The gardens are spectacular in spring and summer; pergolas, bridges, paths and lush lawns are inviting.

Loft Brasserie & Bar
18 Calle Guanajuato   541/482-1116
Dinner: Daily; Brunch: Sat, Sun   loftbrasserie.com
Moderate

Jacqueline and Jeremy Vidalo present an inspiring space offering contemporary American-French fare in their brasserie/bar. As much as possible, the food is organic, all-natural and sourced locally; made from scratch is the rule, not the exception. The full bar has a fun specialty cocktail list and features local and European wines (from the Rogue to the Rhine). Chef Jeremy heads up the kitchen while Jacqueline runs the front of the house. Starters might include steamed Penn Cove black mussels, chicken liver mousse or roasted beet salad; caramelized French onion soup is a must. Entrees include chicken, scallops, duck breast, lamb, steak frites and more. Enjoy enchanting alfresco dining overlooking Ashland Creek or at the fire pit lounge in the expanded bar.

Macaroni's Ristorante and Martino's Restaurant and Lounge

58 E Main St   541/488-3359
Lunch: Seasonal; Dinner: Daily   martinosashland.com
Moderate

If you choose outdoor seating at Martino's, you'll be as close as you can get to the Angus Bowmer Theatre without a ticket! Martino's is upstairs and Macaroni's is downstairs; owner **Marty Morlan** offers the same menu throughout the neo-classic house. You won't be disappointed with the Oregon smoked salmon ravioli served in a mushroom, basil and tomato cream sauce or the rigatoni carbonara made with applewood-smoked bacon. Pizza, Caesar salad and other pasta dishes are also on the menu. This location is handy for after-theater bistro fare, drinks and dessert; try Marty's famous lemon ricotta cheesecake.

Morning Glory

1149 Siskiyou Blvd   541/488-8636
Breakfast, Lunch: Daily   morninggloryrestaurant.com
Moderate

Owner **Patricia Groth** presides over her breakfast and lunch establishment, a favorite of local families and visitors. Inside the 1926 Craftsman bungalow, you'll find some of the most unusual day starters imaginable. Think shrimp cakes with poached eggs and smoked tomato chutney or a steak omelet with mushrooms, red onions and spinach. Also expect whole grain pecan waffles, oatmeal pancakes and other such fare. Lunch service begins at 11 a.m. with interesting sandwiches and homemade soups and salads made with organic mixed greens. A chipotle-flavored Bloody Mary or other libation from the full-service bar is sure to make you bright-eyed and bushy-tailed as you start your vacation or weekend day.

Music Coop
268 E Main St   541/482-3115
Mon-Sat: 10-6 (Fri till 8); Sun: 11-6   musiccooponline.com

In the business since 1975, **Trina and John Brenes** moved lock, stock and record to Ashland in 2001. Their store is one of the largest record outlets between Sacramento and Portland. There are over

GOLD STANDARD BURGERS

How loyal are you to your favorite fast food restaurant? Would you drive hours just to get your favorite meal? You may be one of many willing to make the drive to Medford to indulge at Oregon's first ever **In-N-Out Burger** (1970 Crater Lake Hwy, Medford; 800/786-1000; in-n-out.com). Known for its "gold standard" fast-food burgers, they don't cut corners. In fact, none of their food is frozen or pre-packaged; all patties are 100% pure beef and made in their own facilities, using only the freshest ingredients. You may choose to keep it simple with a classic hamburger, or try one of their secret menu items such as the animal style; a burger with your choice of lettuce, tomato, mustard-cooked beef patty and extra spread. How about a grilled cheese with melted American cheese, lettuce, tomato, spread with or without onions on a freshly-baked bun? Maybe you are thinking about the scrumptious Flying Dutchman with two slices of cheese inside two beef patties, cheese, lettuce, tomato, spread and onions. For those who prefer it gluten free, try the protein style with a beef patty wrapped in lettuce. Even their shakes are memorable. In-N-Out has it all, and the best part is they bring it to you at a reasonable price; now all we need are more locations in Oregon!

20,000 CD titles, hundreds of box-set CDs and the largest selection of vinyl LPs in Southern Oregon. The selection includes everything from rock, hip-hop, jazz, blues and folk to bluegrass and country music.

Northwest Nature Shop

154 Oak St · 541/482-3241
Mon-Sat: 10-6; Sun: 11-5 · northwestnatureshop.com

Northwest Nature Shop stocks a variety of educational books, hiking guides, science toys, bird amenities, cards and gifts, toys and information about the forests and waterways of our state. Treat the birds and wildlife in your yard to a new bird bath, fountain or feeder and accent your home with clocks and decorative pieces.

Oregon Cabaret Theatre

1 Hargadine St · 541/488-2902
Prices vary · oregoncabaret.com

Forget Shakespeare for a bit and book an amusing evening for your party at the Oregon Cabaret Theatre. Five shows (over 270 performances) change throughout the year, but the intimate venue stays the same. You can opt for gourmet dinner or brunch (reservations necessary) before the curtain goes up; choose from a variety of appetizers, soups, salads and desserts or go for the entertainment only. Menus are prepared by the resident chef and change with each show. The 140-seat theater calls the former First Baptist Church home, magnificently renovated in the 1980s.

Oregon Shakespeare Festival

15 S Pioneer St · 800/219-8161
Seasonal · osfashland.org

One of the world's finest venues to celebrate William Shakespeare (along with other performing arts) is in the charming town of Ashland. Established in 1935, the festival boasts the oldest existing full-scale Elizabethan stage in the Western Hemisphere. Throughout the eight-month season, 11 plays by Shakespeare and classic and contemporary playwrights are presented in three venues with varying seating capacities (270-1,190). People come from all around the globe, often an annual outing, to Ashland to experience Shakespeare and Southern Oregon. During busy summer months, lodging and restaurants also play to a full house.

Paddington Station
125 E Main St   541/482-1343
Sun, Mon: 10-5:30; Tues-Sat: 9:30-8   paddingtonstationashland.com

Paddington has been a Main Street fixture for nearly 40 years; a fun spot any time of the year. You'll find three floors of eclectic merchandise — gadgets and goodies, toys, clothing, books, kitchen needs, women's fashions, toiletries, stationery, souvenirs and more. Check out equally interesting sister shops, **Inspired by Oregon** (541/482-1343) and **Paddington Jewel Box** (541/488-1715), also on Main Street.

The Peerless Hotel
243 4th St   541/488-1082, 800/460-8758
Lodging: Moderate   peerlesshotel.com
Restaurant: Moderately expensive to expensive

Historic accommodations are part of Ashland's claim to fame. The Peerless, built in 1900, is charmingly restored and located close to the town's central shopping and gallery core. Most rooms have tromp l'oeil painted ceilings or walls. Amenities include classy Italian linens and access to the Ashland Racquet Club offering full workout facilities. By the way, if you like large bathrooms, ask for the room with two claw-foot tubs. Relax in gorgeous guest rooms decorated with antiques or outside in the private gardens. Breakfast and complimentary evening sherry are provided between mid-February and November. Room service is available from the property's excellent next-door **Peerless Restaurant & Bar** (541/488-6067). Delicious, made-from-scratch full dinners, tapas and nightly sampler plates are served in the dining room, bar and enchanting garden.

Plaza Inn & Suites

98 Central Ave   541/488-8900, 888/488-0358
Moderate   plazainnashland.com

This Shakespearean-theme boutique hotel offers 92 spacious rooms with various options and concierge service. A hot tub and 24-hour fitness center are available, and rooms in the Cascade building are designated for guests with pets. Mornings begin with a continental breakfast and a snack welcomes guests home each early evening. Later (10 p.m. to midnight), a nightcap of freshly-baked cookies, milk and PB&J sandwiches are provided. Many of Ashland's attractions are within easy walking distance.

ScienceWorks Hands-On Museum

1500 E Main St   541/482-6767
Summer: Daily; Sept-May: Wed-Sun   scienceworksmuseum.org
Nominal

Travelers of all ages can stay curious at this museum with fun, hands-on exhibits and activities that explore energy, anatomy, chemistry and more. Stand inside a bubble in the Bubble Room, create pedal energy to push an electric train around its track, encounter optical illusions and think with your hands in Da Vinci's Garage tinkering room. This museum is home to more than 100 exhibits and hosts themed weekends and ongoing educational science programs for all ages.

Standing Stone Brewing Co.

101 Oak St   541/482-2448
Lunch, Dinner: Daily   standingstonebrewing.com
Moderate

Residing in the former Whittle Garage Building, this classy pub serves up microbrews, signature pizzas baked in a wood-fired oven and great food until midnight. The restaurant's display kitchen turns out an extensive menu with usual pub grub; burgers are made with beef raised on their **One Mile Farm** just down the road from the brew pub. The menu includes flavorful ribs, steaks, fish, chicken and pasta dishes, Szechwan green beans, kimchi pork burgers and fresh-cut garlic fries. There is plenty of seating, a back deck with mountain views and regularly-scheduled live music; kids are welcome.

Weisinger Family Winery

3150 Siskiyou Blvd
Tasting room: Summer: Daily; Winter: Wed-Sun

541/488-5989
weisingers.com

Established in 1988 by **John Weisinge**r, Weisinger Family Winery produces limited production craft wines created exclusively from local vineyards. Sourcing only from vineyards within five miles of the winery property, they support local growers and the local economy. The winery specializes in Gewürztraminer, tempranillo, pinot noir, Rhone and Bordeaux varietals, as well as proprietary blends. A one-bedroom Craftsman-style bungalow is adjacent to the vineyard and is equipped with a kitchen and private deck with hot tub and gas grill. Guests receive a welcoming cheese and wine basket and discounts in the tasting room.

Winchester Inn

35 S 2nd St
Lodging: Inexpensive to expensive
Restaurant: Expensive

541/488-1113, 800/972-4991
winchesterinn.com
541/488-1115

Owners **Laurie, Michael and Drew Gibbs** have magnificently transformed five buildings and a hilly lot into one of Ashland's finest inns with gorgeous tiered gardens. Drew is the inn's second-generation owner and certified sommelier. Top-drawer amenities in the house and cottages' 11 rooms and nine suites include down feather beds, pillows and comforters; luxury bed linens and Egyptian cotton towels; imported toiletries; guest phones with data ports and voicemail and complimentary Wi-Fi. Afternoon pastries are delivered to guest rooms, followed later in the evening with turndown service. A sumptuous two-course gourmet breakfast is included with an overnight stay. The nationally-recognized **Alchemy Restaurant and Bar** is excellent! Chef **William Buscher** has assembled a fine dinner selection of small plates, soups, salads and entrees utilizing local and organic products; daily menus change according to the season.

KIDS' ACTIVITIES: SOUTHERN OREGON

ASHLAND

Emigrant Lake and Water Slides (541/774-8183, emigrantlake.org)

Lithia Park and Playground (541/488-5340, lithiaparkplayground. com, lithiaparktrailguide.com)

ScienceWorks Hands-On Museum (541/482-6767, scienceworks museum.org)

CAVE JUNCTION

Great Cats World Park (541/592-2957, greatcatsworldpark.com)

Oregon Caves National Monument (541/592-2100, nps.gov/orca)

Out 'n' About Treehouse Treesort (541/592-2208, treehouses.com)

CRATER LAKE

Crater Lake National Park (541/594-3000, nps.gov/crla)

GOLD HILL

House of Mystery at Oregon Vortex (541/855-1543, oregonvortex.com)

GRANTS PASS

Wildlife Images Rehabilitation Center (541/476-0222, wildlife images.org)

KLAMATH FALLS

Favell Museum of Western Art and Indian Artifacts (541/882-9996, favellmuseum.org)

LAKEVIEW

Warner Canyon Ski Area (541/947-5001, warnercanyon.org)

MEDFORD

Kid Time! Discovery Experience (541/772-9922, kidtime.org)

Rogue Valley Family Fun Center (541/664-4263, rvfamilyfuncenter.com)

WINSTON

Wildlife Safari (541/679-6761, wildlifesafari.net)

Venison may be accompanied by fennel and foie gras jam; pork may be complemented by French triple cream brie macaroni and cheese; fish will be prepared to capture the utmost flavor and homemade pasta choices may showcase creamy sauces and fine cheeses. Fresh scones accompany assorted classic and new brunch dishes. Reservations recommended.

AZALEA

Heaven on Earth Restaurant & Bakery

703 Quines Creek Road 541/837-3700
Breakfast, Lunch, Dinner: Daily heavenonearthrestaurant.com
Moderate

A slice of paradise is 30 minutes north of Grants Pass at exit 86 where **Christine Jackson** makes her restaurant and bakery a requisite visit for folks in Southern Oregon. The rustic eatery is noted for its home-style cooking and use of locally made products. Stop to enjoy or take home some of the tastiest baked goods and gigantic, melt-in-your-mouth cinnnamon rolls (including a humungous family-size version) — a little piece of heaven!

BLY

Aspen Ridge Resort

Fishhole Creek Road 18 541/884-8685, 800/393-3323
Seasonal aspenrr.com
Inexpensive to moderate

This century-old, 14,000-acre working cattle ranch is about 70 miles east of Klamath Falls and 18 miles southeast of Bly. Log cabins, suites and lodge rooms are rustically elegant; the large cabins (sleeps six) feature wood-burning stoves, four-poster beds, lofts and full kitchens. You can fill the long days with hiking, fishing, horseback riding, biking, swimming and tennis. The resort offers guided horseback rides, during which guests take part in the daily ranch work, whether that be keeping tabs on newborn calves, moving cattle or just checking the herd. Generously portioned country breakfasts and dinners are served in the lodge restaurant, and the on-premises Buffalo Saloon is a favorite after-dinner stop for beer, wine and cocktails. Steaks, chicken and baby back ribs are grilled over mesquite on the back deck and served with great-tasting sides; beef tri-tip is the specialty of the house (reservations are a must for guests and drive-up customers). Wi-Fi is available in the lodge; no cell phone service and no pets.

CAVE JUNCTION

The Chateau at Oregon Caves

20000 Caves Hwy   541/592-3400
Seasonal: May-Oct   oregoncaveschateau.com
Moderate

Built in 1934 by businessmen from Grants Pass, this historic lodge features 23 unique rooms. Standard and deluxe rooms are accented with Monterey-style furniture and contain either two double beds or one queen bed; family suites have two rooms and one bath. A focal point is a stream channeled from the Oregon Caves that runs through the dining room. Dinners include fish, beef, bison, pastas and other Northwest-influenced selections. The vintage coffee shop (where you can take a stool at the counter, order a malt and enjoy the nostalgic 1930s soda fountain) is open for breakfast, lunch and dessert. Oregon Caves memorabilia, snacks and gifts are sold in the Gift Gallery.

Great Cats World Park

27919 Redwood Hwy   541/592-2957
Seasonal: Feb-Nov   greatcatsworldpark.com
Reasonable

Great Cats World Park offers animal demonstrations and educational guided tours where cats exhibit natural behaviors. You can get up close and personal with a variety of large and small cats on this ten-acre park. Resident felines include lions, tigers, leopards, serval, ocelots, lynx and more. Snacks are available at the gift shop.

Oregon Caves National Monument

19000 Caves Hwy   541/592-2100
Seasonal: Spring-fall   nps.gov/orca
Nominal

Another of our state's treasures can be found tucked into the Siskiyou Mountains about 20 miles southeast of Cave Junction. Be forewarned that the last ten miles are narrow, steep and winding (travel trailers and large RVs are not recommended beyond milepost

12). Expect snowfall late fall through spring. That being said, the incentives are magnificent marble caves of re-crystalized limestone, hiking, wildlife and nearby camping. Tours of the caves (fee applies) are mid-spring through mid-fall and weather dependent; there is no fee to visit the surface trails and monument facilities. There are two visitor centers; one at the monument and one in Cave Junction.

Out 'n' About Treehouse Treesort

300 Page Creek Road	541/592-2208
Year round	treehouses.com
Moderate	

Kids of all ages have the time of their lives at this unique treesort. This bed and breakfast in the trees has 13 treehouses and three non-treehouses complete with lavatories in the trees and on the ground. Each space has a specific theme and accommodates two, four or more people on one level or two. Furnishings vary and may include queen or twin beds and bunks, kitchenettes and tables and chairs. The loftiest unit is over 40 feet up a tree and accessed by swinging bridges and platforms. Throughout the 36 private acres are child-size forts, seven swinging bridges, six swings, 20 flights of stairs and four ladders; over a mile of zip lines; a swimming pool plus horses. You will not be bored when you go out on a limb for this adventure! Breakfast is included in the stay and is served in the main lodge. A full breakfast with multiple choices is served mid-March through October; continental breakfast is offered the remainder of the year. Reservations are necessary to play out your Tarzan and Jane vacation; no TVs or landline phones.

CENTRAL POINT

Rogue Creamery

311 N Front St	541/665-1155, 866/396-4704
Daily	roguecreamery.com

This creamery's origin dates back to 1933. In the 1940s, the Vella family supplied cheddar cheese to the war effort and was the first major supplier of cottage cheese in Oregon. Today under the leadership of **Cary Bryant** and **David Gremmel**s, Rogue Creamery continues the tradition of award-winning blue and cheddar cheese made locally in Central Point. Rogue Creamery's classic Oregon Blue Vein Cheese was created in 1954 and was the first blue cheese made in caves on the West Coast. In 2002, Bryant and Gremmels created Rogue River Blue followed by the world's first smoked blue cheese, Smokey Blue. You'll find artisan cheeses, specialty foods, local wines and craft beers in the cheese shop as well as grilled cheese sandwiches to enjoy while watching the cheese makers or chilling on the patio. Each March, the annual Oregon Cheese Festival showcases products from Rogue Creamery and other Oregon cheese producers, plus beer, wine, baked goods and chocolates.

CHILOQUIN

Lonesome Duck Ranch & Resort

32955 Hwy 97 N   541/783-2783, 800/367-2540
Moderately expensive   lonesomeduck.com

Debbie and Steve Hilbert preside over a scenic and fun retreat, combining many things for different family members to enjoy (kids love walking the llamas). In a 200-acre setting on two miles of Williamson River frontage, the possibilities are especially attractive for those who relish the outdoor life. Rivers Edge, a full-size log home with two bedrooms, two full baths and a loft area with twin beds is also available. Arrowhead cottage, one of the original ranch houses, features a great stone fireplace, two small bedrooms, kitchen, living and dining rooms. There's a two-night minimum and off-season (November to mid-May) rates are reduced. Each cabin offers superb views. Fly-fishing is first-class, with guides available for half or full days. The Wood River, Klamath Lake, Agency Lake and the Sprague River are nearby; what a thrill to land a trophy rainbow trout! The ranch is near five Klamath Basin refuges, home to more than 430 wildlife species and some 250 bird varieties. Take a tour with ranch manager **Marshal Moser**, a wildlife biologist and naturalist. You can't help but enjoy the flora and fauna, enhanced by Marshal's expert knowledge. With easy access to Crater Lake, horse facilities, barbecues and kitchens in each unit, what more could you ask for? Photographers: this place is for you!

CRATER LAKE

Crater Lake National Park

541/594-3000
nps.gov/crla

Seasonal: 10-4
Lodging: Moderate to expensive
Restaurant: Breakfast, Lunch, Dinner: Daily
Expensive

WINE TOURS

The Rogue Valley is a rich agricultural area known for pear orchards and more than 127 wineries. Choosing which winery to visit can be mind-boggling, and **Wine Hopper Tours** (541/476-9463, winehoppertours.com) aims to simplify the decision. Round trip tours depart daily from Ashland and Medford in a 13-passenger tour van and include an interesting history of this wine region, tastings at featured wineries and a vineyard picnic. Or opt for a relaxing, twilight wine float on the Rogue River. For the more adventurous, book a rafting wine excursion on the Rogue River or a hiking wine trip on the Rogue River Trail. Prices start at $79 per person; reservations required. Custom group trips are also available.

Oregon's only national park brings visitors from around the world to take in the brilliant blue beauty from the caldera rim. The rim road is open until the snow flies, usually open in its entirety from July through October. The scenery is breathtaking as you wind your way around our nation's deepest lake (1,943 feet) encompassing views of two islands (Wizard and Phantom Ship), breathtaking scenery and wildlife. Visitor centers are located at the rim (typically open June to September) and year round at park headquarters. A concessionaire operates seasonal ranger-narrated boat tours around the lake and to Wizard Island. Built in 1915 and beautifully renovated in 1995, the 71-room **Crater Lake Lodge** (888/774-2728, craterlakelodges.com) and restaurant are open mid-May through mid-October. The restaurant features Northwest breakfast, lunch and dinner cuisine. Southwest of the lake, **Mazama Village** (541/594-2255) has a campground, cabins, camper store, fuel, restaurant and gift shop. Various fees apply for vehicles, bicycles and pedestrians entering the park. Allow plenty of time to experience this national treasure and enjoy the pristine surroundings.

EAGLE POINT

Butte Creek Mill

402 N Royal Ave   541/826-3531
Daily   buttecreekmill.com

Debbie and Bob Russell are making their living and keeping history alive as operators of the last commercial water-powered flour mill west of the Mississippi. The mill has functioned since 1872 and is on the National Register of Historic Places. Today you can buy (on-site or online) flours, cereals, stone-ground mixes, grains and other products, organically and otherwise produced, and all of the highest quality. The mill's educational center (call ahead to see when they are milling) offers information on American history, science and technology, ecology and more. The mill is great for family picnics, business retreats, concerts and parties. The adjacent antique store, formerly a cheese factory, is full of toys, advertising signs, country store items and unusual fixtures from an old-time soda fountain, saloon and barber shop.

Oregon Bee Store

14356 Hwy 26   541/826-7621
Seasonal: Mar-Dec   oregonbeestore.com

For a sweet stop in Southern Oregon, visit second generation Wild Bee Honey Farm for honey and honey products. They also sell gourmet honey from around the world and beautiful 100% beeswax candles in a variety of shapes and sizes. Beekeeping supplies, equipment and instruction are available at the store and online.

ELKTON

The Big K Guest Ranch and Outfitters
20029 Hwy 138W   541/584-2295
Year round   big-k.com
Moderate

The Big K Guest Ranch offers great hospitality and service at a beautifully constructed rustic lodge. This classic log structure is elegant with amazing views from huge windows and French doors. The property was established over 100 years ago by Charles Kesterson, and the Kesterson family still proudly runs the ranch. Twenty comfortable cabins house up to four or five people per unit. Packages include lodging only, meals and lodging or custom hunting and fishing outings. Breakfast, lunch and dinner are served in the main dining room. The guest ranch is actually a 2,500-acre working ranch with ten miles of Umpqua River frontage. It is an ideal place for individuals, families or groups. Custom guided fishing trips, scenic jet boat rides, rafting trips and skeet shooting are also available or bring your own horse to explore the outdoors.

Tomaselli's Pastry Mill & Cafe
14836 Umpqua Hwy   541/584-2855
Breakfast, Lunch, Dinner: Wed-Sun   tomasellispastrymill.com
Inexpensive to moderately expensive

Tomaselli's Pastry Mill & Cafe is a convenient destination for refilling coffee mugs and reenergizing with espresso and homemade bakery goodies on Highway 38 between Drain and Reedsport. You can't go wrong with pastries and breads, but don't overlook Tomaselli's for Friday night dinner. The gourmet meals may include sautéed duck breast with cherry sauce, praline-glazed chinook salmon, polenta with beef and Italian sausage, stew or lamb, pork and steak dishes, delicious with wines from local vineyards. There are plenty of great breakfast favorites and combos which are served until noon. Lunch service starts at 11 a.m. with comfort foods, soups, salads, sandwiches and burgers. Pizzas are available starting at noon; opt for one of the house specialties or pick your own combination.

GOLD HILL

Rogue Valley Zipline Adventure
Shuttle location: I-5 exit 40
9450 Old Stage Road, Central Point   541/821-9476
Expensive   rvzipline.com

Where to find a challenging family adventure with the best views in Southern Oregon, led by entertaining guides? Answer: In Gold Hill for an exhilarating off-the-ground excursion on an amazing zip line. Actually, the 2,700-foot course consists of five zip lines; the longest is over 1,300 feet. A van picks up parties at a shuttle stop where they are transported to zip headquarters on private property in gold mining country. From there, participants are outfitted with safety equipment and given important guidelines before hiking to the first platform. Along the way, certified guides impart local history and interesting tidbits about the flora, fauna and landmarks. Allow three to three-and-a-half hours to complete the course. Tours operate all year; sun, rain or snow (although dangerous inclement weather will halt the activities). Post-zipping, visit the general store for snacks and such and catch a ride back to the shuttle stop. What's more fun than a summer afternoon in the trees? A full day (June-Aug) zipping, dipping and sipping. The Zip, Dip & Sip Tour starts on the zip line course followed by a professionally guided seven-mile whitewater rafting trip and lunch at Laurel Hill Golf Course. The last leg is wine tasting at an estate winery. Reservations required for all trips; group discounts available.

GRANTS PASS

Cary's of Oregon
413 Union Ave   888/822-9300
Mon-Fri: 9-5; Sat: 10-2   carysoforegon.com

When you're in Southern Oregon and mention the words "English toffee," the immediate response is Cary's of Oregon. From a long-standing family recipe, **Cary Cound** and his crew make some of the best toffee around — known for its light, crisp texture and a variety of mouthwatering flavors. A factory store carries all sorts of hard-to-resist toffee treats and samples to tempt. The products are all natural and gluten-free. Not going that way? They ship toffee and gift packs nationwide.

Flery Manor Bed & Breakfast

2000 Jumpoff Joe Creek Road   541/476-3591
Moderate   flerymanor.com

A bed and breakfast combined with an art studio is the Flery's unusual hosting formula. This attractive mountainside destination is near the Rogue River and has three suites and two additional nicely decorated rooms; some feature a fireplace and Jacuzzi. Guests enjoy a well-stocked library, and a piano is available for those with a musical flair. Original recipe, three-course organic breakfasts (many times with ingredients fresh from the home garden) feature innovative egg dishes. Guests are invited to experience the art studio where they may dabble in clay, paint, music, photography, writing or other creative art forms. Enjoy a walk or hike around the property to view the ponds, waterfalls and streams and perhaps catch a glimpse of the two resident black swans; more exhilarating hiking trails are on adjacent private property. Less strenuous time may be spent in the hammock or the gazebo enjoying the sights and sounds of nature.

The Haul

121 SW H St   541/474-4991
Lunch, Dinner: Wed-Mon   thehaulgp.com
Inexpensive to moderate

A great place to get a burger is The Haul, serving gourmet pizzas, burgers, sandwiches, soups, salads and entrees like smoked pork chops and chicken picatta. The Bi-Animal burger is a must-try, made with Salant Family Ranch beef, minced house-cured bacon and finished with fresh lettuce, onion and tomato. Food is fresh and locally sourced with numerous vegetarian options. The drink menu is extensive with a long list of non-alcoholic beverages, cocktails, hard cider, wine, bottled beer and draft beer (exclusively serving Conner

Fields Brewing). Oftentimes, they have live music events which are listed on their website. The Haul is a more recent addition to Grants Pass; the warehouse-like setting resembles something you would find in Portland and welcomes customers with its casual, yet intimate, atmosphere. Small tables and picnic benches fill the restaurant, order service is available at the counter with a bar downstairs and a full bar upstairs available for special events and private parties.

Taprock Northwest Grill

971 SE 6th St   541/955-5998
Breakfast, Lunch, Dinner: Daily; Brunch: Sun   taprock.com
Moderate

This beautiful lodge-inspired restaurant sits at the edge of the Rogue River along Highway 99. A man-made waterfall, wildlife sculptures and ample outdoor lighting are welcoming touches. The restaurant has seating for 300 inside, plus more on the wraparound deck and at the hand-hewn bar. The menu reflects its Northwest theme with farm-fresh egg dishes, salmon, Dungeness crab and other seafood, sandwiches, burgers, steaks and pastas. Salads are farm-to-table fresh and offered in two sizes. Start your morning with breakfast favorites of Dungeness crab cake Benedicts, berry French toast and flat iron steak and eggs.

Weasku Inn

5560 Rogue River Hwy   541/471-8000, 800/493-2758
Moderately expensive   weasku.com

Even the pronunciation of this inn's name is welcoming: We-Ask-U Inn. This historic lodge has been home away from home for guests since 1924. Restoration to the lodge and the original A-frame cabin were completed in 1998 retaining the authentic feel and decor. The 11 riverfront cabins and a three-bedroom river house are nicely appointed; stone fireplaces and Jacuzzi tubs in some cabins. Additional amenities include a deluxe continental breakfast, afternoon appetizer reception and nightly freshly-baked cookies and milk. Hollywood legends such as Clark Gable, Carole Lombard and Walt Disney left Tinseltown behind to vacation at this tranquil Rogue River retreat.

Wild River Brewing & Pizza Company

595 NE E St   541/471-7487
Lunch, Dinner: Daily   wildriverbrewing.com
Moderate

The main location is a family-oriented restaurant that features a showcase brewery and in addition to pizza, serves pasta, European-inspired classics, sandwiches and other meals. Down the street (533 NE F St, 541/474-4456), the pub's friendly atmosphere is a good place to grab a pint and watch a sporting event on the big screen. They also serve great burgers, pub fare and entrees from the full-service menus at their other locations in Cave Junction, Brookings and Medford.

IDLEYLD PARK

Steamboat Inn

42705 N Umpqua Hwy   541/498-2230, 800/840-8825
Moderate and up   thesteamboatinn.com

Although this charming retreat is known far and wide by fishermen, others will be just as engaged with the many attractions offered. For over a half-century, anglers have made Steamboat their base camp for some of the best steelhead fishing anywhere. The eight cabins and two suites on the river are breathtaking; the sounds of the rippling water will put even the most restless sleeper into seventh heaven. Also available (and particularly well suited for families) are five hideaway cottages and three 1960s three-bedroom ranch houses. The main building has a charming library and a huge dining table where the legendary fabulous family-style dinners are served. For over 20 years, great winemakers and wonderful chefs have combined their talents to provide remarkable winemakers' dinners at Steamboat Inn. Hikers can enjoy a multitude of waterfalls and wildlife on some of the most fantastic trails in Oregon. Proprietors **Sharon and Jim Van Loan** and **Patricia Lee** are gracious, friendly, guest-oriented hosts. Take fly-fishing instruction, a whitewater raft trip or enjoy a relaxing massage. This is one of Oregon's best!

FESTIVALS & FAIRS IN SOUTHERN OREGON

MARCH-NOVEMBER
Oregon Shakespeare Festival (Ashland, 800/219-8161, osfashland.org)
JUNE
Summer Arts Festival (Roseburg, 541/672-2532, uvarts.com)
JUNE, JULY, AUGUST
Britt Festivals (Jacksonville, 541/779-0847, brittfest.org)
AUGUST
Douglas County Fair (Roseburg, 541/957-7010, Facebook)
SEPTEMBER
Harvest Festival (Central Point, 541/774-8270, attheexpo.com)
Winston-Dillard Melon Festival (Winston, 541/679-4260, winston chamber.org)
OCTOBER
Art Along the Rogue Music and Art Fest (Grants Pass, 541/476-5510, artalongtherogue.com)
Klamath Basin Potato Festival (Merrill, 541/891-3178, klamath basinpotatofestival.com)
Southern Oregon Music Festival (Medford, 866/448-1948, somusicfest.org)
DECEMBER
Klamath Falls Snowflake Festival (Klamath Falls, 541/884-3505, klamathsnowflake.com)

JACKSONVILLE

Britt Festivals
350 1st St   541/779-0847, 800/882-7488
Seasonal: Summer   brittfest.org

Each summer the Peter Britt estate, now a Jackson County park, comes alive with three months of concerts and performances under the stars. Britt was a 19th-century photographer and painter who also appreciated fine music, often enjoying concerts on the lawn of his house on a hill. Since 1963, concert-goers have flocked to

Jacksonville and this spectacular outdoor setting to hear classical, folk, pop, country and blues musicians and comedians. The relaxed venue is dotted with patrons seated on the lawn (bring a blanket) and reserved seating near the stage. Various cultural and fun events occur in conjunction with the concerts; early purchase of single performance tickets is highly recommended. Concert dates for the new season are announced in February each year.

Bybee's Historic Inn

883 Old Stage Road   541/899-0106, 877/292-3374
Moderate   bybeeshistoricinn.com

Experience living history in a classical revival manse built in 1857 by William M. Bybee, a Jackson County farmer, freight driver, settler, stockman, politician and leader. Today, six beautiful guest rooms are tastefully appointed with period antiques and fabric-covered walls and supplied with modern technological amenities; the Americana room on the first floor offers a separate entrance and is wheelchair accessible. Each room in this bed and breakfast inn contains a private bathroom that is outfitted with a two-person Jacuzzi tub (unheard of in the 1850s), walk-in shower or claw-foot tub and luxurious robes, towels and quality bed linens (line-dried in the summer sunshine). Outside, enjoy the manicured three acres with a game of bocce ball and croquet or settle onto one of the porches and patios with a complimentary glass of wine, ice cream or homemade treat. Breakfasts, included with an overnight stay, are a three-course gourmet experience prepared to guests' dietary requests. Bybee's Historic Inn, a National Historic Landmark, is also conducive to high teas and murder mystery dinners and is a spectacular setting for outdoor weddings, showers and other gatherings.

Déjà Vu Bistro & Wine Bar

240 E California St   541/899-1942
Dinner: Wed-Sun   dejavubistrowinebar.com
Moderate

Following a 14-year absence, chef **Bill Prahl** purchased this restaurant in the McCully House Inn's garden room and patio and returned to take the reins of this successful venture, hence the name Déjà vu Bistro & Wine Bar. The emphasis is on local seasonal produce, cheeses, meats and wines from the nearby Applegate and Rogue valleys. The chef's grilled romaine salad is part of his repertoire and is a wonderful accompaniment to a la carte entrees. In lieu of a "greens" starter, you may opt for the housemade soup. Palate pleasing dinner combinations include coffee-rubbed flat iron steak and fingerling potatoes, duck breast with cauliflower puree, seared sea scallops alongside zucchini spaghetti or other main dishes creatively melding organic and seasonal meats and produce.

Elan Guest Suites and Gallery

245 W Main St   541/899-8000, 877/789-1952
Moderate   elanguestsuites.com

This classy boutique lodging includes a first-floor art gallery and secure parking garage with luggage lift. Three stylish and contemporary suites are appointed with private balconies, wood and tile floors, fully-equipped kitchens and state-of-the-art sound systems and technologies. Guests are sure to appreciate original artworks that enhance each suite. Complimentary fresh-baked bagels, scones or breakfast treats are provided by nearby Good Bean Company. Elan Gallery features special art exhibits and events and is open daily to guests. Pure panache!

Frau Kemmling Schoolhaus Brewhaus

525 Bigham Knoll   541/899-1000
Lunch, Dinner: Daily   fraukemmling.com
Moderate

Housed in a former Jacksonville schoolhouse (circa 1908), the restaurant and biergarten are enhanced with Bavarian scenes, historic photos and other German decor. The menu offers authentic German listings with English explanations — fondues, schnitzels, schweinebraten, knodels and so much more. Celebrate Oktoberfest, Winterfest and MaiFest with good German food, good German beer and good friends!

Gary West Meats

690 N 5th St   800/833-1820
Mon-Sat: 10-6; Sun: 11-5 (seasonal)   garywest.com

Gary's grandparents were pioneers in the Applegate area, and Gary is well-schooled in the special flavors of old-time foods that make for memorable ranch meals. A break at this jerky factory and tasting room is fun and different from the usual snack stops. You'll be treated to tasty elk, bison and Angus beef samples. If you're in a buying mood, there are jerky samplers; a great selection of Oregon wines; baskets featuring wild game, sausage and other unusual gifts; hams and buffalo strips.

Gogi's Restaurant

235 W Main St   541/899-8699
Dinner: Wed-Sun; Brunch: Sun   gogis.net
Moderate

Brothers **Gabriel Murphy** and **Jonoah Murphy** pull much of the seasonal produce from their small farm in the Applegate Valley. Intimate dining in chic environs features international cuisine, made in-house using local organic ingredients as much as possible. For starters, try crispy pork belly served with creamy polenta and pickled watermelon rind, soup of the day or crisp salad. Entrees include double-cut New York steak, braised lamb shank, confit of duck leg, seafood and other very good choices. Brunch temptations may include Benedicts (traditional or a cowboy version with steak), Dutch-style cinnamon apple pancakes, housemade corned beef hash and soups, salads and sandwiches served with house-cut potato chips. Outstanding service, fine wines and creative cocktails complete the impressive dining experience.

Jacksonville Inn

175 E California St   541/899-1900, 800/321-9344
Rooms: Moderate; Cottages: Moderately expensive   jacksonvilleinn.com

This historic bed and breakfast (circa 1861) is tastefully decorated with period antiques and reproductions. There are eight rooms with private bathrooms at the inn. The original honeymoon cottage, a small restored historic house, is two blocks away; three replicated cottages, including the Presidential Cottage where President and Mrs. George W. Bush stayed, were built at the same location. Each is private and luxurious. Full breakfast is included with an overnight stay and served in the inn's dining room; choose from a variety of delicious favorites like housemade granola, waffles, hearty egg preparations and such. A wonderful brunch each Sunday starts with champagne or sparkling cider, then work your way through fresh fruit, house-baked pastries, eggs and meats and near-famous scalloped potatoes or select a special of the day. Lunch and dinner are served in the dining room and bistro as well as on a lovely garden patio (weather permitting); the wine list and gourmet menus are extensive. Dinners with fresh, local and seasonal ingredients include the inn's special grilled chicken, veal scaloppini, fish and seafood, flavorful steaks, prime rib and more. Keep the restaurant in mind for off-site catering, banquets (private dining rooms are available) and picnic baskets to take to Britt Festival concerts. Proprietors **Linda and Jerry Evans** also operate the Wine and Gift Shop at this location, fully-stocked with over 2,000 impressive wine selections.

Jacksonville's Magnolia Inn
245 N 5th St   541/899-0255
Moderate   magnolia-inn.com

Magnolia Inn offers nine well-appointed vintage rooms with en suite baths and a veranda overlooking the property's English garden. Delightful hosts, **Susan and Robert Roos** oversee the morning's continental breakfast; a guest kitchen and dining area are located on the second floor. The check-in area is stocked with something for the taking from Susan's treasure trove of baked goods.

Mustard Seed Cafe
130 N 5th St   541/899-2977
Breakfast: Wed-Sun; Lunch: Wed-Sat   Facebook
Inexpensive

You can count on this tiny eatery for a good meal at easy prices and with warm service. What to order? Cinnamon rolls, various scrambles and omelets and corned beef hash for breakfast; burgers, sandwiches and onion rings for lunch or selections from the special value breakfast and lunch menus. If you can't decide, ask one of the regular customers for their suggestions!

Pot Rack

140 W California St   541/899-5736
Daily: 10-5   jacksonvillepotrack.com

Aptly named, this shop sells pot racks as well as pots, pans and cooking utensils to hang on the holders. You'll find other brand name cookware, bakeware, useful and obscure gadgets, colorful table accessories, table linens, aprons, cutlery, attractive gifts and items to inspire your culinary bent.

Terra Firma

135 W California St   541/899-1097
Mon-Sat: 10:30-6; Sun: 11-5   terrafirmahome.com

Merchandise at this gift emporium is best described as fun stuff. The main floor has a unique selection of some of this and some of that—soap by the loaf, candles, jewelry, hardware, housewares, home decor and affordable gifts for your home or best friend. A clearance area for furniture from their home and design location in Medford is located on the second floor.

Touvelle House Bed & Breakfast

455 N Oregon St   541/899-8938, 800/846-8422
Moderate   touvellehouse.com

Touvelle House is distinguished from other lodgings by a number of special amenities, including a seasonal, heated swimming pool, sauna, guest refrigerators and water dispensers on each floor and a library. The six individualized guest rooms, all with private bathrooms, feature luxurious beds and linens, air conditioning, CD players, iPod docks and Wi-Fi. Common areas in the Craftsman-style home are comfortably furnished for reading, playing cards or games, warming by the great room's sandstone fireplace or taking morning coffee.

You may find your niche in the beautifully landscaped grounds for an afternoon siesta. Coffee and breakfast in the dining room start mornings off on the right foot; your hosts will accommodate special dietary restrictions with advance notice. Tea is available all day in the well-decorated period dining room; fresh homemade sweets are set out later in the day. This is a great night's sleep in a superb location.

KLAMATH FALLS

Crystalwood Lodge

38625 Westside Road   866/381-2322
Moderate   crystalwoodlodge.com

When you pack up the family, and the pet dog (or cat) begs to come along, it's no problem if the destination is Crystalwood Lodge. Near the south entrance to Crater Lake National Park and adjacent to the Upper Klamath National Wildlife Refuge, this lodge sits on 130 acres in the center of wonderful fly-fishing, canoeing, golf, hiking, horseback riding, cross-country skiing, snowshoeing, dog sledding, biking and other outdoor activities. Nearby you can visit Train Mountain, a small gauge train ride covering 36 miles of track through the forest. You can also take in Crater Lake Zipline, Oregon's longest zipline that gives you up to three hours of fun flying from tree to tree. Rooms are named after checkpoints in the Iditarod Sled Dog Race, and the owner's sled dog kennel is available for guest tours. Crates (home-away-from-home pet houses) are provided in every room, a dog-washing facility is near at hand and pet day care is available. In lieu of meal service, guests have access to a fully-outfitted commercial kitchen facility, walk-in cooler, freezer and grill. Gathering and meeting space is available year round with catered gourmet meals to groups for reunions, retreats, weddings, workshops

> ## DID YOU KNOW...
>
> ... Oregon grows 99% of all hazelnuts produced in the United States.
>
> ... It is also the country's leading producer of Christmas trees, the tenth largest agricultural commodity in the state.

and such. The lodge primarily caters to groups, but individuals may rent if space is available.

Favell Museum of Western Art and Indian Artifacts

125 W Main St   541/882-9996
Tues-Sat: 10-5   favellmuseum.org
Nominal

Founder Gene Favell assembled this rich and fascinating collection prior to his death in 2001. You'll find both art and artifacts, Favell's fabulous art book anthology, plus one of the finest collections of firearms in the West; many are miniature models. More than 100,000 Indian artifacts are shown including a huge set of ancient and authentic Indian arrowheads. The striking building houses galleries of figurines, art, prints and sculptures that are also offered for sale; there is a comfortable meeting room for public events.

The Klamath Grill and Pancake House

715 Main St   541/882-1427
Breakfast, Lunch: Daily   klamathgrill.com
Inexpensive

It's always fun to check out the local hot spots, and a good place to start in K-Falls is at this Main Street restaurant. Pancakes (ten varieties), waffles, stuffed French toast, pigs in a blanket and egg dishes are breakfast staples. If you're in the mood for lunch, hot and cold sandwiches, burgers and salads are tasty options.

Lake of the Woods Mountain Lodge & Resort

950 Harriman Rt   541/949-8300, 866/201-4194
Lodging: Moderate   lakeofthewoodsresort.com
Restaurant: Moderately expensive to expensive

Spend the day at the lake, then head inside your cozy cabin to rest and rejuvenate for another day of fishing, waterskiing, hiking, scuba diving or winter activities. One- and two-bedroom vintage cabins at Lake of the Woods have varying amenities (full kitchen or kitchenette, jetted tub, gas fireplace, screened porch). One-bedroom park model cabins have living rooms with a sofa sleeper or trundle bed, full kitchens and bathrooms; units may also have sleeping lofts, covered porches or bunkrooms. The **Lake House Restaurant** is open for breakfast, lunch and dinner, and the **Marina Pizza Parlor** serves lunch and dinner (pizza, wraps, salads, sandwiches) daily during the summer season (in winter, the pizza parlor is open Friday through Sunday). A full-service marina offers boat rentals, fuel and moorage.

Mermaid Garden Cafe

501 Main St   541/882-3671
Lunch: Mon-Fri   Facebook
Inexpensive

A mythical marine creature may seem out of place in Klamath Falls, but not at the Mermaid Garden Cafe where mermaid figurines and kitsch decorate **Kelly Hennessey**'s popular establishment. Her family and friends have provided much of the decor; a friend crafted the wooden tables, her father drew colorful images of fish on the table tops and the oil paintings were done by her sister. Lunch consists of wraps, soups, made-to-order salads (choose from a selection of greens, homemade salad dressings and two dozen additions) and a weekly pizza special. Pizzas run the gamut from usual toppings to brie with asparagus and a Thai chicken version. Winning lunch flavors include a New Jersey sloppy joe, turkey curry wrap or spicy portabella panini; each is accompanied by a green salad, Thai cabbage slaw or Southwestern potato salad. This is a hot spot in downtown K-Falls!

Mia & Pia's Pizzeria & Brewhouse

3545 Summers Lane   541/884-4880
Lunch, Dinner: Daily   miaandpias.com
Moderate to moderately expensive

Dozens of beers and ales are on tap at Mia & Pia's. The brewhouse is the outgrowth of a family business started nearly four decades ago. Much of the equipment and hardware is reclaimed from their prior dairy business and is in daily use at the pizzeria and brewhouse. Some 30 pizza varieties are available, or dream up your own creations. Other good eats include appetizers, burgers, broasted chicken, spaghetti, soups, salads and sandwiches. These folks will bring their beer truck to your event for a never-to-be-forgotten party. Remember to fill your growler!

Mr. B's Steakhouse

3927 S 6th St   541/883-8719
Dinner: Tues-Sat   Facebook
Moderately expensive

Take a dinner break where the signature dish is a 20-ounce, ranch cut, bone-in New York steak; smaller steaks are equally big on flavor. Grilled fish and seafood, double pork and lamb chops and other favorites (wiener schnitzel and chicken marsala) are also served as complete dinners. If you're famished, add an appetizer order of mussels or clams, escargot bourguignon or oysters Florentine. Not to worry if you prefer something less filling; options include light dinners with fewer sides, sandwiches and specialty salads. The outdoor garden patio is a summer oasis for families and friends to mingle and dine.

Rocky Point Resort

28121 Rocky Point Road   541/356-2287
Seasonal: Apr 1-Nov 1   rockypointoregon.com
Lodging: Rates vary
Restaurant: Moderate to moderately expensive

If you want to "rough it" but also enjoy a comfy bed and shower each evening, consider a stay at this resort, not far from either Medford or Klamath Falls on the northwest shore of Upper Klamath Lake. You have a choice of cabins, guest rooms, RV spaces—even tent sites. The resort's popular restaurant is open for breakfast, lunch and dinner Memorial Day through Labor Day, Wednesdays through Sundays and weekends only in spring and fall (best to call ahead). Overnighters are welcome to use the well-kept public restrooms, showers, laundry facilities and fish-cleaning station; pick up supplies at the marina store, where you can also rent canoes, boats and kayaks or fuel your watercraft.

Running Y Ranch

5500 Running Y Road   541/850-5500
Lodging: Moderate and up   runningy.com
Restaurant: Moderately expensive

Running Y Ranch is Southern Oregon's premier full-service destination resort. The lodge is a Holiday Inn Resort and features updated guestrooms and amenities, as well as a restaurant, The **Ruddy Duck** (541/850-5582), with a beautiful deck overlooking Payne Canyon. The resort also features larger vacation homes. The **Arnold Palmer Signature Course** (541/850-5580) is ranked one of the state's best, yet non-golfers have plenty to do as well: abundant fishing, birding, hiking, whitewater rafting and more are close at hand. Winter visitors don't have to travel far for snowshoeing or skating at on-property **Ice Sports** (541/850-5758). Additional amenities include the **Sandhill Spa** (541/850-5547) and a sports and fitness center with a year-round swimming pool.

LAKEVIEW

Willow Springs Guest Ranch

34064 Clover Flat Road   541/947-5499
Seasonal: May 15-Sept   willowspringsguestranch.com
Moderate

To get a taste of life in Oregon's Outback, visit **Patty and Keith Barnhart** at their working cattle ranch. You'll be in the midst of a vast population of birds, squirrels, deer, antelope and other critters. With many miles of trails, you can hike or ride your own horses. Part of the fun at Willow Springs is the on-site-generated electricity, with various combinations of solar and wind power. And after a day on the range, you'll have no problem with an early lights out. Accommodations are rustic cabins decorated with exceptional Western artwork, a sunporch just right for meditating and a wood-fired hot tub to soothe those weary cowboy and cowgirl muscles. Rates include hearty ranch breakfasts. Additional fees apply for authentic Dutch-oven cooked dinners, box lunches, guided rides or lodging and feed for your own horse.

MEDFORD

4 Daughters Irish Pub

126 W Main St   541/779-4455
Lunch, Dinner: Daily   4daughtersirishpub.com
Moderate

This property goes back to the early 1900s; it has been a barbershop, theater, billiard parlor and cigar club. Named for the

OREGON'S TOP 12 NATURE AREAS & PARKS

Columbia River Gorge National Scenic Area (Office: 902 Wasco St, Suite 200, Hood River; 541/308-1700): spectacular view areas

Crater Lake (Crater Lake National Park, Crater Lake; 541/594-3000): one of Oregon's seven wonders

Haystack Rock (Hwy 101, Cannon Beach): 235-foot monolith, kid- and pet-friendly

Multnomah Falls (50000 Historic Columbia River Hwy, Corbett; 503/695-2376): exquisite falls, second longest in the U.S.

Cape Perpetua Scenic Area (2400 Hwy 101, Yachats; 541/547-3289): exceptional tide pools and great stop for kids

Columbia River Maritime Museum (1792 Marine Dr, Astoria; 503/325-2323): superb building, great setting and wonderful exhibits

Smith Rock State Park (Hwy 97, nine miles north of Redmond; 541/548-7501): amazing rock formations and great hiking

Shore Acres State Park (Cape Arago Hwy, Coos Bay; 541/888-3732): ocean-front and botanical garden

Lithia Park (59 Winburn Way, Ashland; 541/488-5340): listed on the National Register of Historic Places; 93 acres

High Desert Museum (59800 S Hwy 97, Bend; 541/382-4754): great family stop

Yaquina Head Natural Area (750 Lighthouse Dr, Newport; 541/574-3100): amazing views from the top of the lighthouse

Silver Falls State Park (Hwy 214, Silverton; 503/873-8681): walking trails, waterfalls and great picnic spots

owner's four daughters, this pub is appropriately furnished with a game room including pool and darts. The extensive menu includes small bites, soups and salads, burgers, beer-battered fish and chips, Guinness meatloaf, shepherd's pie and wonderful homemade desserts. Plenty of Irish drink specialties and beers are available. The pub is family-friendly until 10 p.m. daily.

Downtown Market Co.

231 E Main St
541/973-2233
Mon-Fri: 9-6; Sat: 10-4
downtownmarketco.com

Nora LaBrocca's love of food led her to open this downtown market. Brought up in Southern California, the LaBrocca clan raised beef, poultry and game birds for chic Los Angeles-area restaurants. The lunch menu at the Downtown Market's taste kitchen changes every week or so and brings fresh soups, salads, sandwiches, pastries and more to the tables. Beyond lunch this place is a specialty food market and offers culinary classes, wine tastings, flights and pairings and occasional family-style dinners. Two ground floor outdoor patios are pleasantly furnished to feel like a big city rooftop. Large outdoor grills are used year round to prepare panini sandwiches and other delicious offerings (men have been known to drool over these to-die-for grills). Summer picnic baskets are superb!

Elements Tapas Bar & Lounge

101 E Main St
541/779-0135
Daily: 4 p.m.-late
elementsmedford.com
Moderate

At this historic downtown building you'll find Spanish wines and great drinks from the full bar to accompany outstanding food, crafted as much as possible from local produce. Try red grapes encrusted with Rogue Creamery smoked blue cheese and crushed pistachios, Spanish olives, mushroom catalan, roasted beet salad and other delectable choices. Traditional Spanish paellas with vegetables and assorted meats and seafood are made to order from scratch, which allows adequate time to share tasty tapas.

Inn at the Commons

200 N Riverside Ave   541/779-5811
Lodging: Moderate   innatthecommons.com
Restaurant: Moderately expensive to expensive

Hospitality entrepreneurs **Becky and Doug Neuman** purchased the former Red Lion Hotel, renamed it and created a destination property that is warm and comfortable. All 118 guest rooms and suites are outfitted with the latest technology; many rooms offer courtyard views and balconies. Guests are treated to a complimentary hot breakfast buffet. **Larks Restaurant** (541/774-4760) features farm-to-table gourmet fare for lunch and dinner. The inn is Medford's biggest venue for large meetings and conventions with space for up to 800 people.

Jaspers Café

2739 N Pacific Hwy   541/776-5307
Lunch, Dinner: Daily   jasperscafe.com
Inexpensive

It's no secret that I enjoy great hamburgers with all the trimmings and, of course, crispy French fries. If you're in Southern Oregon, this is the place to go. The menu lists classic, gourmet, extreme gourmet and outrageous and wild burgers! Choices include beef in combination with game meats (antelope, elk, kangaroo, bison). Over 20 flavors of hand-scooped shakes and malts reign supreme on the drink menu.

Porters — Dining at the Depot

147 N Front St   541/857-1910
Dinner: Daily   porterstrainstation.com
Moderate and up

Named a National Historic Landmark, Medford's beautifully-restored railroad depot has been home to this restaurant for over a decade. The century old building is magnificent with original Craftsman-style architectural details that are nostalgically impressive; there are over 40,000 red roof tiles, hand-chiseled granite corbels, massive wood beams, working radiators, a ticket-making machine and other memorabilia. Dinners at the depot feature outstanding Southern Oregon produce, cheeses, meats, beers and wines and an excellent selection of fish and seafood. For an appetizer I recommend the Thai lettuce cups with chicken or a bowl of seafood chowder; other starters and shareables, a la carte entrees and nightly specials are ideal for smaller appetites. Standout entrees include slow-cooked rosemary-roasted prime rib of beef (also presented thinly shaved on a sandwich with cheese and onions accompanied by garlic fries) and rack of lamb finished with fresh mint balsamic glaze. Optional surf items and extras may be added to generously-portioned steak and chop entrees to create your favorite combo plate. Jack Daniels bread pudding and a decadent ice cream sundae are two of the half dozen irresistible desserts. Alfresco dining and "get giddy" hour specials are additional features. All aboard!

MERLIN

Morrison's Rogue River Lodge

8500 Galice Road   800/826-1963
Seasonal: May-Oct   morrisonslodge.com
Inexpensive to very expensive

A picturesque stretch of the Rogue River, 16 miles downstream from Grants Pass, offers some of the best whitewater rafting and steelhead fishing in Oregon. Morrison's Rogue River Lodge was originally built in 1946 as a fishing lodge and welcomes guests to rustic accommodations in the main log lodge, nearby cabins (circa 1965 to 1976) and creekside units built since 2007. Guests can choose from a variety of accommodations between nine river-view cottages (with fireplaces, private decks and covered parking) or four rooms in the main lodge. All lodging options feature the conveniences of home, like air conditioners, televisions, Wi-Fi, private baths and more. Two multi-bedroom suites and four cottages are just a brief walk away on Taylor Creek. The property includes a heated swimming pool, putting green, volleyball and tennis and basketball courts. Morrison's is also known for their delicious four-course, *prix-fixe* dinners served outdoors (weather permitting); reservations are a must for both lodge and town guests. The nightly menu may feature prime rib of beef, salmon filet, pork chops, lamb or a chicken dish; housemade orange dinner rolls are a real treat. Here, dinner is always treated as a special occasion. Looking to reconnect with the great outdoors? Book a fishing or rafting package! Fishing season runs from the end of August until the first part of November. Lodge closed for the winter season.

Rogue Wilderness Adventures

325 Galice Road   541/479-9554, 800/336-1647
Seasonal: Apr-Oct   wildrogue.com

Owner-operator **Brad Niva** knows the Rogue River like the back of his hand and will help plan your float trip, ranging from a half-day to three- or four-day journey via inflatable kayak or raft through the Wild and Scenic Rogue River Canyon. Popular multi-day river, fishing and hiking trips include stays at wilderness lodges and wonderful meals. The scenery is indescribable and the experience is sure to create a favorite lifetime memory.

OAKLAND

MarshAnne Landing

175 Hogan Road   541/459-7998
Seasonal: Mar-Dec: Wed-Sun or by appointment   marshannelanding.com

Fran and Greg Cramer's small winery produces cab and syrah blends, merlot, pinot noir and syrah wines and other proprietary blends. The beautiful, serene tasting room showcases local artists' bronze sculptures, paintings, pottery, glasswork, jewelry and fiber art. Special events are scheduled throughout the year in the tasting room and outdoors on the deck overlooking the vineyard. Check out their music schedule which features classical, opera and jazz concerts in the intimate space of their concert hall-like tasting room. It is also a prime wedding and private function venue.

STEP BACK IN TIME

Oakland is nestled in the heart of the Umpqua Valley and is surrounded by rich, rolling farmland, ideal to cattle, sheep, goats, horses and agriculture, especially wineries. This charming town was the first city to be placed on the state's historic register. The first settlers came to the area in 1846 via the Applegate Trail. Many homes and business buildings are listed on the National Historic Registry; more than 80 such properties were built between 1852 and 1890 and have been beautifully preserved. Tourism has become Oakland's number one industry. To get there, drive along the Umpqua River Scenic Byway (to/from Reedsport via Highway 38) which will sweep you past wildlife, waterfalls and whitewater rapids, crossing the Rochester Covered Bridge. Pick up a walking/driving tour map with homes of yesteryear from the Oakland Museum or City Hall. Enjoy a picnic in the park or take a break at **Tolly's Grill and Soda Fountain** (541/459-3796, tollysgrill.com) housed in the town's early mercantile and drug store.

Tolly's Grill and Soda Fountain

115 Locust St   541/459-3796
Breakfast, Lunch, Dinner: Daily   tollysgrill.com
Moderate and up

    This eatery was Oakland's mercantile and drug store in the late 19th century; interesting signage from that era remains. You can't miss the candy counter or graceful curved stairway leading up to the loft as you pass through the Fountain Room on your way to the piano bar. The decor is eclectic (carousel horses, artwork and memorabilia). Sit at one of about a dozen stools that line the soda fountain counter for a quick bite or take a seat at one of the round tables with comfortable wingback chairs for a relaxing lunch or dinner. In addition to a full fountain, look for menu specials such as ranchero omelets and cinnamon roll French toast for breakfast and pulled pork sandwiches with Ninkasi beer barbecue sauce and catfish sandwiches for lunch. Dinners include sea scallops, butternut squash ravioli, steaks or other fine dining choices.

TRAVEL ASSISTANCE

Should you ever need roadside assistance as you visit some of the great places in this edition, your **AAA** (oregon.aaa.com) membership can be a godsend. These folks are available to members 24/7 for vehicle and bicycle roadside service. Travel planning services include maps and tour books for hundreds of destinations, routes and current road conditions; helpful seminars on packing and special offers for cruises and more. Show your AAA card and get discounted rates on hotels, car repair and rental, florists, dining, attractions, computers, eyewear, movie tickets — over 160,000 participating businesses. AAA has insurance professionals and can assist you with a variety of insurance options. You'll find their offices conveniently located across the state in these towns:

Beaverton (8555 SW Apple Way; 503/243-6444)

Bend (20350 Empire Blvd, Suite A-5; 541/382-1303)

Clackamas (10365 SE Sunnyside Road; 503/241-6800)

Coos Bay (1705 Ocean Blvd SE, Suite A; 541/269-7432)

Corvallis (1550 NW 9th St, Suite 104; 541/757-2535)

Eugene (983 Willagillespie Road; 541/484-0661)

Grants Pass (1563 NE F St; 541/479-7829)

Hillsboro (7300 NE Butler St; 503/726-5900)

Lake Oswego (6 Centerpointe Dr, Suite 100; 503/973-6555)

Medford (1777 E Barnett Road; 541/779-7170)

Pendleton (1729 SW Court Pl; 541/276-2243)

Portland (600 SW Market St; 503/222-6767)

Roseburg (3019 NW Stewart Pkwy, Suite 303; 541/673-7453)

Salem (2909 Ryan Dr SE; 503/584-5200)

Springfield (939 Harlow Road, Suite 100; 541/741-8200)

Warrenton (135 S Hwy 101; 503/861-3118)

Wilsonville (30020 SW Boones Ferry Road, Suite 12; 503/570-0199)

Wood Village (22741 NE Park Lane, Suite G; 503/489-2842)

PROSPECT

Prospect Historic Hotel (Bed & Breakfast Inn, Motel & Dinner House)

391 Mill Creek Dr
B&B: Moderate to expensive
Motel: Inexpensive to moderate
Restaurant: Moderately expensive to expensive

541/560-3664, 800/944-6490
prospecthotel.com

Does putting your head on a pillow at a historic 1880s stagecoach-stop hotel sound intriguing? If so, this stop in Prospect is the closest full-service town to Crater Lake and the Rogue River. It is also the jumping-off point for many outdoor activities. Ten bed and breakfast rooms are in the Nationally Registered Historic Hotel; the full hearty breakfast is a delightful start to the morning. All rooms have private bathrooms, handmade quilts and period furnishings. Behind the hotel, 14 modern motel units are outfitted with TVs, coffeemakers, refrigerators and microwaves (some kitchenettes); these units are ideal for families and guests with pets. The dinner house is open May through October as well as most holidays and serves mouthwatering dinners complete with salad, freshly-baked bread and dessert. **Karen and Fred Wickman** are the owners; Karen oversees the dinner house while Fred serves as jack-of-all-trades for the inn. Explore five acres of park-like grounds and three waterfalls that are just a short stroll away and then relax with a local wine or beer on the magnificent veranda.

ROGUE RIVER

Pholia Farm

9115 W Evans Creek Road
Seasonal: May-Aug: Sat or by appointment
Lodging: Inexpensive

541/582-8883
pholiafarm.com

Learn all you never knew about Nigerian dwarf dairy goats and the rich milk and cheese they produce at **Gianaclis and Vern Caldwell**'s farm. The dairy is off-grid, as is the Caldwell's home; alternative power sources (solar, micro-hydro generator and backup bio-diesel generator) supply electricity. The breed's milk is unique and boasts the highest butterfat of all goats; the Caldwell's herd averages 6.5% butterfat and 4.3% in protein, which translates into extraordinary Old World-style cheese. The farm feeds spent brewers grain and local hay to the goats and uses an ale bath during one of the cheese's aging processes. Classes are offered in cheesemaking and herdsmanship for novice goat owners. Cheeses are available from the farm and at a few select retailers. It's best to call ahead if you are going to this off-the-beaten-path enterprise. If you'd like to spend the night at the farm, inquire about guest quarters in the refurbished 1970 Airstream Land Yacht (airbnb.com).

ROSEBURG

Abacela Vineyard and Winery

12500 Lookingglass Road   541/679-6642
Daily: 11-6 (till 5 in winter)   abacela.com

Hilda and Earl Jones searched the U.S. from their Alabama home for just the right growing climate, gave up careers in medical research and began learning more about tempranillo grapes. The established vineyard and award-winning winery produce tempranillo, albariño, syrah, malbec and other varietal wines. Tastings are served in the Vine & Wine Center which includes magnificent views and elegant private tastings.

Brix 527

527 SE Jackson St   541/440-4901
Breakfast, Lunch, Dinner: Daily   Facebook
Moderate

In industrial-chic quarters in downtown Roseburg, Brix 527 is a trifecta of historic buildings joined together to encompass BRIX grill and eatery, BRIX chill (a lounge) and BRIX gather (an event center). For breakfast, the made-on-the-premises real crab cake Benedict is delicious, there are other gourmet selections, too. Soups, sandwiches, salads and tasty lunch specials complete the list. For dinner choose from steaks, seafood, crab cakes, burgers, pasta dishes, chicken and superb salads; there is also a full bar selection.

Delfino Vineyards

3829 Colonial Road   541/673-7575
Daily: 11-5   delfinovineyards.com
Cottage: Expensive

Terri and Jim Delfino's enterprise includes a five-star one-bedroom guest cottage nestled in the picturesque 160-acre site; in-room breakfast basket (or fixings to make breakfast on your own schedule) and a bottle of Delfino Vineyards wine are included. During your stay, amble over to the tasting room, hike the wooded trails, soak in the hot tub, take a dip in the lap pool or snuggle up by the cottage's fireplace. For two couples or a family (no guests younger than 14, please), the cottage has a queen sofa bed; two-night minimum stays

SILVER LAKE

Cowboy Dinner Tree

East Bay Road   541/576-2426
Seasonal: June-Oct: Thurs-Sun; Nov-May: Fri-Sun   cowboydinnertree.net
Moderate

This dinner stop in the heart of Oregon's High Desert country is a unique experience! When you call (reservations are a must), place your order for either a 26-ounce top sirloin steak (think roast) or whole chicken; the trimmings, such as hearty soup, salad, baked potato and homemade dessert, will make you happy you journeyed this far. Portions are gigantic! **Angel and Jamie Roscoe** continue in her parent's footsteps, where, just like her mother, Angel prepares homemade sweet yeast rolls from a secret family recipe; on a busy evening, she'll turn out 80 pans of the melt-in-your-mouth bread. Jamie prepares chickens for the rotisserie and spice-rubbed steaks for the grill. If you want to call it a night at sundown, reserve one of the two rustic cabins (no TV or telephone); the package deal includes dinner. Interesting cowboy memorabilia accents the dining room and cabins. No credit cards; no kidding.

TALENT

New Sammy's Cowboy Bistro
2210 S Pacific Hwy   541/535-2779
Lunch, Dinner: Wed-Sat   Facebook
Moderately expensive

You may need your glasses to find this spot! Venture off I-5 about three miles north of Ashland for one heck of a dining experience. For some 20 years **Charlene and Vernon Rollins** have been filling satisfied customers' plates with awesome food. Chef Charlene consistently produces healthy, organic meals, with homemade breads, entrees made with seasonal ingredients and amazing desserts; Vernon takes care of the front of the house. The restaurant's garden supplies herbs and vegetables; other local producers provide meats and such, including whole suckling pigs. The Rollins' talents have caught the eye of prestigious food magazines, and Charlene has been nominated by the James Beard Foundation for her culinary accomplishments. Reservations are definitely in order.

WINSTON

Wildlife Safari
1790 Safari Road   541/679-6761
Daily: 10-4   wildlifesafari.net
Reasonable

This spectacular drive-through wildlife park continues to attract families to observe over 550 animals roaming natural habitat. Some 76 species of large and small African, Asian and North and South American animals are showcased; to the delight of youngsters, many brush up next to visitors' autos! Before or after your safari, explore the village with unique animals, train and animal rides and a petting zoo, as well as a cafe, gift shop, kids' play area and gardens. Private encounters such as helping feed the bears and tigers are by reservation. Allow several hours to take in all the activities. This popular attraction is committed to research, education and conservation of wildlife.

Index

Featured entries in bold
Cities and towns in italics

NOTES

NOTES

NOTES

NOTES

NOTES

NOTES

NOTES

NOTES